THE SECOND X
THE BIOLOGY OF WOMEN

THE SECOND X
THE BIOLOGY OF WOMEN

COLLEEN M. BELK
UNIVERSITY OF MINNESOTA—DULUTH

VIRGINIA M. BORDEN
UNIVERSITY OF MINNESOTA—DULUTH

HARCOURT BRACE COLLEGE PUBLISHERS

FORT WORTH PHILADELPHIA SAN DIEGO NEW YORK ORLANDO AUSTIN SAN ANTONIO
TORONTO MONTREAL LONDON SYDNEY TOKYO

Custom Publisher	BOB TESSMAN
Director of Digital Publishing	MIKE BEAUPRÉ
Project Editor	ANGELA WILLIAMS URQUHART
Art Director	LINDA WOOTON
Production Manager	MARY BOTELLO
Electronic Publishing Coordinator	KATHI EMBRY

Cover image: Copyright ©1998 Photopia

ISBN: 0-03-025426-4

Printed in the United States of America

PREFACE

WHY A BOOK ON WOMEN'S BIOLOGY?

The title of this book, *The Second X*, refers not only to the biological fact that women have two X chromosomes (while men have one) but also to the revolutionary 1953 work of the French writer, Simone De Beauvoir. In her book *The Second Sex*, De Beauvoir describes the experience of womanhood as one of "otherness." De Beauvoir was one of the first feminists to point out that maleness is considered the norm against which females are measured. Sadly, her basic thesis holds true in medicine and science in many ways even today, more than 40 years after the original publication of her book.

In this text, we hope to do, in a small way, for women's biology what Simone De Beauvoir did so powerfully for the social status of women. *The Second X* presents the fundamental principles of biology unique to women in a manner that challenges the traditional approach that considers women to be modified men. By removing the male lens through which women's biology has traditionally been viewed, we encourage readers to question prevailing opinions of women's (and men's) capabilities and roles in society. Most chapters include several discussion questions that help readers explore alternative ways to frame questions about women's "nature." Many discussion questions help in understanding the real consequences of adopting either traditional or alternative approaches to understanding the biology of women.

The Second X is divided into two basic sections. The first section, Chapters 1 through 3, explores the role of history, the scientific method, and our current understanding of the evolutionary history of humans, especially how women's biology is conceptualized, studied, and valued. In Chapter 1, The History of Women's Biology, we outline the history of negative treatment that women's biology has received by the scientific and medical communities in the distant and not so distant past. In this chapter, we point out how these ideas, once widely accepted, continue to subtly hamper women today. In Chapter 2, Understanding and Evaluating Science, we explore the foundations of the scientific method and discuss strategies for evaluating scientific information. We describe the logic of the scientific method and how its application leads to an understanding of processes we cannot observe directly. Additionally, we explore how social factors, such as a scientist's belief system or limitations on human experimentation, influence what processes are investigated and how these processes are described. Rounding out our explorations of influences on the study of women's biology, Chapter 3, The Evolution of Sex and Gender, allows us to explore hypotheses regarding the biological basis for the two sexes and the relationship of behavior to biological sex. In this chapter, we investigate the evidence for these hypotheses and see that explanations about the evolution of gender roles may serve to limit the potential of both women and men.

The remainder of *The Second X* explores major themes in the life cycles of women. We begin in Chapter 4, Sex Determination, with an exploration of the genetic factors that lead to the development of female bodies in humans as well as in other species. This chapter helps readers understand that sex is not always fixed nor always one of only two states in other species, as well as our own. In Chapter 5, Sex Differentiation and Development, we explain the biological basis of fetal development from an embryo to a newborn and from an adolescent to a sexually mature adult. This chapter provides an opportunity to explore the ever increasing research on the effect of hormones on the central nervous system during fetal development and how much, if at all, fetal hormonal levels affect later behaviors.

In Chapter 6, Women's Bodies I: Anatomy, we describe the skeletal, external, and internal anatomy of women, with an emphasis on the range of variation among women and between women and men. Readers see that for the most part, women are as different from each other as they are different from men—however, the few average differences between women's and men's anatomy may have a strong influence on women's lives. Chapter 7, Women's Bodies II: Muscle, Fat, and Health, explores the average differences between women and men in body composition and shape, again with an emphasis on the wide variation among healthy members of each sex. This chapter also covers some of the unique nutritional needs of women, as well as the physiology and psychology of dieting and eating disorders.

Chapter 8, Menstruation, takes a positive view of this complex, often maligned, and nearly universal female experience. We begin by investigating the evolutionary basis of menstruation followed by an in-depth description of the cycle, again emphasizing the range of normal women's experiences. We also discuss the physiological source of, and treatments for, common menstrual complications and address common social attitudes concerning menstrual blood and the supposed limitations menstruation imposes on women. In Chapter 9, Oogenesis and Fertilization, we describe the production of eggs during intrauterine development and the changes that occur to these eggs before and during ovulation. The role of the egg as an "active participant" in fertilization is discussed, helping to abolish the myth of women as passive receptors of active male sperm. The result of fertilization, Pregnancy and Birthing, is detailed in Chapter 10. This chapter chronicles the dramatic changes that occur in a woman's body while she is supporting the development of another human being. Pregnancy and the process of birthing are presented in a way that emphasizes their naturalness and the opportunities for women to have control over the progress of these events. Chapter 11, Women Postpartum, explores the physiology of lactation, the experience of postpartum depression, and evaluates the research and social factors that influence both of these processes.

In Chapter 12, The Control of Fertility: Birth Control and Assisted Reproduction, we cover the physiology of birth control methods, as well as the causes and remedies of infertility. We discuss the physiological effects and potential risks of birth control methods and address the issue of future birth control technology. Additionally, we investigate the physiological and supposed psychosomatic causes of infertility, the current status of assisted reproductive technologies, from artificial insemination to *in vitro* fertilization, and the individual and social costs and benefits of technological interventions in human reproduction.

The Second X comes full circle in Chapters 13 and 14, which cover processes that typically occur in later life. In Chapter 13, Women and Cancer, we summarize the known mechanisms of cancer and discuss the origin, prevalence of, and treatment options for malignant and benign gynecological tumors. Chapter 14, Menopause and Aging, investigates the biology of menopause with the intent of debunking some of the myths surrounding this stage of life. Included is a review of the current state of research concerning estrogen replacement/hormone replacement therapy as well as an assessment of the body's own sources of non-ovarian estrogen.

By the end of this textbook, readers will have a clear understanding of the state of knowledge about women's biology and the skills to be able to recognize biased notions masquerading as science. In the spirit of Simone De Beauvoir, this awareness will lead to a more accurate understanding of, and a genuine appreciation and respect for, womanhood in and of itself.

ACKNOWLEDGMENTS

This book would not have been possible without the gracious help of many individuals. In particular, the authors would like to thank reviewers Bill Maier, Beth Young, Nancy Grace, Suzanne E. Franks, LeAne Rutherford, Karen Kolias, Judy Seymour, Stacy Ake, and Catherine Podeszwa for their excellent and helpful feedback. This text has been much improved by their conscientious reading. Any errors that remain are the authors' alone.

We would also like to thank the many friends, family, and colleagues who have provided information, support, and guidance throughout the writing process. Elizabeth Borden, Rosemary Quebral, the Thoennes family, Dee Belk, Deborah Shubat, and Judy Seymour all lent support and shared personal experiences of their own biological lives. Merry Jo Oursler, Sandy Christian, Lisa Messerer, and Anne Hershey provided professional expertise and advice.

The authors are indebted to Donald Christian for supporting the development of our Biology of Women course at the University of Minnesota-Duluth. The UMD Commission on Women provided financial support for the inital phases of textbook development. Bob Tessman and Janet Morey of Harcourt Brace were instrumental in bringing this book to the attention of the publisher. Bob has continued to serve as a strong supporter of and advocate for this project.

Virginia Borden would like to especially thank Bill Maier for the tremendous amount of emotional support, thoughtful feedback, and insightful conversation he provided during the production of this textbook. Virginia is extremely grateful for all that he shares with her.

Colleen Belk would like to thank Bob Belk for a lifetime of personal support and Mac for all the love, sweetness, and joy he brings to her life.

Virginia Borden
Colleen Belk

JANUARY, 1998

ILLUSTRATED BY

Kathryn Marsaa
and
David Pfaff

CONTENTS

CHAPTER 1 The History of Women's Biology 1

CHAPTER 2 Understanding and Evaluating Science 11

CHAPTER 3 The Evolution of Sex and Gender 27

CHAPTER 4 Sex Determination 49

CHAPTER 5 Sexual Differentiation and Development 63

CHAPTER 6 Women's Bodies I: Anatomy 81

CHAPTER 7 Women's Bodies II: Muscle, Fat, and Health 107

CHAPTER 8 Menstruation 127

CHAPTER 9 Oogenesis and Fertilization 151

CHAPTER 10 Pregnancy and Birthing 169

CHAPTER 11 Women Postpartum 189

CHAPTER 12 The Control of Fertility 209

CHAPTER 13 Women and Cancer 239

CHAPTER 14 Menopause and Aging 251

For our mothers, Dee Belk and Elizabeth Borden

THE SECOND X

THE BIOLOGY OF WOMEN

CHAPTER 1

This book will help you recognize biased notions masquerading as science.

THE HISTORY OF
WOMEN'S BIOLOGY

WHY A BOOK ON WOMEN'S BIOLOGY?

Since women's biology has traditionally been seen as a deviation from the male norm, a book dedicated to the wonders of women's biology is required to help reshape the manner in which biological events unique to women are viewed. In her classic 1953 text *The Second Sex,* Simone De Beauvoir illustrates the dangers of treating women as "other" in the social and political spheres. This text, *The Second X,* illustrates the dangers inherent in treating women's biology as "other."

The purpose of this chapter is to outline the history of negative treatment that women's biology has received by the scientific and medical communities in the distant and not so distant past. This chapter will also illustrate how the residues of this history have served to legitimize and reinforce stereotypes about contemporary women. These stereotypes, once widely accepted, continue to insidiously and subtly hamper women today.

The remaining chapters of this text will focus on biological phenomena unique to women and, in doing so, will help to dispel many of the negative stereotypes about women's biology that have cultural, not biological, origins. This book will help you recognize biased notions masquerading as science. This recognition should lead to a more accurate understanding of, and a genuine appreciation and respect for, femaleness in and of itself—not as an addendum to maleness.

How Things Were

Disturbances of the womb were thought to cause hysteria, which was "treated" by removal of the uterus, hence the term hysterectomy.

1

While things have improved tremendously for women in the United States, early ideas about women's nature, put forth by respected scientists, philosophers of science, and medical doctors, continue to shape and mold perceptions about the innate abilities of women. It is only through an understanding of the origins and persistence of some of these biased ideas that we can begin to recognize and discount the characterizations of women as "other" and less.

The notion of women as the other, second sex due to their biology can be unearthed in the works of early philosophers of science. Early Greek philosophers such as Plato believed that all humans were originally male and that their punishment for a failure to live a good life was to be reincarnated as a female. Plato's student Aristotle considered femaleness to be a deformity and believed, in fact, that women were underdeveloped males who arose as a result of some defect in the developmental pathway toward maleness. Aristotle wrote,

> Just as the young of mutilated parents are sometimes born mutilated and sometimes not, so also the young born of a female are sometimes female and sometimes male instead. For the female is, as it were, a mutilated male, and the catamenia [menstrual discharge] are semen, only not pure; for there is only one thing they have not in them, the principle of soul.

The residual effects of these philosophies can be seen in the negative aura currently surrounding women's biology. Not many people, male or female, would argue that women should be proud of their biology, while men are urged to do so. Take for example the braggadocio associated with male reproductive processes. Sperm counts are a sign of male virility, while we would never expect to hear a woman boast about her egg counts. Think of how odd it would sound for a woman to say "Why, I ovulated well into my fifties." Or consider the common response to a couple who has given birth to twins: Typically the father of the twins is congratulated by statements such as "I didn't know you had it in you," while it was actually the mother who was exceptionally virile. In the case of dizygotic twins (twins that arise as a result of two separate egg cells being fertilized by two different sperm), the woman actually ovulates twice in one menstrual cycle. Therefore, both of the eggs were probably fertilized by separate sperm from a single ejaculate, yet it is the male who is congratulated for his virility.

Menstruation is another example of a biological process cloaked in shame. Consequently, women are expected to hide their menstruation, and most of us oblige. How many women walk to a public bathroom with a tampon in hand, not hidden in a purse or up a shirt sleeve?

This type of shame is not limited to menstruation itself— indeed, the aura of shame encompasses the whole vaginal region. For example, it is considered normal practice for women to douche in order to alter the natural, normal smell of their vaginas. Small children are taught the word penis, but very few are taught the word clitoris. Some textbooks even leave the clitoris out of drawings of the female reproductive system.

Shame concerning reproductive organs can be tracked back to Hippocrates, the ancient Greek physician considered by many to be the early founder of the science of medicine. Hippocrates thought the womb dried out without intercourse and believed that the womb required the moisture provided by semen. He (whose Hippocratic oath all physicians swear to) prescribed intercourse and pregnancy as the cures for many female illnesses.

The womb has long been the subject of peculiar hypotheses by philosophers and scientists other than Hippocrates. Medieval doctors believed that menstruation caused women to put all their energy into the womb, sparing little energy for the intellect. It was also believed that the uterus moved around inside the body cavities causing maladies as it moved, giving rise to the term "wandering uterus." Disturbances of the womb were thought to cause hysteria, which was "treated" by removal of the uterus, hence the term hysterectomy. Some medical doctors thought that the "foul vapors" caused by the "failure to expel blood" by menopausal women negatively affected women's brains. The effects of this particular idea (and others like it) permeate our culture's description of menopause as a time of loss in spite of the fact that many women do not experience menopause as a time of loss, and it need not be viewed that way.

The clitoris, like the uterus and vagina, did not escape the attention of early physicians. Removal of the clitoris (clitoridectomy) was prescribed for mental afflictions and as a response to female masturbation. Instead of considering legitimate reasons for mental anguish, such as the severe oppression of women, removal of female genitalia was performed. Clitoridectomy in response to masturbation can be viewed as a surgical reinforcement of the inability of most persons to regard women's sexuality as having any purpose other than reproduction.

Arguably, the legacy of many of these ideas continues to be embodied in the cultural acceptance of male sexuality and the lack of acceptance of female sexuality. Males are congratulated for their sexual conquests while females are derided.

This attitude plays itself out to the extreme in the continued derisive references to unwed mothers, teenage mothers, and welfare mothers. These women are railed against in contemporary culture, while most of them would not be in need of society's help if the fathers were doing their share. Where *is* the father in all of this? He is certainly not expected to pay the same price for his sexuality as the mother is.

Other philosophers, like Descartes, believed that women were influenced by passion, not by reason, and that this sex difference was biological in origin. The lasting effects of this philosophy are seen in the division, by gender, of career choices. Traditionally females have the jobs that require nurturing while males have the jobs that require acute analytical skills. For example, females (presumably due to their innate nurturing abilities) are more likely to run childcare centers while males (presumably due to their superior reasoning abilities and capability for aggression) run large corporations. The fact is that the financial rewards for supposed female traits are far exceeded by the financial rewards for supposed male traits. Consider the differences in income and benefits packages between a childcare worker and a CEO. Even in science, most often the investigator analyzing the data and theorizing about its significance is male and the technician doing the lab work is more likely to be female.

The idea that men are more courageous, intelligent, and energetic than women was advanced by the biologist Charles Darwin. He believed that evolution selected for these traits in men and not in women. The not-so-subtle outcome of attitudes like Darwin's can be seen in Hollywood movies season after season. While there are a few notable exceptions (*Alien* and *Terminator* 2 come to mind), it is normally exclusively male characters who are able to perform feats of incredible strength. Somehow, audiences are willing to accept suspensions of reality where male characters are involved, such as one heroic man fighting off many heavily armed "bad guys" with his bare fists. Rarely, however, is the woman in a typical film even able to protect herself, much less fight off several perpetrators at once.

The refusal of early scientists to accept women on their own terms led to the burgeoning of the dubious field of craniology, the study of the size and shape of the skull as a determinant of intelligence. When 19th century craniologists found that women's brains were smaller, they deemed women to be intellectually inferior. The fact that women's brains are actually bigger than men's brains relative to body size did little to dissuade these scientists. Their conclusions matched their preconceived notions, which seemed more convincing than the facts. A popular argument at this time claimed that women's intellectual inferiority was a manifestation of their biology and therefore increasing opportunities for women's education would be useless. In the example of the craniologists, it becomes clear that when scientists have biased notions to begin with, he or she they can interpret "facts" quite subjectively. The fall out of the brain size/intelligence work had powerful effects on women's subjugation during the 19th century and residues can be found today in the onslaught of studies that attempt to ascribe certain qualities to female brains (passivity, nurturance) and male brains (aggressiveness, competitiveness). This argument serves to legitimize the idea that females are better suited to the kinds of roles that require nurturing (generally non-paid jobs like mothering or very low-paid jobs) and males more suited for jobs that reward their aggressive natures.

Another historical figure who can be credited with leaving a lasting hangover of negative female archetypes is the founder of psychoanalysis, Sigmund Freud, who believed (among many other equally deleterious things) that a woman's penis envy could only be overcome by the production of a baby boy. The whole notion of penis envy is one that persists and one that perpetuates the portrayal of women as men without penises. This portrayal has caused countless problems in medical research and treatment. Women are most decidedly not men without penises, they are women, with differences in physiology and both reproductive and nonreproductive anatomy. To begin to think of how silly the concept of penis envy is, consider the rather compelling argument one could make for men having clitoris envy. Why, who wouldn't be envious of genitalia that were protected (not hanging free, exposed to all sorts of hazards), useful solely for a person's sexual pleasure and whose use never resulted in pregnancy? In fact, women don't have penis envy at all. What women are envious of is the range of opportunities supported by, and the innate respect garnered by, the presence of a penis.

While the effects of these philosophies about women's biology have been shown to permeate modern culture, they also began the not so beneficial practice of defining femaleness and maleness as being opposites (consider the phrase opposite sex). Pitting females against males, when femaleness has already been defined as otherness and hence wrong, puts women in the position of having to fight a battle they are destined to lose, a battle they should not even have to fight.

Let's revisit the opinion that women are ruled by passion while men are ruled by reason, which is another way of saying that women are more emotional than men. While it may be true that some women are more emotional than some men, this is certainly not always the case. Even when true, being emotional isn't necessarily bad. Clearly, there are times when it is more rational to be emotional. The problem starts when the male level of emotion is considered the norm, and the female level an unacceptable deviation from the norm. It would be just as easy to define a woman's level of emotionality as the norm and consider the male to be emotionally stilted. However, the historical bias against women's "natures" prevents us from doing so.

It is not the intent of this book to cast femaleness as inherently good and maleness as inherently bad. It is, however, our intent to point out that many views of women's biology are couched in the negative when they need not be. Suggesting that women are more emotional than men, that this is because of their biology, and defining emotionality as bad truly stacks the deck against women and limits both females and males from reaching their full human potential. It implies that we are all, females and males, essentially half people. Females can't be aggressive, and males can't be nurturing. This is clearly not the case. A well-rounded person will want to have access to the full range of traits.

How Things Are

> *The suggestion that women's biology is too complex for them to be included in clinical drug trials is a frightening one for women and leads to what can only be described as sub-par health care for half the population.*

The previous section of this chapter showed that historical ideas about women's biological inferiority continue to have lasting negative effects on women in terms of subtle, insidious biases against women. This portion of the chapter will outline some of the ways in which women continue to struggle to overcome cultural biases that limit their opportunities, especially in the sciences.

If you are unconvinced that our culture limits women's opportunities consider the example of a woman out walking alone at night. This is a right that most males can take for granted, but if a woman is attacked while out on an evening walk through a park, the first question people will ask is, "What was she doing there?" This was a typical response following the brutal rape and beating of a female jogger in New York City's Central Park.

While few people today would suggest that women are less intelligent than men, there are far fewer women than men succeeding in science and medicine, typically viewed as fields open only to intelligent people. More importantly, even when numbers of females and males declaring a science or pre-medicine major are equal upon college entrance, at each level of advancement women are being lost from the so-called pipeline. Biology departments award around 50% of their undergraduate degrees to women. The first loss of women from the pipeline occurs at the decision to attend graduate school. Women make up 42% of biology graduate students. The next level of advancement, post-doctoral research, sees an even greater loss of women as compared to men, and the loss continues such that only about 30% of all employed scientists are female and only 19% of college faculty in the life sciences are women.

This phenomenon is not particular to science. Indeed, there are very few fields where women and men are equally represented in the upper echelons. It's not just a matter of representation either. Women in nearly every work sector earn 12 to 15% less than their male colleagues, even when years of experience are factored in. In academe, that translates into an average starting salary of $28,000 for a female Ph.D. and a $37,000 starting salary for her male colleague. For these reasons, the example of women's lack of success in biology is representative not only of the problems facing women in science and medicine but of the kinds of problems women face in most male dominated fields.

In addition to historically rooted cultural biases about women's capabilities, women's biology is currently negatively impacted by (1) the underrepresentation of women in medical trials, which is caused in part by (2) the lack of women in biology, which can be explained in part by (3) the culture's lowered expectations for women in fields requiring sharp analytical skills and (4) the culture of science itself.

The Underrepresentation of Women in Medical Trials Are women considered in medical trials? The National Institute of Health (NIH) is a governmental organization set up to fund research aimed at improving human health. In the past, the NIH has been remiss about including women in clinical trials of drugs being tested prior to the marketing of these drugs. They too have made the assumption that women's and men's biology are the same, and that drugs tested on males will have the same effects on females. However, women's biology in many cases differs markedly from men's biology, as examples throughout this book will show.

The justification for testing drugs on males only was that it was difficult to sort out the effects of female hormonal fluctuations on drug responses. These hormonal fluctuations were thought of as an extra variable, a variable too cumbersome to include in these studies. The suggestion that women's biology is too complex to be included in clinical drug trials is a frightening one for women and leads to what can only be described as sub-par health care for half the population. Additionally, the logic itself turns out to be flawed because many scientists have shown that males as well as females undergo cyclic changes in hormone levels. So the notion that females are too difficult to study because of their monthly hormonal fluctuations applies to males as well.

While the NIH now requires a higher participation of women in drug trials, recent examples demonstrate that sex differences are not always considered. For example, in 1985, a cholesterol lowering drug (Hamilton, 1995) was tested on close to 4000 males and no females, even though heart disease is the leading cause of death among older women.

There are more examples of important studies neglecting women. For example, the 1990 Multiple Risk Factor Intervention Trial (abbreviated, tellingly, MR FIT) examined mortality from coronary heart disease in close to 13,000 men, but no women. In 1989, the Physicians Health Steering Committee found that low doses of aspirin reduced the risk of some types of heart disease in over 20,000 men but did not test the effects of aspirin on women.

The example of heart disease illustrates another problem with excluding women. Heart disease, often thought of as a male disease, is the leading cause of death in older women. Lack of research on the effects of heart disease prevention drugs on women (whose hearts are smaller in relation to their body size) is in part due to the designation of heart disease as a male disease.

The same situation has revealed itself with AIDS research. AIDS is now increasing more rapidly among women than any other group, and women have different symptoms than men. Again, due to the designation of AIDS as a male disease, research into its effects on women has been scarce. According to Sue Rosser (1991), the limited research on AIDS in women has focused on women as prostitutes or mothers. Viewing women as vectors for transmission to men (prostitutes) or the fetus (mother) has produced little information on the progress of AIDS in most women. Consequently, women die approximately 15 weeks after diagnosis and males die 30 months after diagnosis.

The Lack of Women in Biology   Do women have an equal chance in science? One classic study by D. W. Chambers (1983) suggests that as early as kindergarten, women are not expected to be scientists. Chambers asked 4,807 kindergartners to draw a scientist; only 28 drew a female scientist.

While the perception of science as a male vocation has softened in the past decade, many facts remind us of how far women have to go to be perceived as equals in this field. To begin with, there are fewer women with Ph.Ds in biology than men. Because a Ph.D. is required for positions of power both in academe and industry, fewer women are able to influence the field. Of those women who do have Ph.Ds, many hold non-tenure track positions. In fact, twice as many women with Ph.Ds as men with Ph.Ds are in such positions, which means that they are not eligible for research funds. All of these factors explain why the NIH only awards 20% of its grant money to women investigators. Because scientific success is often bluntly defined by the number of dollars a scientist receives in grants, lower research funding clearly puts women at a disadvantage.

One lesson learned from the success women have had in biology at the college level is that the single biggest predictor of the future success of women is the previous success of women. In other words, when the number of women in a field reaches "critical mass," other women realize that this is a field where women are respected and can succeed and are more likely to follow in the footsteps of these female mentors. Tokenism, such as having one or two female scientists in a large department, is recognized by students for what it is and does not have the same effect as actual parity. From the example of biologists, we have learned that only at critical mass is gender stratification at the college level attenuated. The huge waste of talent at the advanced degree level can be partly explained by the lowered cultural expectations for women.

Lowered Expectations for Women in Fields Requiring Sharp Analytical Skills   Do the cultural biases that label women as biologically inferior translate into a decreased respect for women's analytical abilities and render women more susceptible to dubious judgments about their intellectual achievements and scientific skill? Unfortunately, this appears to be the case as is illustrated by the work of Myra Sadker and David Sadker (1994), who showed that math and science teachers make more eye contact with boys and pay more attention to them than they do to girls in their classes.

According to the Sadkers' recent book, *Failing at Fairness*, boys receive the majority of attention in U.S. classrooms, and girls are rewarded for being quiet and cooperative. This subtle form of discrimination was exemplified by differences in teachers' responses to girls and boys. When girls were called on in class to answer a question, the typical teacher response was "good" or "okay" while the boys more often received probing follow-up questions. This may seem innocuous, but it illustrates one of the many ways in which boys are taught that what they have to say is important, and girls are not encouraged to value their thoughts and ideas. One need only attend a typical college biology lecture to see the effects of this message on women, who are largely mute in the lecture hall.

There is absolutely no data to support the widely held belief that girls are actually biologically inferior to boys in analytic abilities, yet this belief seems to be affecting the way girls are treated in school as well as girls' own self-perceptions. In fact, many researchers have found that upon entry into school, girls outscore boys on achievement tests. In spite of this, by the time girls leave high school, they tend to have less self-esteem than boys. Could this lowering in self-esteem have anything to do with the girls' new-found awareness of the limitations imposed on their behaviors and societal roles? Imagine starting out believing that you could be or do anything you wanted, but then consistently being reminded of your "lower" capabilities by a society that fails to value women. Consider the effects of the slowly dawning awareness that you must keep your body covered, be ashamed of your body's natural processes, be considered promiscuous if you have sex and frigid if you don't, be paid less than a male worker of equal education and skills, and be considered unattractive when your body puts on the body fat it naturally acquires. This would lower the self-esteem of any thinking person.

Perhaps in response to this lowering of self-esteem, many high school girls seem to spend more time on their hair than they do on math. Those girls who do keep up with their math have to battle the clear message that boys are better at it than girls. In reality, "the difference in math ability [between men and women] is so close to zero right now, that we should consider it zero," says Janet Hyde, a University of Wisconsin scientist who recently conducted a massive comparative analysis of math performance and gender (1990). Her study compared the SAT math scores of four million high school students and found that women actually had a slight advantage over men. When women's scores were lower than men's, Hyde found that it was not ability separating the sexes, it was the number of math courses taken in high school.

By graduation from high school, only 28% of all female students have taken three or more years of math and science, compared to 40% of males. This discrepancy leaves many girls ineligible for most college majors requiring math and science, unless they spend years making up this deficiency.

The women who do make it in science continue to fight the uphill battle of lowered cultural expectations for women. Witness yet another study of scientific sexism reported in the June 1996 edition of *The Economist* that showed research papers to a test group consisting of both male and female reviewers. Some of the papers were purportedly written by a Joan T. McKay and some by a John T. McKay. Both the female and male reviewers rated the papers lower if they were attributed to Joan, rather than John. Similar studies have shown the same biased results using "applications" for teaching positions at universities, as well as students' assessments of professor performances. These results would clearly hamper the careers of women scientists. In addition to such outright sexism, women are also subject to something even more difficult to grab hold of and change: the culture of science itself.

The Culture of Science When you think of a typical biological researcher, the image of a driven scientist working late into the night may come to mind. You might think that this image is not an accurate reflection of the actual situation, but in most, if not all, successful labs in the 1990s this is actually the case. A typical work week for a graduate student, post-doctoral researcher, or the laboratory's principle investigator is much closer to 60,

70, or even 80 hours a week than the standard 40-hour work week of most U.S. workers. Many graduate students will sleep in the lab in order to tend to experiments rather than go home and risk an experimental mishap. In most molecular biology and biochemistry labs, weekends are the busiest times because students do not have classes to attend. At the lunch table, scientists trade stories of how late they worked the night before or how early they got to the lab in the morning. In science, extremely hard work is necessary in order to succeed. A scientist who does not work extended hours cannot keep up with new techniques, journal articles, and competitors. Because many people are willing to work such long hours, hard work becomes the norm for those who succeed in science.

Nothing is wrong with hard work per se, but this cultural value evolved at a time when most scientists were either single males or married males with stay-at-home wives. When the first molecular biology labs started operating in the 1950s and 1960s, women scientists were expected to forgo having families. Even today, many women have given up having children in order to succeed in science. One compelling reason for this is that a university professor's tenure decision is usually based on the work they perform in their early to middle 30s, a time when most women with careers are raising small children.

This level of commitment is equally expected of females and males, which is fine for single people who are willing to do the work. However, when a woman (or man) has a family, the demands of a career in science make it very difficult to keep up. Because women still perform the majority of child related duties, even in enlightened marriages, women often have a more difficult time than men. While this culture does not specifically exclude women who choose to have families, women pay a much higher price for their success.

This phenomenon affects men with families as well but seems to result in a higher loss of women from science than men. One explanation might be that men with children are more likely than women with children to have a stay-at-home spouse. Adding to the loss of women from science is the so-called "two-body problem" that arises when scientists marry each other. This arrangement typically deflects women's careers from reaching their highest potential because two career couples often have to relocate to a region where both can find work. This often forces a woman to make compromises in terms of finding a job that best fits her training and provides the most opportunity for advancement.

Science as a whole loses out when people with children are squeezed out, because their different perspectives can lead to novel insights that should not be squandered. Science would be better served by valuing both people who spend long hours in the lab and people who choose to have differently balanced lives.

If our society were more supportive of families some of this problem would be alleviated, but women would still face other gender-related difficulties. In Sweden, for example, long leaves are allowed by federal law. Up to one year of paid leave is allowed for new parents, which the mother and father can split however they choose, to which they can add up to six months of unpaid leave. However, a recent study demonstrated that women are still at a disadvantage. Wenneras and Wold (1997) surveyed scientists and isolated the three factors that had a significant influence on scientific peer review: the scientist's productivity, the relationship between the scientist and the reviewer, and the scientist's gender. For a female scientist to be awarded the same score as her male colleague, she needed to publish three more papers in *Science* or *Nature* (journals so prestigious that most scientists will never publish in them) or 20 more papers in other journals. In other words, a woman must be 2.5 times as productive as a man in order to be considered his scientific equal. Because Sweden is considered to be one of the most egalitarian countries in the world, these results suggest that women scientists in any country must far exceed the accomplishments of male scientists to be considered their equals.

Many researchers are beginning to wonder if women "do science" differently than men. Support for this notion was found by Gerhard Sonnert and Gerald Holton (both of

Harvard), who reported their findings about the attitudes of 800 scientists (males and females), all of whom began their careers with prestigious postdoctoral fellowships. This study was unique in that comparisons were being made between females and males who were already succeeding in science. One interesting result was the finding that women were more likely to try to find their own "niche" rather than to engage in competition in the most active fields of science.

Sonnert and Holton's finding that women prefer to avoid competition is an example of a different perspective that women bring to science. In the culture of science, investigators often go head-to-head in battles to answer the exact same research problem. Even though the head-to-head approach does yield good results quickly in many instances, it also makes sense to ask different questions and use different experimental approaches to answer these questions, a technique that seems to be favored by women.

Sonnert and Holton also found more far-reaching differences between women and men. They found that women are "inclined toward more comprehensive and synthetic work." Evidence for this theory was the number and types of publications women and men had. Women published slightly fewer papers than men, but the citation rate for women's papers was higher. The women in the Sonnert and Holton study published an average of 2.3 papers a year, while the men published an average of 2.8. But the citation rate for the females was much higher—24.4 per paper written by a female and 14.4 per paper written by a male. The higher citation rate of the women's papers would seem to indicate that their work had more widespread and lasting effects than the men's.

Remarkably, even for these accomplished scientists, women's low self confidence endures. While 70% of the men saw their own scientific ability as being above average, only 52% of the women felt the same way. Whether this results from women underestimating their own abilities, or having a more realistic view of their abilities, is difficult to determine. Once again, early socialization results in differing world views for males and females.

Not so surprisingly, the language of science reflects a more male world view. For example, consider the following list of common terms from the field of immunology: invasion, competition, inhibition, penetration. It is possible that viewing science in such warlike terms limits the types of questions one can pose about the process. For example, one might ask how a cell of the immune system knows to attack and destroy foreign particles in the blood stream. Do the cells of the immune system excrete a chemical that will damage the foreign particle (in a manner analogous to a war plane dropping bombs on targets)? Conversely, if one views immunology in less warlike terms, one might ask how the cells of the immune system can tell that a foreign particle is foreign. Do the cells of the immune system wrap themselves around the particle? Do they fuse with the particle and bring it inside the cell in order to determine what the foreign particle is? A language that reflects only one world view is by definition limited in scope. Additionally, the language may serve to dissuade young women from entering the field if they do not feel comfortable with the language itself.

Lastly, females and males appear to operate differently even in the work environment. Mary Frank Fox, at Georgia Institute of Technology, surveyed 3,300 graduate students in various fields (1992). She found a clear female–male divide on most questions. For example, women were more likely than men to make a formal appointment to see a supervisor instead of talking to them during more informal meetings, such as running into them in the hallway. They were also less likely than men to view supervisors as colleagues and preferred collaboration more than men did.

Many women are aware of the difficulties associated with making informal contacts in a male-dominated environment. A lone woman is less likely to go for drinks on Friday afternoon, or be involved in sport outings where much vital informal information is traded and where lasting friendships and collaborations are forged. Again, this type of problem is not the sole province of biology; correlates can be found in corporate America as well.

This chapter should in no way be seen as an attempt to dissuade women from becoming biologists. Rather it is an attempt to raise awareness of potential obstacles so that women can *recognize* what is happening around them, *realize* that it has nothing to do with their scientific ability, and *devise* strategies for dealing with these issues. Whether a woman feels more comfortable adopting the more "male" traits in order to succeed or whether she chooses to succeed in her own way is her decision, and most women will probably do a little of both.

REFERENCES

American Institute of Physicists Conference Proceedings: Report on Physicists Salaries. Jan. 8, 1994.

Aristotle. (1952). On the generation of animals. In Arthur Platt (Trans.), *The works of Aristotle: Vol. 2. The great books of the Western world.* Chicago: William Benton.

Chambers, D. W. (1983) Stereotypic images of the scientist: The Draw a Scientist Test. *Science Education 67,* 255–265.

Chronicle of Higher Education. Sept. 1 Almanac Issue, 1994.

Etzkowitz, H., Kemelgor, C., Neuschatz, M., & Uzzi, B. (1994). In W. Pearsons, Jr., & I. Fletcher (Eds.), *Who will do science? Educating the next generation.* Johns Hopkins University Press.

Fox, M. F., & Firebaugh, G. (1992). Confidence in science, the gender gap. *Social Science Quarterly 73,* 101–113.

Gerson, K. (1985). *Hard choices: How women decide about work, career and motherhood.* Berkeley: University of California Press.

Hamilton, J. (1985). Avoiding methodological biases in gender–related research. *Women's Health Report of the Public Health Service Task Force on Women's Health Issues.* Washington, DC: U.S. Department of Health and Human Services Public Service.

Hyde, J., Fennema, E., & Ryan, M. (1990). Gender comparisons of mathematic attitudes and affect: A meta analysis. *Psychology of Women Quarterly 14,* 299–324.

Multiple Risk Factor Intervention Trial Group. (1990). Mortality rates after 10.5 years for participants in the multiple risk factor intervention trial: Findings relate to a prior hypothesis of the trial. *Journal of the American Medical Association 263,* 1795–1801.

Rosser, S. V. (1991). AIDS and women. *AIDS Education and Prevention 3,* 230–240.

Sadker, M., & Sadker, D. (1994). *Failing at fairness: How our schools cheat girls.* Touchstone, Simon and Schuster.

Sonnert, G., & Holton, G. (1996). Career patterns of women and men in the sciences. *American Scientist 84,* 63–71.

The Task Force. (1988). Leaky pipeline: Task force on women, minorities and handicapped in science and technology. *Changing America: The new face of science and engineering.* Washington, DC.

Wenneras, C., & Wold, A. (1997). Nepotism and sexism in peer review. *Nature 387,* 341–343.

CHAPTER 2

Will taking birth control pills put me at risk for breast cancer?"

"My grandmother died as a result of heart disease. What sorts of lifestyle and diet choices will keep me protected from this disease?"

"My son's babysitter told me that it is unnatural for a boy to be so interested in playing with dolls. Is there something wrong with him?"

UNDERSTANDING AND
EVALUATING SCIENCE

INTRODUCTION

Many of you have probably had questions like these. You may have tried to find answers to these questions by consulting with friends, checking out books from the library, watching a television news special, or talking to your doctor. Often when you consult more than one of these sources, you receive more than one answer to your questions. Then what do you do?

These questions can and have been addressed using scientific research. Information obtained via scientific study is used by governments, organizations, and individuals to help make decisions about important issues. Given the amount of influence science has on our lives, it is astounding (and dismaying) how few people really understand how scientists accumulate information about the world or the process of science itself.

In order to evaluate the accuracy and meaning of scientific information, it is necessary to have an understanding of the scientific process. Reports of scientific research are often announced in the breathless style of "breaking news," only to be refuted or contradicted by later reports. These contradictions have caused much confusion and frustration among consumers of science, and repeated contradictions have caused many people to give up on their attempts to evaluate scientific information. However, contradiction and refutation in media reports mirror the sometimes chaotic process of scientific discovery, a process that has led to many important changes in our lives, environment, and outlook. To effectively participate in the evaluation of scientific results and to choose wisely the courses of action or policy changes based on those results, we need to understand the process by which scientific knowledge is created. One of the goals of this book is to help you deal with the flood of scientific information that surrounds us, particularly information relating to women's lives. This chapter in particular will give you some guidelines for understanding and evaluating the constant barrage of scientific information we all experience.

Increased understanding of the process of obtaining scientific information will also help you understand your own body. In this chapter, we will discuss the influence of society on scientific research about women's health. Both the scientific questions that are asked and the methods by which these questions are answered are influenced by the social environment of scientific researchers. An exploration of the role of science as a source of information about your own body will make you a better consumer of health care of all types. Finally, a better understanding of the science relating to women's lives will help you evaluate information about what constitutes a woman's "nature" and the influence of biology (or lack of biological influence) on many aspects of a woman's life.

SCIENCE AS A WAY OF KNOWING

Science can give us the tools and knowledge that allow us to develop hormonal birth control methods, but the scientific method cannot tell us if it is right, or ethical, to require certain women to use them.

How do we know what we know about the world? Of course, we have learned about the world from our parents and other teachers, who learned it from their parents and teachers before them, and so on. But where did this knowledge come from? In fact, there are many sources of understanding, or ways of knowing, about the world: These include knowledge gained through revelations based on faith, knowledge gained through intuition, through philosophy, and through science.

Science as a way of knowing is distinct because it requires direct observations of the natural world in order to develop knowledge and insight. The process of science starts with some basic assumptions. One is that the natural world has an order that humans can observe and interpret. Additionally, scientists assume that as long as the conditions surrounding an action remain the same, the consequences of that action will always be the same. These assumptions can help us see both the power of science as a way of knowing and its limitations.

With these assumptions as a guiding framework, scientists can make specific predictions about the outcomes of actions. If these predictions are correct, scientists can assume that they understand enough about what they are studying to manipulate that aspect of the world around them. For example, scientists have been able to repeatedly demonstrate that ovulation (release of eggs) is suppressed when levels of estrogen, a hormone produced by the ovaries, are kept constant in a woman's bloodstream. Using this scientific information, pharmaceutical companies produce birth control pills containing estrogen that reliably prevent conception. Birth control pills were made possible, at least in part, through the powerful tool of the scientific method.

On the other hand, because science is limited to measurable, observable phenomena, the scientific method cannot address questions of morality, spirituality, or ethics. Science can give us the tools and knowledge that allow us to develop hormonal birth control methods, but the scientific method cannot tell us if it is *right*, or ethical, to require certain women to use them. Scientific information is basically amoral—that is, the information itself does not imply a moral judgment. Of course, humans are moral creatures, and people will often use scientific justification to support a particular moral standpoint. For instance, science may be able to show that, *on average*, women are less likely to demonstrate certain types of aggressive behaviors than men. (Note that finding this average difference between women and men is not the same as saying "all women are less aggressive than all men" or "women are never aggressive in any situation." We will return to this point in Chapter 6.) People may wish to use scientific information like this to justify excluding women from activities where a certain type of aggression is considered mandatory, like in military combat, particular sports activities, or as top corporate executives, by arguing that such activities are "unnatural" for women. However, the scientific information itself does not address the *morality* of excluding women from activities based on average biological measures. Nor do scientific results regarding the tendency to display aggressive behavior tell us whether it is indeed preferable to have very aggressive individuals in the infantry or in corporate offices. The use of scientific information in our lives is strongly influenced by other ways of knowing about the world, such as faith and philosophy.

In this book we will be presenting the results of scientific research on women's (and men's) biology. All of us have ways of understanding the world based on a faith tradition and/or a personal philosophy that help us decide *how* to use the information gained from scientific research. Throughout this book, we will encourage you to continually explore your feelings about the moral, ethical, and philosophical aspects of the results of the research we present.

■ DISCUSSION EXERCISE 1

Science cannot test questions of morality or philosophy. Which of the following questions, as stated, can be addressed by science and which cannot? For the ones that cannot, modify the question to a form that can be tested.

1.1. Why does our skin lose its elasticity when we age? can

1.2. What is the best way to discipline children? can not

1.3. Do people behave more immorally during a full moon? can not

1.4. Does watching television cause people to have shorter attention spans? can

THE PROCESS OF SCIENCE

You have to decide if you would be willing, for instance, to use a method of birth control that carried with it a small but statistically significant increase in the risk of breast cancer.

The Logic of Hypothesis Testing

Early in the development of an area of knowledge, scientists are engaged in a discovery process and aided by **inductive reasoning**. Induction consists of observing many individual events and inferring a general principle to explain all of them. For example, we might make the following observations:

1. In the early stages of Little League practices, we've noticed that boys were generally more accurate than girls when throwing a baseball.

2. As adults, men are more likely than women to engage in ball sports.

3. We know from anthropological research that in many non-technological human societies, men perform more of the hunting tasks than women.

From these observations, we may make the following inference: (1) Boys are born with brains that are better able to coordinate complex throwing motions than girls. This inferred explanation for the observed difference in throwing ability is called an **hypothesis**. (You may notice that this is only one of a number of different explanations for our observation. Can you think of other explanations for sex differences in throwing skill? We will discuss these **alternative hypotheses** later on in the chapter.)

Once a hypothesis has been developed based on observations, it may become subject to the process of verification by **deductive reasoning**. The process of deductive reasoning involves making a specific prediction about the outcome of an action or experiment. This prediction is the result we would expect if the hypothesis we have inferred is true. Deductive reasoning always takes the form of an "If...then..." statement and can be tested by performing an experiment. A deductive test of hypothesis (1) might be an experiment that tests the following assertion: **If** *boys have an inborn throwing skill and girls don't,* **then** *boys will be more accurate than girls when throwing an object which neither have much experience with —for instance, a javelin.*

Note that not all hypotheses proposed to explain an observation have been subjected to the process of deductive reasoning. Untested hypotheses (which may also be called unsupported assertions) show up regularly in discussions of health and sex differences. Whenever you hear a scientific hypothesis presented, ask yourself if it has been supported by experimentally tested deduction. If the hypothesis has not been tested, it cannot be considered scientific fact.

Even if an experimental test of a hypothesis produces the predicted results, the hypothesis is still not immediately accepted as fact. This is due to the logical structure of deductive reasoning. While deductive reasoning may be used to reject an incorrect hypothesis, it is impossible to prove a correct hypothesis using this method. This shortcoming can be visualized by way of a truth table (Figure 2.1). Consider the possible results of the experiment discussed above: Boys may be no more accurate (or even less accurate) than girls at tossing a javelin, or boys may in fact be better able to target the javelin than girls. What do these results tell us about our hypothesis? In the first case, if girls are better or there is no difference in targeting, we can reject the notion of a natural male superiority in general throwing skill. In the second case, if boys are better than girls at targeting, as we predicted, we can only say that we have not disproven our hypothesis. Why can't we say the hypothesis is true? One reason might be because we can imagine other factors (like those alternative hypotheses generated earlier) that explain why boys are more accurate than girls at a javelin toss. For instance, throwing accuracy may be based more on arm length than on inborn brain connections. Boys may be better, on average, at both baseball and javelin targeting because boys have, on average, longer upper arm bones than similarly sized girls. Our experiment would show a superiority in male targeting (true prediction) but not for the reason we hypothesized (false hypothesis).

The potential always exists that hypotheses that seem to be true (because they have not been rejected by an initial experiment) may be discarded later when the results of a different experiment cause us to reject them. When studies linked consumption of oat bran to reduced cancer risk, foods labeled "made with oat bran" sold very well. Later the cancer-preventing benefits of oat bran were dismissed because continued research showed that study participants that ate large quantities of oat bran also had very healthy diets overall. A healthy diet is a more important factor in cancer prevention than any single component of that diet. Those of us who filled up on fat-laden, sugar-rich oat bran muffins probably did more to add to our cancer risk than reduce it.

FIGURE 2.1 Possible Meanings of an Experimental Outcome

Hypothesis: Boys have an inborn skill that girls do not		Girls' javelin accuracy > boys'	Boys' javelin accuracy > girls'
	True		??
	False	Yes	??

A truth table shows how the results of an experimental treatment can be used to evaluate the truth of an hypothesis. Note that getting the results predicted by the hypothesis does not prove that the hypothesis is correct, because the predicted results could have occurred for some other reason.

The Experimental Method

Does all of this discussion mean that scientific hypotheses can never be proven? The answer to that question is "yes and no." Yes, they can't be proven beyond a shadow of a doubt because of the logical structure of deductive reasoning—the true cause of a particular phenomenon may be found in a hypothesis that has not yet been inferred. However, in a practical sense, we can prove hypotheses "beyond a reasonable doubt." Scientists all accept as truth that changes in estrogen levels are required to trigger ovulation in women. This is accepted as a fact because both all reasonable alternative hypotheses about the immediate triggers for ovulation have been rejected and the remaining hypothesis has *not* been rejected under a variety of carefully controlled experimental situations. (Note that in actuality, ovulation is a very complex process. We will discuss it in more detail in Chapter 8.)

Control has a very specific meaning in science. A control subject for an experiment is an individual who is exactly like an experimental subject but is not exposed to the experimental treatment. Measurements of controls are used as baseline values for comparison of the effect of treatments. You've probably heard controls mentioned (either explicitly or implicitly) in reports about the environmental causes of cancer, among other things. For example, estrogen has been shown to cause a two-fold increase in the rate of tumor formation in lab rats. "Two-fold increase" refers to the number of tumors in lab rats exposed to estrogen (the experimental group) compared to rats in the same lab who were not exposed to estrogen (the control group). A careful control eliminates as many alternative explanations for the observed result as possible. The rats in the study, whether control or experimental subjects, should be from the same group of parents, be the same age, have received the same diet, the same light, air, and water conditions, and have even experienced the same amount of handling by the experimenters. The *only* difference between the two groups should have been the levels of estrogen they were exposed to. The most effective way of ensuring the equivalence of experimental and control groups is by the **random assignment** of animals to these categories. For instance, a researcher might put all the rats' names in a hat, draw out half and designate these rats as the experimental group and the other rats as the control group. In this way, the researcher ensures that she or he does not intentionally or unconsciously affect the results of the experiment by, for example, selecting all of the weaker rats for the control group.

Good controls are the basis of **strong inference**. If we see a difference in tumor formation in exposed and non-exposed rats, and we have limited the differences between the
experimental and control groups, we can eliminate numerous alternative hypotheses to
explain the difference, including differences in their diets, living conditions, and so on. If
we do not reject the hypothesis that estrogen causes cancer in lab rats, a carefully controlled
experiment can allow us to strongly infer that the hypothesis is true.

■ DISCUSSION EXERCISE 2

What are appropriate controls in the following studies?

2.1. Does regular exercise in rats cause a decrease in the rats' appetite?

2.2. Is the growth of house plants stunted by playing loud rock music in their vicinity?

2.3. Do pink walls decrease the number of assaults inside jails?

2.4. What is the control group in the javelin throw experiment described earlier?

A Brief Word About Statistics

The evaluation of experimental data requires the use of a branch of mathematics known as
statistics. To give readers a thorough understanding of statistics would require much more
coverage than we can provide here, but there are aspects of this science that are important
for you to understand when you are evaluating research. In short, with statistics, we can
examine the result of an experiment and determine the likelihood that the data are due to
an unavoidable error in sampling rather than a result of the experimental treatment.

Figure 2.2a illustrates the results of an experiment on estrogen exposure in lab rats. The
two bell-shaped curves indicate the distribution of tumors in treated and control animals. In
this experimental result, the average number of tumors (represented by the peak of the
curve) is higher in the rats treated with estrogen than in the rats that were not exposed.
However, the experiment only included a sample of lab rats in the world. We need to use
a statistical test to tell us how likely it is that an increase in estrogen exposure would lead
to a greater average number of tumors if *all* lab rats were treated.

There are two possible ways our experimental result may have arisen. Figure 2.2b illustrates one possibility. In this scenario, the experimental result is a good approximation of
the "real" effect of estrogen on rats. That is, if we were able to test the entire rat population, we would see an increase in the number of tumors in estrogen treated rats, just as we
saw in the experimental result. However, there is a chance that the experimental result arose
by chance. Figure 2.2c illustrates this possibility. In this case, estrogen does not actually
have an effect on tumor formation in rats. Instead, just by chance, the rats that were selected
for the experimental treatment came from the portion of the rat population that naturally
produces more tumors, while those in the control group came from the portion that is naturally low in tumors. Because of this random sampling error, the experimental result makes
it appear as if estrogen causes an increase in tumors when, in fact, it does not.

Statistical tests help us determine the likelihood that the results of an experiment are due
to the sampling error illustrated in Figure 2.2c. These tests examine factors such as the difference between the experimental and treatment groups (a smaller difference is more likely
to be due to chance) and the sample size (including more subjects in an experiment reduces
the chance that the sample is not representative of the population). Studies that report a **statistically significant** result are reporting that, *given the data that was gathered,* there is a high likelihood (usually 95–99%) that the difference seen between experimental and control groups
is equivalent to the effect of the treatment on the whole population. Of course, 95% is not
100%. With a 95% significance level, there is a 5% chance that the increase in tumors was

FIGURE 2.2   The Role of Evaluating Experimental Results

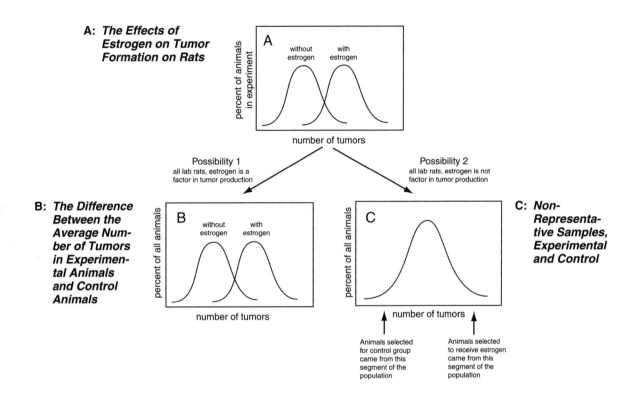

A: *The Effects of Estrogen on Tumor Formation on Rats*

B: *The Difference Between the Average Number of Tumors in Experimental Animals and Control Animals*

C: *Non-Representative Samples, Experimental and Control*

An experimental result can indicate one of two possibilities: Either the outcome of the experimental treatment reflects a real effect, or the outcome resulted from samples that were not representative of the whole population.

due to the bad luck of, by chance, picking animals for the experimental group that would have had more tumors even without any experimental treatment. One out of every 20 times using this standard, researchers report an effect of an experimental treatment that is not a real effect. An experiment with a statistically significant result will still be considered supportive of the hypothesis that estrogen causes cancer in lab rats, but the 1–5% likelihood of sampling error explains why one supportive experiment often does not give us enough information to settle a question. Only after replications (repeats) of an experiment that give the same result do we begin to feel assured that the effect of the experiment is real.

At this point, you may be able to see that a significant result statistically is not always one of **practical significance**. A statistically significant difference between, for example, women's scores and men's scores on a math exam may be a difference of one point in a possible 250 between all men and women who took the test. The practical significance of such a small difference (percentage wise) is questionable. Of course, many statistically significant results will be of practical importance as well. However, because of the different meanings of "significant," you should be careful when evaluating the results of a study. You have to decide if you would be willing, for instance, to use a method of birth control that carried with it a small but statistically significant increase in the risk of breast cancer.

Finally, statistical significance is not a measure of the accuracy of an experiment. Statistical tests all operate with the assumption that the experiment was designed and carried out correctly. Therefore, a statistically significant result should never be taken as the last word on a experimentally tested hypothesis. An examination of the experiment itself is required.

Given the logical limitations of deductive reasoning, the rigorous requirements for controls to eliminate alternative hypotheses, and the calculated level of uncertainty in statistical tests, we can see why definitive scientific answers to important questions are slow to come by. However, a well-designed experiment can certainly allow us to approach the truth. In the next section, we will discuss ways you, as a consumer of science, can evaluate scientific information.

SUMMARY

Scientific inquiry is a process of discovery and verification. Inductive reasoning, the first step, requires the formation of a general rule to explain a number of observations. This explanation can be verified (or rejected) by the process of deductive reasoning. The structure of deductive reasoning allows us to make predictions about the results of an action, but it also limits our ability to prove our proposed explanation, because a prediction may be true even if the hypothesis that generated it is false. One way to increase our confidence in a hypothesis is to test it under carefully controlled conditions that allow us to eliminate alternative explanations for the observed phenomenon. Statistics provide a tool for determining the reliability of the effect we see after completion of an experiment, but statistical tests do not help us decide if an experiment did a good job of controlling for reasonable alternate hypotheses.

EVALUATING SCIENCE

Eliminating all effects of differential social expectations and experience would require selecting girls who were thought to be boys by all the adults and peers in their lives.

Reviewing the Experimental Method

Review your answer to question 2.4: "What is the control group in the javelin throw experiment described earlier?" You may have found this question difficult to answer. Think about what the hypothesis states—boys have a difference in their brains that makes them more accurate when throwing than girls. What then is the experimental treatment? In this case, it is the state of being male. This treatment occurs pretty early in development—at conception when the egg receives either an X-chromosome bearing (female) or a Y-chromosome bearing (male) sperm (see Chapter 4 for a more in-depth explanation of how sex is determined). The control group in this experiment is the group that has not experienced the male developmental event—that is, girls.

But are girls effective controls for boys? Do girls experience everything that boys do, except the Y-chromosome? It's clear from the design of our experiment that we thought that one possible reason the boys were more accurate when throwing a baseball than the girls we observed is that boys are encouraged to spend more time playing catch as small children with their parents and peers. We assumed when we developed our experiment that throwing an object that neither sex has much experience with would control for this probable difference in the amount of practice both sexes had engaged in. This assumption is debatable. It is very possible that differences in sports-like activities early in life lead to differences in later overall sports abilities, like hand-eye coordination for throwing in general, the strength of muscles needed for throwing any object, or general confidence and competitiveness (which may lead girls to give up trying to hit a target sooner than boys). If boys have more training throughout their lifetimes in developing hand-eye coordination in throwing tasks, we might expect them to be better than girls at the javelin throw, even if there is no innate difference in throwing skill.

Imagine the ideal control for the javelin experiment: a group of girls raised *exactly* like their male counterparts. Eliminating all effects of differential social expectations and experience would require selecting girls who were thought to be boys by all the adults and peers in their lives. In fact, to remove any hint of differences in social environment, the girls themselves would have to think that they were boys. This is virtually impossible, and even if possible, of questionable ethics (see Chapter 5 for examples of such research).

The problem of adequacy of control is what makes any branch of science that deals with people (including medicine, psychology, and sociobiology) one of the most contentious, and potentially frustrating and confusing, fields of endeavor. Experiments on humans that conform to the standards of strong inference, that is with random assignment of subjects to experimental and control groups, are relatively rare. Remember that participants in an experiment must all be treated identically except for the experimental treatment. Sometimes this is possible, but imagine testing the effectiveness of a birth control drug by giving a group of women the drug and comparing their rate of pregnancies to another group of women who thought they were getting the drug but who were getting a placebo (sugar pill). To make this a controlled experiment, researchers would be subjecting women to unwanted pregnancies without their consent.

In reality, much scientific research on people is performed using what is called a correlational approach. A correlation describes a relationship between two factors. For instance, to see if estrogen causes cancer in humans, we might look at the cancer rate among women who are long-term users of birth control pills (which contain synthetic estrogen) and compare that number to the rate of cancer among women who have never used the pill. Here we are attempting to correlate estrogen levels and cancer rates in women. That is, do longer periods on the pill, and thus more exposure to estrogen, lead to higher breast cancer rates?

A correlational approach to a question such as this has several complications. As with the javelin experiment, we assume that the experimental and control groups are similar in every way, except, in this case, for their ingestion of birth control pills. Is that a good assumption? We look for the answer to that question in the design of the study. A study on this question that doesn't correct for biases that occur when assignment of subjects to control and experimental groups is not random would not reflect the effect of the pill *only* on cancer rates. Women in the non-pill group are likely on average to be older, of a lower socioeconomic status, and are more likely to be smokers than women on the pill. All of these differences between the two groups could influence their cancer risk. Better correlational studies do their best to match subject groups by only comparing women who are similar in many characteristics. For instance, we should match women according to characteristics that may influence cancer rates—for example, all should be non-smokers. Of course, matching participants does not completely solve the problem of non-randomness. Women who take the pill may have lives that are fundamentally different than women who do not, and these factors may be impossible to control for.

Correlational studies have a second flaw: A correlation between two factors *does not imply* a functional relationship between these factors. For instance, a strong correlation has been shown between foot size and reading ability among school-aged boys—boys with larger feet are at a higher reading level than boys with smaller feet. Of course, feet have nothing to do with one's ability to read. The relationship probably has something to do with age—boys feet get bigger as they grow up, and their ability to read also improves with age. However, correlational relationships are very often used as arguments promoting particular policies or behaviors. For instance, you probably have heard statements like "Children of single mothers engage in more crime than children raised in a two-parent family; therefore, to reduce crime we must reduce the number of children born to single mothers." Of course, this statement ignores all of the factors that may be *associated* with increased rates of single motherhood, like poverty or a history of abuse, each of which may potentially lead to increased crime rates in the children of single mothers. If these factors are the cause, a more effective policy to reduce crime may be to reduce poverty or punish domestic assault rather than to punish single motherhood.

Using Animal Models

Because many experiments on humans suffer from the problem of inadequate control, often researchers will use animals, such as rats, dogs, or chimpanzees, as models for the effects of drugs, environmental factors, or genes on people. As animal researchers argue, many more alternative hypotheses can be controlled for in a lab than in the messy world of human society. Using animals also allows for the testing of a larger number of subjects than testing on humans allows. Large sample sizes are an effective way of including a wide range of natural variation in the experiment and reducing the chance that the experimental or control groups are biased in some way, thus increasing the level of statistical assurance that an observed effect of an experiment is real. Perhaps most commonly, animals are often used as initial test subjects (true "guinea pigs") to determine if an experimental drug, medical treatment, food additive, or pollutant has any negative side effects.

There are serious ethical questions about the propriety of sacrificing large numbers of animals to test experimental treatments. Worldwide, over 100 million animals per year are used in scientific experiments, and many people have serious concerns about the use of animals in this manner. These animals may be subjected to painful treatments, substandard living conditions, and premature death. The use of animals as subjects in experiments that would never be allowed on humans is a major debate among scientists and animal rights activists.

While it is true that using animals as research tools may have some benefits, the applicability of the results of these types of animal studies to humans is questionable. When animals are used in scientific experiments, our ability to predict the results of a similar experiment in people is limited—rats, dogs, and chimpanzees are not humans. Tests of the drug clomiphene citrate provide a notorious example of how humans differ from some animals in basic physiology. This compound was originally tested as a birth control pill in humans in 1961 because research showed that it suppressed ovulation in rats. To the surprise of the women in the clinical trials of this drug, clomiphene citrate did not suppress ovulation in human females— in fact, it *promoted* ovulation. Instead of being a birth control pill, clomiphene citrate is now one of the most common drugs prescribed as a treatment for female infertility (see Chapter 12). The problem of non-equivalence between humans and animals is especially severe in studies that examine animal behavior and purport to reveal reasons for equivalent behavior in humans. (We will discuss this topic in more detail in Chapter 3.)

In addition to the problem of non-equivalence, highly controlled animal studies may miss interactions of drugs and lifestyle that might lead to serious complications. Animal studies of birth control pills did not reveal the dangerous interaction of oral contraceptives and cigarettes. Hundreds of women died before the link between these two factors and fatal strokes was established (see Chapter 12). Animal studies have also been criticized for not imitating the conditions by which drugs or other environmental factors are introduced to humans. Drugs taken orally by humans are sometimes applied directly to the skin of a test animal, while substances that may be absorbed by people through the skin are instead fed to animals during testing.

Research employing animal models has made valuable contributions to our understanding of humans. However, you should read studies that use animal models to predict human health effects with a degree of caution. These studies are only one part of a scientific investigation, which eventually should consist of some type of experiment using human subjects.

Controlled Experiments in Human Biology

Even if a study on humans can use a non-correlational experimental approach (for instance, a study that tests the effectiveness of a drug by comparing the effect of taking the drug to the effect of taking a placebo), there are additional problems to watch for when evaluating experimental studies, especially those on humans. Two serious problems are observer bias and subject expectation. **Observer bias** may influence experimental results in the following way: If a scientist expects a particular result, he or she may unconsciously treat control and experimental subjects differently, systematically err in measuring results, or overlook evidence that might call the hypothesis into question. For example, in the javelin experiment, experimenter bias could take a number of different forms. Perhaps the scientist somehow intimidated the girls and encouraged the boys in their throwing tasks, thus affecting their effort and the outcome. If the researcher knew which sex was hypothesized to be superior in throwing skill, she might make subtle errors in the measurement of accuracy that tended to favor one sex over the other. To avoid the problem of experimenter bias, scientists should design "blind" experiments. In a blind experiment the scientist, doctor, or technician applying the treatment does not know which group (experimental or control) any given subject is in. The results of blind experiments are much more credible than experiments in which all participants know the *expected* outcome.

The problem of **subject expectation** (sometimes called the onstage effect) is similar to that of observer bias. Individual experimental subjects may consciously or unconsciously model the behavior that they feel the researcher expects from them. Women who know that they are being evaluated in a typically male-dominated task in order to compare the sexes may feel intimidated or angry and thus not perform up to their ability. The onstage effect is also a problem in drug trials. Individuals who know they are receiving an experimental drug may be less stressed if they expect a cure, which might cause their condition to improve regardless of the effect of the drug. This problem can be corrected by putting the *subject*, as much as possible, in a blind situation. In experiments concerning drug treatments, this means not telling participants whether they are receiving the drug or a placebo. In experiments on human behavior, this often means intentionally misleading the subject about the purpose of the experiment. In the case of the javelin experiment, the researcher might tell the subject that she is interested in the relationship between the amount of sleep they received last night and their throwing accuracy.

We call experiments on humans in which *both* the research subjects and the technician performing the measurements are unaware of the true experimental hypothesis "double blind" experiments. Double-blind experiments nearly eliminate the effects of human bias on experimental results. When both subjects and researchers have few expectations about the hypothesized outcome of a particular experimental treatment, the results obtained should be considered more credible.

SUMMARY

Science dealing with human biology has unique problems when it comes to experimental design. One problem is adequate control for all alternative hypotheses; because people can rarely be randomly assigned to experimental groups, researchers must use correlation and rely on attempts to match members of already existing groups in society. This may not always control for differences between them. Animals may be able to replace humans in studies when experiments on humans would be impossible or unethical, but it is important to remember that animal biology is not identical to human biology and animals do not have social structures identical to humans. When a question can be tested experimentally, ideally both researchers and subjects should have no expectations about the experiment that may influence the outcome, and experiments should be "double blind."

SCIENCE AND SOCIETY

Scientists usually come into a field of research with opinions and assumptions about which hypotheses are likely to be true. These opinions are usually influenced not only by established science but also by the researchers' own personal ideas about "how the world works."

The Presentation of Science in the Media

Most of us receive information about scientific discoveries through various news media sources. Stories in the general media rarely contain information about the adequacy of controls, the number of subjects, or the experimental design. How can you evaluate the quality of research that supports media statements like "New onion diet leads to 20 pound weight loss in one week" or "Men found to have genetic predisposition to prefer girlish women"?

First and foremost, you should consider the source of scientific reports. Certainly news organizations will be more reliable reporters of fact than entertainment tabloids, and news organizations with science writers should be considered better reporters of the substance of a study than those without. Next, examine the story itself. Use your understanding of the limitations common in experimental design to evaluate the science that is presented. Is the story presenting the results of a scientific study, or is it building a story around an untested hypothesis? (News stories based on untested hypotheses seem especially common when the subject is a supposed evolutionary basis for human behavior.) In addition, look for clues about the adequacy of the reportage. Scientists, generally being a cautious lot, usually discuss the limitations of their research in their papers. Are these cautions noted in an article? If not, the reporter may be overemphasizing the applicability of the results. Note also if the scientific discovery itself is controversial. That is, does it reject a hypothesis that has long been supported? Does it concern a subject that is, in society, controversial (like racial differences or homosexuality)? Might it lead to a change in social policy? In these cases, we should be extremely cautious. New and unexpected research results must be evaluated in light of other scientific evidence and understanding. Reports on research that lack comments from other experts in related fields may miss important problems with a study. Finally, realize that the news media generally will publish only stories on results thought to be newsworthy. For instance, dozens of studies may show no difference in targeting ability between men and women, but the single study that does show a difference may be the one that is widely reported in the news media.

Even after reviewing all of these guidelines, you still may find situations where reports on several scientific studies of a hypothesis seem to communicate conflicting and confusing results. This could mean one of two things—either the reporter is not giving you enough information, in which case you may want to read the researchers' papers yourself, or the researchers themselves are just as confused as you are. This is, as we've already discussed, part of the nature of accumulation of knowledge via science—early on in our understanding of a phenomenon, many hypotheses are proposed, tested, and rejected. It is only by clearly understanding the process and pitfalls of scientific research that you can distinguish "what we know" from "what we don't know."

The Social Context of Science

The challenge of proving hypotheses brought about by the logic of such testing leads to a problem that all researchers and consumers of science face, which we might call "the pet hypothesis problem." Scientists usually come into a field of research with opinions and assumptions about which hypotheses are likely to be true. These opinions are usually influenced not only by established science but also by the researchers' own personal ideas about how the world works. If researchers feel strongly about the truth of a particular hypothesis, they may be unwilling to accept results, even their own results, that would normally cause the hypothesis to be rejected. Thus they might argue that they made some error in the process of performing the experiment that caused them to get negative results (i.e., results that do not support their pet hypothesis). In this case, they may be unwilling to submit for publication experiments that give them unexpected results but may repeat the experiment (sometimes multiple times) with some modifications in an attempt to obtain the result they expect. This tendency not to publish negative results in scientific literature gives readers and users of information a less clear picture of the status of any given hypothesis.

How might society influence the direction of scientific research in general? The opinions and world views of the researchers are not the only factors that impact the science that we see performed. We must add to these perspectives the views of the directors of government funding agencies, legislators, and business organizations that make grants to researchers. Through these channels, both the questions scientists test and the ways in which they are tested are heavily influenced by the society that surrounds them. Consider the following example of current scientific effort. Menopause is a period in a woman's life when menstruation and ovulation have ceased (see Chapter 14). The period of change from menstruating to menopausal is called the climeractic. A variety of physical changes occur during the climeractic and menopause, many of which are associated with changes in the source and amount of estrogen in the bloodstream. Hormone Replacement Therapy (HRT), a drug therapy that includes estrogen, is commonly prescribed to women at the climeractic and is often taken by them for the rest of their lives. Given the link of estrogen to tumor formation in animals, many researchers are interested in whether there is a link between HRT and various forms of cancer. The effort that has been put toward addressing this question is much greater than the effort that has been put toward finding non-pharmacological ways of alleviating the "symptoms" of the climeractic and menopause. This difference in effort is at least partially due to common world views that define menopause as a pathological condition (i.e., an illness) and then seek medical or technological solutions for the changes associated with this life stage. This world view is supported by enormous and financially powerful health care interests and pharmaceutical firms. It is also supported by many other organizations that profit from a population searching for easy ways of maintaining the characteristics of youth. There are certainly many other perspectives on menopause besides pathological perspectives, including seeing the climeractic as a bridge to another stage of life in much the same way as we currently view adolescence.

Throughout this book we will encourage you to ask questions about the models of medical care, women's biology, and social systems that are presented. We hope that it becomes clear that it is as important to question "why we don't know what we don't know" as it is to understand "how it is that we know what we know."

■ DISCUSSION EXERCISE 3

3.1. How might viewing the climeractic in much the same way we view adolescence change the characteristics of the research and treatments described earlier?

3.2. Who funds medical research? Who gets the funding? How might this influence what research is done and how it is done?

3.3. Choose an area of women's biology with which you have some experience. Are there ways of thinking about the process you have chosen that are not reflected in the research you have heard about it or the understanding you have of it?

3.4. Some people think that having more women in control of medical research would change the subjects and methods of research. Do you agree? If so, how and why would science change?

SUMMARY

Presentations of science in the media can be checked for clues about the adequacy of the experimental method, discussion of the limitations of the experiment, and comments from other researchers in the field. Many times reports will indicate that our understanding of the phenomena under study is very incomplete. The social environment of scientists, funding agencies, and institutions supporting research affect the science that is done. Not all scientific questions are asked or investigated at any given time in history.

■ ANSWERS TO DISCUSSION EXERCISES

1.1. Why does our skin lose its elasticity when we age?

Yes, this question can be addressed by scientific research.

1.2. What is the best way to discipline children?

This question cannot be addressed as stated because science does not allow us to make judgments about what is "best." We can ask the question "What is the most effective way to discipline children if our goal is X?", where "X" may be any of several desired outcomes like "total peace and quiet" or "the production of creative and self-directed adults."

1.3. Do people behave more immorally during a full moon?

This question cannot be addressed as stated, because we have not specified what immoral behavior is for the purpose of study. We could ask the question "Are more murders committed during a full moon?" in scientific research, but we make judgments about the morality of these acts using other ways of knowing.

1.4. Does watching television cause people to have shorter attention spans?

Yes, this question can be addressed by scientific research.

2.1. Does regular exercise in rats cause a decrease in the rat's appetite?

After matching rats along as many variables as possible, the researcher should select half of the rats to be placed on a mandatory exercise program and half to remain relatively inactive. Food should be weighed before it is offered to the rats and removed and weighed after a specified period of time.

2.2. Does playing loud rock music in their vicinity stunt the growth of house plants?

Similar house plants should be selected, watered at regular intervals, exposed to the same light and temperature environment. One group should experience loud rock music; the other group should experience silence.

2.3. Do pink walls decrease the number of assaults inside jails?

An experiment like this is a little more challenging to control. The researchers have a few options. One is to compare different jails, one painted pink, the other painted a more typical color, such as battleship gray. The assumption is that the prisoners are treated similarly and have similar characteristics in both jails. A better control would be to paint different areas within a single jail pink and others institutional gray and compare numbers of assaults among prisoners in each area. Again, areas inside the prison would have to be matched for prisoner treatment and background as much as possible.

2.4. What is the control group in the javelin throw experiment described earlier?

See the section on Reviewing the Experimental Method.

REFERENCES

Ambrose, H. W., & Ambrose, K. P. (1995). *A handbook of biological investigation* (5th ed.). Hunter Textbooks.

Longino, H. E. (1990). *Science as social knowledge: Values and objectivity in scientific inquiry.* Princeton University Press.

Platt, J. R. (1964). Strong inference. *Science 146,* 347–353.

Stern, P. C., & Kalof, L. (1996). *Evaluating social sciences research* (2nd ed.). Oxford University Press.

Tavris, C. (1992). *The mismeasure of woman.* Touchstone.

CHAPTER 3

[A] reason many in our society may have strong negative reactions to individuals who send unclear or atypical gender signals is the assumption that gender is a natural part of sex.

THE EVOLUTION OF SEX AND GENDER

INTRODUCTION

Many discussions of the capabilities of women rely on arguments about woman's nature. These arguments are often based on hypotheses of humans' evolutionary history. In this chapter, we will describe some of the evolutionary explanations for differences in women's and men's behavior as well as investigate the evidence for and against these hypotheses. Readers will develop the skills needed to evaluate the evidence for a supposed inborn woman's nature. You will also begin to understand the often negative consequences of assuming that hypotheses about instinctive human behavior are true.

■ DISCUSSION EXERCISE 1

1.1. When you first meet or see a stranger, how do you identify that person's sex? Are the clues you use primarily biological differences or cultural differences (i.e., in clothing, typical occupation, etc.) between the sexes?

1.2. List all of the differences you can think of between women and men. How many of these differences are clearly biological? How many are clearly cultural? How many are unclear in their origin?

SEX AND GENDER

The words "sex" and "gender" have many different meanings. Sex can refer to an activity, such as intercourse, to an individual's group as assigned by sexual anatomy and physiology, to a particular body organ, to an organism's assignment based on the size of their sex cells, or to an individual's group identity (e.g., transsexual, heterosexual). Gender can refer to an individual's group as assigned by anatomy and physiology, or their group according to behavior, or even to categories of words in certain languages (e.g., feminine and masculine nouns in Spanish or French). With these multiple, often overlapping definitions, discussion of sex and gender differences can become confusing and seemingly nonsensical. In this chapter, "sex" will only be used to refer to the group to which one is assigned based solely on *sexual anatomy*. "Gender" will be used to refer to an individual's identification according to typically sex-associated *behaviors*.

Sex Assignment

Sex in humans can usually be clearly defined on the basis of anatomy. At birth, all babies are assigned to a sex: male if a penis is clearly present and female if it is not. Once that distinction is made, a whole suite of additional sex-identifying signals is usually put in place (e.g., pink clothes for girls, blue for boys) that replace the need to examine a child's genitals to determine its correct sex assignment. After puberty, however, additional biological signals help us identify the sex assignment of individuals we are meeting for the first time, including the development of breasts in females, increased muscle development in males, and differences in patterns of fat storage and hair growth. (Chapters 6 and 7 discuss in detail many of the physical sex differences between women and men.)

In the majority of humans, sex assignment is relatively straightforward. It arises from the biological developmental process that starts with the fusion of an egg with a sperm carrying either a female-determining X chromosome or male-determining Y chromosome. (Sex determination is discussed in more detail in Chapter 4). However, even a process as seemingly simple as biological sex determination does not always give unequivocal results. While at birth most infants demonstrate the presence or absence of a penis fairly clearly, occasionally infants are born whose external genitals are ambiguous. In these cases, a decision is typically made by the parents (with the advice of doctors) about which sex the child should be raised as (sometimes plastic surgery is performed so that the genitals more closely match the assigned sex). Sometimes, a child's external genitals do not match their internal sexual organs. In most cases, parents may not realize there is a mismatch until around the time of puberty, when secondary sex characteristics begin to appear that conflict with the child's sex assignment. The activities and lifestyle of individuals whose biological sex is misidentified are especially interesting to scientists looking for the relative importance of hormones versus social expectations on gender identity. Studies of these cases are discussed in detail in Chapter 5.

Gender Assignment

Unlike sex differences, most gender differences are quite malleable—many of the behaviors and the appearances of women and men change from culture to culture and from time to time. Gender differences are reflected, for example, in traditional clothing styles. Consider the universal symbol for woman and man often used as signs for restrooms (Figure 3.1). The only obvious difference between these two figures is in clothing style — wearing a skirt is characteristic of the female gender. Clearly, these easily recognizable symbols for the two sexes do not reflect a biological difference.

Gender differences between the sexes can reinforce and exaggerate biological differences. For instance, while men generally have longer, darker body hair than women, in

FIGURE 3.1   The "Universal Symbols" for Female and Male

Note that the only difference between these figures is in clothing style.

our culture women are more likely to remove body hair. Thus women appear even less hairy in relation to men than they naturally are. (Chapter 6 and 7 describe more of these socially maintained physical gender differences.)

Our cultural understanding of gender is important in social interactions. When we believe we have identified the sex of a person (by either biological traits or by gender signals of sex), we can assign to them a number of behavioral characteristics (gender stereotypes) that enable us to know more about their personalities and aptitudes. For example, a woman is supposed to be more sympathetic than a man, and men are supposed to be more interested in competition than women. While most people realize that these stereotypical behaviors may or may not be expressed in each individual, we assume that most people of a particular sex will conform to most gender stereotypes, and we rely on these preconceptions to help us relate to others.

When individuals give us ambiguous clues about their sex and/or gender, we may become angry with or disgusted by them, because so many seemingly basic traits of their personality remain a mystery to us. On the North American television comedy show, Saturday Night Live, an individual of indeterminate sex and gender (Androgynous Pat) was the subject of a series of skits that poked fun at how this uncertainty led to the frustration of Pat's friends and coworkers.

Another reason many in our society may have strong negative reactions to individuals who send unclear or atypical gender signals is the assumption that gender is a natural part of sex. If gender is inherited with sex chromosomes, than those who don't conform to gender stereotypes are abnormal. If these individuals appear to be consciously rejecting their biologically determined roles, they may be viewed as committing a crime against nature.

Do sex-associated behaviors in women and men stem from a difference between them in sex chromosomes? An anthropological survey of gender indicates that some behaviors that are linked to a single sex in our culture are found in both sexes in many other cultures. In fact, many cultures incorporate more than two distinct genders in their social structures. This phenomenon is particularly well-described in native North American peoples. Several groups, such as the Papago, Yuma, and Navajo of the Southwestern United States, recognize four genders. These include dichotomous male and female genders as well as genders that represent blends of these two roles—berdaches who are anatomically male, but who adopt some traditional women's behaviors such as fiber artistry and food preparation, and amazons who are anatomically female, but who adopt some traditional male behaviors, such as hunting or property ownership. Both berdaches and amazons in these societies may also take on social roles that are assigned specifically and uniquely to their particular gender. As in societies with two genders, these gender assignments play a part in social interactions. Berdaches and amazons are understood to conform to a particular role in society and are interacted with accordingly by others.

The existence of genders in other cultures that do not match sex assignment may suggest that biology clearly does not determine sex-associated behaviors. However, some scientists would explain the existence of other genders in these societies as resulting from some abnormality in biological makeup or early development. We know that some humans have unusual mutations that result in atypical physical characteristics, such as lack of skin pigment (albinism) or diseases such as cystic fibrosis. If biology determines behavior, perhaps berdaches and amazons represent biologically unusual individuals who display the "wrong" behaviors. These two hypotheses about the origins of other genders in these societies still leave us with the question: Does biological sex cause gender?

SUMMARY

Sex, which we define as sexual anatomy, is determined by the sex chromosomes a child receives at conception. Gender is defined as sex-associated behaviors, such as clothing style, typical occupation, and behavioral tendencies. There is debate over whether most aspects of gender are biological (a result of genes on the sex chromosomes) or culturally determined, especially since gender differences change over time and because many other cultures have more than two genders.

THE EVOLUTION OF SEXUAL REPRODUCTION

[A] pair of organisms with only four different genes could produce 256 different types of offspring, while a pair with only eight genes could produce over 65,000 different types of offspring.

Hypotheses about the biological basis for gender often rely on discussions of evolutionary history. To understand the possible evolutionary basis of gender differences, we need to go back to the very beginning—the evolution of two different sexes. Two sexes originated when sexuality and fertilization became required in order to produce offspring.

If you've ever propagated plants from cuttings, you know that these organisms can produce offspring without engaging in sexual reproduction. This process, called asexual reproduction, results in the production of offspring that are exact copies, or clones, of the parent. The budding of yeast cells in bread dough, the multiplication of algal blooms in lakes, and the production of suckers in plants (e.g., the production of young spider plants from a large specimen as shown in Figure 3.2) are examples of asexual reproduction. Asexual reproduction occurs when cells in the parent replicate themselves to form the basis of another adult organism.

Sexual reproduction, on the other hand, requires the fusion of two different cells. Each of these sex cells (called gametes) contains one half of the genetic information found in the adult cell. (See Chapter 9 for a detailed description of the production of gametes and the process of fertilization in humans.)

FIGURE 3.2   A Spider Plant With Suckers

These small spider plants are produced via asexual reproduction of the large plant.

While there are important exceptions (plants, for instance), asexual reproduction is confined to relatively simple organisms, such as bacteria and yeast. Among those more complex organisms that engage in asexual reproduction, nearly all engage in sexual reproduction as well. Many organisms reproduce exclusively via sexual reproduction (humans, for instance). The prevalence of sexual reproduction has led a number of investigators to speculate about the benefits of this strategy. After all, sexual reproduction is usually more expensive than asexual reproduction. It requires developing and maintaining specialized organs for the production and transport of gametes, finding a mate, and often a time- and energy-consuming courtship process.

In reality, there is no way of knowing exactly why sexuality exists—we cannot turn back the clock to witness the moment when sexual reproduction evolved. However, at least two major hypotheses have been proposed to explain its origin. Both rely on arguments that claim it arose through the evolution by natural selection of asexually reproducing organisms.

A Primer on Evolution by Natural Selection

Evolution occurs when, over many generations, the characteristics of a population of organisms change in some way. Nearly all biologists agree that organisms evolve over time—that the characteristics of today's organisms are different from the characteristics of their ancestors. For example, since the advent of antibiotics, many strains of bacteria that are harmful to humans have changed from being susceptible to various antibiotics to being resistant. Let's consider the case of *Stapholoccus aureus*, a bacteria that can cause life-threatening infections in humans. Some strains of *S. aureus* have become resistant to ampicillin, a common antibiotic. When ampicillin was first introduced, many bacteria died in the presence of this antibiotic and very few lived. Today, 50+ years after the introduction of ampicillin, many *S. aureus* cells are resistant to this antibiotic and only a few are susceptible to its effects. This change in the characteristics of *S. aureus* strains from susceptible to resistant to ampicillin has occurred over many bacterial generations. Thus, according to the previous definition, these bacterial populations have evolved.

The evolution of a population such as the *S. aureus* strain described above may occur by many different means, but the most commonly cited is natural selection. Natural selection as a primary mechanism for evolutionary change was first theorized by Charles Darwin and Alfred Russell Wallace in 1865. According to the theory of natural selection, in order for a particular trait to become prevalent in the population, it must confer some advantage to the organism in survival or success in reproduction. In the case of *S. aureus* (Figure 3.3), resistant individuals had a much greater chance of survival in the presence of ampicillin than susceptible individuals. The ampicillin resistant individuals reproduced, but many of the susceptible individuals could not (because they were killed or quite disabled by the antibiotic). Because resistance is a trait that can be passed on to offspring, the next generation of *S. aureus* contained a higher proportion of resistant individuals than the previous generation. Therefore, over a few generations of exposure to ampicillin, the bacterial population that resulted was one in which most individuals are resistant to treatment by this antibiotic.

Most of the variations that are subject to natural selection arise in populations through mutation. The ability to digest ampicillin before it affects the cell may have arisen due to a mutation of the ability to digest a different protein. Being able to digest ampicillin means that the cell is unable to digest something else. In an ampicillin-free environment, these ampicillin resistant cells may have lower survival rates than cells that are susceptible to the antibiotic. In this environment, ampicillin resistance would not be favored by natural selection, and the trait would not increase in prevalence in the population. Natural selection selects among the variations present in a given environment—populations of organisms may evolve in one direction under one set of conditions and in the completely opposite direction under a different set of conditions.

Natural selection can lead to evolution in any population of organisms in which any type of inherited characteristic results in greater survival or reproductive success than other inherited characteristics. The two major hypotheses about the evolution of sexuality from asexuality both assume that sexual reproduction evolved through the process of natural selection.

FIGURE 3.3   The Evolution of Antibiotic Resistance

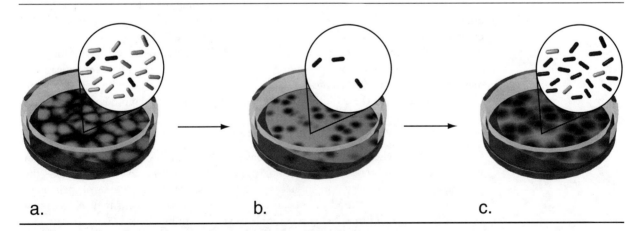

a.   b.   c.

Evolution of antibiotic resistance in a Stapholoccus aureus *strain. Light cells are susceptible to antibiotic, dark cells are resistant.*

  a. Petri dish containing population of mostly susceptible cells.

  b. Same petri dish immediately after antibiotic is applied. Few bacteria survive, but those that do are resistant.

  c. Same petri dish after 2 days and several bacterial generations. The cells surviving antibiotic treatment reproduced, producing a population in which most cells are resistant and only a few are susceptible.

Hypothesis I: Sexual Reproduction Evolved Because It Increases the Variety of Offspring   The most widely cited hypothesis about the origin of sexuality asserts that sexual reproduction is more prevalent than asexual reproduction because sexually produced offspring are more diverse. This hypothesis is illustrated in Figure 3.4. Essentially, asexual reproduction is successful only when environments are unchanging. In these conditions, organisms that are well suited to the environment will produce large numbers of well-suited offspring. In this case, sexually reproducing organisms may produce a wider range of offspring types, only a fraction of which are successful. However, if the environment changes enough, the asexually reproducing line may not be able to survive and will disappear completely (Figure 3.4). In this case, the sexually reproducing forms are favored because they have a greater chance of producing offspring that are able to withstand the environmental change. As long as environments change often, sexually reproducing individuals will be favored by natural selection over asexually reproducing

FIGURE 3.4   The Advantage of Sexual Reproduction

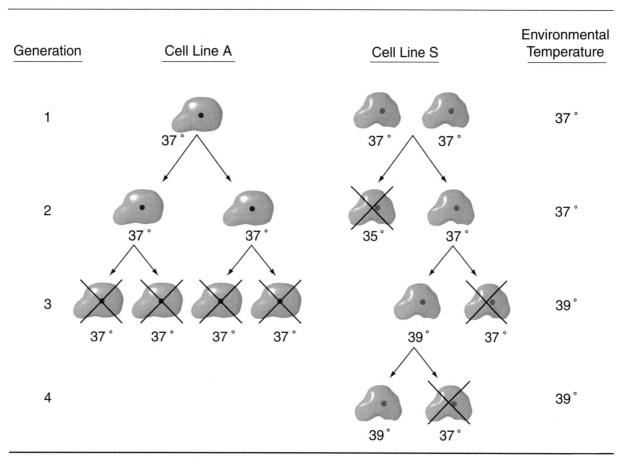

Figure 3.4 illustrates the widely cited hypothesis that sexual reproduction is more common than asexual reproduction because sexually reproducing organisms are more likely to have offspring who survive environmental change. Cell line A is asexually reproducing; cell line S is sexually reproducing. In the first generation, both cell lines produce the same number of offspring but, because the environment is stable, a greater number of cell line A's offspring survive. In stable environments, asexual reproduction is more successful than sexual reproduction. However, in the second generation, the environment changes. Cell line A cannot survive in the new environment because the offspring are exact copies of the parents. Cell line S has produced at least some cells that can survive the new temperature conditions. In changing environments, sexual reproduction is more successful than asexual reproduction. According to this hypothesis, because most environments are variable over time, sexual reproduction is more common.

individuals. This hypothesis asserts that sexual reproduction is common despite its extra expenses because so many environments are variable over time.

To get an idea of how much variety can be introduced into offspring by sexual reproduction, imagine an organism with two genes (Figure 3.5). Genes are bits of chemical information about how to develop that are transferred from a parent to its offspring. In this two-gene organism, each gene comes in two forms (Gene A may be in form A or form a, Gene B may be in form B or b). Most sexually reproducing animals have two copies of each gene; if the two copies of a particular gene carried by an individual are different from each other, we call the organism heterozygous for that gene. When the two copies are the same, we call the individual homozygous

FIGURE 3.5   How Sexual Reproduction Increases Variety

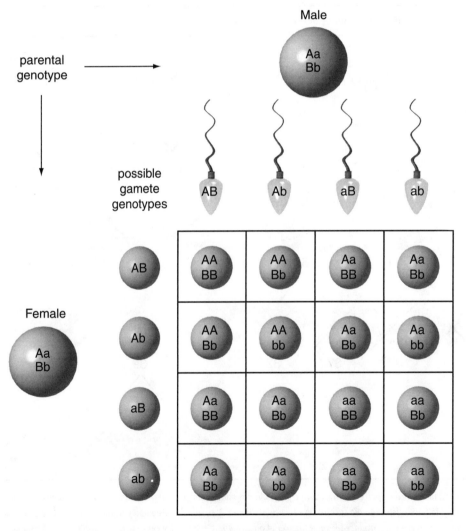

Sexual reproduction increases variety among offspring because it results in different combinations of genes. Identical parents, who both have two different copies of two genes, can produce nine different gene combinations among their offspring.

for that gene. If an individual of this species that is heterozygous for both genes reproduces asexually, all offspring are identical and are heterozygous for both genes. If this individual sexually reproduces, however, one copy of each gene is placed in a gamete (sex cell) and fuses with a gamete that carries one copy of each gene from another individual. Some offspring will be heterozygous for both genes, homozygous for both, or homozygous for one or the other gene. As Figure 3.5 illustrates, two heterozygotes of this species that are sexually reproducing can produce nine different offspring gene combinations, only one of which is identical to themselves. The number of different combinations increases dramatically as the number of genes goes up. For instance, a pair of organisms with only four different genes could produce 256 different types of offspring, while a pair with only eight genes could produce over 65,000 different types of offspring. The number of variants produced would very likely result in some offspring surviving the next moderate environmental change. In fact, individual organisms with high levels of genetic diversity are nearly always more successful than organisms with low genetic diversity.

Of course, the potential variety introduced by sexual reproduction is somewhat limited. Even though with more genes, more variety among offspring is possible, this variety is constrained by the basic biology of the organism. While one of the offspring possible from the sexual reproduction of a pair of fish may have a different color pattern, none of the possible variants will have two fully functional legs instead of fins. The evolution of dramatic changes requires the mutation of genes, not just the different mixes introduced by sexual reproduction.

Hypothesis II: Sex for Reproduction Is a Side Effect of a Cell Survival Strategy
While the first hypothesis is appealing because it describes a direct benefit of sexual reproduction, cell biologists in particular have criticized it because it lacks evidence. For instance, the reproductive success of modern asexual species does not seem to be lower than the success of closely related sexually reproducing species. These biologists suggest an alternative hypothesis that emphasizes the direct benefits of cell fusion itself. According to this hypothesis, obligate sexual reproduction evolved secondarily to cell fusion.

This alternative hypothesis is best set forth by Lynn Margulis and Dorian Sagan. Their explanation of the origin of sex is more complex than the first hypothesis, and probably for that reason it has not replaced it as the most cited explanation. According to Margulis and Sagan, one part of sexuality—the fusion of cells—first occurred during stressful periods early on in the evolution of cells. Individual asexually reproducing organisms in environments where food or water was becoming scarce would fuse with each other to form "megacells" with two or more sets of genetic information. Fusion in response to stress is common today among many simple single-celled organisms. These megacells are better able to survive harsh environmental conditions than cells that do not fuse. When the environment improves, cells are again able to gather enough energy to reproduce. However, reproducing megacells, if simply producing clones, would need significantly more energy to duplicate their increased amount of genetic information. During good times, cells that had not fused would reproduce more rapidly and produce more clones than these megacells. With natural selection favoring megacells in some environments and pared down cells in others, cells that fused with others during stressful periods but could reduce their amount of genetic material during good times would be the most successful. The process of dividing in half the amount of genetic material in a cell is called meiosis. (Meiosis is explained in detail in Chapter 9.) Meiosis probably evolved from basic cell division.

According to this hypothesis, meiosis and cell fusion quickly became linked with reproduction in organisms made up of many cells. Multicellular organisms such as humans produce many different types of cells such as blood, bone, immune system, and nerve cells. When mature, these cell types differ from each other because they turn off some genetic information and amplify other information during development. Attempting to use one of these mature modified cells for reproduction would end in failure because the resulting offspring would be expressing incomplete genetic information. According to Margulis and Sagan, the process of meiosis serves as a method of checking that the cells participating in reproduction contain all necessary components for development. A body cell that is not able to express all genes cannot perform meiosis. If meiosis is required before reproduction, it also cannot participate in this process. The requirement of meiosis before reproduction also leads to a requirement for cell fusion to complete the process. Because a daughter cell of meiosis contains only half of the genetic information required to produce an adult organism, it must fuse with another daughter cell of meiosis to return to the appropriate chromosome number. In this way, sexuality (meiosis followed by cell fusion) has become inextricably linked to reproduction in multicellular organisms.

It is possible that the origin and maintenance of sexual reproduction is a result of both explanations. In nearly all animals, sexuality requires the fusion of gametes from two distinct individuals. Even organisms that are hermaphroditic (that is, contain both female and male reproductive organs) cannot produce offspring singly. The requirement for two individuals to contribute to a reproductive effort may have evolved because it results in the production of a wider variety of offspring, as described by the first hypothesis. Humans and other animals may be sexually reproducing because of the explanation offered by Margulis and Sagan, but they may require mating with another individual because this results in offspring with more variety, leading to better long-term survival.

SUMMARY

Sexual reproduction, which requires the fusion of two cells, probably evolved from asexual reproduction, or cloning. Despite the costs associated with sexual reproduction (producing sex organs, locating a mate, courting), it is extremely common in multicellular organisms and is required for reproduction in most. Two hypotheses exist to explain the origin of sexual reproduction. One is that sexual reproduction increases variety in offspring, leading to better survival over time in a changing environment. The other hypothesis explains that meiosis evolved in cells that fused in poor environments but "lightened their genetic load" in good environments. Meiosis then became required for reproduction in multicellular organisms because it ensured that reproducing cells had accessible all the information necessary for development. In this case, meiosis must be followed by cell fusion in order to reproduce offspring with the same number of genes as the parent. Both hypotheses may help explain why sexuality involving two different individuals is both so common and often necessary for reproduction.

THE EVOLUTION OF TWO SEXES

The essential difference between females and males in all species is the size of the gametes that the different sexes produce. Individuals that produce large gametes are classified as females and individuals that produce small gametes are classified as males. In birds, a female produces 3 to 5 eggs that each weigh 15 to 20% of her weight. In the same breeding season, males may produce trillions of sperm, that in aggregate weigh less than 5% of his body weight. In humans, women produce eggs that are one million times larger than a single sperm. This distinction between female and male is made regardless of the particular anatomical structures we typically associate with the different sexes. For instance, in plants, pollen is produced in male structures while ovules (which become seeds) are produced in female structures, even though these structures bear little resemblance to the sex organs of humans (except perhaps in Georgia O'Keefe's paintings).

Biologists agree on one, fairly simple explanation for why sex differences in gamete size exist. Once sexuality evolved as a method of reproduction, the formation of two different sexual types (i.e., female and male) was probably inevitable. This diversification occurred through the process of natural selection and is diagrammed in Figure 3.6. When a range of gamete sizes are produced in a population, individuals producing gametes near either the

FIGURE 3.6   The Evolution of Gamete Size

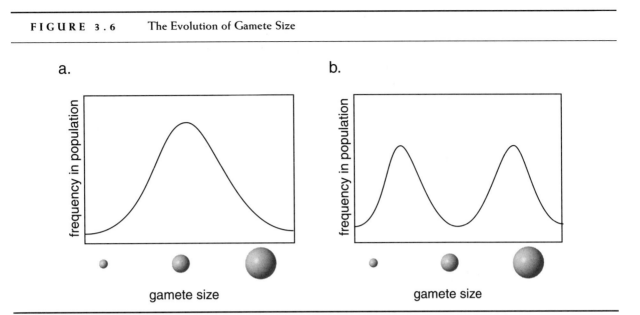

Natural selection resulting in two successful gamete production strategies. Both individuals producing small gametes and individuals producing large gametes are favored over individuals producing mid-sized gametes. The existence of both strategies in the same population is the most stable outcome. By convention, we call the sex that produces small gametes male *and the sex that produces large gametes* female.

small or large ends of the size distribution will be more successful than individuals who produce medium-sized gametes. Imagine three different ways of distributing the same amount of energy into gametes: one could produce many small gametes, few large gametes, or a moderate number of medium-sized gametes. Individuals that produce few, but large, gametes provide a large supply of nutrients in each cell. These individuals will therefore have larger, healthier offspring at birth. Their offspring, because of their size and hardiness, will be better able to compete for food than offspring produced from smaller gametes. Accessing more food allows these offspring to have a large number of offspring of their own. Thus, individuals that produce few large gametes will have more grandkids than individuals who produce a greater number of mid-sized gametes. By the process of natural selection, individuals with large gametes should therefore become prevalent in the population.

On the other hand, individuals who produce many small gametes can potentially parent more offspring than those who produce fewer gametes, because they can distribute these abundant gametes more widely. In addition, small gametes may be more likely than larger gametes to win the race to fertilization sites because they can move faster. Natural selection would favor individuals who produce many small gametes over individuals producing fewer, larger ones.

The two successful gamete production strategies described previously coexist in populations because each strategy individually is unstable. In a population where all gametes were large, individuals that appeared who produced smaller gametes would be successful at parenting offspring because they could fertilize many other gametes. Where all gametes were small, individuals that appeared with larger gametes would be more successful at producing grandkids. The most stable situation is a population where 50% of the individuals produce few large gametes and 50% produce many small gametes. This sex ratio (50/50) is common in nearly all obligately sexually reproducing species.

While the essence of sex differences is gamete size, other physical differences between the sexes arise because of this variation. The production of few large gametes requires different organ architecture than the production of many small gametes. Thus, the gonads (gamete producing organs) of females and males differ. In humans and other animals, the female gonad is the ovary, while the male gonad is the testis. The organs affecting gamete release may be different as well. In mammals, the initial difference in gamete size has led to more dramatic sex differences in physical traits. Recall that the female reproductive strategy is successful because females provide nutrients to their offspring in the form of large gametes. Female mammals have taken this provisioning of nutrients to an extreme—not only are their gametes large and nutrient filled, they also provide nutrients throughout the development of these offspring during pregnancy and after birth via milk. Female mammals thus also have uteri and mammary glands that male mammals lack, all as a result of this difference in successful gamete production strategies.

SUMMARY

The evolution of two sexes occurred through natural selection on gamete size. Females who produce few, large gametes are favored by natural selection because they produce a greater number of grandkids than individuals with smaller gametes. Males who produce many, small gametes are favored by natural selection because they can father more offspring than individuals who produce fewer, slower gametes. The two sexes coexist because neither strategy is stable on its own. Many physical differences between the sexes are a direct result of differences in gamete production strategy.

THE EVOLUTION OF GENDER

(Basic) reproductive behaviors are far from universal, and their applicability to animals with such a large capacity for learning, like ourselves, is questionable.

We have seen that differences in gamete production strategy have led to differences between female and male anatomy. Might this fundamental difference lead to differences in sex-related behavior as well?

Sociobiologists (scientists who study behavior) have hypothesized that in most animals, the differences between female and male behaviors are indeed caused by the differences in gamete size described above. Whether this explanation is true, especially when applied to humans, is subject to highly spirited debate in the scientific community. Evolutionary hypotheses such as this are extremely difficult to test. Despite controversy among scientists and the problems of verification, a large literature on instinctual animal sexual behaviors exists and books, articles, and television shows using these hypotheses to explain the origins of our behaviors remain very popular. Given how commonplace these explanations have become, and because these explanations can have an effect on the lives of women and men, an understanding of the supposed biological basis of human gender roles is important for anyone interested in the biology of women.

■ **DISCUSSION EXERCISE 2**

2.1. Do you think that there is a woman's nature? If so, what does it consist of?

2.2. What evidence do you have to support your view?

The Evolution of Behavior

In this chapter we have discussed the evolution by natural selection of physical traits like changes in antibiotic resistance, the rise of sexual reproduction, and diversification in gamete size. Natural selection as described by Darwin can also cause the evolution of behaviors in animals when behaviors are linked to particular genes.

We call gene-linked behaviors instincts or reflexes. Many animal behaviors studied by scientists are, to a large degree, instinctive. Moths will move toward bright light, young birds will build nests in the right environment, and fruit flies raised in isolation will perform the courtship displays characteristic of their species when introduced to the opposite sex. Because these behaviors can occur in individuals who haven't had an opportunity to learn them, they must have a genetic basis. A gene, or more likely a set of genes, contains the biochemical instructions for performing the behavior in response to a particular stimulus.

As with physical traits, behavioral traits that are associated with genes are subject to the process of natural selection. Individuals who exhibited a particularly successful behavior would have more offspring, and the gene or genes for this behavior would become more prevalent in the population. Less successful behaviors would tend to diminish in prevalence. Several experiments have shown that instinctual behaviors common in a population can be modified by selection. In most cases, experimenters imposed the selective pressure. For example, from a group of organisms displaying a range of behaviors researchers can remove individuals that are behaving in a particular manner and allow only these animals to breed. If the behavior is instinctual, the next generation (when raised in isolation from their parents) should have a higher proportion of individuals displaying the selected behavior than in the original group. Researchers have selected for many different behaviors among, for example, fruit flies: moving away from light, moving toward light, tolerance of crowded conditions, aggressiveness when in crowded conditions, quickly triggered mating behavior, and slowly developing mating behavior.

Genetically based behavioral differences between natural populations may have also evolved in response to natural selection. For example, in two populations of garter snakes (slug-eating and slug-refusing) from California, newborn garter snakes from the slug-refusing population will not eat slugs, while newborns from the slug-eating population will happily devour them. When these snakes are raised to adulthood and slug-eaters are mated with slug-refusers, offspring raised in isolation from their parents will be variable with respect to slug preference. This variable behavior among offspring demonstrates that the behavioral food preferences in these snakes are most likely genetic—regardless of the environment they are raised in, they must carry the right genes in order to choose slugs for dinner. The fact that slug-eating and slug-refusing behaviors are genetic lends support to the hypothesis of this behavior's evolution via natural selection in different environments. Specifically, in environments where slugs are plentiful, we may infer that snakes that preferred slugs were successful and left more offspring than slug avoiders. Where slugs are less plentiful, and where preferring slugs means that you might eat potentially fatal leeches, snakes that avoided slugs were successful and left more offspring than slug preferrers. In this manner, slug-avoiding populations may have evolved in low slug environments while slug-preferring populations evolved in slug-plentiful environments.

Not all behaviors are instinctual, even among non-human animals. Non-instinctual behaviors must be learned from adults or by trial and error. Many bird species will sing if raised in isolation, but their song sounds much different from the typical song if they have not heard an adult sing. Predatory mammals, like large cats, will attempt to hunt prey but are ineffective without adult teachers to model for them. Rats can be taught to display certain behaviors in order to receive food or avoid electric shock. In general, animals with larger brains and/or who live in variable environments display many more learned behaviors than animals with small brains or narrow habitats. Humans, with our large brains and wide habitat range, display an incredible capacity for learning.

The Behavioral Consequences of Reproductive Strategies

In animals whose behavior relies heavily on instinctual responses, there are some common themes among sex-related behaviors. In this section we explore the basic female and male reproductive strategies and consider some of the numerous variations on this basic strategy.

Female Behavior   Female animals, like all female organisms, invest their energy in gametes in a way that increases the success of individual offspring. As discussed previously, this reproductive strategy decreases the total number of offspring they can produce. Because they have fewer chances to produce successful offspring, individual offspring are fairly precious to a female. Therefore, we expect that female reproductive behavior should have evolved to maximize the health and success of each (or most) offspring.

According to this hypothesis, successful female animals should choose male partners who will provide the most support to the next generation. On the most basic level, male support for offspring means providing healthy and successful genes. Females should therefore be selective about which males they will allow to fertilize their eggs. For example, if a female mated with a male with inadequate food gathering instincts, her offspring might also have low success with food gathering. Female offspring with this poor food gathering trait would be less likely to have successful offspring themselves, and the trait would not spread in the population. However, if a female had a genetic trait that allowed her to evaluate the food gathering capabilities of males, she could mate with only the best male food gatherer, ensuring that many of her offspring will be equally skilled at obtaining food. Her offsprings' success at gathering food would lead to reproductive success. Hence, the instinct to choose the male with better food-gathering abilities would spread in the population.

Females can evaluate the health and success of males in any of several ways. In some species, females evaluate male quality by examining particular physical features. These physical signals of quality are usually structures or coloration that seem to have no survival value. The bright colors of many male birds, the loud calls of male amphibians, and the large antlers of many hoofed mammals (see Figure 3.7) may increase the risk of predation or the energy needs of these animals. Sociobiologists hypothesize that these types of male structures and behaviors have evolved in response to females choosing males to mate with who can survive

---

FIGURE 3.7   The Result of Sexual Selection in Elk

The antlers on this elk probably evolved as a result of sexual selection rather than natural selection. Female elk may have preferentially mated with male elk with large antlers, if producing and maintaining antlers is a measure of the overall health and quality of the male. In this way, ornaments like these antlers—which do nothing to increase the survival of males and may in fact reduce their survival—may have become more common in the elk population.

despite these handicaps. For instance, a male elk that can afford to support a large antler rack must be healthy and strong—females should choose these males to produce healthy and strong offspring. Because these structures probably reduce male survival, the process of their evolution is distinguished from natural selection—Darwin termed it sexual selection.

Besides simply choosing the male with the brightest colors or largest antlers, females may also be able to evaluate male quality based on courtship displays. Many animals engage in courtship displays before mating. Evolutionary biologists have speculated that these displays may have evolved as a method to synchronize the reproductive state of females and males. Especially among animals who range widely and do not come in contact with the opposite sex regularly, individuals who could induce fertility in themselves and a partner were probably more successful than individuals who were limited to a particular breeding season. In modern animals with a specific breeding season or in those where contact between the two sexes is common, courtship displays may have been modified to serve as a vehicle for female choice. Females choosing males displaying the correct sequence of courtship behaviors ensure that they are mating with the correct species. Hybrids between two related species often have low reproductive success, and females who mated with males of the wrong species would have fewer successful grandkids than females who chose males only of their own species. Females may also be able to evaluate male success by observing the vigor displayed by the male during the courtship period. Male displays also often include modified food gathering, predator escape, and, in species where the male assists in rearing offspring, parental care behaviors. These displays allow the female to choose males who are likely to produce offspring with successful feeding and escape behaviors or males who will continue to provide care for offspring after they are born.

Finally, females may evaluate male quality and receive additional energy supplies for their offspring by requiring food gifts before mating or choosing males based on the quality of the territory the males are defending. Food gifts are made prerequisite by females of many insect species, including the Mormon cricket and the hanging fly, as well as by bird species, including the Red Billed Gull and Eastern Screech Owl. Female choice based on territory quality is very prevalent in birds but is also found among insects, fish, and some mammals.

Male Behavior While females who maximize the success of individual offspring are favored by natural selection, typically males who maximize the number of females they fertilize are successful. Because the amount of resources in their individual gametes is so small, males typically do not contribute much to the head start of their offspring. Because males' gamete contribution does little to increase the short-term survival of offspring, successful males distribute these gametes as widely as possible. The more eggs a male fertilizes, the more likely one or a few of those eggs were produced by a successful female and will result in surviving offspring. In general, males who are promiscuous in their reproductive behavior should, therefore, evolve via natural selection.

Because their gametes are individually rather inexpensive, males are willing to take the risk of wasting sperm in their attempts to fertilize eggs. Promiscuous males may waste sperm by mating with infertile or unhealthy females or even attempting to mate with organisms of different species or with inanimate objects. Flowering plants have taken advantage of this tendency among males of some insect species. For instance, some species of orchid have flower parts that are shaped like a female wasp. These flowers attract male wasps that attempt to mate with it. The wasp's sperm is wasted in this futile attempt at fertilization. In the meantime, however, the male wasp will pick up pollen or drop some from another flower, and thus complete the steps necessary for the flower's sexual reproduction. Because sperm are so small and easy to make, this mistake on the part of the wasp costs it very little. A male wasp who is not tricked by the flower has a higher threshold for mating attempts (i.e., a lower libido) than the tricked male, so despite its lack of sperm waste, it may attempt to mate with fewer real females and, therefore, father fewer offspring.

In species that have a defined breeding season, males may increase their reproductive success by outcompeting other males for access to females or for prime territorial sites. Evolutionary biologists have proposed that size differences between the sexes (known as sexual dimorphism) result from this male/male competition. As long as males can increase the number of females they can mate with by being larger than other males, large males will be favored by natural selection.

After reading this section, you may conclude that the different reproductive strategies of females and males lead to universal behavioral differences in the two sexes. That is, because of differences in gamete size, females have evolved to withhold sex (in order to evaluate male quality), while males have evolved to mate as often and as widely as possible. You may be tempted to explain the supposed promiscuity of men compared to women or the supposed coyness of women using these evolutionary arguments. However, one should be extremely cautious when extrapolating these supposed universals onto humans. As we shall see, these reproductive behaviors are far from universal, and their applicability to animals with such a large capacity for learning, like ourselves, is questionable.

Sex Role Reversals

Although female selectiveness and male promiscuity are the rule in species where parental care is non-existent or wholly the function of the female, for many animals the investment in offspring is more than simply providing energy and nutrients in the egg and sperm. As discussed, males of some species will provide energy-rich gifts to females during courtship. These gifts represent investments of time and energy in the reproductive success of the offspring, in addition to the energy required for sperm production. In other species, including some bird species, as well as in seahorses, some species of darter fish, the Giant Water Bug, and the South American Frog, males provide the majority of the post-fertilization parental care (usually until the eggs hatch). In these species, the male is choosy about his mates. This sex role reversal results from the same process that leads to female choosiness in animals that provide no post-fertilization parental care. Selectivity in mating increases the success of the parent with the higher level of investment in individual offspring. Among species that display this sex role reversal, the female sex is often large, colorful, and performs elaborate displays.

In many species, both females and males must be involved in provisioning for the young in order to ensure their success. These species include most birds and some mammals. Where both females and males have large investments in the young, both may attempt to evaluate mate quality through mutual displays. In addition to situations where either males or both females and males are choosy, males are not more promiscuous than females in all species. In birds and some mammals, males rarely mate with more than one female per breeding season. When birds mate with individuals other than their primary partner, it is unclear whether the male or the female initiates these contacts. While these situations do not qualify as sex role reversal, they are a clear modification of the basic sex roles.

SUMMARY

The difference between the sexes in gamete production strategy has led to basic differences in sexual behavior. In species where parental investment after fertilization is minimal or where females provide all post-fertilization care, females are expected to be choosy of their mates while males are expected to be promiscuous. However, these basic behavior patterns are not universal among animals. When males contribute to the success of offspring after fertilization, the difference between the sexes in parental investment is not as great and both males and females may be choosy of mates.

Gender in Mammals

To summarize, successful reproductive strategies clearly may vary among animals. Certain behaviors that are successful among males of species who provide little post-fertilization care are not found among males of species who do aid in individual offspring survival. However, you may have noticed that few examples of actual sex role reversal exist in mammals. Because humans are mammals, it is important to explore which features particular to this group of animals contribute to their reproductive behaviors.

Mammals differ from other groups of animals in that the young develop internally and are provisioned early in life with milk produced by the mother. Unlike birds, in which both sexes incubate eggs and provide food for young, female mammals are the only direct source of energy and nourishment for developing offspring until weaning occurs. Given this biology, it is nearly impossible for male mammals to make a larger investment in an individual offspring than females. If sex role reversal exists in mammals (a thorough literature search by the authors revealed no examples), it is exceedingly rare.

Many mammal species display the basic sex role behaviors. Among hoofed mammals, for example, males are larger than females and often have more extensive antlers (presumably for display) while females choose males based on various measures of male quality. In these animals, such as deer, elk, and impala, male post-fertilization investment is small or non-existent.

However, in many mammal species, especially those that live in groups (i.e., social mammals), both sexes are involved in support of the young. Among many carnivores and primates (such as fox, wolf, and orangutan), males provide food for a pregnant and lactating mate or care for milk-feeding young while the mother recharges her energy stores by feeding or resting. In these cases, the investment of a male in individual young may approach the investment of the female. Many of the mammals who share parental care duties are monogamous, that is, they mate with one partner for the period of the mating season (and sometimes for life). These monogamous pairs often form when both females and males choose partners. For example, among wolves, both the males and females in a group establish a dominance hierarchy. Once this is established, high-ranking females will only mate with high-ranking males and vice versa.

Besides the increased investment of males in offspring in these species, social mammals are also more behaviorally flexible than other mammals. The behavior of social mammals is, to a large degree, learned. The ability to learn allows social mammals to live in a wider range of environments and to exploit a larger number of resources than most solitary mammals. This flexibility also means that fewer behaviors in social mammals are entirely instinctive. For instance, carnivores have a basic hunting instinct, but they are ineffective hunters unless trained by adults. The ability to learn allows parents in different environments to transmit to their offspring the learned skills necessary for success in their own home range. Many social mammals display an astonishing degree of behavioral flexibility. Individuals of the same species in different environments exhibit different behavior patterns. Lions, for instance, vary their group sizes depending on habitat conditions. When their prey is large, lions form large groups; when their prey is small, they form small groups. Group sizes change even within a population over time, as with lions in sub-Saharan Africa, who respond to their prey base as it oscillates throughout the year from large animals to small and back again.

Even sexual behavior is flexible within species. Among primate species known as tamarins, all types of sexual systems are displayed within a single large population. These systems include monogamy, polygyny (one male with many female mates), and polyandry (one female with many male mates). The sexual system adopted by a subpopulation depends on the number of males and females in the group as well as environmental factors. For instance, when food is scarce and widespread, tamarins that are in polyandrous groups may be more successful, but when food is found in discrete clumps, polygyny may be more likely. According to scientists who study primate behavior, among great apes (the group to which humans belong), few sexual behaviors are instinctive. Among social animals, sexual behavior is often not confined to reproductive functions. According to some sociobiologists, sexuality may be used as a way to bond the members of a group together. Recent observers of primate groups in the wild have noted that females are seemingly as interested in copulation and sexual play as males. Among pygmy chimpanzees (one of our closest relatives), sexual liaisons between non-fertile females and males, and between two females or two males, are a common occurrence. Pregnant (thus obviously infertile) females of African elephants, baboons, chimpanzees, and rhesus macaques have been observed engaging in sexual intercourse. Sexual intercourse in humans also fills a variety of social needs not related to reproduction, including the physical expression of deep caring. Clearly, sexual behavior in social animals is important for several reasons.

Humans are the most behaviorally flexible species on the planet. As you would expect, and as you may have experienced, human behavior and social organization vary from culture to culture and in different environments. Human populations display the entire range of sexual systems, from polyandry to monogamy to polygyny. While 70% of human cultures do practice polygyny, in 50% of these cultures, non-monogamous couples are rare. Only extremely resource-rich men in these cultures have more than one female partner. Additionally, one would not expect in humans the "basic" male and female reproductive behavior described in the beginning of this section. Human infants are helpless for many years, and their successful rearing depends on the assistance of many adults, including the male parent. Even if some human sexual behavior is instinctive, given the needs of a human infant we might hypothesize that natural selection would favor human males who provided a large amount of post-fertilization support. According to this hypothesis, we would expect human males to have evolved to be monogamous and not especially promiscuous.

SUMMARY

Because female mammals provide support to developing offspring throughout pregnancy and early infancy, male mammals are unlikely to be able to make a larger parental investment than females. However, in many mammals, male investment during their mate's pregnancy and lactation of the young is very high. Especially among social mammals, males are likely to be as choosy as females of mates and unlikely to be very promiscuous. Additionally, much of the reproductive behaviors displayed in primates, especially humans, is learned rather than instinctive.

OTHER GENDER ROLE BEHAVIORS IN HUMANS

According to this hypothesis, females have evolved into good care givers and secretaries but must rely on maps to find their way around, while men have evolved the perfect skills for business leadership and never need to ask for directions.

While hypotheses about human sexual behavior (i.e., male promiscuity, female coyness) rely on descriptions of the evolution of different gamete production strategies, the difference between the women and men in many non-sexual behaviors (e.g., typical employment) has an hypothesized explanation that depends on more recent human evolution.

The Gender Division of Labor

The world of work in U.S. society is to a large degree sexually segregated. Women are more likely to be daycare providers, nurses, secretaries, and homemakers than men, while men are more likely to be doctors, politicians, college science professors, and upper-level corporate executives than women. This gender division of labor has been explained by some sociobiologists as due to the evolutionary legacy of our human ancestors.

According to these sociobiologists, early human societies adopted a gender division of labor out of necessity. Women, who were likely to be pregnant or caring for a breast-feeding infant, were less able to range freely than men. These women primarily collected food by gathering roots, nuts, and berries, and hunting small game near their campsites. Men, who were more mobile than women and who could leave their offspring for longer periods, could range far from the camp in order to hunt large game. This hunter-gatherer lifestyle led to the evolution of different skills and behaviors in the two sexes. Successful females were the ones who were adept at anticipating and meeting the short-term needs of their children, who had the rapid fine motor control necessary to efficiently gather tiny fruits and nuts, and who were able to easily identify likely food-producing plants by visually keying in on physical habitat characteristics. Successful males were the ones who worked well in all male groups, had good spatial skills (in order for the spear to connect with the game animal), were able to find their way to and from far-ranging hunting grounds, and were aggressive in their pursuit of prey. According to this hypothesis, females have evolved into good care givers and secretaries but must rely on maps to find their way around, while men have evolved the perfect skills for business leadership and never need to ask for directions.

The evidence commonly cited in support of this hypothesis is that the gender division of labor is nearly universal and consistent in most human cultures. Despite the fact that different cultures approach hunting and gathering tasks quite differently, sociobiologists argue that cultures where females and males share hunting, gathering, and child care duties are the exception to the biological rule. Additionally, sociobiologists have searched for physical evidence to support an evolutionary cause for the division of labor. This physical evidence began with studies that showed differences in average skill level between women and men on various tests. For instance, some researchers have demonstrated that men score higher on math tests than women, while women score higher on certain verbal tests than men. When critics argued that differences on skills tests today are likely due to differences in training and treatment in the past, sociobiologists began to search for sex differences in brain structure and development. Sex differences in brain structure have been found in some studies but not in others, and often studies that find a difference in one direction will be contradicted by other studies that find a difference in the opposite direction. Studies of sex differences in the brain are described in more detail in Chapter 5.

While sociobiologists can describe logically sound hypotheses giving evolutionary explanations for the gender division of labor, they are as with all evolutionary hypotheses, extremely difficult to prove. Additionally, equally likely alternative hypotheses have been proposed that take into account humans' incredible capacity for learning and behavioral flexibility.

Alternative Hypotheses to Explain Gender Differences   The hypothesis of an evolutionary basis for our modern gender division of labor assumes that this division is universal and basically identical among human cultures. However, this is not the case. We already know that humans are remarkably flexible behaviorally. We know that cultures can change rapidly when the environment changes (from nomadic to settled agriculture, for instance). We also know that the specific jobs that women and men take differ among cultural groups. Clearly, women have until recently been the primary food source for infants—this was a biological fact. Women's role in feeding infants does place some limitations on their traditional activities, just as men's inability to nurse infants places limitations on their roles. That this basic biology has led to divisions of labor in different societies is not a surprise — just as the wide variety of ways in which cultures have worked within this biological necessity and their environmental conditions to find an efficient lifestyle should be no surprise. Finally, just because a gender division of labor exists in different cultures does not mean that the specific task skills required for these labors are based on genetic differences that evolved via natural selection.

As discussed in Chapter 5, the physical evidence used to support the hypothesis of inborn biological difference between women and men is suspect. Even if differences between the sexes in brain structures are found, any link of brain differences with behavior differences is a correlation (see the limitations of correlations in Chapter 2). Only a small portion of brain development occurs before birth. A baby's brain doubles in size by the end of the first year, and quadruples in size by the end of the fourth. Childhood experiences obviously can have a strong influence on brain structure. The acquisition of language clearly demonstrates this principle. Children under the age of twelve can quickly pick up additional languages. Often these children will have little or no accent from their first language impacting the pronunciation of their second language. In contrast, older children and adults have a more difficult time learning additional languages and, when they do, often have heavily accented pronunciation. This phenomenon occurs because language-associated brain structure becomes fairly stable in adolescence. While learning a new language modifies that structure in both children and adults, children's brains are more flexible. Less is known about the development of brain structures associated with spatial skills and math ability but, presumably, early childhood experiences in these areas may affect later ease of learning. If little boys are encouraged to engage in more sports-oriented play than little girls, we might expect to see developed differences in their brain structures as adults. Therefore, in humans, showing a difference in brain structure does not prove a genetic origin for that difference. While one may argue that genetic differences between males and females lead to differences in the brain and therefore different behaviors, another could convincingly argue that differences in the treatment of females and males during early childhood lead to differences in learned behavior and therefore differences in brain structure. Which came first, the brain architecture or the learning?

Gender differences in behavior may have other explanations rather than biology. Cultural differences also lead to behavioral variation between groups. For example, people raised in Italian-American communities on the East Coast may be louder and more direct in conversation than individuals raised in Norwegian-American communities in the upper Midwest. A man's ability to understand directions given in terms of compass points is just as likely due to his modeling of his father's behavior as it is to a genetic legacy that differs from a woman's. A woman's dislike of math may have as much to do with her understanding of expectations about women in her culture as it does with a relic of her evolutionary history.

■ DISCUSSION EXERCISE 3

3.1. Are there differences between women and men that everyone can agree on? What differences are in dispute?

3.2. How could you determine if one of these disputed differences are fixed (i.e., genetic)?

3.3. Is it important to determine which gender differences are fixed and which are not? Why or why not?

Consequences of Accepting That There Are Some Natural Human Behaviors   One reason evolutionary explanations are so appealing to us is that they reinforce our existing beliefs about human nature. After all, many people feel that it is perfectly clear that men are more promiscuous than women, that women are better care givers than men, and that men are better in economic competition. However, there are serious consequences of accepting as true hypotheses about the naturalness of human behaviors. For instance, the founder of sociobiology, Edward O. Wilson, once despaired that a certain degree of gender role division is inevitable. He wrote about the apparent mismatch between women's desires for social equality and their intrinsic capabilities.

> I am suggesting that the contradictions are rooted in the surviving relics of our prior genetic history, and that one of the most inconvenient and senseless, but nonetheless unavoidable, of these residues is the modest predisposition toward sex role differences.

In other words, try as they may, women will never be able to perform as well as men in certain tasks (nor men as well as women in others). If we believe Wilson's explanation of the naturalness of these differences, we might as well give up working for gender equality now.

In addition, accepting certain behaviors as natural in certain sexes implies that all members of a certain sex should conform to that behavior. If gender roles are built into the genes, we should not expect men to take on primary care giver roles. When they do, we must assume that they are not as skilled as women, and that they are actually abnormal. Interestingly, if we accept current gender roles as natural, males are subtly steered away from low-paying, typically female jobs (or primary care giving within the family), while women are steered away from high-paying, typically male jobs. Accepting a natural difference in aptitude and attitude will continue to relegate women to their current second-class economic status—a working woman currently receives about $0.70 for every $1.00 a working man receives.

As you will discover in the next exercise, evolutionary explanations for human behavior are very easy to propose. Because they are based on easily followed arguments and conform to our beliefs about universal experience, many people find these hypotheses easy to believe. However, simply because a logically sound hypothesis exists does not imply that the hypothesis is true (see Chapter 2). To be accepted as fact, all unproven hypotheses must be rigorously tested. This is where sociobiology faces a serious quandary. Testing an evolutionary explanation for a behavior (or even for a structure) is extremely difficult. We cannot travel back in time to observe the behavioral characteristics of our ancestors, and we cannot effectively compare ourselves to related species, since we have been evolving away from each other for millions of years. Other than cross-cultural studies, which lead to problems associated with defining universal behaviors, we cannot perform the types of experiments required to determine which behaviors in humans are instinctual and which are learned. These experiments would require raising a child without a social environment, surely unethical and also likely to result in an adult with behaviors that are very difficult to interpret.

Humans were subject to natural selection during our evolution, and it certainly is possible that some of our behaviors originated in a similar fashion to other traits, such as an upright stance or the loss of thick body fur. However, if particular human behaviors have a basis in biology, they are also subject to influence from social tradition and learning. These three factors interact with each other throughout human development and are nearly impossible to separate. Additionally, we do know that any biological imprint on human behavior is weak and not deterministic. The role that instinct plays in determining the limits of human learning has not been clearly determined for even the simplest human behaviors. For example, even behaviors associated with eating, a basic human response to feelings of hunger, are learned. Some people have learned to starve themselves despite intense feelings of hunger, while others may eat even when they are not hungry. Clearly, humans are not restricted to narrow ranges of instinctive behaviors, even if behavioral instincts exist.

Finally, as with other social animals, behaviors that once had just a biological function may now have a number of different social functions. Consider this example from Anne Fausto-Sterling:

> The ability to experience thirst is localized in a particular area of the brain, yet the act of drinking has many meanings. We go out to a bar not to quench our thirst but to be sociable. We raise our glasses in unison at a party to celebrate an important event, not to meet our physiological need for water. Even this act, which can fill a biological need, cannot be understood outside of its social context. (*Myths of Gender*, 1985).

Because we have no way of distilling from human behavior the essence that is constrained by our biology, and because we know that human behavior is incredibly flexible and changes rapidly in response to environmental and social changes, efforts to explain the evolutionary basis for particular human behaviors should be approached with skepticism. When you come across these explanations, evaluate the quality of the evidence supporting the hypotheses. Ask yourself what may be lost by accepting this hypothesis without further evidence. Any biological hypotheses that may result in limitations on human potential need to be held to the highest standard.

■ DISCUSSION EXERCISE 4

4.1. Imagine a world where women have control over the economic and social life of the community. Make up an evolutionary explanation for why female superiority is "natural" in humans.

SUMMARY

Non-sexual gender roles in humans have been hypothesized to arise from the gender role divisions in our early evolutionary history. Because women supposedly were engaged in fruit and vegetable gathering and men were involved in hunting large game, different skills were favored by natural selection in the sexes. This hypothesis is meant to explain current gender divisions of labor (e.g., women are childcare employees, men are executives). However, there is little evidence that gender roles are fixed in different cultures, and the role of learning in humans' expression of gender role differences is clear. Even if some aspect of gender roles is genetic, we have no evidence for this, and the consequences of assuming limits to human possibility can be negative for both women and men.

REFERENCES

Alcock, J. (1984). *Animal behavior: An evolutionary approach.* Sinauer Associates.

Arnold, S. J. (1980). The microevolution of feeding behavior. In A. Kamil & T. Sargent (Eds.), *Foraging behavior: Ecological, ethological, and psychological approaches.* Garland Press.

Bleir, R. (1986). Sex differences research: Science or belief? In R. Bleir (Ed.), *Feminist approaches to science.* Pergamon Press.

Darwin, C. (1871). *The descent of man, and selection in relation to sex.* Appleton Publishers.

Fausto-Sterling, A. (1985). *Myths of gender: Biological theories about women and men.* Basic Books.

Gowaty, P. A. (1992). Evolutionary biology and feminism. *Human Nature* 3(3), 217–249.

Haraway, D. (1989). *Primate visions: Gender, race, and nature in the world of modern science.* Routledge Publishers.

Hardy, S. B. (1981). *The woman that never evolved.* Harvard University Press.

Kevles, B. (1986). *Females of the species.* Harvard University Press.

Laumann, E. O., Gagnon, J. H., Michael, R. T., & Michaels, S. (1994). *The social organization of sexuality: sexual practices in the United States.* University of Chicago Press.

Lewinton, R. C., Rose, S., & Kamin, L. J. (1984). *Not in our genes.* Pantheon Books.

Maynard-Smith, J. (1977). Parental investment—A prospective analysis. *Animal Behavior* 25, 1–9.

Mies, M. (1986). *Patriarchy and accumulation on a world scale: Women in the international division of labour.* Zed Books.

Terborgh, J., & Janson, C. H. (1986). The socioecology of primate groups. *Annual Review of Ecology and Systematics* 17,111–135.

Trivers, R. (1972). Parental investment and sexual selection. In B. Campbell (Ed.), *Sexual selection and the descent of man, 1871–1971,* pp. 136–179. Aldine Press.

Williams, W. L. (1992). *The spirit and the flesh: Sexual diversity in American Indian culture.* Beacon Press.

Wilson, E. O. (1975). *Sociobiology: The new synthesis.* Harvard University Press.

CHAPTER 4

An understanding of the true mechanism of sex determination could have prevented the divorce of Catherine of Aragon and the beheading of Anne Boleyn, former wives of King Henry VIII, each of whom were blamed for not producing a male heir to the throne.

SEX DETERMINATION

SEX DETERMINATION

Your sex was genetically determined when your mother's egg fused with your father's sperm. Egg cells have one X, or sex, chromosome and 22 non-sex determining chromosomes, called autosomes, for a total of 23 chromosomes. All the rest of a female's cells have two X chromosomes and 22 pairs of autosomes, for a total of 46 chromosomes. When a female's ovaries generate egg cells, the number of chromosomes in the precursor cells is divided in half. A cell on its way to becoming an egg cell begins the process with 46 chromosomes and ends the process with 23. During this division, one of the two X chromosomes is placed into each egg cell, along with one member of each pair of the 22 pairs of non-sex chromosomes. (This process, called meiosis, is described fully in Chapter 9). Males have 23 pairs of chromosomes as well, but male sex chromosomes are not two X's as seen in females. All of the cells in a man's body (except the sperm cells) have 22 pairs of autosomes and one X and one Y chromosome. Males can therefore generate sperm that contain 22 unpaired autosomes and either an X or a Y sex chromosome.

If an egg cell, which always carries an X chromosome, fuses with a sperm bearing a Y chromosome, the embryo which develops from this fertilized egg cell will have one X chromosome and one Y chromosome and therefore be genetically male. If the egg cell fuses with a sperm which also has an X chromosome, the embryo that develops from this fertilized egg cell will have two X chromosomes and therefore be genetically female (Figure 4. 1). It is in this manner that the male of our species actually determines the sex of the embryo.

An understanding of the true mechanism of sex determination could have prevented the divorce of Catherine of Aragon and the beheading of Anne Boleyn, former wives of King Henry VIII, each of whom were blamed for not producing a male heir to the throne. Both of these wives (he had six in all) did, however, produce female offspring, indicating that their fertility was not necessarily the "problem." Catherine of Aragon was the mother of future Queen Mary I (born 1516), and Anne Boleyn was the mother of future Queen Elizabeth I (born 1533).

S U M M A R Y

The combination of sex chromosomes at fertilization determines the sex of the early embryo. Human females have two X chromosomes, while males have one X and one Y chromosome. One of a female's X chromosomes is obtained from her mother's egg cell and the other X chromosome is obtained from her father's sperm cell at fertilization. Since a female can contribute either of her two X chromosomes and a male can contribute either his X or his Y chromosome, genetic sex is determined by the male in the human species.

The Structure and Function of DNA

> *It is interesting to think that you most likely have some DNA nucleotides in your body thta were once part of a carrot's or a cow's DNA.*

Now that you know how sex is determined, you may be wondering exactly what these X and Y chromosomes are. Chromosomes are long pieces of DNA (**deoxyribonucleic acid**) wrapped around proteins. It is estimated that if you were to take all the DNA out of one cell in your body and lay it end to end, there would be six feet of DNA! If you took all the DNA out of each and every cell in your body, you would have a length of DNA equal to the distance required to travel to the sun and back 100 times. This incredible amount of DNA

FIGURE 4.1   Genetic Sex Determination

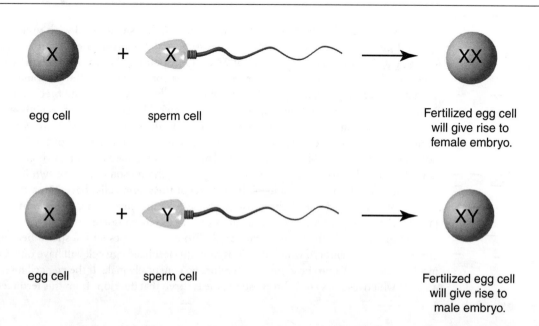

egg cell   sperm cell   Fertilized egg cell
                                                                  will give rise to
                                                                  female embryo.

egg cell   sperm cell   Fertilized egg cell
                                                                  will give rise to
                                                                  male embryo.

is wrapped around proteins in much the same manner that you have probably wrapped the long thin string of a kite around a stick to prevent it from becoming tangled. You have 46 of these DNA and protein complexes, called chromosomes, in every cell of your body (except sperm cells and egg cells, which have 23).

If we examine the DNA molecule itself, starting with the three-dimensional structure and taking a series of steps inward toward the molecular structure (Figure 4.2), we would see that DNA is comprised of two strands of chemicals that wind around each other to form a double helix. Each strand of the helix is composed of a series of chemical building blocks called nucleotides. Nucleotides are composed of a sugar, a phosphate, and a nitrogen-containing base. The nitrogenous bases of DNA have one of four different chemical structures. Each different nitrogenous base has a different name: adenine (A), guanine (G), cytosine (C), or thymine (T). Nucleotides are thus composed of a sugar, a phosphate, and one of the four nitrogenous bases A, G, C, or T. The order of nucleotides on one strand determines the order of nucleotides on the other strand because A always pairs with T and G always pairs with C (and vice versa). The order of nucleotides differs from gene to gene.

To better visualize the DNA molecule, think of taking a rope ladder and securing one end of it to the ceiling and twisting it to form a double helix. The upright sides of the rope ladder would correspond to the sugars and phosphates of the DNA backbone, and the rungs would be made of the paired nitrogenous bases.

Only 4 nucleotide bases.

FIGURE 4.2   The Structure of DNA

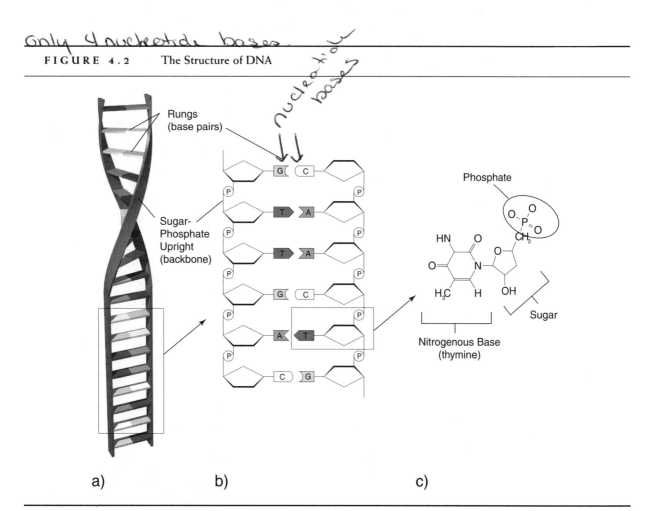

nucleotide bases

a)   b)   c)

When the DNA molecule needs to be copied during cell division, the DNA is split apart up the middle of the helix (similar to a zipper being unzipped), and new nucleotides are added to each side of the original parent molecule, maintaining the A-T and G-C pairings. Individual nucleotides are synthesized by your body and provided by the food you eat. Anything that you eat which at one point was alive, such as fruit, vegetables, and meat, has DNA that can be broken down into its component nucleotides. These nucleotides can then be incorporated into your DNA while your cells make copies of themselves. It is interesting to think that you most likely have some DNA nucleotides in your body that once were part of a cow's or a carrot's DNA. The reason you do not resemble a cow or a carrot is that your body does not incorporate entire genes into your DNA. Rather your body breaks down the cow and carrot genes into component nucleotides and incorporates these into your DNA when your DNA is duplicated.

SUMMARY

Your cells contain chromosomes that are made of DNA wrapped around proteins. DNA is a double helical molecule made up of many nucleotides joined together. A lengthwise series of nucleotides joined together can make up a gene. Different genes are composed of the same four nucleotides arranged in different orders.

How Genes Make Proteins

How can different sequences of nucleotides lead to such different appearances and abilities as those seen in carrots, cows, and humans? All of these organisms have different genes that provide information to cells concerning which proteins to synthesize. Carrots make proteins that enable them to perform photosynthesis, proteins that humans and cows do not make. While this is just one example of how carrots, cows, and humans differ, all the genetic differences between them are due to these organisms having different genes which, in turn, results in the synthesis of different proteins.

Proteins are molecules that serve a wide variety of roles in your body. They help your muscles move, your eyes focus, and your brain think. One of the major roles of intracellular proteins is to function as enzymes, which are biological catalysts that speed up the chemical reactions your body performs. All of the molecules your body needs to be healthy, e.g. proteins, lipids, (fats), and sugars, are metabolized (broken down) by enzyme-catalyzed reactions. When you eat proteins, fats, and carbohydrates, your body breaks these nutrients down in order to convert them into a form of energy your body can use. Many of the vitamins you need to be healthy work together with enzymes to perform these chemical reactions.

While you may now understand that genes are made of DNA and that different stretches of DNA code for different proteins, you may be wondering how exactly genes *code* for proteins. The first thing you need to know is that proteins are made of different combinations of the 20 naturally occurring amino acids (Figure 4.3). Different amino acids have different chemical properties, and different proteins are composed of different sequences of amino acids. If you consider all of the novel ways in which the 20 amino acids could be arranged to make proteins of varying lengths, you quickly realize that there are almost an infinite variety of proteins that could be produced by a cell. The proteins that a cell produces are prescribed by the active genes in a given cell type. Genes code for which proteins will be produced through the order of their nucleotides. The order of nucleotides in a gene determines the order of amino acids in a protein, and each gene codes for only one protein.

How exactly does the order of nucleotides determine the order of amino acids? The first step in the process of going from a gene to a protein is called *transcription*. The process of transcription is the process of copying the DNA into a messenger RNA transcript. (Think of the process of obtaining a copy of your course work and grades. This is called getting a transcript.) RNA stands for ribonucleic acid. The structure of RNA differs a little from the structure

FIGURE 4.3   The Twenty Naturally Occurring Amino Acids

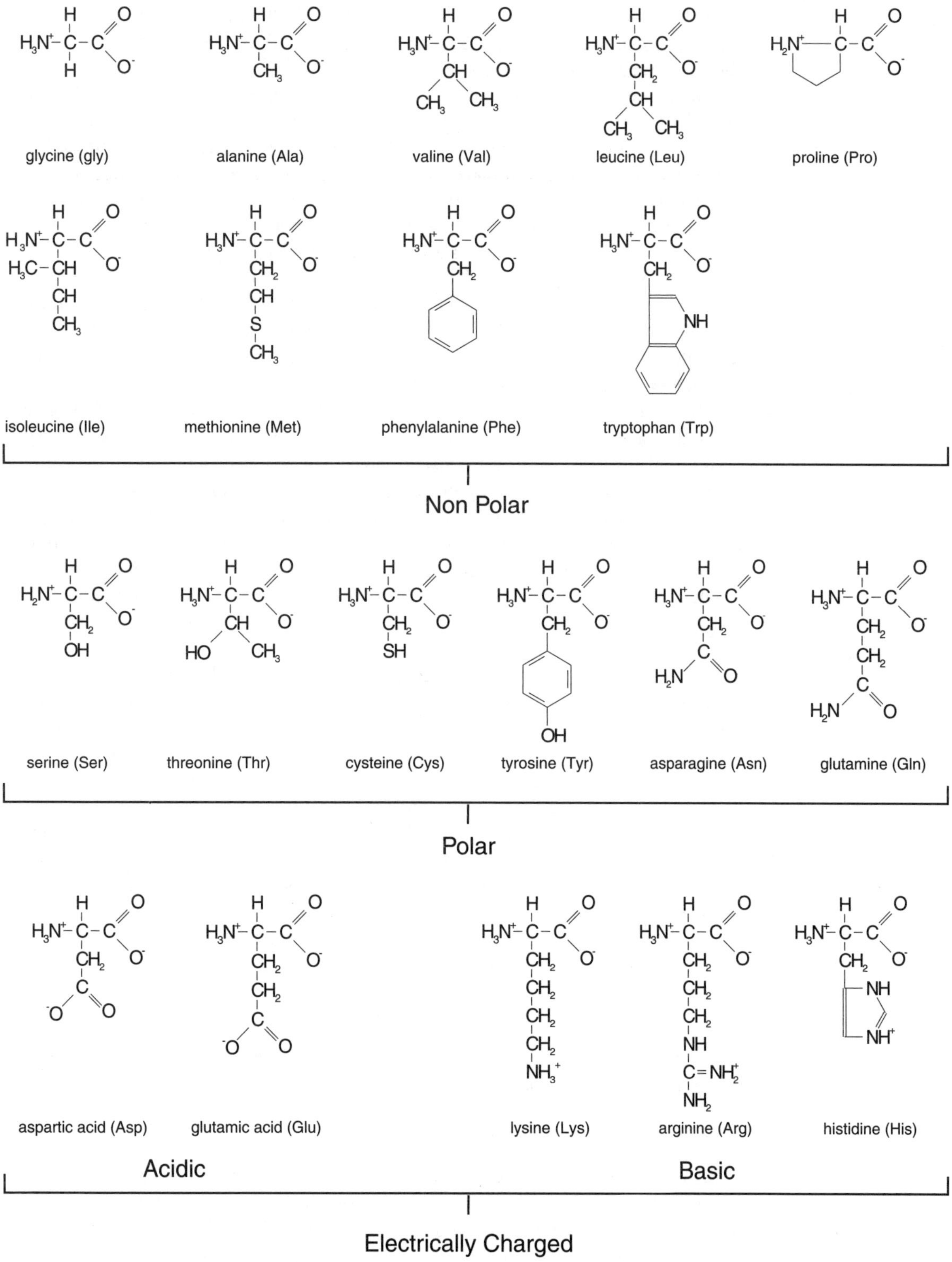

glycine (gly)   alanine (Ala)   valine (Val)   leucine (Leu)   proline (Pro)

isoleucine (Ile)   methionine (Met)   phenylalanine (Phe)   tryptophan (Trp)

Non Polar

serine (Ser)   threonine (Thr)   cysteine (Cys)   tyrosine (Tyr)   asparagine (Asn)   glutamine (Gln)

Polar

aspartic acid (Asp)   glutamic acid (Glu)   lysine (Lys)   arginine (Arg)   histidine (His)

Acidic   Basic

Electrically Charged

of DNA, in as much as the sugar in RNA is ribose (not deoxyribose as is the case with DNA), and the thymine bases are replaced with uracil bases. Using a DNA gene as a template, nucleotides are added to the complementary strand according to the base pairing rules. In RNA, C and G still make a base pair, but A now pairs with U. This process makes a new copy of the original gene. This copy is called messenger RNA because it carries the "message" of the gene out of the nucleus to the cytoplasm of the cell where it can be translated.

The process of translation involves taking information in the form of nucleotides (the mRNA transcript) and translating it into the language of amino acids. Translation is, therefore, also an apt name if you think of a translator as a person who takes information in one language and translates it into another language so that others can understand.

Cellular translation occurs in the cytoplasm of the cell on subcellular structures called ribosomes. Ribosomes function as workbenches where translation can occur. Molecules called transfer RNAs carry amino acids around in the cytoplasm and bind to the nucleotides found on the transcript. Particular transfer RNAs, carrying their specific amino acid, recognize particular nucleotide sequences on the RNA molecule. The amino acid is then incorporated into the growing protein, which is being constructed on the ribosome workbench. Overall, the sequence of nucleotides on the DNA dictates the sequence of amino acids that makes up the protein the gene codes for.

All of this seems very complicated until one sees the similarities the process of protein building shares with the more familiar process of planting a garden. Let's suppose you are going to plant a large garden. In order to do so, you will need a blueprint, indicating what size and shape garden to build and what vegetables to plant and where to plant them. Certain vegetables will be planted in a region where they will be exposed to lots of sun and some will grow better in the shade. Others will be planted around the periphery and serve as pest deterrents. Larger plants will provide shade for smaller plants. In this sense, the whole garden, composed of many plant sub-units, could be likened to a functioning protein. The blueprint is similar to a cell's DNA. You would most likely need to make a copy of the blueprint so that the blueprint is not ruined if it gets rained on or misplaced. Once you have this copy (mRNA transcript), you can take it to the land on which you plan to build your garden (ribosome). Once there, you will need the seeds, flowers, and seedlings to plant (amino acids). These will be carried to the garden in wheel barrows (transfer RNA molecules) and removed from the wheel barrows when the copy of the blue print calls for them to be planted in various arrangements to make a functional garden (protein).

Getting back to the X and Y chromosomes, you may now be able to suggest a hypothesis for how the X and Y chromosome differ. They differ in that they are composed of some different genes. While there are genes that are similar on the X and Y chromosomes, the genes that are different on these two chromosomes lead to the production of different proteins. This small difference in the types of proteins made by the sex chromosomes leads to physical sex differences between females and males like the development of breasts, ovaries, vagina, and uterus in females but not in males.

SUMMARY

Genes code for the production of proteins. The X chromosome and the Y chromosome carry some different genes. These different genes direct cells to produce a small number of proteins that differ in males and females. Some of the genes on the sex chromosomes, through the actions of the proteins they code for, result in biological sex differences.

Genes on the X Chromosome

What are some of these genes on the X and Y chromsomes? Each X chromosome contains around 5% of a human's total number of genes and is roughly 160 million nucleotides long. The Y chromosome is about 25% as long as the X chromosome and contains comparatively few genes (around 12).

Genes on the X and Y chromosome are called sex-linked genes because inheritance of these genes occurs along with sex determination. Most examples of sex-linked inheritance involve X linkage, since so few genes are located on (linked to) the Y chromosome. Because females carry two X chromosomes, each X-linked gene is represented twice (once on each chromosome).

For autosomal chromosomes, any given gene is represented twice, once on each chromosome. These duplicate copies of the gene are called alleles and code for allelic proteins. Because each allele was inherited from a different parent, there can be differences between them. In our gardening metaphor, alleles would be similar to different varieties of squash or tomatoes. Alleles can be dominant, meaning that they can exert their effects when present on either one or both of the paired chromosomes. Recessive alleles must be present on both chromosomes of a pair in order to exert their effects. An example, using a gene on a non-sex chromosome (autosome) is the disease cystic fibrosis. Cystic fibrosis (CF) is fairly common among white persons of northern European descent. People who have two dominant alleles of the CF gene make two proteins that help transport chloride ions out of cells. People who have one dominant and one recessive allele of the CF gene make one normal chloride transporter and one defective protein that cannot transport chloride out of the cells. One normal CF allele is enough to prevent a person from having the disease. Persons with two recessive alleles make two defective transporters and chloride ions build up inside their cells. In the lungs of these people, fluid accumulation results in severe damage and can lead to death at an early age.

Females have two alleles of every gene. Males have two alleles of every gene, except the genes located on the X and Y chromosomes, because males have only one of each of these chromosomes. Many diseases are the result of recessive alleles. A person with only one copy of a recessive allele and one copy of a dominant allele will not have the disease. In males, however, a single copy of a recessive allele on their X chromosome is enough to produce the disease, because there is no normal allele on the Y chromosome to provide a normal protein. Males, therefore, will express all genes on their X chromosome whether they are dominant or recessive, and thus are affected with X-linked disorders much more often than women are.

Some of the genes located on the X chromosome that show this sex-linked pattern of inheritance lead to colorblindness, hemophilia, Duchenne muscular dystrophy, and, some researchers believe, homosexuality. Below is a description of how each of these traits is thought to be inherited. Figure 4.4 shows their location, if known, on the X chromosome.

Colorblindness: Red-green color blindness affects approximately 4% of all males. Red blindness is an inability to see red as a distinct color. Green blindness is an inability to see green as a distinct color. Both red and green blindness are X-linked traits. When normal (in this case, the dominant allele is normal), these genes code for the production of opsins. Opsins are present in eye cells and function in binding to pigments. Pigments are chemicals that absorb light of various wavelengths. A lack of opsins results in an insensitivity to light of red and green wavelengths. People with normal vision see the three primary colors: red, green and blue. All other colors are seen as mixtures of primary colors. The genes that code for opsins that absorb green and red wavelengths are at one end of the X chromosome. Males carrying one mutant gene see both red and green as red, and males carrying the other mutant gene see both red and green as green.

Hemophilia: Hemophilia is a defect in the blood clotting mechanism resulting from a gene which leads to the production of a nonfunctional form of a protein called clotting factor VIII. Without this protein, an individual may bleed to death following a minor cut. Treatment requires blood transfusions of normal blood carrying required clotting factors.

FIGURE 4.4   The Locations of Some of the Genes on the X Chromosome

---

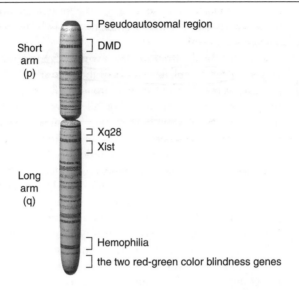

Queen Victoria of England was a carrier; she had one copy of the recessive allele, and one copy of the dominant allele. She passed on the recessive allele to several of her children. Many members of the royal families of Europe subsequently inherited this allele. The current British Royal family is free of this disease because they are descendants of an unaffected son of Victoria's, Edward the VII. A mutation to this X-linked gene arose either in one of Victoria's parents (in her father's sperm cell or mother's egg cell) or in Victoria herself. Victoria's granddaughter, Alexandra, carried one recessive and one normal copy of this allele too. Alexandra married Czar Nicholas II of Russia. Their son Alexis, heir to the throne of the 400-year-old Romanov dynasty, had hemophilia. Because medical doctors could not cure their son, the royal couple placed their faith in the monk Rasputin. While under Rasputin's care, young Alexis recovered well from several episodes of bleeding, and the family became believers in Rasputin's spiritual powers. They began to trust him to help them make decisions not only about their son's health but also about governance as well. Many historians believe that Rasputin's influences on the royal family contributed to the revolution that overthrew the throne. This overthrow occurred during the communist revolution of 1917 and resulted in the deaths of Alexis (who was 14 years old), his mother, and the Czar.

Duchenne muscular dystrophy (DMD): DMD is a progressive, fatal disease of muscle wasting that affects approximately 1 in 3,500 males. The onset of muscle wasting occurs between 1 and 6 years of age and, by 12 years of age, affected boys are often confined to a wheelchair. The gene, which is defective in DMD, is one that normally codes for the dystrophin protein. When at least one allele is normal, dystrophin stabilizes cell membranes during muscle contraction. Presumably, the absence of normal dystrophin proteins allows muscle cells to break down and muscle tissue to die.

Homosexuality: Malfunctions in single genes leading to specific outcomes are actually relatively rare. Most traits that people find interesting, such as intelligence, personality, and sexuality, are under the control of many genes and the environment. This reality has not stopped numerous researchers from attempting to find single gene causes for aspects of these behaviors.

Recent and controversial studies by Dean Hamer and Simon LeVay (1994, 1995) have attempted to find a gene associated with male homosexuality on the X chromosome. In these studies, the X chromosomes of families with homosexual brothers were examined. These researchers found that 2/3 of the 32 pairs of homosexual brothers shared matching nucleotide sequences in an X chromosome region called Xq28. Because brothers would be expected to share chromosomal regions 50% of the time (because a mother can pass on either of her two X chromosomes) the correlation between the presence of this region and homosexuality was thought to be significant. The inference drawn was that this region on the X chromosome might be involved in steering men toward homosexuality.

After much criticism of this original experiment, scientists looked at the X chromosomes of the heterosexual brothers of the homosexual men and found that less than the expected percent of the heterosexual brothers shared the same Xq28 region. Later investigators also looked for, but did not find, any correlation between X chromosome regions and sexual orientation in women.

These studies received much attention in the popular press, and the notion of a "gay gene" persists. However, it is crucial to point out that each member of the 32 pairs of brothers shared his Xq28 region with his brother and not with any of the other men in the study. There is no single Xq28 region associated with homosexuality and, therefore, no single "gay gene." Further critical evaluation of these studies has led many researchers to question why some heterosexual brothers would have the same Xq28 sequence as their homosexual brothers yet not be homosexual themselves. Additionally, LeVay and Hamer's own research also showed that many homosexual brothers did not share this region. Clearly, the correlation between presence of similar Xq28 regions in homosexual brothers does little to explain the origin of this complex behavioral trait.

Another strong criticism of these studies is that they are predicated on the unproven belief that homosexuality has a biological basis. While it may turn out that there is some level of biological predisposition toward homosexuality in males, this has never been proven—and many researchers would argue for a cultural influence as well. Many studies of homosexual males have been based on the presumption that homosexual males are sexually somewhere between men and women, and that this intermediate state is the result of abnormal biological development. One must wonder if the support for these theories derives as much from their appeal to cultural ideologies (i.e., homosexuals are abnormal) as from their scientific merit. This argument is especially compelling because other scientists have tried to repeat these experiments and failed. Moreover, healthy skepticism is required when scientists posit yet another theory that blames the mother (in this case because she donates the "defective" X chromosome) for any behavior a child exhibits that deviates from the norm. All in all, even though the notion of a "gay gene" persists in the popular press, there is no scientific evidence supporting the idea of a single gene being responsible for the inheritance of any complex behavioral trait.

SUMMARY

There are many genes on the X chromosome for which there are no alleles on the Y chromosome. Because of this, males are far more susceptible to inheriting X-linked recessive traits than females are.

Genes on the Y Chromosome

Genes on the Y chromosome are passed from fathers to sons. Although this distinctive pattern of inheritance should make Y-linked genes easy to identify, very few genes have been localized to the Y chromosomes. Of the 12 or so genes thought to be on the Y chromosome, most are located in the pseudoautosomal region at the tip of the Y chromosome, which has genes similar to those found in the pseudoautosomal region on the X chromosome. These regions are called pseudoautosomal because they behave more like non-sex chromosomes (autosomes) than like sex chromosomes but are not actual autosomes. Autosome-like behaviors include the fact that these regions undergo recombination with each other, and the genes are present in two doses in both males and females. Recombination is the physical exchange of portions of one chromosome with another. In this case, portions of the X chromosome are exchanged for portions of the Y chromosome.

One gene thought to be located exclusively on the Y chromosome is called the SRY gene. In Chapter 5 you will see that expression of this gene triggers a cascade of events that leads to development of testes and some of the specialized cells required for male sexual characteristics. Genes other than SRY, on chromosomes other than the Y, code for proteins that are unique to males but are not expressed unless testes develop.

One of the other genes on the Y chromosome may be required for the production of healthy sperm. Deletion of this gene results in infertility due to an inability to produce sperm. These are the only genes on the Y chromosome to have been unambiguously characterized to date.

SUMMARY

The Y chromosome has very few genes. Those that are present code for proteins, and this leads to the development of male sexual characteristics.

X Inactivation

We now know that most of the protein products of genes on the X chromosome have nothing at all to do with the production of biological sex differences. Accordingly, females and males should require equal doses of the products of X-linked genes. How can we account for the fact that females, since they have two X chromosomes, could receive two doses of X-linked genes, while males receive only one?

The answer comes from a phenomenon called X inactivation that occurs in all of the cells of a developing female embryo. This inactivation guarantees that all females actually only receive one dose of the proteins produced by genes on the X chromosomes. Inactivation of the genes on one of the two X chromosomes takes place in the embryo at about the time the embryo implants in the uterus. This inactivation is random with respect to parental source—either of the two X chromosomes can be inactivated in a given cell. Inactivation is also irreversible and, as such, is inherited during cell replication. (Once a maternal or paternal X chromosome is inactivated in a cell, all descendants of that cell continue inactivating the same chromosome.)

It appears that a gene on the X chromosome called *Xist* (for X inactivation specific transcript), which is present on both X chromosomes but is expressed only on the inactive X chromosome, starts the inactivation process. The *Xist* gene produces a very large RNA molecule that wraps itself tightly around the inactive X chromosome, thus making transcription of genes on most of this chromosome impossible. The genes in the pseudoautosomal region are not affected by the product of the *Xist* gene and therefore not inactivated in males or females.

An inactivated X chromosome is called a Barr body, named after its discoverer, Murray Barr, who was the first to find these darkly staining chromosomes. The presence of an inactive X chromosome in normal females was first hypothesized by British scientist Mary Lyon in the 1960s, hence the process of inactivation is sometimes referred to as Lyonization.

The example of calico cats is a good one to illustrate the effects of X inactivation or Lyonization. Certain cats carry genes for fur color on their X chromosomes. If a male cat with orange fur mates with a female cat with black fur (or vice versa), a female kitten could have one X chromosome with the gene for orange fur and one X chromosome with a gene for black fur. Early on in development, when the kitten embryo consists of around 16 cells, one of the two X chromosomes is randomly inactivated in each cell. Thus, some cells will be expressing the orange fur color gene and others will be expressing the black fur color gene. The pattern of inactivation (maternal X chromosome or paternal X chromosome) is passed on to the daughter cells of the 16-celled embryo, resulting in the patches of orange and black fur color seen in calico cats. On rare occasions, male cats can have calico coloring. This can happen only if a male cat has two X chromosomes and one Y chromosome (a situation that does occur, though infrequently).

An example of the effects of X inactivation in human females is a skin disorder called anhidrotic ectodermal dysplasia in which an affected individual, with two recessive alleles, has no sweat glands. In a heterozygous female, (a female with one normal and one recessive allele), random X inactivation results in a mosaic pattern of sweat glands. Patches of skin are normal, due to the inactivation of the X chromosome with the recessive allele, while other patches of skin have no sweat glands, due to inactivation of the X chromosome with the normal allele (Figure 4.5).

SUMMARY
One X chromosome is inactivated in every cell of a female resulting in mosaicism of gene expression in females.

The Evolution of the Sex Chromosomes

> *... the Y chromosome is a degenerate X chromosome.*

Most scientists now believe that the X and Y chromosomes started out nearly identical, differing only in the region that bore what would become the SRY gene. This gene eventually became the sex-determining gene and, from then on, evolution favored clustering the genes that control traits beneficial to males but harmful to females around the sex determining region on the Y chromosome. This clustering would be selected for because it would prevent the production of infertile intersexes. Over time, the stretches of DNA in

---

FIGURE 4.5 Random X Inactivation

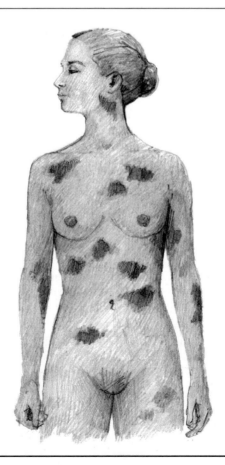

this region of the Y chromosome became increasingly different from the corresponding segments on the X. Eventually, the X and Y became so different that they stopped recombining. Supression of recombination has a price, in the sense that a Y chromosome bearing a damaged gene can no longer swap it for a healthy copy on the X chromosome. The Y chromosome therefore accumulates damaged copies of genes. The X chromosome can continue to exchange damaged copies for healthy copies by recombining with other X chromosomes. Eventually, the functions of the once normal genes on the now damaged Y chromosome are taken over by other, non sex chromosomes. Ultimately, genes on the Y become so badly damaged that they are nonfunctional and the Y chromosome slowly shrinks, because there is no selective advantage to hanging on to damaged genes. It is for this reason that researchers now believe that the Y chromosome is a degenerate X chromosome. Taken to its ultimate extreme, this process might well eliminate the Y chromosome all together. In fact, in most animals with an X-Y system of sex determination, the Y chromosome has diminished function. Some fruit flies and fish have even evolved so that the females are XX and the males are X.

Humans with one X chromosome develop into healthy, albeit infertile adults, while those with one Y chromosome abort early in development. Simply put, the X chromosome has the resources for human development that the Y does not.

SUMMARY

The human Y chromosome evolved from the human X chromosome.

Modified Sex Ratios

You have probably noticed that there are roughly equal numbers of males and females born. This is because the statistical probability of having a girl baby equals the statistical probability of having a boy baby. Because the sex of human offspring is determined by the presence of two X chromosomes or one X and one Y chromosome, and because most males produce equal numbers of X-bearing and Y-bearing sperm cells, the ratio of males to females born should be 1:1. This ratio is called the sex ratio. Interestingly, the sex ratio in humans is not 1:1 at fertilization, birth, or death. Only in adulthood, around 20 years of age, is the ratio actually 1:1. Thereafter females outnumber males in ever-increasing proportions.

The difference in numbers of females born as compared to males is an interesting one. This has been extensively studied from records of registered births. It is thought, though largely unexplained, that there are fewer girls conceived than boys (100:120), but by birth this disparity has receded to 100 girls for every 106 boys. Also, it is impossible to account for the affects of female infanticide and the selective abortion of female fetuses on these statistics. Lastly, it may be that an increase in family size is related to the sex of prior children. A recent study shows that when the second child is male, there is a reduced likelihood of further children. Clearly this would skew the sex distribution.

The larger proportion of females later in life is probably due to both genetic factors, for example, the deleterious effects of X-linked recessive inheritance on males and environmental factors, and more deaths due to accidents in young males than in young females. The female to male death ratio from homicide is 1:4. The female to male death ratios for accidents, cirrhosis, lung cancer, suicide, and heart disease is 1:2. Between 30 and 50 years of age, the higher frequency of heart disease in males accounts for most of the sex difference in death rate. By the age of 65, 16% of U.S. females have died and 30% of U.S. males have died. On average, females live about eight years longer than males.

The birth ratio also seems to vary between different races, with African Americans giving birth to more females than males. Some researchers have found that the sex ratio varies with season, resulting in fewer girls being born in summer and more in late fall and winter and that increased numbers of female births follow hormonally induced ovulation. Some researchers feel that timing intercourse in relation to ovulation helps a couple to select the sex they prefer. (See Chapter 9.)

■ DISCUSSION EXERCISE 1

> 1.1. Would you be inclined to continue having children until you gave birth to one of a desired sex?

SUMMARY

The ratio of females to males is not 1:1 at fertilization, birth or throughout most of life. More boys are conceived and born than girls, but males have shorter life spans for many reasons, both genetic and environmental.

Sex Determination in Other Species

In order to broaden your perspective about the biological determination of "femaleness and maleness" and to undermine the impression that the state of femaleness is the state of lacking (in this case a Y chromosome), we will describe mechanisms of sex determination in other living organisms.

In most vertebrates (fish, amphibians, reptiles, birds, and mammals) gonadal sex is fixed at fertilization by specific chromosomes. This type of sex determination is the same as is seen in humans and is called genotypic sex determination. In humans, females have two of the same chromosomes, and males have two different chromosomes. However, there are variations in nature on which sex has two of the same chromosomes and which sex has two different chromosomes. Organisms with two of the same sex chromosomes are called homogametic (the prefix *homo* means same and *gametic* means sex cell); organisms with two different sex chromosomes are called heterogametic (the prefix *hetero* means different). Females are the homogametic sex in most mammal and fly species, but the reverse is true in butterflies, fish, and birds. In these species, it would be the female who determines the sex of the offspring.

In many egg laying species, gonadal sex (ovaries or testes) is not irrevocably fixed by genetic sex. In these organisms, gonadal sex depends on which genes (coding for hormone receptors) are activated during embryonic development. In many reptiles, gonadal sex is determined by the incubation temperature of the egg, a process known as temperature dependent sex determination. Incubation temperature modifies the number and placement of several enzymes and hormone receptors in the egg. Some researchers have found that a drop of the female hormone estrogen applied to the shell of an incubating egg will produce female offspring in temperature conditions that would normally yield all male hatchlings.

In wasps, ants, and bees, sex is determined by the presence or absence of fertilization. In bees, males (drones) develop from unfertilized eggs. Females (workers and queens) develop from fertilized eggs.

Some species of bony fishes even change their sex after maturation. This mode of sex determination is one in which individuals are deflected from developing as females as a result of social signals, in response to dominance interactions. Males are derived secondarily as a result of an environmental condition that deflects them from the female pathway.

The nematode *Caenorhabditis elegans* normally exists as one of two sexes, a self-fertilizing hermaphrodite or a male. Hermaphrodites have both male and female reproductive organs.

In a particular type of marine worm, *Bonellia*, all eggs develop into small larvae of a sexually indifferent kind. Those that settle onto the sea floor develop into females. Each female has a long proboscis at its front end. Those eggs that settle on the proboscis of a female don't develop much more and become dwarf males that remain permanently attached to the female body. The sex–determining factor is the carbon dioxide tension that is higher at the surface of living tissue than on the surface of the sea floor.

The level of plasticity displayed by some organisms belies the rigidity of sex determination seen in humans. Unusual forms of sexuality challenge our notions of what it means to be female or male and help to reinforce the concept of sexuality as a complex combination of behavorial, anatomical, and physiological characteristics.

SUMMARY

Sex can be determined at fertilization by the kind of chromosomes present or by a variety of environmental cues. Chromosomal sex determination is rather inflexible, but many species whose sex is not determined chromosomally show a much greater degree of plasticity in determining an organism's sex than do humans.

REFERENCES

Byne, W. (1995). Science and belief: Psychobiological research on sexual orientation. *Journal of Homosexuality* 28(3–4), 303–344.

Crews, D., Bergeron, J. M., & McLachlan, J. A. (1995). The role of estrogen in turtle sex determination and the effect of PCB's. *Environmental Health Perspectives* 103(7), 73–77.

Hamer, D., & LeVay, S. (1994). Evidence for a biological influence in male homosexuality. *Scientific American* 270, 44–49.

Hu, S., Patatucci, A. M., Patterson, C., Li, L., Fulker, D. W., Cherny, S. S., Kruglyak, L., & Hamer, D. H. (1995). Linkage between sexual orientation and chromosome Xq28 in males but not in females. *Nature Genetics (BRO)* 3, 248–256.

James, W. H. (1987). The human sex ratio. Part 1: A review of the literature. *Human Biology* 59(5), 721–752.

Mandel, J. L., Monaco, A. P., Nelson, D. L., Schlessinger, D., & Willard, H. (1992). Genome analysis and the human X chromosome. *Science* 258, 103–109.

Nobbe, G. (1993). Gender bending. *Wildlife Conservation* 96(Nov/Dec), 7.

Osman, M. I. (1985). A note on the human sex ratio and factors influencing family size in Japan. *Journal of Heredity* 76, 141.

Reijo, R., Alagappan, R. K., Patrizio, P., & Page, D. C. (1996). Severe ologozoospermia resulting from deletions of azoospermia factor gene on chromosome Y. *Lancet* 347 (9011), 1290–1293.

Rennie, J. (1993). Spot marks the X: In females, one chromosome may lock itself inside an RNA. *Scientific American* 268, 29–30.

CHAPTER 5

Differentiation and development of reproductive structures occurs such that every human fetus will become female, unless deflected from that pathway by androgens.

SEXUAL DIFFERENTIATION AND DEVELOPMENT

FROM FERTILIZED EGG CELL TO YOUNG WOMAN

In the previous chapter you learned that embryonic sex is determined by the combination of sex chromosomes present at fertilization. This chapter will explain how a human embryo is destined to develop into a female unless deflected from that pathway by androgens, how puberty in adolescent girls progresses, and what (if any) effect embryonic androgens have on the brain of the developing embryo.

Development From Fertilization to Week Seven

For the first seven weeks after fertilization, development proceeds in precisely the same manner in female and male fetuses. Immediately after the fusion of egg and sperm, a series of rapid mitotic cell divisions (see Chapter 9 for a discussion of mitosis) called *cleavage* takes place. During this process, the fertilized egg cell makes copies of itself so that after one round of cell division there are two cells, then four cells, then eight cells, and so on. These copied cells remain together in a ball, which does not increase in size from that of the original fertilized egg cell. As cleavage occurs the fertilized egg cell moves via muscular contractions of the oviduct (the normal site of fertilization) toward the uterus, which has been hormonally prepared for the implantation of the embryo. In fact, the first division is completed in the oviduct about 36 hours after fertilization. The second and third divisions, which also take place in the oviduct, are completed by 72 hours post-fertilization. It is at this point, around three days after fertilization, that the embryo is propelled into the uterus.

63

From this description you can see that cell division alone would produce a ball of identical cells, which is not the same thing as producing a human with many different types of cells, such as eye cells, liver cells, and brain cells. In order to accomplish this transformation, cells must differentiate or take on specialized functions. For example, the cells that will give rise to the eyes must be light sensitive, and the cells of the liver must be specialized for detoxifying the blood, while the cells of the brain must be specialized to be able to interpret many different types of stimuli.

The type of specialized cell that a given undifferentiated cell will become depends, in part, on what portion of the egg cell it came from. This is because the fertilized egg cell contains cytoplasm that differs in biological molecules from one region to the next. In other words, if you were to measure the concentration of a certain molecule in one region of the egg cell, a different region of the egg cell would most probably have a different concentration of that molecule.

The organization of an egg cell can be likened to the organization of a grocery store. While a grocery store should have all the different types of food a person would need to survive, the grocery store is partitioned into different sections for meat, fruits and vegetables, bread, and so on. These areas are specialized into the butcher shops, produce sections, and bakeries that make up the entire grocery store.

When the egg cell begins to divide, each resulting cell ends up with differing proportions of cellular constituents. When these differing constituents are taken up by cells as they subdivide inside the fertilized egg cell, they act as messengers that tell these cells to turn on different genes. While each of these cells is genetically identical, some genes are transcribed (turned on) in a given cell with given messengers while others are not. A cell with different messengers will transcribe a different set of genes. Therefore, due to the heterogeneity of the egg cell, cells in different regions are exposed to different messengers that turn on different genes, yielding differently specialized cells.

One week after fertilization, the embryo is composed of about 100 cells and is superficially implanted in the uterine lining. At this point, the inner portion of the embryo will develop into the embryo proper, while the outer portion will develop into the fetal portion of the placenta and the amniotic membrane (the so-called "bag of waters"). When the embryo first reaches the uterus, it secretes enzymes that penetrate the uterine lining, and the cells of the uterus and outer portion of the embryo join forces to make the placenta.

Placentation begins during the second week of development and allows the embryo to become firmly implanted in the uterus. This process establishes the physiological connection between the mother and the fetus. The blood that circulates in the placenta brings oxygen and nutrients from the maternal blood to the embryo and carries away carbon dioxide and other waste products. Although tissues of maternal and embryonic origin are closely apposed in the placenta, there is little actual mingling of the tissues, resulting in a separation of the circulation of the mother from that of the embryo. The placental barrier, however, does allow some substances to pass through so that the embryo obtains nourishment.

During the third week of development, layers of tissue develop that will give rise to organs and organ systems. To accomplish this, differentiated cells of similar type begin subdividing into regions that will give rise to the whole organ systems. Initially, a mass of cells is set aside for an organ system, for example, the cardiovascular system, and subsequently further subdivided into the various parts of the organ system, such as the heart, capillaries, and veins. In this manner, early development of the cardiovascular system and central nervous system (brain and spinal cord) begins during the third week. All of the other organ systems develop during weeks four through eight, as do all major external and internal structures.

SUMMARY

During the first seven weeks of development, a single fertilized egg cell divides rapidly. Implanted in the uterine wall and nourished by the placenta, the fertilized egg begins to differentiate into the specialized cells required for the formation of tissues, organs, and organ systems.

Gonadal Differentiation and Development

Until week seven, development proceeds in precisely the same manner regardless of whether the embryo is female or male. It is only during the differentiation of the gonads (ovaries and testes) that development in females and males begins to differ. Development of the gonads begins when the cells, which will differentiate into either ovaries or testicles, find their way to a region in the abdomen of the embryo called the gonadal ridge. Once at the gonadal ridge, these cells proliferate (rapidly make copies of themselves) yielding two indifferent gonads. The indifferent gonads consist of the inner medulla and the outer cortex and are considered indifferent in the sense that they could become either the paired ovaries of a female or the paired testicles of a male. Inside these indifferent gonads are cells which could become either the structural and estrogen secreting cells of the ovary (the granulosa cells and the theca cells) or the structural and testosterone secreting cells of the testes (the Sertoli cells and the Leydig cells).

The indifferent gonad shows an intrinsic tendency to feminize: Unless there are androgens present (male hormones, including testosterone) ovarian development will occur. Embryonic androgens will be synthesized (largely) only in the presence of a gene on the Y chromosome called SRY. If there are two X chromosomes present, hence no SRY gene, the cortex of the indifferent gonad proliferates, the medulla regresses and the development of ovaries occurs. In the presence of the Y chromosome and its SRY gene, the medulla of the indifferent gonad proliferates, the cortex regresses and the gonads become testicles. Thus the type of sex chromosomes present at fertilization determine the gonadal sex of the individual (Figure 5.1). The SRY gene itself codes for the production of a transcription factor (a protein that regulates transcription), which turns on several of the genes required for the production of testicles.

Once differentiated, the gonads determine the hormonal environment of the embryo. The cells of the ovaries do not start to make estrogen in large quantities until puberty. The cells of the embryonic testes make testosterone, which then influences the development of one of two internal duct systems and the formation of the external genitalia. To better understand how hormones can influence development, a brief introduction to endocrinology follows.

FIGURE 5.1   Determination of Gonadal Sex

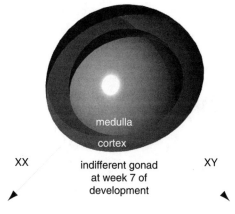

XX   indifferent gonad   XY
                      at week 7 of
                      development

Cortex proliferates / medulla regresses   Medulla proliferates / cortex regresses
           ovaries develop   testes develop

Endocrinology

Endocrinology is the study of organs and glands that secrete hormones and of how these hormones affect their target cells. Hormones are chemicals that are synthesized by specialized cells and then secreted into the blood stream. Once in the blood stream, hormones travel to distant sites and exert their effects on target organs and cells. Each hormone has a specific chemical structure that can be recognized by only the target cell; therefore, a given hormone elicits a specific response from selected target cells but has no effect on other cells. Hormone and hormone receptor interactions can be likened to the opening of a door lock. You may try several keys before you select the right key, whose structure is the only one capable of turning the chamber in order to open the door.

Sex hormones like estrogen and testosterone are steroid hormones, because their synthesis requires the steroid cholesterol as a precursor. Steroid hormones are fat-soluble and can cross cell membranes readily. The term sex hormone derives from the fact that these hormones are produced by the gonads and are known to be responsible for many of the anatomical sex differences we see in human females and males.

Sex hormones exert their effects only on target cells that have receptors for them. These sex hormone receptors are generally found inside the sensitive cells. Once a sex hormone passes into the cell and binds to a receptor, the hormone and receptor move together to the cell nucleus and either enhance or inhibit the transcription of different genes. For example, at puberty the ovaries secrete high levels of estrogen that travel through the blood stream and enter the cells of the breast tissue. Once inside the breast cell, estrogen binds to its receptor. The estrogen and its receptor then bind to the DNA to increase the transcription of genes in breast tissue that are required for the growth and development of the breast at puberty (Figure 5.2). Because males have lower levels of estrogen and fewer estrogen receptors in their breast tissue, the genes responsible for breast development are not turned on at puberty, and the breasts do not develop to the extent that they do in females.

There are many organs involved in the endocrine system, five of which are involved in the production of sex differences. These are the hypothalamus, pituitary, adrenals, ovaries, and testes. Figure 5.3 shows the location of the hypothalamus, pituitary, adrenals, and

FIGURE 5.2   Steroid Hormone Interactions

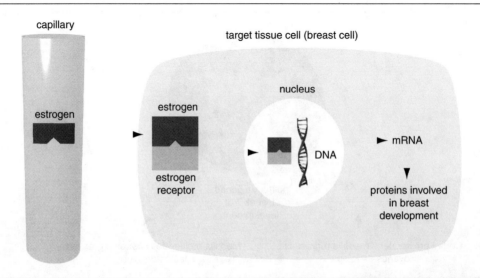

ovaries in a typical female. The hypothalamus, pituitary, and adrenals are regulated largely in the same fashion in females as in males.

Hypothalamus and Pituitary

The hypothalamus of both females and males secretes gonadotropin-releasing hormone (GnRH), which in turn regulates the pituitary gland. GnRH is secreted through a complex of veins routed directly to the pituitary gland located at the base of the skull. For this reason, GnRH is largely, but not entirely, excluded from circulation through the blood stream. GnRH is released in spurts at intervals of about 80 minutes.

Once it reaches the anterior portion of the pituitary gland, GnRH stimulates the synthesis and release of the two pituitary gonadotropins, follicle stimulating hormone (FSH) and luteinizing hormone (LH). Gonadotropins are hormones that act on the gonads. In females, FSH stimulates the synthesis of estrogens and the production of ova. In males, FSH stimulates the development of sperm. LH stimulates ovulation in females and the secretion of androgens in males.

Gonadal hormones can, in turn, regulate the hypothalamus to complete the loop of regulation. In females, increasing estrogen levels produced by the ovary stimulate the production of GnRH, which triggers the pituitary to release the LH required for ovulation.

Adrenals

You are probably familiar with the hormone adrenaline, which is secreted from the adrenal glands in response to stress or excitement. The adrenal glands that produce adrenaline are named after this hormone, but these glands produce other hormones as well. One adrenal gland lies on top

---

FIGURE 5.3   The Endocrine Organs Involved in Sex Differentiation and Development

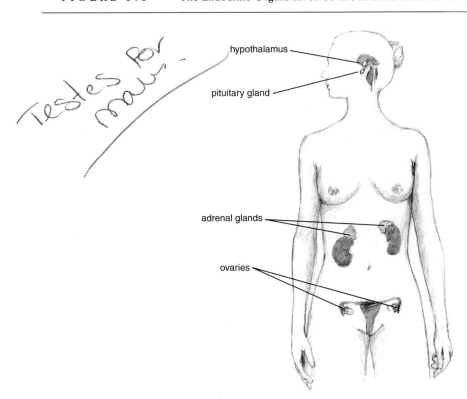

Testes for males –

hypothalamus

pituitary gland

adrenal glands

ovaries

of each kidney. The cells of the outer covering (the adrenal cortex) are able to synthesize steroid hormones from cholesterol and to secrete them. While cholesterol can be synthesized in many body tissues, further differentiation into steroid hormones takes place only in the adrenal cortex, the ovaries, and the testes. Adrenal androgens are weak androgens and do not exert masculinizing effects when they are produced in normal amounts. The adrenal androgen androstenedione has only 1/10 the potency of testosterone, which is produced by the testes, and is converted to estrogen in fat tissues. However, excess adrenal androgens excreted during development can masculinize the genitalia of females (see below) and in adult females can cause growth of facial hair, the clitoris and muscles and may lead to some types of baldness. The adrenal androgen dehydroepiandrosterone (DHEA) is produced in large quantities and may serve as a circulating store of androgen from which other steroids are built in both females and males.

Ovaries

There are three major estrogens secreted by the ovaries (Figure 5.4). Estradiol, the most potent of the three major estrogens, is produced by both granulosa and theca cells of the ovary. Estrone can be formed from estradiol, but its major precursor is androstenedione (also a testosterone precursor). Estriol is formed from both estrone and estradiol and is the weakest of the estrogens.

Ovarian hormones have multiple functions. They are involved in menstruation, the development of egg cells, breast development, pregnancy, and menopause. The biosynthesis of the major naturally occurring sex hormones is shown in Figure 5.5. Cholesterol is the starting material for the synthesis of both estrogens and androgens. In the ovaries it will be converted to estrogen, in the testes to testosterone.

SUMMARY

The organs of the endocrine system synthesize and secrete hormones. The hypothalamus responds to circulating hormones by secreting gonadotropin-releasing hormone (GnRH), which causes the pituitary gland of females and males to release follicle stimulating hormone(FSH) and leutinizing hormone (LH). The adrenal glands of

FIGURE 5.4   The Three Major Estrogens

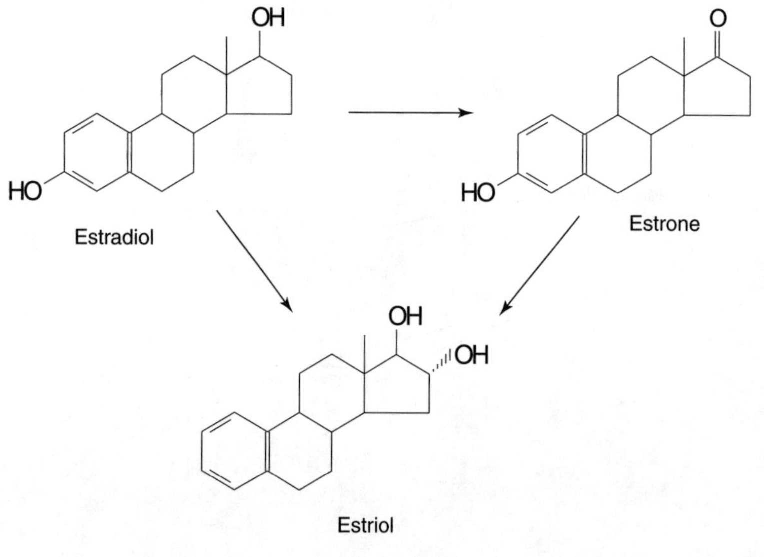

FIGURE 5.5   Biosynthesis of Sex Hormones

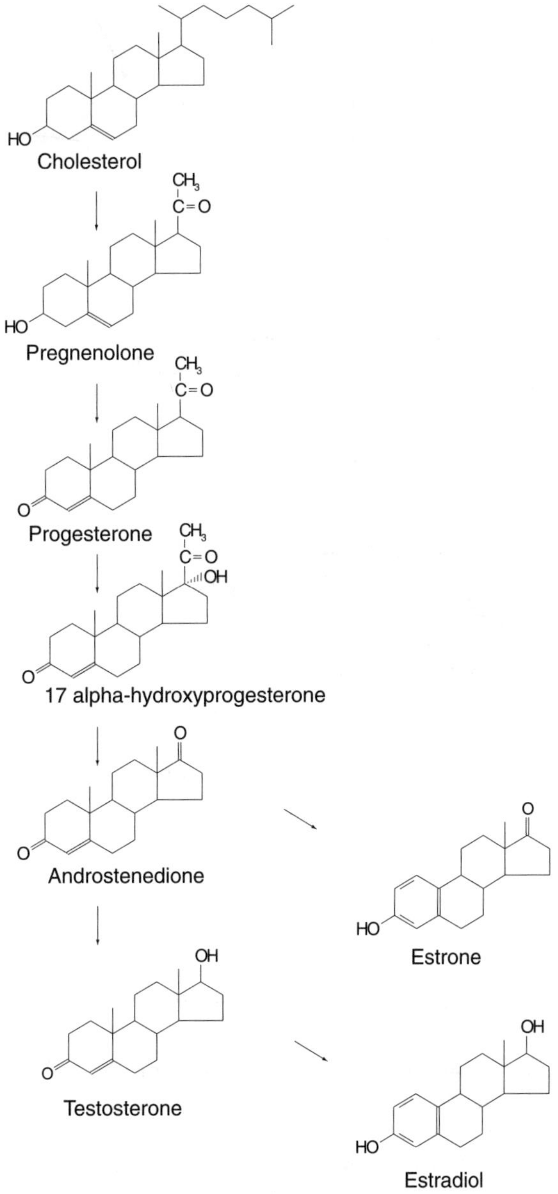

females and males synthesize and secrete androgens into general circulation. The ovaries of females synthesize and secrete three different kinds of estrogens, and the testicles of males synthesize and secrete testosterone.

Duct System Differentiation

Duct system differentiation (Figure 5.6), like the gonadal differentiation preceding it, will produce female structures unless deflected from this pathway by androgens. In the absence of androgens, the female embryonic duct system will give rise to the internal reproductive structures including the oviducts, uterus, and upper vagina.

FIGURE 5.6   Differentiation and Development of the Internal Duct System

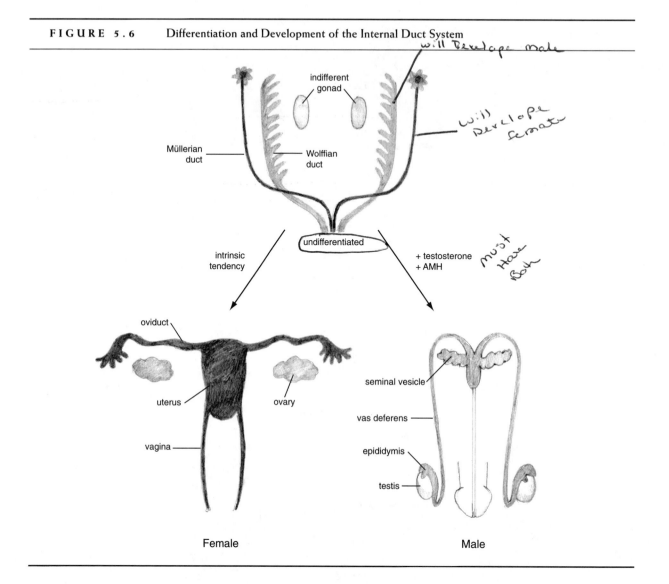

The embryonic duct system consists of the Wolffian and Müllerian ducts, which exist side by side in all embryos until the eighth week of development. From then on, the Müllerian duct persists in females and the Wolffian duct regresses. In fact, even in the absence of gonads, Müllerian duct development takes place.

Persistence of the Müllerian duct is due to the absence of Sertoli cells in female embryos. Sertoli cells in the testes of male embryos produce anti-Müllerian hormone (AMH), which causes regression of the Müllerian duct. Subsequently, in males, testosterone is secreted by the fetal testes and stimulates development of the Wolffian duct system into the sperm-carrying epididymis, vas deferens, and urethra. The development of the Wolffian duct system does not require the conversion of testosterone into DHT; the development of the external genitalia does require this conversion.

External Genitalia Differentiation

Left to their own devices, the external genitalia, like the gonads and internal genitalia, will follow a female developmental pathway. As is true of the gonads, the external genitalia exist in a bipotential state and are able to develop into either male or female structures depending on hormonal signals. This is in contrast to the embryonic duct system in which both male and female systems coexist, with only one developing further. In male and female embryos, the bipotential genitalia consist of a genital tubercle, a urogenital sinus, and two labioscrotal swellings (Figure 5.7).

In females, the genital tubercle becomes the clitoris. The urogenital sinus remains open, forming the labia minora and further differentiates into the vagina and urethra. The labioscrotal swellings fold to form the labia majora.

FIGURE 5.7   Differentiation and Development of the External Genitalia

Biopotential Stage

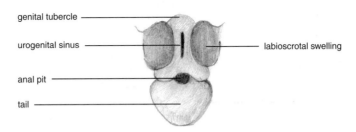

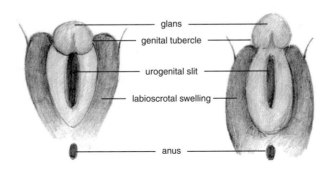

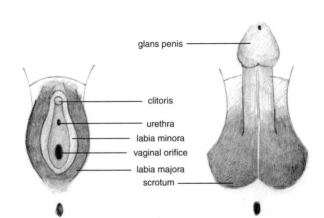

In the presence of dihydroxytestosterone (DHT), an androgen formed from testosterone, the external genitals develop into typical male structures. In males, the genital tubercle forms the penis, the urogenital sinus fuses to form the urethra, and the labioscrotal swellings fuse to form the scrotum, which houses the descended testes.

SUMMARY

Differentiation and development of reproductive structures occurs after week seven and displays an intrinsic tendency to feminize. Unless deflected from this pathway by androgens, the bipotential gonads become ovaries, the Müllerian duct system differentiates to yield the oviducts, uterus and upper vagina, and the bipotential external genitalia become the clitoris, labia majora and minora, lower vagina, and urethra.

Puberty and the Development of Secondary Sexual Characteristics

From birth to puberty, the gonads of both sexes secrete very low levels of hormones. Around the age of seven or eight, these levels begin to slowly increase due to age-associated changes in the hypothalamus. Before puberty, the release of FSH and LH is inhibited by the low levels of gonadal hormones secreted. As the brain matures, the hypothalamus begins to override the negative feedback effects of the gonadal steroids and begins GnRH secretion. GnRH secretion causes FSH and LH secretion, which initiates the process of preparing egg cells for ovulation in females and the process of sperm production in males. Once the testes have begun producing sperm, testosterone secreted by the adolescent testes has a negative feedback effect on the hypothalamus, thereby decreasing the amount of FSH and LH produced in males.

Puberty in girls is marked biologically by breast development, pubic and axial hair growth, accelerated skeletal growth, and the beginning of menstruation. All of these events occur over a period of roughly 4.5 years.

Breast Development

Breast development or thelarche (the suffix *arche*, from the Greek *arkhe*, means beginning) occurs as a result of the increased estrogen levels seen at puberty. Increased estrogen at puberty yields increased size and pigmentation of areola, the formation of a mass of breast tissue under each areola, and development of milk glands. Estrogen also stimulates the growth of the ductile portion of the breast. This stimulation of the ducts can continue to occur in response to estrogen (and progesterone) during each menstrual cycle and may result in pain and swelling of the breasts. Increased estrogen at this time also causes the enlargement of the uterus, vagina, labia, and clitoris.

Pubic and Axillary Hair Growth

Pubic hair and axillary (armpit) hair growth occurs as a result of increased adrenal androgen secretions. This increased adrenal function occurs from about age 6 or 7 through adolescence and is called andrenarche. The events of andrenarche are independent of other hormonal events at puberty. Generally, andrenarche precedes the growth spurt by two years. Because both males and females have similarly regulated adrenal glands, this event occurs similarly in both sexes. However, hair growth is more apparent in males because they have thicker, coarser hair than females.

Accelerated Skeletal Growth

Skeletal growth rapidly increases as a result of initial gonadal secretion of low levels of estrogen, which increases the secretion of growth hormone. Growth hormone is secreted from the pituitary and increases during sleep. This occurs in females and males, with the testes supplying small amounts of estrogen for males. The growth spurt in girls begins around the age of 11 or 12, which is about two years earlier than in boys. During puberty, bone density increases 10 to 20%, and it is thought that calcium supplementation during adolescence (13–15 years of age) results in significant increases in bone density, affording protection against developing osteoporosis later in life.

Menstruation

The beginning of menstruation, or menarche, usually occurs after the growth spurt has passed. The average age of menarche in the U.S. is 12.8. Menarche occurs as levels of estrogen increase. High levels of estrogen increase the amounts of GnRH released by the hypothalamus, which stimulates a midcycle surge of LH required for ovulation and the first menstruation. Often the menses directly following menarche are anovulatory (no egg is released), irregular, heavy, and painful.

SUMMARY
FSH and LH levels rise moderately before puberty and are followed by a rise in estrogen levels. Increased estrogen secretion results in the development of breasts (thelarche) and skeletal growth and culminates in the beginning of menstruation (menarche). Adrenal androgens stimulate the pubic and axillary hair growth (andrenarche) seen during this time.

Abnormal Sexual Differentiation

Development does not always follow the path described thus far. In fact, it is estimated that around 0.2% of children born in the U.S. have genitalia that are neither clearly female nor clearly male. These ambiguous genitalia vary in form and usually result from abnormal sex hormone exposure during development. This exposure can arise as a result of a genetic condition or as a result of synthetic hormones being administered to pregnant women.

Very rarely, individuals are born with ambiguous genitalia and gonads consisting of both ovarian and testicular tissues. These children are considered to be true hermaphrodites (from Greek mythology, Hermaphrodites, son of Aphrodite and Hermes, was half woman and half man) and can be raised as either girls or boys. This decision is made, in part, based on whether the external genitalia can be made to resemble typical female or male genitalia more readily.

Another form of hermaphroditism (called pseudohermaphroditism) exists when an individual has internal genitalia of one sex and the external genitalia of the other. Female pseudohermaphrodites have ovaries and masculinized external genitalia, a condition that occurs if females are androgenized *in utero*. Male pseudohermaphrodites have testes and female external genitalia. An example of male pseudohermaphroditism is 5-alpha-reductase deficiency, which results from a recessive mutation. 5-alpha-reductase is the enzyme that converts testosterone to the form required to act on external genitalia, dihydroxytestosterone (DHT). Absence or malfunction of this enzyme results in external genitalia that are not masculinized. The Wolffian ducts, however, respond to testosterone (not DHT), and, therefore, are masculinized. At puberty, conversion of testosterone to DHT is not required and the typical male secondary sex characteristics arise. These include increased muscle mass and strength, the descent of the testes, voice deepening, penis growth, erections, and ejaculation through the urethra (which is attached to the sperm carrying vas deferens).

A genetic defect in androgen receptors results in XY individuals who produce normal androgens and Müllerian duct inhibitor, but whose cells can't respond to the presence of androgens. Therefore, the Müllerian ducts are inhibited. The Wolffian ducts, whose cells have non-functional androgen receptors and can only develop in response to testosterone, do not develop. Because the external genitalia are also unresponsive to androgen, they will be feminized, and the baby will be thought to be a girl. At puberty, the testes release androgens and a small amount of estrogen. The child will, therefore, experience breast development. Since this child has no internal duct structures, menstruation will not occur, nor can she become pregnant. However, she will look like a female and will, most often, have been raised as one as well.

Masculinization of female genitalia is a condition that arises when XX females are exposed to androgens *in utero*, resulting in an enlarged clitoris and fusion of the labia to form a scrotum. This exposure occurs either because the mother was administered a drug containing androgens or through the overproduction of androgens by the adrenal gland. While the external genitalia are masculinized, absence of Müllerian duct inhibitor allows for the development of uterus and oviducts. Because there are no testes secreting testosterone, the Wolffian duct structures do not develop. When it is determined that these babies are actually girls, surgery is often performed in order to convert the scrotum into the labia and to fashion a vagina.

People with these types of developmental abnormalities have been studied extensively by social scientists in an attempt to determine the roles of genetic sex and sex of socialization in determining personality traits and abilities.

GENDER AND BRAIN DIFFERENCES

Is the Male Brain Androgenized?

Some scientists believe that the androgens, which are secreted by the developing testes of boy babies, act on their brains, thereby programming them for male specific behaviors. These scientists argue that this prenatal androgen exposure results in a large difference in the physical brains of males and females, which lead to many of the behavioral differences between the sexes. The remainder of this chapter will focus on this research and its social implications.

To consider whether the male brain is androgenized requires us to look more closely at hormone actions on the human brain. It is important to keep in mind that testosterone never interacts with the brain directly. Instead, testosterone secreted by the developing embryo must be converted to estrogen in order to affect the brain. Figure 5.8 shows the two major pathways of testosterone metabolism. It is currently believed that low levels of estrogen are required for female brain development, whereas high levels of estrogen generated in the male brain cells by conversion of testosterone induce so-called masculine differentiation.

In order to understand whether differences between the genders have a biological or social basis, researchers have utilized cases where there is discordance between genetic sex and sex of rearing and cases in which girl babies have been exposed to excess androgens *in utero*. If the sex-typical behaviors of these individuals are affected, these scientists then argue that the person's biology was able to override their socialization.

An example of this type of research was performed by Julianne Imperato-McGinley (1979) in the Dominican Republic where she found a large population of individuals with 5-alpha-reductase deficiency. Recall that these XY children are born with feminized genitalia and are often raised as females but acquire male secondary sex characteristics at puberty. On the surface, it would appear that if these children had female gender identities, in spite of being XY males, the effects of their upbringing had overcome their biology. However, if they adopted a male gender identity, this could be seen as an argument for a strong biological influence on gendered behavior.

Imperato-McGinley studied 19 children with 5-alpha-reductase deficiency and found that, even though these children were raised as girls, at puberty 17 of them underwent gender identity reversal—they felt and acted as though they were males.

FIGURE 5.8   The Two Major Pathways of Testosterone Metabolism

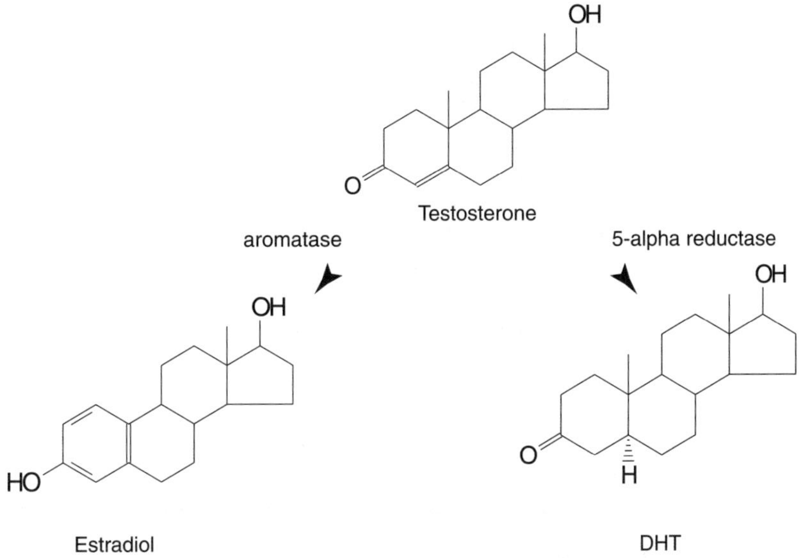

At first glance, this study seems to show that brain androgenizing influence is stronger than socialization. According to the brain androgenization hypothesis, the brains of these XY babies would presumably have been androgenized since the aromatase enzyme, which converts testosterone to estradiol, is not affected by a deficiency in 5-alpha-reductase. In addition, their socialization was purportedly typical of that of any girl. However, upon closer inspection, the androgenizing hypothesis breaks down. One mitigating factor is that for the people of the Dominican Republic this condition is not rare, and, therefore, parents and community members are comfortable with and aware of children with this enzyme deficiency. The people of their villages called these children Huevodoces, which is slang for eggs or testes, at 12. It is very possible that the switch from female to male gender identity was made easier by the culture's acceptance of this occurrence among its adolescents. These children may well have known that something was amiss since their genitalia, while feminized, does not always look exactly like that of other girls. These children may have chosen maleness later on since it offered a chance at feeling more normal about themselves. Also, if the parents (both of whom may have had family members with this condition) were aware that their child might switch gender roles at puberty, they may have allowed these children a wider range of behaviors than just female or male typical behaviors. Lastly, in a culture where male and female gender roles parallel those of the U.S., children who were raised as girls might be able to see quite clearly the social and economic advantages of being a male.

In any case, the fact that 10% of the Huevodoces studied did not undergo gender reversal at puberty is evidence that biological sex does not always override sex of rearing. However, in spite of this study's limitations, the idea that there is a biological basis for gender identity was advanced to the point where the most widely used reference text for clinical obstetricians and gynecologists (Speroff, 1994) cites it in a brief section about androgenization of the central nervous system.

Another study, which tried to determine the effects of androgenization, surveyed girls who had been androgenized *in utero*. Some pregnant women in the late 1960s were treated with synthetic hormones in an attempt to avert miscarriages. These hormones turned out to be androgenic, and girl babies were, therefore, born with masculinized external genitalia. According to the brain androgenization hypothesis, the brains of these girls would have been androgenized too. However, these fetally androgenized girls are genetic females, and at puberty they menstruate, ovulate and become fertile. So, androgenization obviously had no effect on the region of the brain that regulates these reproductive processes.

To elucidate any brain differences this presumed androgenization had on these girls, Money and Ehrhardt (1972) studied 25 of these females from 1967 forward. According to these two researchers, these girls were more similar to boys than to other girls. Money and Ehrhardt referred to them as "tomboys" because these girls liked sports, rough and tumble play, functional clothing, and boys' toys. They also concluded that these girls had higher IQs than the general population. Again, on the surface these results appear to make a compelling argument for brain androgenization and for increased intelligence associated with androgenization. This study is cited repeatedly in the literature as evidence for brain differences between females and males. However, there are many crippling criticisms of this study and its conclusions.

■ DISCUSSION EXERCISE 1

    1.1. Are there other explanations for the data Money and Ehrhardt collected? Are there factors that Money and Ehrhardt have not properly controlled for?

One other major outcome of the Money and Ehrhardt study was the perceived positive correlation between androgen exposure and IQ. Again, this study is commonly cited in the literature as the basis for further studies on the effects of androgen on IQ. However, the IQs of the girls in this study were no higher than their non-affected sisters and brothers. These girls did not have high IQs because of their androgenization, they had high IQs because they came from families with high IQ parents and siblings.

Since studies like these require large groups of children with rare developmental anomalies, and because it is very difficult to sort out the effects of socialization from those of biology, many researchers have turned to anatomical studies of the brain to answer the age-old nature/nurture question.

The study of brain sizes, shapes, weights and volumes was in the past called craniology or phrenology. This type of research is recognized by most people now to have been bad science awash in cultural bias. The point of these studies was to show that brain differences relegate women and minorities to the lowered social status they were experiencing, and that improving education and opportunities for these people would be of little value. However, as ludicrous as this sounds, current research on brain differences seems to have the same flavor and, as you will see, has led to many ambiguous and conflicting results.

One area of research currently under investigation is the phenomenon of lateralization. Lateralization is the localization of functions to the two different cerebral hemispheres (Figure 5.9). Many neurologists believe that the left hemisphere is associated with language functions and the right hemisphere with nonverbal perception and visiospatial abilities. Since these functions correlate with perceived sex differences, researchers have tried to show (with mixed results) that there is a corresponding anatomical difference in the brains of females and males, with increased specialization of the left hemisphere in females and greater specialization of the right hemisphere in males.

Remarkably, all of this research is predicated on the assumption that there are differences in verbal and visiospatial abilities between females and males when there are no clear-cut differences in either. All girls are not better than all boys at verbal tests. When one compares large groups of girls with large groups of boys, the means (averages) may be slightly different, but this tells us nothing about any one girl or boy. Girls and boys also have the same range of scores on verbal and visiospatial tests, so neither sex shows an overall

FIGURE 5.9   The Hemispheres and Corpus Callosum of the Human Brain

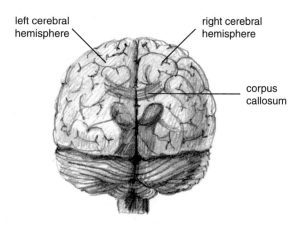

proficiency or deficiency in either area. A study by Jacklin (1981) collated approximately 30 major studies on verbal skills involving close to 70,000 children and found that sex differences in verbal ability account for only 1% of the variance in these studies. In other words, 99% of the differences in test scores had nothing at all to do with the sex of the person taking the test.

Somehow this information has not dissuaded scientists from continuing to perform these studies on brain lateralization. Some scientists claim that anatomical sex differences in the structures that connect the two cerebral hemispheres may, in part, underlie sex differences in cognitive function and cerebral lateralization, despite the fact that no differences in cognitive function or cerebral lateralization have ever been unequivocally proven. Nevertheless, the structure that provides connection between the two cerebral hemispheres, the corpus callosum, has been extensively studied, and not surprisingly, there are as many reports showing a size difference in favor of females as there are showing no difference at all.

Scientific studies have a hard time even proving differences in FSH and LH secretion between human males and females. It has been shown in rats that estrogen stimulates a release of LH from the pituitary (triggering ovulation) in females and not in males. This is clear-cut evidence that the hypothalamus is responding differently in female rats than in male rats. Further studies in rodents suggest that androgens produced by fetal males suppress the ability of hypothalamic neurons to respond cyclically. However, in primates like Rhesus monkeys, estrogen stimulates the same quantity and duration of LH surge in males as females. Furthermore, in humans, androgens do not suppress cyclicity, and ovulation and pregnancy in human females exposed as fetuses to high levels of circulating androgens are possible.

Another type of anatomical study focuses on a region of the hypothalamus called the SDN-POA (sexually dimorphic nucleus of the preoptic area). Some researchers have showed this region to be smaller in females than in males. One researcher, Simon LeVay (1991), found that the volume of one particular region of the SDN-POA is lower in women and homosexuals. From this data he concluded that homosexual males have brains which resemble those of females. This led to a flurry of press reports about homosexual brain differences. However, LeVay only measured SDN-POA volumes from homosexual males who had died of AIDS. Since he reported his results, many researchers have speculated about whether the decreased levels of testosterone known to exist in males with HIV could not have led, independent of their sexual orientation, to smaller regions of the SDN-POA. Other studies have shown no difference in either volume or cell number between the SDN-POA of homosexual and heterosexual men.

SUMMARY

There are very few anatomical differences between female and male brains and, as of yet, none have been shown to have any effect on human behavior.

Social Implications of Brain Sex Differences Research

You may wonder why it is that the authors of this textbook are so interested in exposing the lack of evidence for brain differences between the sexes and the fact that no brain differences in humans have been shown to correspond to sex-typical behavioral differences. The reason for this is the inherent danger in describing behaviors that do not have equal value as immutable parts of a person's biology. Consider the importance of supposed biologic differences in justifying and legitimizing gender inequality as you read the words of renowned feminist and neurobiologist Ruth Bleier (1984):

> The reasoning starts with the observation that women do not share equally with men in positions of leadership, authority, or power and are far from equally represented in industry, business, the university, the arts, engineering, science and other professions, government, sports, and crafts. The suspicion follows, then, that perhaps this situation has less to do with ideologies and institutions, with sex-role stereotyping and channeling from babyhood on, or with conscious and unconscious, legal and illegal discrimination against women in education and employment opportunities than with women's innate ability to perform equally with men, either because of our naturally nurturant, passive, noncompetitive and unambitious temperaments or because of biological limitations on the capacities and skills required to achieve in our kind of society.
>
> *Science and Gender: A Critique of Biology and Its Theories on Women*, p. 81

Contrast Bleier's thoughts with those of the leading and most often cited researcher in the field of brain differences, Doreen Kimura. In a 1992 issue of *Scientific American* she states that women and men differ not only in physical attributes and reproductive function but also in the way in which their brains work. To bolster her claim that male and female brains differ, she has shown that three-year-old boys are better at throwing than three-year-old girls and that females are better at remembering whether items have been misplaced than males. She then claims that differences in throwing ability and the ability to find misplaced objects are the result of differing levels of testosterone, which changed the brains of males and their behaviors early in life.

Kimura believes that brain differences between females and males extend to all known behaviors in which males and females differ, thereby excluding any effect of socialization. According to Kimura, three-year-old boys are better at throwing tasks because males have been evolutionarily selected for on the basis of throwing ability, not because their parents are more likely to play catch with them than with their sisters. She believes that this difference translates into better visiospatial ability in adult males than adult females. As evidence for her hypothesis that human males have better visiospatial abilities (which is itself an unproved assertion) as the result of their differently evolved brains, she cites the work of Gaulin (1986) on polygamous voles, small mouse-like mammals in which single males mate with many females. Polygamous male voles, Gaulin claimed, have been subject to evolutionary pressures that helped them to develop enhanced navigational ability so that they can find their way from female to female in order to mate.

The whole field of sex differences research appears to revolve around explaining gender inequalities based on hormonally induced differences in abilities and temperament.

However, we would argue that the explanations proffered by these researchers only reflect and reinforce the ideology that sex-typical behaviors are natural and normal when those behaviors actually arise as a result of strong political and social forces.

■ DISCUSSION EXERCISE 2

2.1. Brainstorm a list of commonly accepted sex-typical behaviors (for example, "females are more nurturing than males" or "males are more aggressive than females"). Do you think these differences are "real"? Why or why not? Have you heard biological arguments for why these differences exist? What are they? Can you think of non-biological arguments for why these differences exist?

■ ANSWERS TO DISCUSSION QUESTIONS

1.1. Is it possible that androgens affect the muscle more than the brain?

Increased muscle and bone growth caused by androgen exposure could make "rough and tumble" play more likely. Did the parents of these girls, who knew that their daughters were born with masculinized genitalia, treat them any differently than they would have otherwise? Did the parents of these girls simply remember more "tomboy" behaviors being displayed by these girls since they were likely to be more concerned about "masculine" behaviors by these daughters? How does all the scrutiny of these girls' genitalia, including major surgery to "correct" it, affect their gender identity? Many of these girls underwent a complete removal of their clitoris, the effects of which are not addressed by this study. At what age were the genital surgeries performed? It turns out that over half of these girls had a penis and scrotum for $3\frac{1}{2}$ to $7\frac{1}{2}$ (or more) years. Having a penis and scrotum during the time gender identity is formed argues much more strongly for a societal influence on gender identity than it does for a biological role.

2.1. Brainstorm a list of commonly accepted sex-typical behaviors (for example, "females are more nurturing than males" or "males are more aggressive than females"). Do you think these differences are "real"? Why or why not? Have you heard biological arguments for why these differences exist? What are they? Can you think of non-biological arguments for why these differences exist?

Biological arguments about the reason for typical behavior patterns in females and males usually have to do with the role of women as child bearers and the role of men as meat providers. However, there is very little evidence that females and males differ strongly in their capacity for typical behavior patterns, but much evidence that certain behaviors are rewarded when performed by girls and punished when performed by boys and vice versa. Few parents encourage nurturing behavior in their male children by giving them baby dolls to play with and boys that engage in "female" activities are considered unusual.

REFERENCES

Allen, L. S., & Gorski, R. A. (1991). Sexual dimorphism of the anterior commissure and massa intermedia of the human brain. *Journal of Comparative Neurology 312*(1), 97–104.

Bleier, R. (1984).Hormones, the brain, and sex differences. In *Science and gender: A critique of biology and its theories on women*. Pergamon Press.

Gaulin, S. J. C., & FitzGerald, R. W. (1986). Sex differences in spatial ability: An evolutionary hypothesis and test. *The American Naturalist 127*, 74–88.

Hoffman, M. A., & Swaab, D. F. (1991). Sexual dimorphism of the human brain: Myth and reality. *Experimental Clinical Endocrinology 98*(2), 161–70.

Imperato-McGinley, J., Terson, R. E., Gautier, T., & Sturla, E. (1979). Androgen and the evolution of male gender identity among male pseudohermaphrodites with 5-reductase deficiency. *New England Journal of Medicine 300*, 1233–1237.

Jacklin, D. (1981). Methodological issues in the study of sex-related differences. *Developmental Review* (1), 266–273.

Karsch, F. J., Dierschke, D. J., & Knobil, E. (1973). Sexual differentiation of pituitary function: Apparent difference between primates and rodents. *Science 179*, 484–486.

Kimura, D. (1992). Sex differences in the brain. *Scientific American* (Sept.), 119–125.

LeVay, S. (1991). A difference in hypothalamic structure between heterosexual and homosexual men. *Science* (253), 1034–1037.

Money, J., & Ehrhardt, A. (1972). *Man and woman, boy and girl*. Baltimore: Johns Hopkins University Press.

Speroff, L., Glass, R. H., & Case N. J. (1994). *Clinical gynecologic endocrinology and infertility* (5th ed.). Williams and Wilkins.

CHAPTER 6

In most cases, greater differences are found within the sexes than between them. The height difference between the shortest woman and the tallest woman is much greater than the average difference between women and men.

WOMEN'S
BODIES I: ANATOMY

INTRODUCTION

A chapter titled "Women's Bodies" has the potential to reinforce the idea of a physical dichotomy between women and men. However, in nearly all respects, female and male human bodies are identical. For example, of the 206 bones in a human skeleton, only five show fairly consistent average differences between the sexes. No one who studies anatomy could identify the difference between a woman's and a man's lungs, liver, heart, and pancreas. Consider how *you* identify the sex of an unknown person. You probably begin by observing hair and clothing style. These are not basic biological differences but are a consequence of social differences between the sexes. Biological differences that do exist between women and men can be emphasized and reinforced by social differences. For instance, women tend to have shorter and finer body hair than men, but many women take great pains to remove much of their body hair, thus making the difference in "hairiness" more apparent. Men generally have a higher percentage of muscle for their weight than women, but differences in lifetime activity levels, as influenced by social expectations, can increase the differences between the sexes in muscular appearance. One function of this chapter and the next is to help you understand the physical characteristics of women, both basic biological differences and those differences that are affected by social expectations.

Many of the physical differences between women and men are *average differences*. We intentionally emphasize "average" because individual human beings vary widely within a single sex. On average, men are 8.7% larger than women. This figure generally applies to height, weight, bone length, and even to the size of the cranium, or skull. Does this mean that *all women* are 8.7% smaller than *all men*? Of course not. You probably know taller than average women and shorter than average men. Figure 6.1 shows the distribution of heights of women and men in the U.S. population. Note that the difference in average heights of men and women is approximately 15 centimeters but that the distributions in the two populations overlap, such that the shortest 22% of men are shorter than the tallest 10% of women. In fact, for many traits, the difference between women and men is small, which means that the range of variation within a sex overlaps almost completely with the range of the other sex. You can also see from Figure 6.1 that the height difference between the shortest woman and the tallest woman (40 cm) is much greater than the average difference between women and men (15 cm). In most cases, greater differences are found within the sexes than between them. Average differences between the sexes tell us little about what we should expect *individual* men and women to be like.

Even though many of the average differences between women and men are small, some consistent differences do exist between the female and male body. Women's reproductive organs are obviously different from those of men, and while there is significant variation within each sex in the characteristics of their reproductive systems, there is virtually no overlap. There are differences between the sexes related to the amounts of various kinds of hormones produced, in part, by these reproductive organs. For instance, a woman at the same level of physical activity as a man will almost certainly have a higher percentage of body fat. Even among elite athletes, the percent of body fat in women is 12%, double the 6% found in men. Given our culture's current obsession with fat, many

---

FIGURE 6.1   Average and Range of Heights of Women and Men

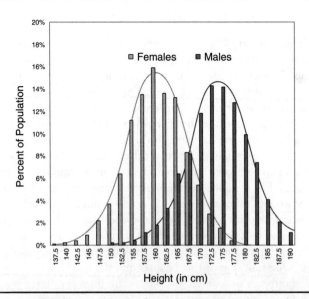

The average height of women is 160 cm, while the average height of men is 175 cm. Notice how much overlap exists between the two distributions, however. The shortest 25% of men are shorter than the tallest 25% of women. You can see from this figure how saying that the "average woman" is shorter than the "average man" is not the same as saying "all women are shorter than all men."

women may find this information dismaying—if fat is bad, doesn't this mean that women are less healthy? However, a healthy level of body fat for women *is* different from a healthy level in men. Understanding the female body will help you see how, in some cases, measuring women against a male standard is self-defeating and unfair.

■ DISCUSSION EXERCISE 1

1.1. What physical differences do you see between women and men? Which of these do you think are biological? Which do you think are due to differences in social roles? Can you think of other differences that might be biological but which are emphasized by social practices?

SKELETAL ANATOMY

The angle that forms between the kneecap and the femur, called the Q angle, increases as the broadness of the bony pelvis increases... Some anatomy textbooks refer to a large Q angle as "miserable alignment syndrome," although it is not clear that there are any negative implications of a larger angle. Instead, the alignment may be considered "miserable" because it differs from the perceived ideal alignment that is characteristic of most men.

Figure 6.2 illustrates a human skeleton, highlighting the five bones that are typically different between males and females. Three of these bones are found on the head: the mandible, or jaw bone, which is larger in males; the temporal bone, found near the temple, which in males has a larger opening to allow connection of thicker muscles to support the large jaw; and the frontal bone of the cranium, or the forehead, which in females is generally more rounded and has a less pronounced ridge above the eyes.

The other two bones that show general differences between men and women are the two ossa coxae, which form the bony pelvis (Figure 6.3). Although each os coxa is a single large bone, it actually arises from the fusion of three smaller bones: the ilium, which you can feel part of as your hip bones, the ischium, which are the projections you're sitting on, and the pubis, which is the bone you can feel at the front of your pubic region. These two bones are joined at the front of the body by the pubic symphysis. At the back of the body, the ossa coxae are attached to the base of the spine, called the sacrum, at a point called the sacroiliac joint (i.e., the junction between the sacrum and the ilium). Both the pubic symphysis and the sacroiliac joint are immobile connections except during pregnancy and birthing, when they soften to permit a degree of flexibility for the passage of a child.

The differences between the pelves of men and women relate to different reproductive capabilities. While there is considerable amount of overlap between the sexes, 76% of women have rounded pelvic inlets (see Figure 6.3), whereas 78% of men have inlets that resemble elongated ovals (i.e., the inlet is longer from front to back than from side to side). Rounder inlets generally permit the easier passage of a child's head through the birth canal, although women with less round inlets are capable of giving birth.

Besides these differences in the shapes of bones, women and men differ in the robustness of their skeletons and their relative body proportions. Bone mass, or weight, averages 4.4 kg in females, but 5.8 kg in males, a 32% difference. This difference of 1.4 kg is due in small part (about 30% or .42 kg) to the overall sizes of the respective skeletons and in large part (about 70% or .98 kg) to differences in the density (weight per volume) and diameter of each bone.

From infancy to adulthood, humans grow in overall size, but a larger proportion of growth occurs in our extremities (legs and arms) than in our torso. (Think of how short toddlers' legs look in relationship to their bodies.) Our final growth spurt occurs during adolescence and

FIGURE 6.2   Five Bones That Typically Differ Between the Sexes

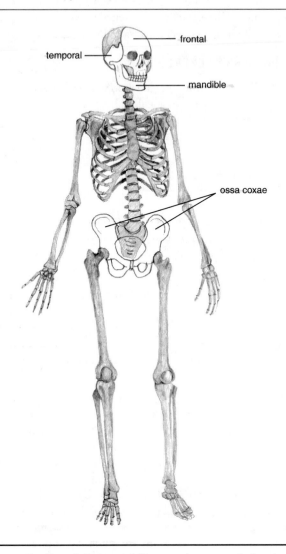

Human female and male skeletons are virtually identical. Consistent differences in bones are only found in the five labelled above: the mandible, temporal bone, frontal bone, and the two ossa coxae.

puberty, again with a larger proportion of growth occurring in the arms and legs than in the torso. In part because puberty both occurs later and lasts longer (on average) in men than in women, the average adult man has longer arms and legs than the average adult woman. In fact, if we measure the contribution to height made by leg length, females' legs equal, on average, 51.2% of their height, while males' legs make up 56%. Men and women sitting together tend to be closer in height than men and women standing together because of this difference in relative length.

The Effect of the Skeleton on Posture, Body Shape, and Sports Injury

The round pelvic inlet that is typical of the majority of women is produced by a bony pelvis which is flatter and broader than a pelvis with an oval inlet as typical with the majority of men. The bony

FIGURE 6.3   Differences Between Female and Male Pelves

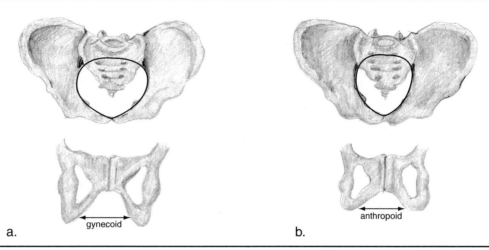

a.   b.

A top view of the average female and male-type pelves: The line indicates the dimensions of the pelvic inlet. Notice that the pelvic inlet is wider in females than in males.

pelvis is tipped forward (that is, the pelvic inlet is about 50–60° from the horizontal, as in Figure 6.4), so that the part of the ilium which we think of as the hip bone and the pubic symphysis are on the same vertical plane on the front surface of the body. A flatter pelvis requires a greater degree of tipping to bring the hip bones to the front of the body. This tip is maintained by the curvature of the lower spine. The spinal curvature and greater pelvic tilt in individuals with broad pelves elevates the buttocks and gives a curvy appearance to the side profile.

FIGURE 6.4   Angle of Pelvic Tilt

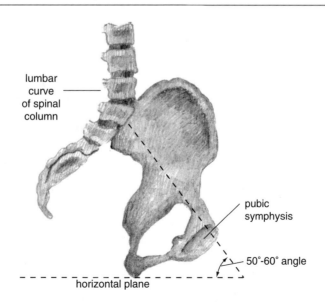

Side view of a bony pelvis, indicating its position in a standing individual. The pelvis is "tilted forward" when we stand. The angle of pelvic tilt, indicated by the line, is greater in women than men.

When you bring your feet together to walk or run, your femurs, or thigh bones, extend diagonally to your knees from where they attach at the hips. A broader pelvis means that the femurs are further away from each other at the point of attachment than femurs attached to a narrower pelvis. Therefore, the angle that forms between the kneecap and the femur, called the Q angle (Figure 6.5), increases as the broadness of the bony pelvis increases. Some anatomy textbooks refer to a large Q angle as "miserable alignment syndrome," although it is not clear that there are any negative implications of a larger angle. Instead, the alignment may be considered "miserable" because it differs from the perceived ideal alignment that is characteristic of most men.

An increased Q angle has been assumed to be a risk factor for knee injury, since the muscles in the thigh would tend to pull the knee cap up and towards the outside of the knee. For instance, among basketball players, knee injuries are much more common among women, who generally have greater Q angles, than among men, who generally have lesser Q angles.

FIGURE 6.5   Q Angle in Women and Men

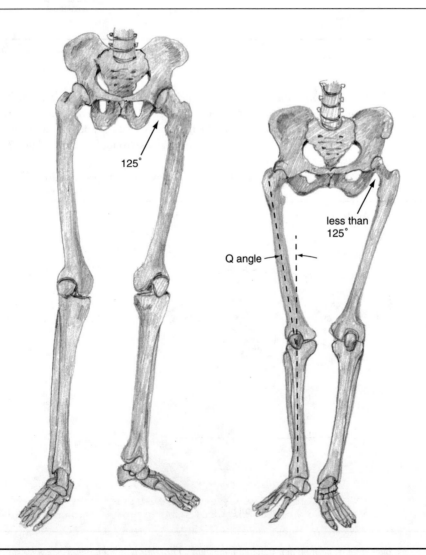

The Q angle is indicated by the lines. Q angles in women are typically larger than Q angles in men.

However, many scientists studying sports injury are quick to point out that because of social differences in early physical activity and conditioning, many women may not have developed the leg muscle strength that can support the knee-stressing movements typical of basketball. In fact, recent analysis indicates that most injuries are sport specific rather than gender specific. Even if differences in Q angle do lead to differences in likelihood of knee injury, these injuries may be less debilitating than ones suffered by men. In a study of the 1992 West Point class, women experienced two times as many leg injuries as men, but men recovered more slowly from leg injuries. The difference in injury occurrence and recovery time balances out. Thus, males and females were excused due to injury from full activities for an *equal* amount of time over their four-year career at West Point.

The Skeleton and Gender Roles

The average differences between women's and men's skeletons contribute to average differences in success in certain physical activities. Because women generally have long torsos relative to their leg length, their center of gravity (the point on the body where the weight above equals the weight below) is lower than on men. Individuals with a lower center of gravity are better able to maintain balance. Competitive gymnastics recognizes this difference in center of gravity—women, but not men, compete on the balance beam apparatus. While men, with their generally longer legs and arms, have more difficulty balancing, they bring more power to activities that rely on the lever action of their extremities. Because a longer lever can transmit more force, men are generally better jumpers and stronger throwers than women, relative to their size.

While the size and shape of the human skeleton is strongly influenced by genetics, hormones, and nutrition, bones also respond to physical stresses and pressures applied to them. Increased stress, caused by increased physical activity and muscle use, causes bones to increase in weight and size. A portion of the 1.4 kg average difference in bone mass between men and women is due to differences in participation in weight-bearing exercise throughout life. Low bone mass, or osteoporosis, has serious consequences for aging adults (see Chapter 14). Since differences in expectations about the appropriate activity levels of women and men throughout their lifetimes contribute to differences in average exercise amounts, bone density in women is exceptionally small. Thus, women on average experience an increased risk for osteoporosis. Women and men who have engaged in regular weight-bearing exercise throughout their lives are less likely to experience the repeated fractures and spine deformation characteristic of osteoporosis.

Even bones that are similar between women and men may be influenced by differential treatment throughout our lifetimes. Women's and men's feet are virtually identical, but women are three times more likely than men to develop the bony protrusion called a bunion on their big toes. A bunion forms when the tip of the big toe is forced towards, or even overlaps, other toes (see Figure 6.6). The stress produced by this positioning, along with an increase in pressure on the toe, causes the bone at the base of the big toe to enlarge. The protrusion rubs against shoes, and the tissues around it may become inflamed and painful. Although there seems to be some natural differences among women in their susceptibility to bunions, these growths are more likely to form on the feet of women who wear high-heeled shoes with narrow toes. These types of shoes both reposition the big toe and subject it to more weight than when the foot is flat on the ground. Often associated with bunions are hammer toes, which form when bones in the smaller toes bend downward in response to pressure from the overlapping big toe. As long as high-heeled, narrow-toed shoes are considered appropriate attire for women in many situations, bunions and hammer toes will remain more common among women than men. (Incidentally, high-heeled shoes also contribute to back pain, since the forward tilt of the body must be counteracted by the

---

FIGURE 6.6   A Bunion on the Large Toe

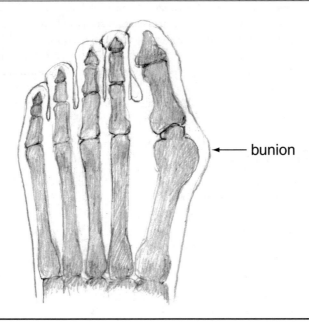

bunion

Bunions are much more common in women and are formed when the toes are forced together and support most of the body's weight.

spine, which increases curvature and muscle stress in the lower back. Yet another reason to wear flat-heeled, supportive, and comfortable shoes!)

SUMMARY

Only five bones and the overall size and proportion of the skeleton differ between women and men. Average sexual differences in the pelvic bone result in differences in posture and stance, which may or may not have an effect on sports injury. Some gender differences in skeletal anatomy are caused or reinforced by differences in social behavior, rather than by biological differences between the sexes.

EXTERNAL ANATOMY

Most sociobiologists would agree that there is no biological basis for particular beauty fads such as the hair style considered most attractive in a particular culture at a particular time. Whatever the contribution of innate behavior to our feelings about beauty, clearly we learn many of our values regarding physical appearance from our culture.

The integument, also known by its components the skin, hair, nails, and various glands, is the largest organ of the human body. The integument functions as a sensory organ and a waste organ and protects the body from stressful conditions in our environment. We also are probably more concerned with the condition of our skin and its associated features than any other organ. Our self-image is closely associated with our physical appearance. There are some average sex differences in the skin and its associated features; many of these differences are subject to social behaviors that emphasize and exaggerate our biological differences.

Figure 6.7 illustrates a cross-section of human skin. Notice that skin consists of three layers: the epidermis, which is primarily multiple layers of dead or dying cells underlain by their source layer; the dermis, which nourishes the epidermis and contains the fibers that support the skin; and the hypodermis, which binds the skin to underlying organs and contains much of the subcutaneous (under the skin) fat. On average, the hypodermis is 8% thicker on women than men, which tends to smooth out the irregular appearance of the muscles beneath. Even among elite athletes, women will typically appear to have less muscle definition than men because of this difference in hypodermis. Within the dermis are found hair follicles, sebaceous glands, sweat glands, and mammary glands (see Figure 6.8). Nails are a modified, hardened layer of epidermis.

The skin's appearance is strongly influenced by the condition of the epidermis and dermis as well as the activity of the sebaceous glands. The color of skin is primarily related to the amount of pigment found in cells called melanocytes located in the lower layer of the epidermis. The pigment in these cells is called melanin, and while all individuals have basically the same number of melanocytes, the amount of melanin produced

FIGURE 6.7   A Cross-Section of Human Skin

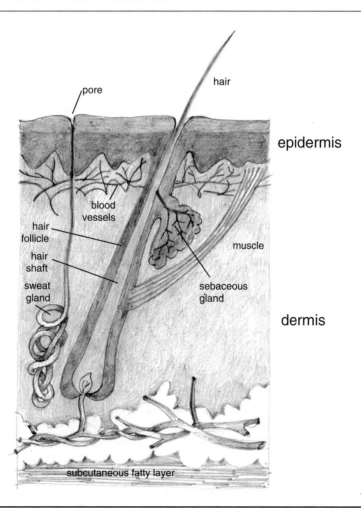

and its dispersion is influenced by both genetic differences and sun exposure. While there are no biological *sex* differences in melanin production, human populations from different environments display genetic differences in this trait. In general, populations experiencing high levels of exposure to direct sunlight (as at the equator) produce more melanin than populations experiencing lower light levels (as in northern regions). The difference between populations in baseline melanin levels is due to the role of sunlight in the synthesis of vitamin D. Humans exposed to low sunlight levels may fail to produce adequate amounts of this vitamin. If people in low-light environments have lower levels of melanin, they are better able to absorb sunlight for vitamin D synthesis. Thus, populations that evolved farther from the equator have paler skin to compensate for the lack of intense sunlight at high latitudes.

Skin color can also be affected by environmental conditions. Melanin production increases and the pigment itself darkens in contact with sunlight. These changes in melanin amount and appearance is why your skin color changes when you tan. The darker skin acts to protect the cells of body from ultraviolet (UV) light, which can damage DNA and interfere with the normal growth and maintenance of underlying tissues.

Additionally, skin color may be affected by an individual's physical condition. Unhealthy individuals often appear pale or ashen, and certain skin tones can indicate the presence of disease. In healthy people with low levels of melanin, blood vessels in the dermis may affect the color of the skin. If blood vessels are dilated (for example, under conditions of stress, sexual excitement, or high body temperature) or are found near the surface of the skin, pale skin will appear pinkish or ruddy. Some scientists have speculated that rouge and lipstick make women seem more beautiful because these cosmetics make women appear sexually excited. According to sociobiologists, men will be more attracted to women who, in subtle ways, appear receptive to their sexual advances. Of course, like most sociobiological hypotheses, this assertion is essentially impossible to test.

■ **DISCUSSION EXERCISE 2**

2.1. Can you think of alternative hypotheses to explain why rouge and lipstick cause women to appear more beautiful? How could you test these hypotheses?

Sex, Sun, and Skin

In the past, differences in skin color between women and men in the same population were due to differences in social role. Men were more likely than women to work outdoors and consequently were more likely to have increased melanin and darker skin. Pale skin was considered beautiful in women, especially because it was a signal of wealth. Women from wealthy backgrounds did not need to spend time assisting with the work of the men in their families and thus did not experience the skin changes associated with sun exposure. In some situations, you'll notice that this social sex difference in skin tone is still expected. Advertisements that include photos of a scantily clothed woman and man embracing nearly always present a darker-skinned man and a pale-skinned woman. We apparently still find the image of the self-sufficient, tanned man (i.e., hard-working) and the reliant, fragile, and pale woman (i.e., protected from work) appealing.

More recently, tan skin has become the standard of beauty among women, because, like pale skin in the past, a tan is now a sign of wealth. Wealthy women and men sport tans as a signal that they can afford travel and leisure required to develop this skin tone. Since a tan has become a beauty ideal for both women and men, questions about the health risks and benefits of tanning have become more interesting to both sexes.

Some types of DNA damage lead to the formation of cancer cells—cells that divide without any control (Chapter 13). Although melanin affords some protection from DNA damage due to UV light, 80 to 90% of epidermal cancers occur in sun-exposed sites on the body, indicating that melanin protection is not complete. Epidermal cancers affect approximately 600,000 people in the United States each year and result in 2,000 deaths (.03% death rate). Moderate sun exposure thus leads to a slight increase in the risk of death due to this form of skin cancer.

Melanoma, another type of skin cancer, affects fewer people but is more deadly (approximately 20% of those diagnosed die within five years). Melanoma is associated with the prolonged sun exposure that leads to severe sunburn. In this case, skin, which has not been exposed recently to high intensity sunlight, is suddenly exposed for an extended period, causing damage to the epidermal layer. Because the exposure is so sudden and the level so high, melanin production does not occur in time to protect the skin, and ultraviolet light is able to inflict damage to the DNA of the underlying cells.

Interestingly, *moderate* sun exposure, while increasing the risk of epidermal cancer, may actually *decrease* the risk of melanoma. Our bodies require sunlight in order to synthesize vitamin D. One important function of this vitamin seems to be in the suppression of cancer cells. Vitamin D has been shown to inhibit the growth of melanomas, as well as breast and colon cancer tumors in laboratory situations. Moderate exposure to sunlight would then be expected to have a net positive effect on cancer survival. In fact, a variety of studies have shown that death due to melanoma is actually negatively associated with lifetime sun exposure.

Although the exact relationship between levels of sun exposure and melanoma is still not definitively established, sunlight definitely affects the skin's overall texture. In addition to increasing melanin production to block UV light, the epidermis produces more layers in response to sun exposure so that radiation is more effectively reflected from the body's surface. The extra layers cause the skin to appear leathery. Sunlight that does penetrate the epidermis damages the supportive proteins (collagen and elastin) in the dermis. As these fibers are lost or broken, the skin loses its underlying elasticity and will crease and wrinkle. You can see how sun affects the texture of the skin by comparing the skin on parts of your body that are commonly exposed to parts that are usually covered. Protected areas of skin have a smoother appearance than exposed areas. One of the main reasons a baby's skin is so smooth is that it has not been exposed to the sun as much as an adult.

The skin's appearance is also affected by the activity of sebaceous glands (often referred to as "pores") embedded in the dermis. These glands are most commonly associated with hair follicles (see Figure 6.7) , although they may be found separately, such as on the lips, penis, labia minora, clitoris, areola, and nipple. Sebaceous glands produce an oily substance called sebum, which is made of the remnants of gland cells that have died and degraded. Sebum is either released onto the hair shaft and drawn up onto the surface of the skin or released directly onto the skin's surface. The oily properties of sebum help to maintain the water levels in the skin by slowing down water evaporation from the skin's surface. Accumulated sebum gives skin an oily appearance while low amounts of sebum (especially combined with low water intake or high water loss) cause skin to appear dry. Frequent washing aggravates dry skin by continually removing sebum from its surface. Moisturizers used to combat dry skin reduce the rate of water evaporation from its surface and often contain lanolin, which ironically is purified, processed sheep sebum.

Acne occurs when sebum accumulates within a sebaceous gland. Acne can take several forms: a blackhead forms when the gland is simply plugged, a pimple occurs when a plugged gland becomes infected and inflamed, and a whitehead forms when the accumulation of sebum is permanent (Figure 6.8). Hormones called androgens (see Chapter 5) increase the activity of sebaceous glands, so acne is associated with changes in hormone production such as those that occur during puberty and with the menstrual cycle. Acne also can result from changes in sebaceous glands caused by drugs or diet and from reactions to

FIGURE 6.8   Forms of Acne

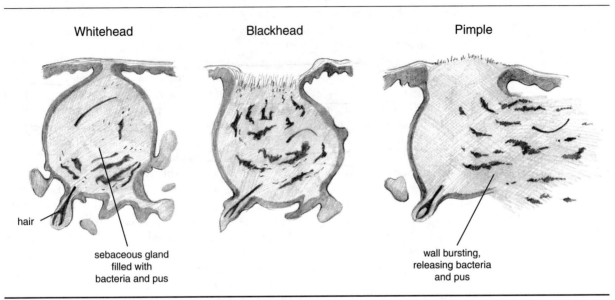

Whitehead   Blackhead   Pimple

hair

sebaceous gland
filled with
bacteria and pus

wall bursting,
releasing bacteria
and pus

Acne forms when a sebaceous gland is plugged and/or infected. The diagram shows a cross-section of a pimple, which is an infected gland; a blackhead, which is a temporarily plugged gland; and a whitehead, which is a more permanently plugged gland.

cosmetics. Glands usually become unclogged, and inflamed glands heal over time. However, this process is not helped (and in fact may be hurt) by harsh scrubbing or other treatments. Acne may be prevented on oily skin by treatments that dry the skin, which increases the rate of shedding and carries away dead cells that may clog sebaceous glands.

Hair

An obvious average difference between men and women in some populations of people is in the location and appearance of body hair. While both sexes as adults have thick hair on their scalps, armpits, and genitals, men in these populations also have thicker growth on their faces, and coarser, longer hair on the rest of their bodies. The number of hairs on the body is determined by the number of hair follicles in the dermis. While there is great variation among individuals within a sex, males and females have, on average, the same number of hair follicles. The difference in the appearance of body hair relates to the characteristics of individual hairs; that is, adult men have thicker and longer hairs on their bodies than women. The thickness and length of hair produced by some individual follicles is influenced by sex hormones in the bloodstream. Before puberty, levels of testosterone and estrogen are low in both girls and boys. Thus, children have very fine, light hair on their bodies. At puberty, testosterone levels increase in both men and women and act on the hair follicles, especially those on the lower abdomen, thighs, chest, pubic area, and underarms of both sexes, and on the faces of men. Testosterone, which generally circulates in higher levels in men's bloodstreams, causes thicker, longer hair to be produced by sensitive follicles, while estrogen, which is in higher levels in women, opposes testosterone action. Once a hair follicle has been stimulated to produce this thicker "sexual hair," all subsequent hairs produced by the follicle will be of this type. Thus, within a population men generally appear hairier than women.

A few women may experience increased sexual hair growth. This condition is often caused by the presence of a tumor on an ovary and could signify an underlying problem.

FIGURE 6.9   Changes in Popular Women's Hairstyles Over the Last 30 Years

1940s   1960s   1980s

Perceptions of beauty and stylishness shift rapidly in Western culture.

However, nearly all women experience some increased sexual hair growth as they age. Because estrogen levels decline slowly throughout adulthood and then drastically at menopause (see Chapter 14), new sexual hair growth is stimulated due to the decreased opposition to testosterone action.

Hair color is determined by the type and amount of pigment found in the hair shaft. Darker hair contains high levels of melanin, while blonde hair contains very little melanin. Another pigment, called trichosiderin, lends a reddish hue. As humans age, the amount of pigment produced by the hair follicle and embedded in the hair declines, eventually to nothing. White, or actually unpigmented, hair is produced by these follicles.

Standards of Beauty

Sociobiologists have sought to prove that our general standards of beauty have a biological basis. However, specific standards of beauty are flexible and may change dramatically over time. Most sociobiologists would agree that there is no biological basis for *particular* beauty trends such as the hairstyle considered most attractive in a particular culture at a particular time (Figure 6.9). Whatever the contribution of innate behavior to our feelings about beauty, clearly we learn many of our values regarding physical appearance from our culture.

Because skin and hair make up a large part of our outward appearance, they are subjected to a larger degree of superfluous modification than any other part of our bodies. We make many of the modifications to conform to socially determined ideals. These modifications may emphasize biological differences or create differences that do not naturally exist. Currently in Western society, beauty is equated with a youthful appearance, especially for women. The result of these beauty standards is that in many Western populations, natural differences in appearance between women and men are exaggerated.

Consider the average differences between men and women in skin qualities. Apparent differences in the amount and severity of facial wrinkling between men and women are partially due to social differences affecting lifelong amounts of sun exposure. The social factors that led to this difference are changing (that is, fewer men have outdoor jobs, and both white men and white women value the tan that is produced by long-term sun exposure). However, because a youthful appearance for women is highly valued in Western society, many women are more averse to wrinkles than men and will seek methods to minimize their appearance. Techniques for reducing wrinkles include removal of the outer layers of skin (dermabrasion) and removal of "excess" sagging skin (face-lift). A prescription drug called Retin-A, a form of vitamin A, partially reverses the collagen damage caused by sun exposure but is effective only as long as it is in the bloodstream—once a patient stops ingesting the pills, wrinkles return. Wrinkles are more apparent on dry skin, so lotions and creams that prevent water loss may minimize their appearance. Recall however that the skin is nourished by the tissues and blood vessels within and beneath it. Very few substances can actually be absorbed into the skin from the outside, including collagen, which is often promoted as an ingredient in wrinkle remover creams. All of these techniques for reducing the appearance of wrinkles are much more likely to be employed by women than men, and all of these treatments have a cost. Wrinkling is a normal part of aging. Outside of prevention (limiting sun exposure), all other "beauty treatments" are expensive and short-lived.

When androgen levels increase in both girls and boys during puberty, the levels of acne increase. Because androgen levels are higher in boys, they are more likely to experience severe acne during adolescence. However, among *adults*, women tend to report more acne than men. The difference in acne may be due to a biological difference (e.g., differences in response to naturally fluctuating levels of androgen), or it may result from social sex differences in the *likelihood* of reporting acne. Since the look of youthfulness that is valued in women includes smooth skin, women may be more concerned with the blemishes that result from sebum accumulation. Thus, women may be more prone to visit the dermatologist when they experience outbreaks of acne. Alternatively, the cosmetics used almost exclusively by women to mask their natural variation in skin tone and texture may increase acne. Some dermatologists believe that ingredients in cosmetics can cause acne by physically blocking the glands, much as sebum and dead cells may do, while other dermatologists believe that cosmetic-associated acne results from an allergic reaction to particular cosmetic ingredients.

In fact, many ingredients in cosmetics are associated with inflammations of the skin and allergic reactions. Unfortunately, since cosmetics are only loosely regulated by the Federal Food and Drug Administration (FDA) in the United States, cosmetics that are associated with allergic reactions or other negative effects may not be easily identified. The FDA does keep a database of adverse reactions associated with certain cosmetics that are voluntarily reported by manufacturers, but this database is incomplete and often outdated due to lack of reporting. For the most part, cosmetics appear to be safe, although the occasional horror story can be found. For instance, a beauty cream imported from Mexico in 1992 contained 6 to 10% mercury, a potent brain toxin, and resulted in the poisoning of three women in the United States. Two-thirds of tested samples of kohl, an eyeliner commonly used by Middle Eastern women, have been found to contain high levels of lead, which has serious affects on brain growth and function.

If the FDA exercised stronger regulatory control over cosmetics, manufacturers would have to prove that their product is safe and effective before being allowed to sell the product, much the way drug manufacturers are required to do. Currently, cosmetics manufacturers can make any claim about the efficacy and safety of their products without documenting these claims. Thus, women pay for cosmetic products that may not perform as they claim and may pay an additional physical price for cosmetics with hazardous ingredients

Beauty enhancing modifications to women's hair are a complicated reflection of both sexual differences and an age standard. Women remove "excess" hair on their faces and bodies by shaving it, pulling it out, or by electrolysis, which kills the hair follicle by burning it with an electric current. Does this standard reflect the difference between women and men in amount of sexual hair, or the difference between adults and adolescents in amount of sexual hair? Many men who produce beards do shave their faces, which de-emphasizes the body hair difference between men and women. Both men and women are also likely to mask gray scalp hair as well. These practices may be evidence that the standard of beauty for both sexes reflects the relative hairlessness of the body and full, colorful hair of the scalp typical of youth. Regardless of its origin, the removal of hair exaggerates a difference in the natural amounts of body hair in both sexes. As is the case with cosmetics, maintaining hair standards is an expense. Shaving and tweezing hair are short-term solutions that must be repeated regularly. Electrolysis removes hair permanently but is tedious, labor-intensive, and costly

SUMMARY

The skin and its associated structures form a layer of protection and of self-presentation between us and the world. Skin is affected by genetic factors, such as the number of hair follicles, baseline melanin production, the activity of glands in the skin, and by environmental factors, like sun exposure, nutrition, and voluntary modification. Many of the voluntary and socially caused modifications humans make to their skin and hair exaggerate differences between the sexes and, according to current fashion, seek to imitate youthful characteristics.

REPRODUCTIVE ANATOMY

> *A term for the female genital region in use not very many years ago was pudendum, which comes from the Latin word* pudere, *meaning "to be ashamed." This term is no longer in common usage, but it still captures the embarrassment many women feel about their bodies.*

The differences between women and men in reproductive anatomy are much more clear and consistent than the features we have discussed thus far. Of course, there is a wide variation in these structures within each sex, and a small number of individuals have reproductive structures that superficially represent an "intermediate" condition between female and male structures (see Chapter 5). In this section, we will present only female reproductive anatomy in order to help women and men begin to understand the form and function of women's bodies.

Breast Anatomy

Breasts, or mammae, are found primarily in only a single class of animal, the mammals, of which humans are a part. Mammae contain specialized skin glands called mammary glands. Mammary glands are found in both sexes but are rudimentary and non-functional in men and well developed in women. Mammary glands in women, as in all female mammals, produce milk for the sustenance of newborn young. (Chapter 11 discusses the production of milk after the birth of a child.) Figure 6.10 illustrates the structure of an average female breast. The glands themselves are modified sweat glands and are made up of 15 to 20 lobes. These lobes are subdivided into lobules and then further subdivided into sacs called alveoli, where milk production actually occurs. Each lobe of the gland ends in a lactiferous duct, which opens at the nipple. These ducts contain a reservoir, called the lactiferous sinus or ampulla, where milk is stored during lactation. Muscles around the nipple control the flow of milk and will contract and relax in response to stimulation. On the surface of the breast, the nipple is surrounded by an obvious darkened area called the areola.

The mammary gland in a non-lactating woman is approximately equivalent in size to a Ping-Pong ball. However, the lobules of the gland are separated and supported by connective tissue and surrounded and cushioned by fat. Most lobules are found in the lower portion of the

FIGURE 6.10   Long Section of a Female Breast.

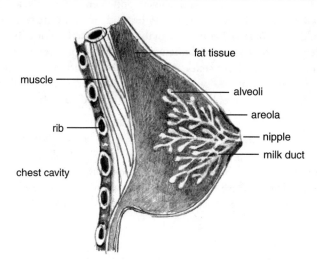

breast and toward the underarm, which gives breasts a typically sloped appearance. When women perform breast self-exams, they can feel the lumpy lobes of the gland. It is important for women to be able to understand the structure of their breasts in order to notice when unusual lumps appear. The size of a woman's breasts is determined by the amount of fat that is stored there, which is a function of genetic and environmental factors, and the extensiveness of connective tissue, which is a function of a woman's genes. Because all women have essentially the same amount of mammary gland tissue, the size of a woman's breasts is completely unrelated to her ability to produce milk.

Women's breasts change in response to hormonal change. Chapters 10 and 11 discuss the changes that occur during pregnancy and postpartum in breast tissue, but breasts also respond to women's monthly hormonal cycle (described more fully in Chapter 8). Estrogen, increasing near the middle of the cycle (approximately one week after menstruation), stimulates cell reproduction in the alveoli, while progesterone, released towards the end of the cycle (immediately before menstruation), stimulates more changes to the alveoli and increases blood flow to the gland. Thus, right before menstruation, women experience lumpiness due to increased gland size and heaviness and tenderness due to increased fluid in their breasts. The gland begins to regress immediately after menstruation, but since estrogen soon begins to increase and stimulate growth, full regression cannot occur. Therefore, with every menstrual cycle, the size and extensiveness of the mammary gland increases. This increase in gland size causes a small increase in breast size over the course of a typical woman's life, but since women also gain weight as they age, most of the increase in breast size over our lifespans is caused by fat accumulation.

Cyclic changes in breast tissue seem to promote the formation of both benign (non-cancerous) fluid-filled cysts and fibroid tumors, which are also non-cancerous growths of connective tissue. Fibroid tumors are more common among young women, while the incidence of cysts increases from age 30 on. Both are lumpy to the touch, although they usually differ from the lumpiness of breast cancer because they are often movable, regular in shape, and changeable in size from day to day. Although the occurrence of cysts and fibroid tumors in breasts has been called "fibrocystic disease," it is not associated with illness in any way. These conditions are found in 70 to 90% of women and are not related to an increased risk of breast cancer. The majority of breast lumps found in premenopausal women (about 11 of every 12 found) are these non-malignant types. After menopause, about 1 of every 2 lumps discovered is cancerous. Of course, any new lumps found in breasts should be evaluated by a clinician.

Some women find benign lumps painful or disturbing, and both fibroid tumors and cysts can often be removed. Pain associated with these lumps is often related to cyclic changes, and can be lessened by hormonal treatments that moderate the cycle. Women must weigh the relief gained by this treatment against the slightly increased risk of cancer that is associated with hormonal therapy (see Chapters 12 and 14).

External Genitals

A term for the female genital region in use not very many years ago was pudendum, which comes from the Latin word *pudere*, meaning "to be ashamed." This term is no longer in common usage, but it still captures the embarrassment many women feel about their bodies. While we have come a long way from the practice common 150 years ago of doctors performing gynecological exams under a blanket, many gynecologists still shield women with lap cloths during exams. Women's reluctance to observe these parts of their bodies is not characteristic of any other parts that we need a mirror to see, such as our teeth, and has the unfortunate result of requiring that women rely on doctors to tell them if they are healthy. This reliance on professionals to tell women about themselves need not be the case, as the following sections will demonstrate.

The Vulva and Clitoris Figure 6.11 illustrates the appearance of a woman's external genitalia. The most obvious feature of the genitals is a structure called the vulva. The vulva consists of two sets of lips, or labia: the labia majora, which are fatty and have a hairy external surface, and the labia minora, which contain neither fat nor hair. The word vulva comes

---

FIGURE 6.11   Female External Genitalia

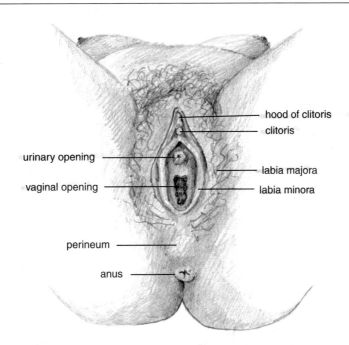

from the Latin word *volvere*, meaning "wrapper," but protection of the genitals is only one of the roles of the vulva. The vulva is erotically sensitive and filled with spongy tissues (called vestibular bulbs) that fill with blood during sexual arousal. This congestion of blood in the vulva is an important component of a woman's sexual pleasure.

The inner surface of the labia majora and the surfaces of the labia minora contain many sebaceous glands that release sebum directly onto the skin's surface. The sebum covering the genitals probably has a protective function, because it repels urine, menstrual blood, and bacteria. These sebaceous glands are subject to becoming clogged. Glands that remain clogged can become enlarged and filled with solidified sebum; these are known as sebaceous cysts. These cysts are harmless and are basically equivalent to large whiteheads. Sebaceous cysts may disappear after a short time, but many women have them for several years without any noticeable discomfort.

On the front end of the vulva, the labia minora divides around the clitoris to form the prepuce of the clitoris, or clitoral hood. Most of the 2.5 cm length of the clitoris is embedded in the surrounding tissue, so only the very tip of the clitoris is apparent on visual inspection. You can feel most of its length, however, as an elongated, firm cylinder in the surrounding fat of the labia majora.

In developing female babies, the clitoris arises from the same tissue as the penis in males (see Chapter 5), and like the penis, the clitoris contains multiple nerve endings and erectile tissue. Unlike the penis, which is also used for excretion of urine and as a passageway for gametes, sexual arousal and orgasm is the only role of the clitoris. During arousal, erectile tissue in the clitoris becomes engorged with blood, often nearly doubling its diameter. As a woman becomes more stimulated, the clitoris retracts into the labia majora directly above the pubic bone. In this position, the clitoris can respond to pressure, either directly applied or transmitted by the labia minora which moves and is pulled on during intercourse. Continued stimulation of the clitoris is required for orgasm to occur. (Some of the other physiological changes that occur during orgasm are described later in the chapter.)

Evolutionary biologists have engaged in long debate over the "significance" of the clitoris, since its only function is triggering sexual arousal and orgasm. Orgasm in women is not assured during every instance of sexual intercourse and is not required for conception to occur. Some sociobiologists have hypothesized that the somewhat unpredictable occurrence of female orgasm during intercourse ensures that women will engage in frequent intercourse, since experiments have shown that other animals are more likely to continue an activity if they are not able to predict when they will be rewarded for it. Frequent intercourse increases the likelihood of conception, so that women who have random orgasms will more likely leave many offspring than women who do not orgasm (or, presumably, orgasm regularly) during intercourse. In this way, the clitoris has evolved as an adaptation to increase the likelihood of conception. On the other hand, the evolutionary biologist Stephen J. Gould argues that the clitoris has no adaptive function but is simply the result of a common developmental program in males and females. The clitoris in females is equivalent to nipples in males—not important to survival but a remnant of our shared biological history.

As with most sociobiological debates, the function of the clitoris is easy to hypothesize but difficult to prove through collection of definitive scientific data. Regardless of its "real function," some feminists have argued that the hypothesizing and debating over the function of the clitoris is a symptom of societal ambivalence about women's sexuality. This discussion may be a subtle way of deciding if regular female orgasm is "natural." If regular orgasm is not natural, perhaps a woman who complains to her partner about the infrequency of her orgasms during sex is being "unnatural," thus selfish and pleasure seeking. Interestingly, there is very little sociobiological literature on the function of the pleasurable aspects of male orgasm. After all, if women with fewer assured orgasms have more reproductive success than those with regular orgasm, shouldn't the same be true of men? Rather, it seems from the little discussion about the issue that consistent pleasurable male orgasms during sex are obviously necessary for successful reproduction. Presumably, there is no question that regular male orgasm is both "natural" and "right."

The "Vestibule"   The area of a woman's genitals enclosed by the vulva has been traditionally called the vestibule. The word "vestibule" comes from the Latin for "courtyard, or entrance," and its use to describe female genitalia reflects the view that women are primarily acted on or entered by men. Considering that *most* of the functions of the organs in this region concern the exit of substances from the body (i.e., excretion of urine, loss of menstrual blood, birth of children), naming this area after an entrance seems rather ironic.

Almost immediately below the clitoris, the outlet of the urethra may be visible as a tiny vertical slit. The urethra is the tube that serves as a passageway for urine from the bladder. The urethra in women is short (4 cm) compared to the male urethra (18 cm). Partially due to the difference in length, women are more susceptible to bladder infections, because bacteria (primarily the species of bacteria found in our intestines) have a shorter distance to travel from the outside of the body. Bladder infections may be more common when the genitals are kept moist, as when a woman is wearing sanitary pads.

A few centimeters below the urethral opening is the vaginal opening. The inside of the opening is surrounded by an irregular membranous fold known as the hymen. The function of the hymen is unclear, although as evidenced by its name (Hymen was the Greek god of marriage) it is the subject of a great amount of mythology. Many people believe that the hymen is mostly intact until a woman's first intercourse, when it is ruptured with much bleeding and pain on the part of the woman. Thus, an intact hymen is thought to be a sign of virginity. However, in most active women, the hymen is no longer intact by young adulthood—it becomes stretched and broken while girls are running, jumping, tumbling, and biking throughout childhood. Women may have a fair amount of hymenal tissue even after becoming sexual active. There is no way to clearly determine if a woman has had sexual intercourse simply by observing the condition of her hymen.

SUMMARY

Women's sexual anatomy includes the breasts, vulva, clitoris, and vestibule. There is variation in the healthy appearance and feel of these organs among women. The names of and beliefs about these organs often reflect socially constructed ideas about the nature of women's sexuality.

Internal Genitals

Figure 6.12 illustrates the internal genitalia of a typical woman. The organs that make up the internal genitals—the vagina, uterus, and ovaries—function in reproduction and also are hormone producing, or endocrine, tissues. The hormones produced by tissues in a woman's genitals influence many aspects of a woman's biology, not just reproduction. The role of hormones is discussed more completely in Chapter 5.

The Vagina   The vagina is a muscular organ that primarily acts as a passageway in and out of the uterus. Menstrual tissue, babies, and placentas may all pass out of the body via the vagina; sperm is introduced into the uterus via the vagina. The structure of the vagina reflects this diverse traffic. Although in diagrams the vagina is depicted as a hollow tube, in actuality, most of the tube is collapsed. The vagina is more potential space than typically empty space. The walls of the vagina conform around any objects inside it—from a slender tampon to a full term baby's head and shoulders—and thus the walls are highly folded.

The internal surface of the vagina is made up of hairless skin and glandular structures. This surface is highly resistant to infection by bacteria because there are few irregularities for the bacteria to invade. The chance of infection is also reduced by the continual casting off of outer layers of tissue, which carry away most bacteria that have been introduced into the

FIGURE 6.12   Female Internal Genitalia

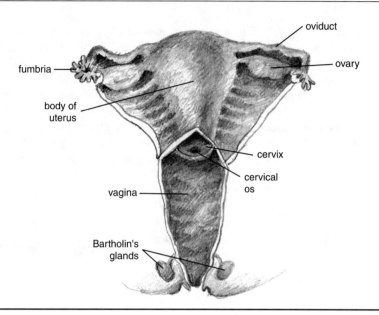

vagina. The moisture in the vagina comes from the breakdown of these cells, mucus produced by the cervix, and vaginal lubrication, which is a product of specialized glands (vestibular glands) at the entrance of the vagina and water released by blood vessels near the surface of the vaginal walls. These blood vessels respond to sexual stimulation as well, and the increased water loss that occurs from them during arousal is experienced as wetness by women. Typically, the discharge from the vagina is odorless, clear or milky in color, and non-irritating. As an additional protection against infection, the degraded cells and liquid discharged into the vagina are fed upon by bacteria, called lactobacilli, that produce lactic acid as a waste product. Few other microorganisms can survive long in the acidic environment that results from lactobacilli activity. The microorganisms that inhabit the vagina are called the "vaginal flora."

Yeast, fungi of the genus *Candida*, are microorganisms typically found in low density in the vaginal flora. When there is a decline in densities of other members of the vaginal flora, yeast may proliferate, causing an often painfully itchy and disturbing yeast infection. These infections are usually characterized by a thick discharge from the vagina, which often smells sweet, or like baking bread. Women on antibiotics are most likely to experience yeast infections as the antibiotics kill the lactobacilli normally prevalent in the vagina. Pregnancy also changes conditions in the vagina that may lead to yeast infections. Any condition that suppresses the immune system, such as AIDS, immunosuppressive drugs, and stress, may also upset the balance of the flora and trigger yeast or bacterial infections. Bacteria, viruses, and fungi that do infect the vagina (as well as other parts of the female genitals) are often sexually transmitted. A more thorough description of the biology and effects of sexually transmitted diseases (STDs) is presented in Chapter 12.

Douches, which are tools that introduce fluid into the vagina under slight pressure to "wash" it out, are often advertised as a hygienic method for keeping the vagina clean. However, since the vagina is self-cleansing, douches contribute little to cleanliness and may in fact cause harm. A douche that introduces water at too high of a pressure may force bacteria from the vagina into the uterus, potentially causing a serious infection. Douches may disrupt the vaginal flora, leading to yeast and other infections. The natural secretions of the vagina are quite capable of keeping this organ clean and healthy.

Vaginal Orgasm and the "G Spot" Although the vagina has relatively few nerve endings, especially compared to the clitoris, many people have assumed that women should be able to experience orgasm through vaginal stimulation only. This belief has been supported over the past 100 years since the psychologist Sigmund Freud stated that clitoral orgasms were "immature" in women. According to Freud, becoming an adult woman entailed, psychologically, the transfer of pleasure from the penis-like clitoris to the womanly vagina. Thus, he felt that psychologically healthy women should experience vaginal orgasms only. As we shall see, orgasm achieved through vaginal stimulation only is quite rare in women.

Studies by William Masters and Virginia Johnson in the 1960s demonstrated that triggering the physiological responses associated with orgasm required clitoral stimulation in nearly all women in their sample. These results set back the proponents of the primacy of the vaginal orgasm, now lacking definitive proof of its existence. The setback lasted only until the work of the gynecologist Ernest Grafenberg was rediscovered in the late 1970s. Grafenberg had described women who were aroused to orgasm by stimulation of a spot on the anterior (front) wall of the vagina. He noted that women thus stimulated "ejaculated" a clear fluid from their urethra. The spot on the vagina was later termed the "G spot" in his honor, and a best selling book of the same name was released.

Since the initial hoopla, however, the evidence for an erogenous zone for all women on the anterior wall of the vagina has, shall we say, a spotty record. The sensitive area Grafenberg described corresponds to tissue that forms both the anterior wall of the vagina and the posterior wall of the urethra. The urethra has nerve endings to help control the flow of urine, nerve endings which are also sensitive to pressure. The makeup of the "female ejaculate" may or may not be mostly urine. It is also clear that a sensitive G spot is not characteristic of all women, nor do all women experience orgasm in response to G spot stimulation. Some women may find stimulation of this area erotic, while others may not.

At this point, we should note that sexual pleasure is not confined to orgasmic experiences. Many women experience intense sexual pleasure simply through closeness to their partner's body. The discussion over the relative importance of the G spot versus the clitoris as the site of orgasm also demonstrates our culture's belief that there is one "right" way to experience sexual pleasure. Carol Tavris, who with Leonore Tiefer reviewed the cultural history of the G spot, believes that it provides a good model for many of our societal discussions of sexuality.

> [S]ex occurs in many places, beginning in the brain, and including, but not limited to, various interesting anatomical parts...The G spot was popular because it pandered to the popular notion that sex is in the cells...[O]h for a G spot! Like the clitoris before it, it promises unlimited bliss. All you have to do is push the right button, once you find it.
> C. Tavris, *The Mismeasure of Woman*, pp. 241–242

While stimulation of the vagina is not required for orgasm to occur, the response of the vaginal muscles contribute greatly to the sensation of orgasm. Masters and Johnson referred to the spasmodic and involuntary contractions of the muscles of the vagina and vulva as physiological orgasm. Different women experience this physiological response in different ways, ranging from intensely pleasurable to mildly pleasurable to slightly painful. Certainly, for many women, the experience of orgasm is a small part of the pleasure of sex. Struggling for the "right way" to experience orgasm can be frustrating and angering for women who feel a need to conform to a sexual ideal.

The Uterus   When a woman is standing, her vagina is typically at a 45-degree angle to the floor, extending up and back into her body. At the top of the vagina, and usually resting at a 90° angle to it, is the uterus, commonly called the womb. Some women can feel the very tip of their uterus (the cervix) by inserting a finger into their vagina.

In about 80% of women, the uterus lies on top of the bladder (see Figure 6.12), while in the other 20% it angles away from the bladder and lies on top of the rectum. This condition, sometimes called a "tipped" or "retroverted" uterus, has been blamed for a variety of woes, including difficulty becoming pregnant and dysmenorrhea (painful menstruation). As it has become more obvious how common this alternative position is, it has also become clear that a tipped uterus represents just one state in the normal variation found among women's bodies. Neither position of the uterus is superior for conception, pregnancy, or childbirth.

Some women have an unusually shaped uterus due to the effects of a drug taken by their mothers during pregnancy. DES (diethylstrilbestrol) is a synthetic estrogen that was given to some pregnant women until 1971 in the mistaken belief that it would prevent miscarriage. DES had little effect on the rate of miscarriage and had the terrible side effect of damaging the reproductive system of a developing fetus. "DES daughters" often have very small uterine cavities, giving the uterus a T-shaped appearance. These women may have difficulty sustaining a pregnancy to term due to this malformation. Happily, nearly 80% of DES daughters eventually have successful pregnancies.

The uterus is about size of fist in a woman who has never been pregnant and only slightly larger in women who have. The wall of the uterus is thick (1 cm) and made of some of the most powerful muscles in the human body. These muscular walls contract rhythmically during labor, childbirth and orgasm. The internal surface of the uterine wall is called the endometrium, which changes in thickness and character during the course of a menstrual cycle. The lower 1/3 to 1/2 of the uterus is narrower than the upper portion and is called the cervix. The cervix produces a mucus that also changes in concert with hormonal changes of the menstrual cycle. (Changes occurring during the menstrual cycle are discussed in more detail in Chapter 8.)

The opening from the cervical canal into the vagina is called the cervical os. During labor and birthing, the os dilates from the size of a pinhead to at least 10 cm in diameter (for a full term birth) to allow the passage of the baby's head. While the os closes again after the birth is complete, the shape of the os is irreversibly changed by the event. Thus, the os appears as a "dot" on the end of the cervix in women who have not given birth and as a "dash" or more irregular opening in women who have had one or more deliveries. Because of this change, clinicians can readily determine if a woman has given birth in the past.

The cervical os also dilates slightly during orgasm and remains open for about 30 minutes afterward. This response may increase the passage of sperm into the uterus after intercourse and may increase the likelihood of conception by increasing the number of sperm that come in contact with the egg. The sexually stimulated opening of the cervical os can, in concert with the uterine contractions that also occur during orgasm, help relieve cramping during menstruation by increasing the flow of endometrial tissue from the body.

The Oviducts   The oviducts (sometimes called the "Fallopian tubes" after the anatomist Gabriello Fallopio, who first described them) are actually an extension of the top surface of the uterus. These tubes extend out from the body of the uterus towards the ovaries, which are suspended within the body cavity. The oviducts are not attached to the ovaries directly. Instead, they end in a brushy-bordered funnel (called the infundibulum). The brushy ends of the the infundibulum move over the surface of the ovary as a woman moves. These movements, along with suction inside the oviducts, direct eggs released by the ovary into the oviducts. The infundibulum can catch eggs regardless of the surface of the ovary from which the egg is released. Rarely, an egg is released that is not directed into the oviducts. This egg is typically reabsorbed by tissues in the body cavity. An egg that does not enter the oviducts can be fertilized outside of the uterus. The resulting embryo can implant on other structures in the abdominal cavity. These kinds of pregnancies are dangerous because of the high risk of internal bleeding, but some have been successful, resulting in the delivery of normal babies via incision through the abdominal wall.

Oviducts are lined with tiny hairs, called cilia, that move back and forth (or "beat") causing a net movement of liquid towards the uterus. This movement both creates suction that pulls the egg from the ovary and propels the egg towards the uterine cavity. Sometimes a blockage (due to scar tissue or a DES-caused deformity) causes the egg to stall in the oviduct. If this egg becomes fertilized and implants in the walls of the oviduct, an ectopic pregnancy results. Because the tube is so narrow, these pregnancies are never successful, and the inevitable rupture of the tube can cause severe internal bleeding. See Chapter 10 for a fuller discussion of ectopic pregnancies.

The vagina-uterus-oviduct represents the only natural pathway in humans directly from the outside to the inside of the abdominal cavity. This means that women can experience bacterial infections of their abdominal cavity (called peritonitis) without experiencing an injury that punctures the cavity wall or a rupture of an infected internal organ. Peritonitis is most likely to occur in women who have an infection, often sexually transmitted, of their uterus or oviducts. Adolescent girls who are sexually active are especially susceptible to sexually transmitted infections of the uterus or oviducts, because the cervix physically becomes more resistant to infection (via changes in its shape and surface) as a woman matures. Peritonitis is a rare but life-threatening complication of sexually transmitted disease in women and is a result of the anatomy of their reproductive system.

The Ovaries   The ovaries are the primary sex organs in women; that is, they are the organs that produce the sex cells, or gametes. In addition, the ovaries are a primary source of the sex hormones that circulate in a woman's body during her reproductive years. Ovaries are surprisingly small, about the size of a walnut, but at birth contain about 2 million ova (eggs) each. The development of ovaries is described in Chapter 9. During nearly every menstrual cycle, one or more eggs mature and are released from a structure on the ovary called a follicle. The follicle is a fluid-filled sac containing the developing egg, surrounded by its associated tissues, and additional liquid. The follicle is an endocrine structure, which releases the ovarian hormone estrogen. During ovulation, the follicle ruptures (much like a blister popping) and releases the egg, which is usually picked up by the oviducts and moved toward the uterus. The remnant of the follicle is called the corpus luteum, which secretes both estrogen and progesterone. The process of egg development, ovulation, and fertilization is described in more detail in Chapters 8 and 9.

Abnormally formed fluid-filled sacs are typically called cysts, and because ovaries produce one or more fluid-filled follicles every month or so, these organs are prone to developing cysts that remain intact over several months. The majority of ovarian cysts are harmless and either occur because the egg-containing follicle does not rupture or because the corpus luteum continues to grow after the egg is released. These types of cysts are called functional cysts, because they are related to the normal function of the ovary. When ovulation ceases at menopause, functional cysts are less likely to occur. Drugs that suppress ovulation (like birth control pills) will also suppress the formation of functional cysts. Large ovarian cysts may cause pelvic pain as they press on other organs or if they rupture, but most functional cysts disappear on their own after one or two menstrual cycles.

Other non-cancerous cysts may appear on ovaries, including teratomas that develop from cells triggered to grow and differentiate into various organs, including bone, hair, and teeth. Teratomas are discussed in more detail in Chapter 9. For the most part, cysts that appear on the ovaries are benign, but any growth on the organ, especially in post-menopausal women, should be carefully evaluated.

FIGURE 6.13   Speculum

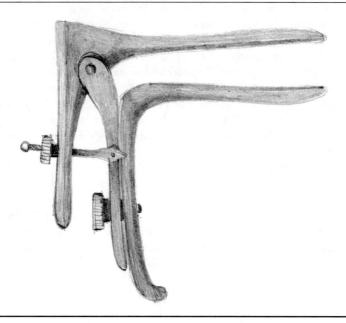

This instrument is typically used by clinicians during internal pelvic exams.

Pelvic Exams

We are hopeful that the preceding description of the typical condition and variations in female genitalia has removed some of the mystery that surrounds these organs for many women. Women who observe changes in their own bodies are likely to note and investigate any problems before they become serious. However, because of the location of these organs and the physical and social challenges involved in self-inspection, most women rely on clinicians for thorough examinations of their reproductive systems. The benefits of regular pelvic examinations in young women who do not have any disease symptoms and are not pregnant are questionable, but most women submit to an exam every two years. Clinicians encourage yearly pelvics for post-menopausal women, women taking hormonal contraceptives or using IUDs or diaphragms, women with a family history of reproductive cancer, and DES daughters.

During a pelvic exam, the clinician typically performs four examinations: external, internal (or speculum), bimanual, and rectovaginal. During the external examination, the clinician will first examine the vulva for any growths, discolorations or unusual discharge. To inspect the cervix and the interior of the vagina, the clinician will use a speculum (Figure 6.13), a tool that is shaped somewhat like a duck's bill and is inserted into the vagina and opened to spread apart the vaginal walls. Insertion and opening of the speculum should at its worst be only slightly uncomfortable. Women experiencing pain during this procedure should notify their clinician, who may be able to use a smaller speculum or reorient the tool for relief.

Next, the clinician visually inspects the vagina and cervix, and, if applicable, checks the position of an IUD or the fit of a diaphragm. The clinician will also take samples for a "Pap test" during the internal examination. During the test, a small brush, cotton swab, or spatula is used to remove a few cells from the cervical os. These cells are smeared on a slide and later analyzed for any irregularities in appearance. This procedure can reveal cancer of the cervix at a very early stage and when it is most easily cured. Atypical Pap test results do not necessarily indicate cancer, because infection of the cervix or vagina may also cause cell changes. Unless there is a strong reason to suspect cervical cancer, clinicians usually advise women with one atypical Pap result to return for another test in a few months. If the result does not change, a small sample (biopsy) of the cervix may then be taken.

A clinician can also indirectly assess the condition of the other internal genitals during a pelvic exam. The bimanual examination requires the clinician to insert one or two fingers into a woman's vagina while using the other hand to press on her abdomen. In this manner, the clinician can determine the position and state of the uterus, ovaries, and oviducts. Ovaries are very small and difficult to feel and firm pressure on a woman's abdomen may be needed to locate them. During a rectovaginal examination, the clinician inserts a finger in the rectum and another in the vagina to feel the internal genitals from another angle.

The nature of pelvic exams means that they are psychologically uncomfortable for many women. A woman is on her back with her legs spread and elevated, which exposes her genitals to the best view and access by the clinician. Often a cloth is put over the patient's lap, restricting her view, and the clinician may not speak much during the exam. If a woman finds a pelvic exam especially difficult, she should discuss her feelings with her clinician. It may be beneficial for these women to seek out a more sensitive and gentle practitioner.

SUMMARY

The internal genitalia of a woman consists of the vagina, uterus, oviducts, and ovaries. These organs also show a wide degree of variation among women in terms of shape, placement, and response to stimulation. Pelvic exams can help identify unusual features that appear to be outside of the normal range of variation.

REFERENCES

Ainsleigh, H. G. (1993). Beneficial effects of sun exposure on cancer mortality. *Preventative Medicine* 22, 132–140.

al-Hazzaa, S. A., & Krahn, P. M. (1995). Kohl: A hazardous eyeliner. *International Ophthalmology* 19(2), 83–88.

Boston Women's Health Book Collective. (1992). *The new our bodies, ourselves.* Touchstone.

Carlson, K. J., Eisenstat, S. A., Ziporyn, T. (1996). *The Harvard guide to women's health.* Harvard University Press.

Ciullo, J. (1993). Lower extremity injuries. In A. J. Pearl (Ed.), *The athletic female.* Human Kinetics Publishers.

Fausto-Sterling, A. (1992). *Myths of gender.* Basic Books.

Krogman, W. M., & Iscar, M. Y. (1986). *The human skeleton in forensic medicine.* Charles C. Thomas.

McBride, J. T., Meade III, W. C., & Ryan, J. B. (1993). Incidence and pattern of injury in female cadets at West Point Military Academy. In A. J. Pearl (Ed.), *The athletic female.* Human Kinetics Publishers.

Tavris, C. (1992). *The mismeasure of woman.* Touchstone.

CHAPTER 7

Although the mechanism for this is not clear, sex hormones also seem to regulate where fat is stored on women and men....As fat mass increases, women see an increase in the size of their hips and thighs ("saddle bags"), while men see an increase in the size of their abdominal fat mass ("spare tire").

WOMEN'S BODIES II: MUSCLE, FAT, AND HEALTH

BODY COMPOSITION

The physical characteristic that in Western society commands the most attention and has primary psychological relevance for many women is weight and body shape. As many as 40% of American women attempt to lose weight through dieting at any given time, although this estimate varies depending on the source of the survey.

In overall size and proportion, women are about 92% as large as men, but this relationship does not hold for differences in body composition. In other words, women do not have 92% of the muscle, 92% of the fat, and 92% of the bone mass of men. As we discussed in Chapter 6, an average woman's skeleton is about 13% lighter than an average man's, even though she is only about 8% smaller in stature. Women also have 34% less lean body mass (that is, the portion of body weight that is not water or fat) than men, primarily due to differences in muscle mass. This difference in muscle mass corresponds to a difference in strength. Because a higher proportion of their weight is muscle, men are 20% stronger than women at the same weights. Of course, differences in exercise training will exaggerate or alleviate this strength difference, but men at the same weight and training level as women will inevitably have more muscle and greater strength.

While men have more muscle, women carry more fat stores. Twenty-two percent of an average woman's weight consists of body fat, compared to 14% in males. These percentages can also change depending on an individual's energy intake and expenditure, but at the same level of elite aerobic training, female athletes have twice the body fat per weight of males (12% and 6%, respectively).

Sex differences in fat storage and muscle mass are primarily caused by dissimilarity between the sexes in levels of certain hormones in the bloodstream. The sex organs of women (ovaries) and men (testes) make all three classes of sex hormones: progestins, estrogens, and androgens. However, these sex organs produce different *ratios* of these hormones. Ovaries produce more estrogens and progestins than androgens, while testes produce primarily androgen (specifically, testosterone) and only low levels of the other two classes.

As discussed in Chapter 5, steroid hormones can easily cross cell membranes. Once inside a cell, a receptor for the hormone must be present for the hormone to have any effect. If a receptor is present, the hormone will bind to it, and the whole hormone-receptor complex will move to the nucleus where it affects the transcription of specific genes. Thus, in the presence of steroid hormones and their receptors, certain proteins will increase or decrease in production. Testosterone in muscle cells increases the levels of proteins that trigger cell growth and multiplication, as is evidenced by individuals who take this steroid to improve athletic performance. At natural levels, men's higher levels of testosterone produce larger muscles.

The roles of sex hormones in fat cells (adipocytes) are more complex and are summarized in Figure 7.1. Adipocytes have androgen receptors in their cytoplasm. When an androgen such as testosterone and its receptor move to the nucleus of an adipocyte, the levels of proteins that cause fat (lipid) breakdown increase inside the cell. Therefore, the rate of lipid degradation increases. The component parts of these degraded lipid molecules are used to power the activities of the cell or are released into the bloodstream. There, they are available for uptake and use in energy generation by other cells. The presence of testosterone in adipocytes also causes changes in the cell membrane that limit the amount of lipid these cells take from the bloodstream.

While adipocytes do not have receptors for either estrogen or progestin, estrogen does affect the production of testosterone receptors, such that cells exposed to high estrogen levels produce few testosterone receptors. In this case, rates of lipid degradation are low and uptake of lipids is high. Thus women are more likely than men to store fat in adipocytes and less likely to use the fat that is stored there for quick energy generation.

Given our cultural beliefs about the costs of fat, it may seem that men's bodies have a more efficient system than women's for dealing with fat. However, because adipocytes in men are less likely to take up fat than those in women, the levels of fat circulating in men's bloodstreams may be greater. When men's diets are high in fat, the excess begins to accumulate in blood vessels, narrowing their diameter and causing arteriosclerosis, a major risk factor for heart disease. This consequence of high fat diets is also true of women after menopause, when estrogen levels decline.

Sex hormones also seem to regulate where fat is stored on women and men, although the mechanism for this is not clear. In the presence of high estrogen and low testosterone, fat is stored in alpha adipocytes on the extremities, while in the presence of low estrogen and high testosterone, it is stored in beta adipocytes in the abdomen. Because these cell types are found in different regions of the body, the appearance of women and men is affected by fat storage. At typical fat mass levels, this causes a difference in the waist to hip ratio (i.e., the diameter of the waist divided by the diameter of the hips), which in women averages 0.74

FIGURE 7.1   The Effects of Estrogen and Testosterone on Adipocytes

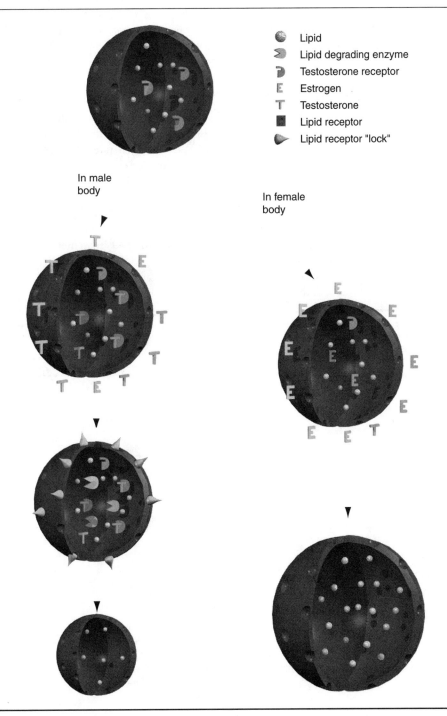

Cells exposed to testosterone produce more lipid degrading enzymes and allow fewer lipid molecules inside, resulting in lower levels of lipid storage. Adipocytes exposed to high levels of estrogen have few testosterone receptors, which minimizes the effects of the already low levels of testosterone in a woman's body on these cells. Thus, women's adipocytes are more likely to retain and store lipid molecules than men's adipocytes.

and in men averages 0.9 (see Figure 7.2). These different patterns of storage remain even when fat amounts are above average. As fat mass increases, women see an increase in the size of their hips and thighs ("saddle bags"), while men see an increase in the size of their abdominal fat mass ("spare tire"). Women see changes in patterns of fat storage when estrogen levels decline after menopause. At this stage, they begin to store fat in abdominal stores, and their waist to hip ratio approaches that of men.

Physiological Effects of Body Composition

Our movements are controlled by muscle cells, which are stimulated to contract when they receive a signal from the brain. In order to perform this function, muscles need to be supplied with energy. As energy is used, wastes are generated that need to be removed from the cell before they interfere with its normal processes. The bloodstream performs both of these functions, bringing energy to and removing wastes from active tissues. Compared to muscle tissue, fat is relatively inactive, and it requires fewer immediate sources of energy and less rapid removal of waste. Thus, the number of blood vessels in fat tissue is much smaller than the number in muscle tissue.

Because women have a higher fat to muscle ratio (.42) than men (.24), and muscle tissue has more blood vessels than fat, men have more blood vessels for their size. There are two consequences of this difference. Men have a greater blood volume per body weight and to move this blood, they require a larger heart per body weight.

Because men have more blood than women, they have more hemoglobin, a protein which carries oxygen. Cells require oxygen for efficient energy use. When energy use is required but

FIGURE 7.2   The Average Waist to Hip Ratio of Women and Men

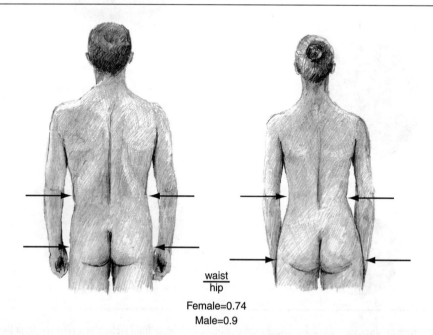

waist / hip

Female=0.74
Male=0.9

Hips are measured at their widest point. Because of differences in pelvis anatomy and fat storage, women have a lower waist to hip ratio than men.

oxygen is not available, cells can still function but markedly less effectively. In addition to lowered efficiency, body cells using energy without oxygen produce a waste product called lactic acid. Lactic acid causes cells to tire and makes the muscle tissue feel sore where it is accumulating. The muscle "burn" you feel during intense exercise is due to lactic acid buildup. When women and men are using the same groups of muscles in the same exercise, men are able to continue to supply the muscle with oxygen for a longer period than women, since men both carry more hemoglobin and can move it into tissues more rapidly with their bigger pumps.

The difference between men and women in the delivery of oxygen to working muscles may explain why the male world record holder in all track distance events is approximately 11% faster than the female world record holder. During exertion, women more quickly begin producing lactic acid then men, and thus their muscles may fatigue earlier. However, it is also possible that, as is true in other sports, women's training is not equivalent to men. While lactic acid production may be higher in elite women athletes, women's bodies may have different ways of handling this acid load, such that their muscles are more resistant to fatigue. Women do regularly beat men in ultra-marathons, which are foot races of 100 miles or more. This could be due to the relative novelty of the sport (i.e., both men and women have only recently begun to train for these events) or due to a difference in physiological needs between short and very long distance running (i.e., the relative non-importance of lactic acid buildup at these extremely long distances). Given that the first women's marathon in the Olympics was held in 1984, it may be that the gap between the top men's time and the top women's time will continue to narrow as more women become involved in track events. (In fact the number of women participating in sports has grown markedly over the past 25 years. In 1972, the number of women high school athletes was about 300,000 compared to 2,360,000 in 1997.)

While the fastest man may always be faster than the fastest woman and the strongest man stronger than the strongest woman, it is important to remember one of the principles described in Chapter 6— knowing differences between the average individuals of each sex, or the extreme individuals of each sex, can tell us very little about the capabilities of all members of each sex. The fastest woman in the 100 m dash (currently Florence Griffith-Joyner, at 10.49 seconds) is faster than the vast majority of men as well. Additionally, the capabilities of individuals at the extreme of a distribution are not necessarily representative of an entire sex. Occasionally sports fans will state, "There's never been a female basketball player who had the same athletic ability as Michael Jordan." Remind them that there's never been another male Michael Jordan (or Mary Lou Retton), either.

Fat has many roles in the body. It cushions internal organs, provides a layer of insulation to maintain body temperature, stores fat-soluble vitamins, and provides for the long-term storage of energy in the body. Because women have more fat and less muscle per weight than men, they conserve more food energy. Ingested calories in women are more likely to go into storage than to be used building and maintaining energy expensive muscle tissue. Because of their larger fat mass, women have a much greater ability to wait out hard times than men and to have adequate physical resources in the form of fat to support pregnancy and breast feeding. We commonly hear that women's bodies are adapted for reproduction, the implication being that the male body is the normal type, from which women represent a modification or an imperfection. However, it is impossible to determine which body type is "normal" and which is the "modification." Male bodies may in fact represent a modification of the conservative female ideal, since greater strength in men would help them compete with other men for access to females or resources to attract them. (See Chapter 3 for a discussion of the evolution of men and women.). In a modern society where food is abundant, the ability to conserve energy in the form of fat is not seen as an advantage. However, women's ability to maintain high body fat levels was crucial to the survival of both individuals and entire human populations during periods of lower food abundance.

SUMMARY

Women's bodies have more fat per weight and less muscle per weight than men's bodies. These differences are primarily due to differences in levels of androgen and estrogen hormones in each sex. Body composition has an effect on physiological characteristics and influences an individual's performance of physical tasks.

NUTRITION

Fat is the macronutrient that receives the most attention in American society, and reasonably so, because high fat intake is associated with heart disease. Fat is also the most likely nutrient to be overconsumed because most of us enjoy the flavor it adds to our foods.

Our body composition and size affects how much energy is required to maintain a healthy condition. Food energy is measured in calories. A **food calorie** (which is actually 1000 of the standard scientific units "calorie") is the amount of energy required to raise the temperature of a liter of water by $1°$ Celsius. We can determine the number of calories in a food item by burning it to ash in an apparatus called a calorimeter and measuring the amount of heat energy given off. Essentially, the cells in our bodies "burn" food as well, but the energy released is used for other work in the cell *before* being lost as heat, rather than converted directly to heat as in a calorimeter. Because men are larger than women, they require more calories to sustain their bodies. In fact, even though men are typically only about 8% larger than women, they require about 19% more calories. Men's additional energy needs are caused by a difference in body composition: Men have, on average, greater muscle mass than women, and muscle requires more energy than fat for maintenance. Although calorie needs vary from person to person, the average adult woman requires 2,100 calories a day, while the average adult man requires 2,500, according to the National Research Council of the United States. Caloric needs also change throughout our lifetimes. For instance, we all need more calories during adolescence but fewer as we age, and women need more calories during pregnancy and when breast feeding.

Besides energy, our bodies require essential nutrients. These include molecules that we need in large amounts (macronutrients), such as carbohydrates, fats, and protein, and those important nutrients we need in smaller amounts (micronutrients), such as vitamins and minerals. The majority of people in the United States receive enough calories in their diet. However, important exceptions include people with low incomes, those with drug or alcohol addictions, those on highly restrictive diets, and some of the elderly population. Many of the health problems associated with nutrition in the well-fed population have to do with an imbalance in the levels of different nutrients in individual diets. While specific recipes about the appropriate levels of nutritional needs vary from person to person, a good general rule is to eat a balanced diet, consisting of more grain, fruits, and vegetables and fewer fats, oils, and sugars than most Americans consume.

Vitamins and Minerals in Women's Health

This chapter is not intended to serve as a guide to nutrition, but certain vitamins and minerals are important in a woman's diet and deserve attention here. These micronutrients include calcium, iron, and folic acid.

Calcium   Calcium is a major component in bones and teeth, as well as an important player in many cell processes. Essentially, our bones serve as a dynamic storage area for the mineral: Ingested calcium is stored there, and calcium for use in the cells is obtained via release from the bone. The ratio of buildup to breakdown of bone changes over our lifetimes. A net gain of bone occurs until young adulthood when the rate of bone loss begins to increase. During adolescence, when bones are growing rapidly, calcium needs are relatively high. According to the federal government, adolescent girls and boys should take in about 1,200 milligrams (mg) of calcium per day (equivalent to four 8-ounce glasses of milk). Calcium needs are also high during pregnancy, when a mother is supplying calcium for the fetus's bone growth, and during breast feeding, when calcium is expressed in milk.

Non-pregnant and non-lactating women before menopause have a lower requirement for calcium, around 800 mg per day. After menopause, when bone degradation outstrips bone growth, the requirement jumps to 1,500 mg a day. Many American women do not consume close to this level of calcium. In fact, the typical postmenopausal woman only receives about one third of the recommended allowance, or 500 mg a day. At this low level, the body will rob the bones of calcium to supply the needs of its cells. For women with small, low density bones, this additional loss may be serious, leading to multiple bone fractures and spinal deformities.

Calcium is obtained in a normal diet from dairy products and leafy green vegetables such as spinach, kale, and chard. The absorption of calcium from the diet is affected by other nutrients. Calcium is absorbed adequately only in the presence of vitamin D and may be inhibited by fat, protein, sodium, and caffeine. Many women increase their calcium intake by taking supplements. Calcium supplements are relatively safe, although at very high levels of intake (>3,000 mg a day), calcium can interfere with absorption of other minerals and may cause nausea, diarrhea, and the hardening of soft tissues. As with most minerals, increasing calcium intake is often more effectively and safely done through diet modification. An easy way to do so is to add non-fat milk powder to foods during cooking.

Iron   Women also require relatively high levels of iron in their diet. Iron is an important component of hemoglobin, the oxygen-carrying molecule of the blood. In fact, the iron in hemoglobin is, in part, what gives blood a reddish color. An iron deficiency results in the production of fewer red blood cells and affects the transport of oxygen. This condition is called iron deficiency anemia and results in fatigue, lightheadedness, decreased tolerance for exercise, and pallor. Any type of blood loss, including menstruation, takes iron from the body. During a typical menstrual period, a woman may lose 20 to 40 mg of iron. Thus, premenopausal women require 50 to 70 mg of iron per day compared to only 30 mg per day for men. Pregnancy also leads to the loss of iron, because the fetus requires it for blood production.

A woman is diagnosed with iron deficiency anemia when the volume of red blood cells in a given volume of whole blood (called the hemacrit level) is less than 36%. Iron deficiency anemia is treated in the short term by supplements of iron. Although supplements are safe if taken as directed, too much iron interferes with the absorption of other minerals, and can lead to constipation or diarrhea, liver damage, heart disturbances, and arthritis. A diet rich in red meats, liver, rice, beans, potatoes, eggs, and dried fruit will also supply adequate iron.

Anemia can also be caused by other conditions besides iron deficiency, including internal bleeding and inadequate amounts of other nutrients. Pernicious anemia is caused by an inadequate intake of vitamin B12 and may result in permanent neurological damage. This type of anemia is more common than would be expected in populations of African American women. B12 deficiency usually results from low levels of animal products (meat, eggs, and cheese) in the diet.

Folic acid   Folic acid, or folate, is a vitamin needed in very small amounts on a daily basis. However, folate seems important for the proper development of fetuses in pregnant women. Studies have found that the risk of neural tube defects (such as spina bifida) in newborns is much lower if the mother has taken in at least 0.4 mg of folate per day during pregnancy.

Because of folate's role in reducing birth defects, some nutritionists have recommended that folate be added to flour or some other staple, much as the important nutrient vitamin D is now added to milk. However, one risk of folate supplementation is that at levels greater than 1 mg per day, folate may mask the symptoms of pernicious anemia, which has serious consequences in adults. Folate can be lost from foods when they are processed (e.g., canned, boiled, or frozen) and is best obtained from fresh vegetables. Once again, a balanced, healthy diet should contain adequate levels of folate to ensure the healthy development of a fetus.

Macronutrients in Women's Health: Fat

The primary source of calories in our diets come from the three macronutrients: fat, protein, and carbohydrates. Because most Americans have ready access to a wide variety of foods, few of us suffer from a deficiency of any one of these nutrients. In fact, many Americans consume excessive amounts of one or all of these nutrients. Fat is the macronutrient that receives the most attention in American society, and reasonably so, because high fat intake is associated with heart disease. Fat is also the most likely nutrient to be overconsumed because most of us enjoy the flavor it adds to our foods. You've probably noticed the difference in taste between whole milk ice cream and fat-free ice cream, or butter and low-fat margarine.

The proper amount of fat in an individual's diet depends on her or his family history, personal history, current health status, and lifestyle. According to most recommendations, a balanced diet consists of approximately 12% of calories from protein, 58% from carbohydrates, and 30% from fat. (One gram of fat contains more than two times the number of calories of a gram of either protein or carbohydrate, so the mass of fat in the ideal diet is actually less than 30%.)

Fat in our diets and in our bloodstreams actually comes in two classes: triglycerides (what we call fat) and cholesterol. Both of these can also be made in our bodies from the excess carbohydrate and protein that we eat. Triglycerides are important parts of our diets because they carry with them the fat-soluble vitamins. Although our bodies can make many types of triglycerides, two essential fats must be ingested because we cannot manufacture them ourselves and they are required for proper growth and development. Non-essential triglycerides can be stored after they are ingested or may be converted to cholesterol, which is essentially a method for moving fats around the body. Cholesterol can also be ingested directly from the animal-based foods we eat, because fat in animals is also converted to this form. In addition to its role in fat transport, cholesterol is an important component of cell membranes and forms the building blocks for steroid hormones like estrogen.

We can measure the consequences of an individual's diet by looking at the levels of cholesterol in her or his bloodstream. Cholesterol comes in two forms: LDL (low density lipoprotein, or "bad cholesterol") and HDL (high density lipoprotein or "good cholesterol"). LDL is a measure of the fat that is moving around the body looking for a home—LDL fats are going into storage. HDL is a measure of the fat released to power body activities—HDL fats are going to be used up. If LDL levels are high, the fat is looking for a settling place. If this fat is not incorporated into adipocytes, it may build up on the inner surfaces of blood vessels, causing arteriosclerosis or "hardening of the arteries." If arteriosclerosis is especially severe in the blood vessels supplying the heart, portions of the heart may suffer injury due to a low oxygen supply—this is basically what occurs during a heart attack. Although genetic factors play a role in determining an individual's LDL levels, fat intake is also associated with LDL and HDL. In particular, diets high in saturated fat (see Figure 7.3) increase LDL levels, while diets low in fat or with a high percentage of polyunsaturated fats lead to low LDL levels.

A high fat diet is an important risk factor in heart disease, but we still don't know whether having large fat *stores* also causes heart disease. In the next section, we'll discuss the definitions and consequences of what has been considered an excess amount of fat in the body.

FIGURE 7.3   Chemical Structure of Saturated and Unsaturated Fats

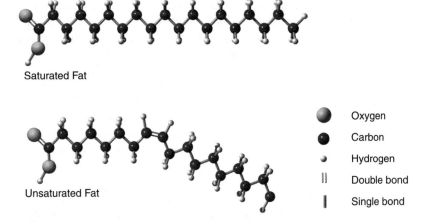

Saturated Fat

	Oxygen
	Carbon
	Hydrogen
||	Double bond
		Single bond

Unsaturated Fat

Unsaturated fats are less likely to build up on artery walls because of the irregular shape of the molecule.

SUMMARY

Women require fewer calories than men because of their smaller size and lower muscle to fat ratio. However, women need a few micronutrients in higher amounts than do men: calcium, iron, and folic acid. Fat is the one macronutrient many Americans overconsume, to the detriment of their health. High fat diets are associated with high levels of blood cholesterol, which can lead to arteriosclerosis and heart disease.

■ DISCUSSION EXERCISE 1

Before reading the following section, answer these true/false questions.

_____ Your weight is a direct result of your diet.

_____ Obesity is a disease.

_____ You can only become overweight by eating too much and being inactive.

_____ Most fat people are unhealthy.

_____ Because men have less fat on their bodies, men are healthier than women.

_____ Fat people, on average, are less active, less happy, and more emotional than thin people.

_____ Low-calorie diets are an effective way to ensure long-term weight loss.

_____ You can never be "too thin."

BODY WEIGHT AND HEALTH

Overweight is often defined using a standard height/weight table generated in 1983 by the Metropolitan Life Insurance Company (Table 7.1). These tables contain desirable weights for individuals of different heights and various frame sizes. Desirable weight is the weight at which which the risk of death risk is lowest, based on information obtained from 4 million of Met Life's policy holders. In recent studies, overweight has been defined as approximately 20% or more above the desirable weight listed on these tables. For individuals of average height (women, 5'4"; men, 5'9"), this is equivalent to a body weight above 72 kg (158 pounds) in women and above 85 kg (187 pounds) in men. [Note that while the concept of "overweight" is acceptable in our culture, there is no such condition as "overheight," and no equivalent tables of "desirable height" exist. A normal distribution of heights is unquestioned, but this is not the case with body weight.]

A more common measure of weight now in use in scientific studies is the Body Mass Index, or BMI. BMI is equivalent to weight in kilograms divided by the square of height in meters. (For those who are unaccustomed to using metric measures, BMI can be calculated using this formula: BMI = [703 x weight in pounds]/height in inches, squared.) Using this measure, overweight has been generally defined as a BMI of 27.3 or more in women and 27.8 or more in men. This is approximately equal to the definition of overweight generated from the Metropolitan Life tables.

Using these standards, a large number of American adults belong in the overweight category — approximately 34 million people, or 24% of men and 27% of women. The percentage of individuals in this category has been steadily increasing over the past several decades. Between 1960 and 1980, the prevalence of being overweight among Caucasians increased by 3% in women and 6% in men and in African Americans by 7% in women and 28% in men. A high prevalence of overweight individuals is primarily an American phenomenon. For instance, the percentage of individuals in the population with a BMI greater than or equal to 30 is three times greater in the United States than in France.

TABLE 7.1
1983 METROPOLITAN INSURANCE COMPANY HEIGHT AND WEIGHT TABLES

Weights at ages 25 to 29 that correspond to lowest mortality

Weights in pounds for individuals of medium frame size

Men		Women	
Height	**Weight**	**Height**	**Weight**
5'2"	131–141	4'10"	109–121
5'3"	133–143	4'11"	111–123
5'4"	135–145	5'0"	123–126
5'5"	137–148	5'1"	115–129
5'6"	139–151	5'2"	118–132
5'7"	142–154	5'3"	121–135
5'8"	145–157	5'4"	124–138
5'9"	148–160	5'5"	127–141
5'10"	151–163	5'6"	130–144
5'11"	154–166	5'7"	133–147
6'0"	157–170	5'8"	136–150
6'1"	160–174	5'9"	139–153
6'2"	164–178	5'10"	142–156
6'3"	167–182	5'11"	145–159
6'4"	171–187	6'0"	148–162

Reprinted with permission from Metropolitan Life Insurance Company, Statistical Bulletin.

While these statistics may indicate that the U.S. population is suffering from an epidemic of obesity, they should be interpreted with some caution. For instance, note that the Metropolitan Life tables are generated from a subset of the American population, that is, those individuals who were insured by this particular company. This population is certainly not representative of the entire U.S. population, since it is primarily made up of the portions of our society who can afford life insurance policies. These tables also demonstrate a principle we discussed in Chapter 2: A correlation between two factors does not prove that one factor is responsible for the other. In other words, although Metropolitan Life has shown that the risk of death increases above particular weights, this relationship does not mean that being over these weights *causes* death.

What Are the Health Consequences of Being Overweight?

While most people have heard the message that being overweight is unhealthy, there is surprisingly little solid evidence that a large body mass in and of itself is a health risk. There are two major health concerns common in overweight individuals: diabetes and risk factors associated with heart disease.

Diabetes is a condition that occurs when the body experiences a change in the way it processes sugar. Insulin, a hormone that stimulates most body cells to take up circulating sugar from the bloodstream, is released after eating to help normalize sugar levels in the blood. If insulin is not produced, or if cells do not respond to it, sugar remains in the bloodstream and is excreted in the urine. Because sugar is not available as a fuel, in severe cases of diabetes the body may break down fat as a fuel. The waste products of this process may build up in the blood and can become life-threatening. Most cases of diabetes are not as severe, and the symptoms, including fatigue, headaches, and excessive thirst, are less threatening. Non-insulin dependent diabetes mellitus (NIDDM), a condition in which many tissues of the body are resistant to insulin, is more likely to occur in extremely overweight individuals. NIDDM is rarely a life-threatening condition, although it can obviously interfere with quality of life. NIDDM can be easily controlled by drugs, modification of diet, and exercise.

A BMI above 25 has been associated with risk factors for cardiovascular disease, including high concentrations of LDL, low concentrations of HDL, and increases in blood pressure (high blood pressure compounds the severity of arteriosclerosis development). The increase in risk factors at higher weights may correspond to an increase in heart disease and death. In most large, long-term, well-designed studies, the lowest morbidity (disease) and mortality rates occurred in adults with a BMI between 19 and 25. However, the *amount* of increase in mortality rate above a BMI of 25 is unclear. For instance, a long-term study of over 48,000 people in the Netherlands indicated that men with BMIs greater than or equal to 30 had a death rate 150% higher than men below this standard. The increase in likelihood of death was almost entirely due to increases in heart disease.

On the other hand, a study of Italian death records indicated that body weights 10 kg (22 lbs) above the desired weight (in most cases, this corresponds to preceeding definitions of overweight) increased the risk of death only minimally. The relationship between weight and risk of heart disease is especially unclear in women. Nearly all studies that test for a relationship between these factors have been performed on middle-aged men. In fact, in the study in the Netherlands, *no* relationship between weight and death due to heart disease was seen in women.

The variable results of studies on the relationship between weight and risk of death have caused researchers to modify their ideas about the relationship between body size and health. Clearly, not all overweight people have risk factors for heart disease, and many individuals classified as "desirable weight" suffer heart attacks. Several researchers have proposed that heart disease is not related to stored fat but instead is related to levels of fat in the bloodstream. Individuals with many fat cells, that are partially filled (and so can continue to store fat), demonstrate fewer risk factors than individuals with fewer fat cells that are completely filled. The risk of death may not be determined by total body fat but by an interaction between the amount of fat in the diet and the number of fat cells in the body.

There is experimental support for this hypothesis. In animal studies, restricting calories in genetically obese individuals reduces their risk factors below those of full-fed, thin animals even though the thin animals have much less body fat. These same results have been observed in humans as well. Measures associated with high risk of heart disease in overweight people (such as LDL concentration and blood pressure) often decline to normal levels with appropriate physical activities, dietary habits, and a small weight loss. This decline is maintained even when body weight remains above the recommended level.

The results of these studies may help explain other correlates of heart disease. In humans, regardless of BMI, the *distribution* of fat on the body has been associated with an increased risk of heart attack. There is a positive relationship between waist to hip ratio and prevalence of heart disease. This relationship probably corresponds to a difference in adipocytes in different regions of the body. Recall that adipocytes on the abdomen are more likely to release fat from storage into the bloodstream. Individuals who store fat here will have higher levels of circulating fat than individuals who store fat on the extremities, in adipocytes that are less "willing" to release stored fat. Like people with filled fat stores, individuals who store weight in abdominal adipocytes have more fat in the bloodstream. In both cases, higher levels of circulating fat probably correspond to higher levels of arteriosclerosis.

Is Your Weight Determined by Your Genes?

Your body weight reflects a complex relationship between your genetic makeup, your developmental environment, and your current environment. The number of fat cells you have is, at the very least, the result of both your particular genetic makeup and the amount of fat you stored when you were an infant. However, because of a persistent interest in finding single-factor causes for particular traits, there has been much recent research interest in discovering the "fat gene," which presumably causes obesity in its mutated form.

Studies of genetically obese mice have thus far identified two genes responsible for weight regulation in these animals. One, called the obese (*ob*) gene, codes for the hormone leptin. Leptin is produced by fat cells and functions as a signal of fullness. Mice that carry two nonfunctional copies of the *ob* gene do not produce this signal and will continue to eat even when their fat stores are full. The other mutation identified in some strains of obese mice is in the receptor for leptin. This receptor is found in the hypothalamus, a region of the brain that acts as a regulator for many body processes (e.g., the hypothalamus helps to regulate body temperature by signaling blood vessels in the skin to open or close to release or conserve heat). Mice who have two mutated copies of this gene may produce leptin but cannot respond to it. At this point, no equivalent mutations have been found in humans, although humans also produce leptin. In fact, studies of obese humans have found that leptin production in these individuals is relatively high. So, while injecting leptin-deficient mice with this hormone will cause them to lose weight, a similar magic bullet seems unlikely in humans.

Although your adult weight may not be set by your genes at birth, evidence is accumulating that adult weight is extremely difficult to modify. You are probably already aware of how strongly your body temperature is controlled. Despite radical changes in the temperature of your environment, your body temperature rarely strays from its set point, around 37° C (98.6° F). Your brain exhibits strong control over your body weight as well. If it did not, an increase in your food intake of just two chocolate chip cookies a day would lead to a weight increase of about 10 pounds in a year. Some scientists have argued for the existence of a physiological set point, which corresponds to the fat mass that your body will attempt to maintain. Some scientific evidence exists for this hypothesis. For instance, the activity of enzymes that promote fat storage in adipocytes increases as the volume of fat in these cells decreases, indicating that adipocytes attempt to actively maintain a certain degree of fullness. Evidence for a set point can also be seen from studies that show that most individuals who participate in restrictive diets to lose weight return to pre-diet weights within five years of ending the diet. Finally, analyses of several exercise-based weight loss programs have indicated that only modest weight loss (of <1 kg [2.2 lbs], and never more than 3 kg [6.6 lbs]) occurred even under the most strenuous training regimen. Our bodies, it seems, will stay close to a set weight point as long as we are eating to physical satisfaction.

SUMMARY

Overweight is defined according to standards set by a life insurance company, although little evidence exists that being overweight causes death. The health risks of fat may be related to the the amounts of fat in the bloodstream, rather than the size of an individual's fat stores. Genes that control weight have been identified in mice, and homologous genes have been found in humans, but obese humans have functional copies of these genes, unlike obese mice. The amount of fat stored on the body may be difficult to modify from an individual's physiological set point.

WOMEN AND WEIGHT

In order for a woman with average-sized hips to approach Barbie ® in appearance, she would need to increase 24 inches in height, 5 inches in bust size, 3.2 inches in neck length, and decrease 6 inches at the waist.

According to various surveys, as many as 40% of women but fewer than 25% of men are trying to lose weight at any given time. Given that the health risks of being overweight are unclear and so far seem to be more severe in men, it is interesting that so many women feel compelled to diet. (In fact, women are remarkably more healthy than men. According to the U.S. government, the life expectancy of a white female born in 1992 is 79.8 years, while for a white male it is only 73.2 years.) In a survey of 33,000 female readers of *Glamour* magazine, 75% indicated that they felt "too fat." Of these women, 45% were underweight according to the Metropolitan Life Insurance tables. Although readers of *Glamour* are not representative of the entire population of American women, a more recent random survey of 8,000 American women indicated that nearly 50% regarded themselves as overweight. Clearly, health risk is not the primary concern for many women who are trying to lose weight. In fact, in the segment of the American population that has the lowest death rate and probably is the least concerned about long-term health—teenagers—dieting to lose weight is astonishingly common. By the age of 13, 60% of girls have dieted to lose weight, by age 18, 80% have done so. Dieting is common among high schoolers despite the fact that the majority of these women are at or *below* normal weight.

Women's perceptions of ideal weight are heavily influenced by societal factors, as is evidenced by how quickly and often this ideal changes. Feelings about weight are also different among racial groups within our current society. For instance, in contrast to the feelings of the underweight white women described above, 40% of overweight African American women surveyed in Washington, D. C., noted that they consider their bodies attractive or very attractive. Because issues of weight control seem to be driven by societal norms rather than health concerns, this section will cover both the physiological and psychological consequences of the preoccupation with weight experienced by many women.

Dieting and the Body

Most women employ some form of restrictive, or low-calorie, diet in their efforts to lose weight. This strategy is sensible when the goal is rapid weight loss. If your energy intake (calories ingested) is lower than the energy required to sustain your current activity levels, your body will turn to energy stored in body tissues to survive. When you burn up your body tissues for energy, your weight drops.

One consequence of restricting your diet to below your daily energy output is the nearly constant feeling of hunger. Some dieters attempt to reduce this feeling by taking appetite-suppressants. Sales of appetite suppressants surpassed $526 million in the United States in 1996. These pills usually contain amphetamines ("speed"), which, in addition to suppressing appetite, cause nervousness, sleeplessness, and may increase blood pressure. The powerful appetite-suppressing drug cocktail fenfluramine/phentermine (commonly called "fen-phen"), was prescribed to millions of Americans for weight loss purposes before its association with irreversible damage to the heart and lungs was identified. The combination was taken off the market by the FDA in 1997, but only after at least 12 women died and countless others suffered severe consequences. Consumers of these types of drugs are primarily women, who pay a large physical and financial cost to conform to a socially determined ideal.

When calorie consumption drops below a critical level (i.e., for most women, 1,000 calories per day), the body makes several adjustments to maintain itself. The brain requires large amounts of energy for survival, but that energy must take the form of glucose. The breakdown of fat does not produce glucose. In order to provide this nutrient, the body of an individual on a very low-calorie diet begins breaking down stored protein, which is primarily found in muscle. Thus, some weight lost during these kinds of diets is due to the loss of skeletal muscle, not body fat. In addition, one waste product of the breakdown of stored fats in the body is ketone bodies. The body can handle small amounts of ketones in the bloodstream, but at high rates of fat breakdown, ketones can cause several unpleasant side effects, such as dizziness, headaches, and lethargy. After several weeks, the body adjusts to these higher levels of ketones and the side effects moderate.

As discussed in the section on weight and genetics, weight loss due to dieting is usually not maintained once the diet ceases. This means that many dieters, especially women, will engage in many diets throughout their lives. This cycling in weight over the course of a lifetime has been associated with negative health outcomes. Studies of this phenomenon have shown a positive relationship between weight variability and mortality from heart disease; that is, the more one's weight cycles, the more likely one is to suffer from heart disease. As with any correlation, this relationship does not indicate that weight cycling *causes* heart disease, but further study may be valuable for determining the relationship between these two factors. It may be the case that yo-yo dieting is as dangerous to good health as being overweight.

Eating Disorders

The average woman weighs approximately 64 kg, or 140 lbs. In 1990, the average weight of professional female models in the United States was 49 kg, or 109 lbs. This 23% difference between average women and the women who are our models of beauty is probably one of the major reasons so many women in the United States are dissatisfied with their bodies. The number one reason women state for engaging in restrictive diets is "to look better," followed by a much smaller number who diet to improve their health. An increased significance of thinness as a beauty trait can be seen in other affluent cultures as well. In Japan, the average weight per height of young women has steadily decreased from the 1950s through the 1980s. The researcher that documented this trend believes that the most important reason for this trend is a desire for "increased beauty" in this age group. The message that "thin is beautiful" is not confined to just adult models. Barbie®, one of the most popular toys in the United States, is a model of the successful, beautiful woman for even very young girls. However, Barbie's ® proportions are much different than the typical woman's. In order for a woman with average-sized hips to approach Barbie ® in appearance (Figure 7.4), she would need to increase 24 inches in height, 5 inches in bust size, 3.2 inches in neck length, and decrease 6 inches at the waist.

With such unrealistic models of beauty and the additional message that "fatness" is a condition to be reviled, it should be no surprise that most women are concerned about their weight and that some women engage in extreme behaviors to conform to these standards. The American Psychiatric Association has defined two classes of eating disorders associated with attempts at weight loss in the most recent volume of their Diagnostic and Statistical Manual (DSM-IV): anorexia nervosa and bulimia nervosa. Ninety-five percent of individuals diagnosed with anorexia or bulimia are women. Most of these women are young and relatively affluent. Table 7.2 lists the DSM-IV criteria for both of these diseases.

Essentially, bulimia is characterized by recurrent episodes of binge eating (eating food past the point of fullness) followed by some behavior that attempts to rid the body of excess calories. This behavior is commonly called purging and refers to either physical purging through self-induced vomiting, ingestion of laxatives or diet pills, or bouts of high intensity exercise. The physical side effects of bulimia depend somewhat on the method of purging. Self-induced vomiting can disturb heart rhythms, force stomach fluid into the lungs causing pneumonia, and damage dental enamel and the lining of the esophagus. The overuse of laxatives can also damage the heart and lead to mineral imbalances that may cause seizures and muscle weakness. Abuse of diet pills can cause high blood pressure, cerebral hemorrhages, and strokes.

FIGURE 7.4   Is Barbie ® a Real Woman?

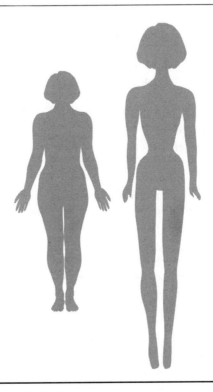

Barbie's ® silhouette compared to an average woman's silhouette. Notice the differences in relative leg length, waist size, and thinness.

TABLE 7.2
DSM-IV CRITERIA FOR DIAGNOSIS OF EATING DISORDERS

Bulimia Nervosa

1. Inconspicuous, recurrent episodes of binge eating

2. Consumption of high calorie, easily ingested food during bingeing

3. Termination of bingeing by abdominal pain, sleep, social interruption, self-induced vomiting

4. Repeated attempts to lose weight with severely restricted diets, self-induced vomiting, or use of cathartics or diuretics

5. Frequent significant weight fluctuations

6. Awareness that eating pattern is abnormal, fear of not being able to stop voluntarily

7. Depressed mood and self-deprecating thoughts following binges

Anorexia Nervosa

1. Weight loss of at least 15% of original body weight

2. Intense fear of becoming obese, which does not diminish

3. Distortion of body image

4. Loss of menstrual period

5. Excessive physical activity

6. Food binges followed by fasting, laxatives, or vomiting

Bulimia is remarkably common among college-aged women, with estimates ranging from 5 to 20% of women in this group conforming to the DSM-IV criteria. Nearly 79% of college age women have bulimic episodes. The prevalence of these behaviors has caused some feminists to ask why they are considered symptoms of a psychiatric disorder, because this would require defining the *majority* of college-age women as psychologically abnormal.

Although less common, anorexia is more dangerous than bulimia and is characterized by a body weight of 15% below original weight. Chronic and extreme caloric restriction may lead to loss of heart muscle tissue resulting in heart failure or the general failure of organ systems that are not receiving adequate support. The mortality rate of individuals with anorexia is approximately 5%. Anorexics are less likely than bulimics to see that they are engaging in dangerous behavior and more likely to be resistant to intervention. These women are extremely fearful of being obese and may literally starve themselves to death in their attempt to lose weight.

The most common physical consequence of dramatic weight loss is experienced both by women who are diagnosed with anorexia and bulimia and women with less serious eating disorders. Some aspect of eating disorders, probably either nutritional imbalance or changes in blood sugar, disrupts certain hormone production pathways causing a dramatic drop in estrogen levels in the body. At these low levels, menstruation ceases and the rate of bone loss increases, much as bone loss increases when estrogen declines after menopause. Women experiencing long periods with low estrogen levels are at a greater risk of developing stress fractures and the other symptoms of osteoporosis. A recent study of women athletes indicated that amenorrheic athletes had significantly lower bone density at most points of measurement than athletes with normal menstruation. Because osteoporosis is irreversible, estrogen declines in youth may lead to consequences that remain throughout life. Intervention, in the form of hormone replacement therapy, calcium supplementation, nutritional therapy, and changes in training schedule, can help to reduce or stop the decline in bone density experienced by these women.

As many as 30% of professional tennis players, 33% of elite cross country runners, and 62% of college gymnasts practice some extreme form of weight control. Eating disorders and subsequent osteoporosis and loss of menstruation may be more common among female athletes than other women. In fact, these three associated conditions have been termed the "Female Athlete Triad" by researchers studying these athletes. Besides the general social pressure that puts a premium on thinness, many sports physicians argue that female athletes experience extra pressure from coaches, judges, and peers to conform to a particular body type associated with success. Whether athletes actually do have higher rates of eating disorders, amenorrhea, and low bone density than nonathletic women is still an open question, however, and some researchers have proposed calling these three associated states the "Female Triad."

Although the psychological and physiological events that trigger the onset of eating disorders are unclear, restrictive dieting itself may trigger obsessive eating behaviors. One of the most revealing experiments having to do with the effect of starvation on the body was performed in the late 1940s at the University of Minnesota. In this experiment, 36 young, healthy, emotionally stable young men were put on a six month diet of semi-starvation, in which their caloric intake was reduced by one half (not an unusual diet for women seeking rapid weight loss). After losing 25% of their body weight, the men became increasingly preoccupied with food, experienced some form of emotional disturbance (such as depression, anger, and psychosis), were less able to function effectively in work and social contexts, and experienced relentless hunger, followed by powerful urges to break the diet (including engaging in binge/purge behavior). None of these behaviors was associated with any measured psychological characteristics of the participants before the diet. Frighteningly, many of these problems persisted after the men were taken off the diet. Thus, women who diet in response to pressure to conform to a social ideal may be putting themselves at risk for developing a disabling eating disorder.

The effects of the social pressures of the thin ideal are not confined to women with eating disorders. That some women react more strongly to these pressures is well within the realm of normal human response. Individual women can make a contribution to reducing the numbers of, or impact on, women with these disorders. This is true because all individuals in this society are in part responsible for supporting the beauty norms that contribute to eating disorders.

> Each time we diet, each time we judge our personal value on the basis of appearance, each time we criticize others or feel better than them based on how they look, each time we positively reinforce weight loss, or even each time we sit around in groups and complain in a comradely way about our bodies, we contribute to the perpetuation of the pressure to be thin. . . Overcoming weight preoccupation, giving up dieting, or accepting one's body as it is, is by no means easy, but the only way off the treadmill is for women themselves to reject the value of thinness and rebel against its tyranny. We need to recognize the strength and courage it takes to rebel against predominant social values. Most importantly, we must recognize the necessity of our doing so.
>
> C. Brown, *Consuming Passions: Feminist Perspectives on Weight Preoccupation and Eating Disorders*, *pp. 67–68*

In order for women to lead happy and healthy lives, our preoccupation with obtaining an ideal weight must be discarded. All of the research discussed in this chapter indicates that a healthy lifestyle is not measured by the number of pounds read on a scale but by a balanced diet and sufficient exercise. In addition, health for women is also related to characteristics of their social lives. For instance, for working women, death, malignancy, and stroke are much less common when they are in a supportive work atmosphere. Women interested in maintaining their and other's health should work for improving the lives of all women. This includes supporting and promoting the acceptance of all of the shapes, sizes, and colors that make up the wonderful diversity of women.

SUMMARY

Many women engage in restrictive dieting for reasons of appearance rather than for health. Restrictive dieting can have several unpleasant side effects including a constant feeling of hunger, lethargy, headaches, loss of muscle tissue, and, if followed by weight regain, possibly heart disease. A societal focus on a particularly thin ideal of beauty may contribute to eating disorders, which have several severe side effects, including osteoporosis and organ failure. The prevalence of eating disorders may only decline when discrimination against fatness is eliminated.

■ DISCUSSION EXERCISE 2

This exercise expands on Discussion Exercise 1. *All of the statements you evaluated in that exercise are false.*

Imagine that you are starting a new society. You and your class strongly believe the truth of one of the statements in Exercise 1 (pick one). You want to affirm, promote, reinforce, support, and expand this idea throughout your new society. What will you do? Brainstorm for 5 to 10 minutes on this issue.

Then, consider the following questions:

2.1. How does your society compare with our own? What are the similarities? What are the differences? How would fat people in this society feel?

2.2. How much do you apply this myth (or the others discussed) to yourself or others? How do you act out or reinforce this myth?

2.3. Do you think that the "average person" believes this myth to be true? Given your knowledge of biology, how can you act to dispel this myth? How would your imaginary society change if you dispelled this myth? How would our society change?

[Exercise adapted from Christian, (1995). S. S. *Working With Groups to Explore Food and Body Connections.*]

REFERENCES

American Psychiatric Assocation. *Diagnostic and Statistical Manual of Mental Disorders* (4th ed.) American Psychiatric Association, 1994.

Abernathy R. P. & Black, D. R. (1996). Healthy body weights: An alternative perspective. *American Journal of Clinical Nutrition 63* (3Suppl), 448S–451S.

Attie, I., & Brooks-Gunn, J. (1987). Weight concerns as chronic stressors in women. In R. C. Barnett, L. Biener, & G. K. Baruch, *Gender and stress.* The Free Press.

Ballor, D. L. (1996). Exercise training and body composition changes. In A. F. Roche, S. B. Heymsfield, & T. G. Lohman (Eds.), *Human body composition.* Human Kinetics Publishers.

Bjorntorp, P., & Eden, S. (1996). Hormonal influences on body composition. In A. F. Roche, S. B. Heymsfield, & T. G. Lohman (Eds.), *Human body composition.* Human Kinetics Publishers.

Blackburn, G. (1995). Effect of degree of weight loss on health benefits. *Obesity Research 3* (Suppl. 2), 211s–216s

Bouchard, C. (1996). Genetic influence on human body composition. In A. F. Roche, S. B. Heymsfield, & T. G. Lohman (Eds.), *Human body composition.* Human Kinetics Publishers.

Brown, C. (1993). The continuum: Anorexia, bulimia, and weight preoccupation. In C. Brown, & K. Jasper (Eds.), *Consuming passions: Feminist approaches to weight preoccupation and eating disorders.* Second Story Press.

Brownell, K. D., & Napolitano, M. A. (1995). Distorting reality for children: Body size proportions of Barbie and Ken dolls. *International Journal of Eating Disorders* 18(3): 295–998.

Carlson, K. J., Eisenstat, S. A., & Ziporyn, T. (1996). *The Harvard guide to women's health.* Harvard University Press.

Christian, S. S. (1995). *Working with groups to explore food and body connections.* Whole Person Associates.

Hamann A., & Matthaei, S. (1996). Regulation of energy balance by leptin. *Experimental & Clinical Endocrinology & Diabetes* 104(4), 293–300.

Hibbard, J. H., & Pope, C. R. (1993). The quality of social roles as predictors of morbidity and mortality. *Social Science and Medicine* 36 (3), 217–225.

Jeejeebhoy, K. H. (1996).Body composition in weight loss and pathological states. In A. F. Roche, S. B. Heymsfield, & T. G. Lohman (Eds.), *Human body composition,* pp. 275–283. Human Kinetics Publishers.

Kumanyika, S., Wilson, J. F., Guilford-Davenport, M. (1993). Weight related attitudes and behaviors of black women. *Journal of the American Dietetic Association* 93(4), 416–422.

Londeree, B. R. (1993). Gender differences in circulorespiratory and metabolic variables related to endurance performance. In A. J. Pearl (Ed.), *The athletic female.* Human Kinetics Publishers.

Malina, R. F. (1996). Regional body composition: Age, sex, and ethnic variation. In A. F. Roche, S. B. Heymsfield, & T. G. Lohman (Eds.), *Human body composition,* pp.217–256. Human Kinetics Publishers, 1996.

Menotti, A., Descovich, G. C., Lanti, M., Spagnolo, A., Dormi, A., & Seccareccia, F. (1993). Indexes of obesity and all-causes mortality in Italian epidemiological data. *Preventative Medicine* 22, 293–303.

National Center for Health Statistics. Anthropometric reference data and prevalence of overweight, United States, 1976–1980. *Vital and Health Statistics, Series 11,* No. 238.

Rencken, M. L., Chesnut III, C. H., & Drinkwater, B. L. (1996). Bone density at multiple skeletal sites in amenorrheic athletes. *Journal of the American Medical Association.* 276(3),238–240.

Seidell, J. C. (1996). Relationships of total and regional body composition to morbidity and mortality. In A. F. Roche, S. B. Heymsfield, & T. G. Lohman (Eds.). *Human Body Composition,* pp. 345–353. Human Kinetics Publishers.

Seidell, J. C., Verschuren, W. M , van Leer, E. M., & Kromhout, D. (1996). Overweight, underweight, and mortality: A prospective study of 48,287 men and women. *Archives of Internal Medicine* 156(9): 958–963.

Takahaski, E. (1986). Secular trend of female body shape in Japan. *Human Biology* 58(2), 293–301.

Tavris, C. (1992). *The mismeasure of woman.* Touchstone.

Thornberry, O. T., Wilson, R. W., & Golden, P. (1986). Health promotion and disease prevention: Provisional data from the National Health Interview Survey: United States, January–June, 1985. *Vital and Health Statistics of the National Center for Health Statistics,* 119, 1–16.

VanItallie, T. B. (1996). Prevalence of obesity. *Endocrinology & Metabolism Clinics of North America* 25(4), 887–905.

Viru, A. (1995). *Adaptation in sports training.* CRC Press.

Williamson, D. F. (1993). Descriptive epidemiology of body weight and weight change in U.S. adults. *Annals of Internal Medicine* 119(7),646–649.

Wooley, S. C., & Wooley, O. W. (Feb. 1984). 33,000 women tell how they really feel about their bodies. *Glamour.*

CHAPTER 8

Menstruation is one of the most remarkable events in biology. It is a cycle that depends on intricate interrelationships between the brain, the pituitary gland, the ovaries, and the uterus.

MENSTRUATION

INTRODUCTION

Given that menstruation is an experience universal to women, it is surprising how little it is discussed (except, usually, in negative terms) and even more surprising how little many women and men know about this cycle. Many women may remember the myths they heard about menstruation as they were growing up—that you shouldn't exercise or bathe when you're menstruating, that intercourse during menstruation is dangerous, or that "that time of the month" is much more psychologically difficult than any other time.

Thankfully, women learn through experience with the menstrual cycle that these myths are just that, and most women become accustomed to the physical changes that occur during a typical month. However, many women have learned little about the real menstrual cycle beyond what they were told by the school nurse in elementary school, and some women find menstruation extremely debilitating and view their periods with dread and loathing.

In this chapter, we hope to promote honest discussion of women's menstrual experience. Menstruation is not an illness, nor is it without effect on women's lives. The more women and men understand this cycle, the less it will be shrouded in potentially damaging myth and taboo.

THE EVOLUTIONARY ORIGIN OF MENSTRUATION

Humans, like nearly all mammals and some fish, sharks, and amphibians, give birth to live young that the mother has nourished inside her body. This is in contrast to the many other vertebrate animals that lay eggs and whose embryonic development occurs outside the body.

Animals that support the developing offspring inside the mother's body require a place in the adult female body for this development to occur and a nutritive connection between the mother and offspring. In mammals, that place is the uterus, and the lining of the uterus—the endometrium—provides early nutritional support for the developing embryo.

Interestingly, while the endometrium does provide some nutritional support to a developing offspring, it may have evolved from an inflammatory reaction. An embryo is not genetically identical to its mother and, unless protected from her immune system, would be detected as a foreign invader and destroyed. In reptiles and birds, the eggshell can function to encapsulate the embryo and maintain it separately from the mother's bloodstream. Mammals, without this protective covering, prepare the uterus as if *in anticipation of* an infection. The buildup of tissue in the uterus before ovulation parallels the inflammatory reaction mammals experience when an infectious organism attacks a portion of the body, lending support to this hypothesis of origin.

Endometrial tissue requires energy for maintenance. In all mammals, the lining of the uterus waxes and wanes in response to ovulatory cycles. In *most* mammal species, the buildup and regression of the endometrium occurs internally—the endometrial tissue proliferates before ovulation and is almost completely *reabsorbed into the body* if fertilization does not occur. This process is known as the estrus cycle. A female mammal with this cycle is in estrus (sometimes called "in heat") immediately before and during ovulation. The word *estrus* comes from the Latin word for "frenzy," which refers to the behavior of both sexes during this time period. During estrus, females will actively solicit mates by releasing scent and increasing their tolerance of male company. Male mammals, in response to these solicitations, will often engage in ritual combat with other males in order to advertise their qualities as male parents. Because these behavioral changes make animals less cautious, human hunters have learned to take advantage of this biological process when hunting mammals—hunting season for deer, moose, and bear all correspond to the estrus season. Although in these large animals estrus occurs only once a year, smaller mammals have more rapid estrus cycles. In rats, for example, estrus can occur once every five days.

The menstrual cycle differs from the estrus cycle in that the endometrial lining is shed from the body instead of reabsorbed if fertilization does not occur. Menstruation occurs in humans and some other primates, but not in any other group of mammals. Mammals with menstrual cycles do not exhibit as large a degree of behavioral change as mammals with estrus cycles. Thus, the exact time of ovulation appears to be hidden in menstruating mammals as well.

The origin of the menstrual cycle in primates has proven a continuing puzzle to evolutionary biologists. Some scientists have speculated that menstruation evolved to protect the uterus from disease-causing organisms introduced in semen. According to this hypothesis, regular menstruation would be advantageous to women because it dislodges infected tissues and carries disease organisms from the body. However, tests of this idea have shown that there is no difference in the number of bacteria in a woman's uterus before and after menstruation. Additionally, although within a species females with more partners are more susceptible to sexually transmitted disease, there is no relationship among the primates between how many sexual partners an average female has and the average amount of tissue she loses during menstruation. Menstruation does not seem to have evolved as a method of protecting female primates against sexually transmitted diseases.

Other scientists have hypothesized that bleeding during menstruation may be simply a result of having large babies. Large babies require a large uterus, and primate babies, especially humans, are quite large at birth compared to the size of the mother. It may be the case that menstruation occurs because women simply cannot reabsorb all of the endometrial tissue lining of this large uterus in a short amount of time. In fact, women and other female primates reabsorb about two thirds of the endometrium. The blood and tissue lost during menstruation may just represent excess material that was impossible to reabsorb.

Because there are few distinct changes in the sexual behavior of female animals that menstruate, some sociobiologists have hypothesized that menstruation is a "side effect" of hidden ovulation. Female mammals with estrus cycles advertise their ovulatory status. Males can thus be assured that their attentions have a good probability of resulting in a fertilization, and they will be less likely to invest energy in supporting non-estral females. Females that hide ovulation can "trick" males into supporting them even when they are not actually fertile, since in order to ensure fathering an offspring, males would have to spend long periods of time with a female. If male help increases the amount of food available to a pregnant female supplies food for any additional children, females with hidden ovulation should have more successful offspring than females who advertise their fertility status. Perhaps menstruation is simply a physiological necessity for females who hide ovulation.

As with most sociobiological hypotheses (see Chapter 3), the "true" origin of hidden ovulation is impossible to determine through experimentation. However, this hypothesis assumes that in menstruating species ovulation is in fact hidden. On the contrary, both obvious and subtle changes occur in human females around the time of ovulation, and these changes may have acted as signals in the past, even though our current cultural conditions make them seem hidden. An obvious change that occurs in females before ovulation is in the amount and consistency of the mucus produced by the cervix. The cervix is the portion of the uterus at the top of the vagina (see Chapter 6). Immediately before ovulation, the cervical mucus changes from scant and gummy to copious and slick in texture. Most women can easily observe changes in the mucus throughout their cycle and with practice can pinpoint the time of ovulation with a reasonable degree of accuracy. Women also experience increases in sensory acuity, increases in feelings of sexual arousal, and significant changes in body temperature (see below) around the time of ovulation. More subtle changes occur around ovulation that may be observable as well. Women may become more symmetrical in appearance as they approach ovulation. A recent study demonstrated that the size difference between the left and right ears and fingers on the left and right hands decreased markedly in women immediately before ovulation. If both men and women can observe these cues, the timing of ovulation is not as hidden as once thought. Regardless whether ovulation in women is in fact hidden, sociobiologists do not explain why hiding ovulation may *cause* menstruation. Explanations of why hidden ovulation might exist do not help us understand why women experience monthly periods.

Menstruation and the Moon

Women have long been aware of the relationship between the lunar cycle (from new moon to full moon and back) and the menstrual cycle. In fact, although the typical menstrual cycle is often described as 28 days, the *average* (but not most common) length is 29.5 days— the same length as the lunar cycle. However, little evidence exists that the lunar cycle actually *determines* the course of the menstrual cycle. Many biological cycles become entrained to environmental cycles. For instance, the circadian rhythm, that governs our sleep/wake cycle is, in most people, entrained to day length. When people experience artificially altered light/dark cycles that differ from 24 hours, their sleep/wake pattern entrains to the new light rhythm. However, light cycles do not "control" the circadian rhythm. Humans exposed to a constant light environment will gradually adopt a day cycle of 24.87 hours, which is longer than the solar day but equal to the lunar day. In this case, humans are probably entrained to moon-caused changes in the Earth's electromagnetic field.

Entrainment with environmental cycles is very likely not limited to the circadian rhythm. The moon's affect on menstruation may also be related to changes its cycle produces in the Earth's electromagnetic fields. Events in a woman's menstrual cycle may be entrained with the electromagnetic changes associated with a particular moon phase. Clearly, even this possible entrainment relationship is not strong, because the vast majority of women do not have a menstrual cycle length that *equals* the lunar cycle length. So, while some of the slang expressions for menstruation (e.g. "she's on her moon") reflect the similarities between the lunar cycle and the menstrual cycle, there is no reason to suspect that the menstrual cycle is any different from the other environmentally influenced biological cycles humans experience.

The "Typical" Cycle

Although the average length of the menstrual cycle is around 29.5 days, descriptions of menstruation tend to utilize a menstrual period of 28 days for convenience. Few women have a cycle of 28, 29, or 30 days—in fact, it is estimated that only 30% of women fall in this range. Cycles range from 20 to 40 days in length and tend to shorten from menarche (first menstruation) through the beginnings of menopause. Women who have tracked their menstrual cycles know that their cycles vary around an average length, some considerably. In a number of surveys, 15% to 20% of women identify themselves as having irregularly occurring periods. On average, menses (the actual period of bleeding) lasts about 5 days, although again there is considerable variation from month to month and from woman to woman. During menses, an average of 2 ounces of blood is lost.

The menstrual cycle is tied to the ovarian cycle, although menses can occur without ovulation. The percentage of cycles with no ovulation (anovulatory) decrease from 38% of cycles in women aged 20 to 24 to 9% in women in their early 30s, a time considered to be their reproductive "peak."

SUMMARY

The development of a protective lining in the reproductive organs is limited to animals who give birth to live young. This lining serves both as protection from the immune system of the mother and as a nutritional supply for a developing embryo. The menstrual cycle is unique to primates and differs from the estrus cycle—in menstruation some of the endometrium is expelled, whereas in the estrus cycle the endometrium is almost entirely reabsorbed. The origin of the menstrual cycle is in dispute, but it may be a side effect of having a large uterus, making complete reabsorption of the endometrium physically impossible. The link of the menstrual cycle to moon cycles is at best indirect. Women's menstrual experiences vary, but most women have relatively regular cycles.

PHYSIOLOGY OF MENSTRUATION

Menstruation is one of the most remarkable events in biology. It is a cycle that depends on intricate interrelationships between the brain, the pituitary gland, the ovaries, and the uterus. During the course of a single menstrual cycle, a woman's body prepares an egg for possible fertilization, prepares her uterus for a potential pregnancy, "evaluates" whether pregnancy has occurred, and if it hasn't, reabsorbs and excretes the uterine lining and begins a new cycle (Figure 8.1). The more women know about the events of the cycle, the more they will understand and successfully anticipate the complex changes that result from its function.

In the interest of clarity and simplicity, we include in this chapter a discussion of only the major events and primary hormones of the cycle. Readers should realize, however, that our understanding of menstruation is continually being modified and that the cycle is substantially more intricate than the process depicted here.

Hormones

The menstrual cycle is regulated by changes in the levels and frequency of release of a number of hormones. Recall that hormones are chemicals secreted in one area of the body, and are carried through the bloodstream, and they are recognized by and have an effect

FIGURE 8.1   Figurative Expression of the Events of the Menstrual Cycle

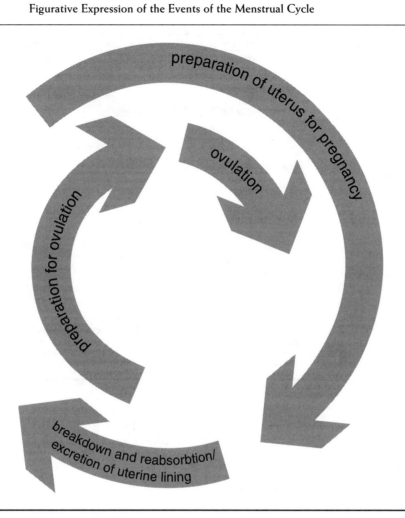

on target cells in other parts of the body. The key hormones of the menstrual cycle are produced in the pituitary, hypothalamus, ovaries, and endometrium. The major hormones of the menstrual cycle and their functions are summarized in Table 8.1.

The pituitary gland, located near the base of the brain, secretes the Follicle Stimulating Hormone (FSH) and Luteinizing Hormone (LH), which directly effect the ovaries. Because these hormones act directly on gonads, they are called *gonadotropic*. The amount of FSH and LH released from the pituitary into the bloodstream is controlled by another hormone produced by the hypothalamus. This hormone, called Gonadotropin Releasing Hormone (GnRH), is secreted by cells in the hypothalamus directly into the veins serving the pituitary, which are located below it in the brain. GnRH is released from the hypothalamus in pulses.

FSH and LH are stimulated by different GnRH pulse frequencies. When GnRH stimulus occurs in slow pulses, the pituitary is stimulated to produce FSH. An increase in GnRH pulse frequency will cause a shift in the pituitary to LH synthesis. The pulse frequency of GnRH is partially regulated by levels of ovarian hormones.

FSH and LH help to regulate the activities of the ovaries. Ovaries produce the hormones progesterone and estrogen in response to stimulation by these hormones. In a complicated feedback relationship, these ovarian hormones in turn regulate GnRH, LH, and FSH levels.

TABLE 8.1
HORMONES OF THE MENSTRUAL CYCLE

Hormone	Where Produced	Stimulated by	Target	Function
GnRH	hypothalamus	low estradiol very high estradiol	pituitary	stimulates production of LH and FSH
FSH	pituitary	low frequency GnRH pulses	ovary	stimulates follicle growth
LH	pituitary	high frequency GnRH pulses	ovary	triggers ovulation
estradiol (estrogen)	ovarian follicles	FSH stimulation of ovaries	breasts, cervix, endometrium, hypothalamus	stimulates mammary gland growth, changes in cervical mucus, some endometrial proliferation
progesterone	corpus luteum (ovary)	LH stimulation	endometrium, breast	stimulates proliferation of endometrium, some breast development
prostaglandin	endometrium	progesterone stimulation of endometrium	uterus, other	induces muscle contractions to propel egg down oviduct and endometrial tissue out of body

The endometrium, which grows in response to stimulation by estrogen and progesterone, also produces a hormone called prostaglandin. Changes in prostaglandin levels lead to the loss of blood and tissue during menses.

A Month in the Life

In standard practice a cycle of 28 days, divided into shorter phases, is used to illustrate the changes that occur in ovarian and menstrual cycles. This text will conform to this practice, although so-called cycle and phase length vary greatly from this average.

Figure 8.2 illustrates the changes in hormone levels, endometrium condition, and ovaries that occur throughout the model 28-day cycle. You may wish to refer to the figure frequently to help you understand the complex, interrelated processes that occur during a typical "month in the life" of a menstruating woman.

Follicular Phase   Although the cycle is typically said to begin with the first day of menstruation, it is easier to describe the changes that occur beginning with day 6 and ending with menstruation, on days 1 through 5. Days 6 through 12 are called the follicular phase and are marked by the ripening of a single ovarian follicle.

During menstruation and the early part of the follicular phase, FSH and LH levels are relatively high. As you might guess by its name, FSH stimulates the growth of follicles in the ovary. Follicles consist of an egg cell and the cells immediately surrounding it (see Chapter 9). FSH levels begin to rise before menstruation occurs and stay at relatively high levels until late in the follicular phase.

During the follicular phase, FSH stimulates the multiplication of the follicle cells surrounding the egg. Numerous follicles on both ovaries begin to develop in response to FSH stimulation. When follicles reach 9 millimeters in diameter, they begin to produce

FIGURE 8.2   The Events of the Menstrual Cycle

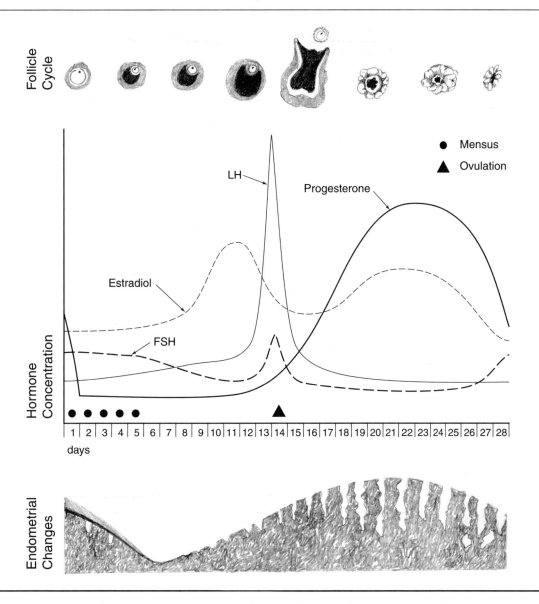

Changes in hormone levels, endometrial condition, and ovarian follicles over the course of the menstrual cycle. The first day of menstrual flow marks the first day of the cycle as drawn here.

the most common form of estrogen, estradiol. Moderately high levels of estradiol inhibit GnRH production by the hypothalamus, which in turn slows FSH synthesis. Estradiol also directly inhibits FSH production by the pituitary, and these two effects lead to a dramatic decline in FSH production.

As FSH declines, ovarian follicle development slows down, except for a single, dominant follicle (rarely, there may be two or more dominant follicles that are ovulated). Although the mechanism of dominant follicle selection is not yet clear, it appears that the largest follicle somehow "captures" the remaining FSH and continues to develop and synthesize additional estradiol. The dominant follicle also begins to synthesize relatively small amounts of progesterone, the hormone typically associated with the second half of the cycle. The remaining, nondominant follicles will regress and the material is reabsorbed by the ovaries.

Estradiol stimulates the thickening of the endometrium, and days 6 through 12 are sometimes called the proliferative phase to reflect the changes occurring in the uterus. Estradiol also seems to affect the production of cervical mucus. The mucus, which had been thick and gummy, increases in abundance, thins, and becomes slick in texture. This change facilitates the passage of sperm from the vagina to the oviducts, where fertilization occurs (see Chapter 9).

At the end of the follicular phase, FSH levels are low, estradiol levels have increased dramatically, and the endometrial lining is well developed.

Pre-Ovulatory Phase   Day 13 in our example cycle marks the peak of estradiol production by the dominant follicle. Although estradiol suppresses GnRH release at moderately high levels (i.e., those seen during the follicular phase), it has the opposite effect at very high levels—GnRH production is suddenly induced, and GnRH pulse frequency rapidly increases. This rapid GnRH stimulation of the pituitary favors LH production and, on day 14, LH reaches its highest level in the cycle. FSH production is also stimulated, but this may simply be a side effect. Recall that low frequency GnRH pulses stimulate the production of FSH. This hormone is probably produced as the GnRH pulses are rapidly increasing in frequency in response to the estrogen peak. The LH and FSH surge lasts only 24 hours.

LH stimulation of the follicle triggers progesterone production, and progesterone begins to rise immediately after the LH peak. Progesterone also inhibits continued LH production; the LH surge is immediately inhibited by the ovarian hormones it stimulates.

Ovulation   Ovulation occurs 10 to 12 hours after the LH peak, around day 15 of the typical cycle. The dominant follicle has reached 2 centimeters in diameter by this time and has produced receptors for LH. In response to the LH surge, the egg is stimulated to develop (see Chapter 9). The follicle then literally bursts open, releasing the egg into the body cavity where it is drawn into the oviducts.

Prostaglandin, the hormone produced by the endometrium, also rises in level in response to the LH surge. Prostaglandin stimulates muscle contraction and aids in propelling the egg down the oviducts. These muscular contractions cause lower abdominal pain, known as Mittleschmerz, in some women.

Sperm can live for 2 to 3 days outside of the testes, but an egg will survive for only about 12 to 24 hours after ovulation. If fertilization occurs, implantation will take place around day 19. If not, the egg breaks down and is reabsorbed or leaves the body through the vagina.

Immediately after ovulation, progesterone levels increase dramatically. This rise in hormone level causes a rapid rise in body temperature (typically about 0.5° C). Various methods of birth control use this temperature change to determine when ovulation has occurred (see Chapter 12).

Luteal Phase   After ovulation, a follicle becomes a corpus luteum (Latin for "yellow body," indicating the color of this structure on the ovary). The luteal phase during a cycle that does not result in pregnancy is characterized by the effects of the corpus luteum as it slowly regresses. The luteal phase occurs from day 16 to day 23 of a typical cycle.

The corpus luteum is an hormone-producing (endocrine) tissue that makes progesterone and estradiol. These hormones stimulate production of the endometrium, which becomes much more well-connected to the woman's bloodstream during the luteal phase. Because the endometrium is itself an endocrine tissue, its increased mass contributes to an increase in the production of prostaglandins. Prostaglandin in turn inhibits the corpus luteum.

While progesterone production by the corpus luteum reaches its peak early in the luteal phase, estradiol production lags behind slightly behind. Rising estradiol levels again inhibit

GnRH production, and LH levels begin to decline. The combined effects of decreased LH and increased prostaglandins produced by the enlarging endometrium cause the regression of the corpus luteum.

By the end of the luteal cycle, progesterone and estradiol levels are high, LH levels are low, and the yellow body itself is shrinking in size.

Premenstrual Phase   The premenstrual phase lasts from day 24 to day 28 and is marked by a rapid decline in progesterone and estradiol and the disintegration of the corpus luteum and endometrium.

The final disintegration of the corpus luteum, a process that began in the luteal phase, causes an immediate and dramatic decline in progesterone and estradiol production. The rapid loss of these two hormones causes the arteries supplying the endometrium to spasm (contract strongly). The endometrial tissue is thus deprived of its nutritional support.

The loss of endometrial tissue is an active process and is caused by an increase in an enzyme that breaks down collagen, a fibrous protein that serves as the base for the endometrium. The production and activity of this enzyme is tightly controlled by different levels of estrogen and progesterone, and it is more active in the premenstrual phase. Without degradation of collagen, the endometrium would be maintained indefinitely.

If fertilization has occurred, the process of endometrial breakdown is halted. The life of the corpus luteum is lengthened by a hormone produced by the placenta, a membrane produced by the developing embryo, and the endometrium. With the corpus luteum intact, progesterone and estradiol levels remain high, and thus the endometrium is maintained. In pregnant women, the corpus luteum finally disintegrates about week 6 or 7 of pregnancy, when the placenta begins to produce progesterone (see Chapter 10).

Menstrual Phase   The menstrual phase, days 1–5 of the cycle, are actually rather uneventful compared to the rest of the cycle. Of course, this contrasts with women's experience, since most women are relatively unaware of their cycle *except* during these days. The menstrual phase is characterized by menses, the loss of endometrial tissue and blood through the cervix and vagina. Prostaglandin, which has been rising in level as the endometrium proliferated, is abundant in menstrual blood. Recall that this hormone promotes muscular contractions—prostaglandin speeds the rate of blood and tissue loss by causing contractions of the uterine wall. Because these muscles are rapidly and rhythmically contracting, they may fatigue. Menstrual cramps are thus like other muscle cramps that occur after intense exercise. Prostaglandin may also cause contractions of other nearby muscles, like those surrounding the intestinal tract. Many women find that gastrointestinal discomfort accompanies the first day of menstruation because of this effect.

Estradiol levels remain low during the menstrual phase, and thus are not inhibiting GnRH or FSH production. As FSH levels rise, follicles begin to ripen, and the cycle begins anew.

SUMMARY
The progress of the menstrual cycle is summarized by Figure 8.2. The cycle is marked by complex interrelationships between the hypothalamus, the pituitary, the ovaries, and the endometrium.

MANAGEMENT OF MENSTRUATION

Typically, only two types of excretion are not under the voluntary control of an adult—perspiration and menses. While abundant perspiration is often considered undesirable, very little social censure is associated with normal levels of perspiration. We *expect* that athletes will perspire profusely during activity, actors and people at press conferences will perspire under intense lighting, and that everyone perspires in hot, humid weather. However, displaying any evidence of menses, also an extremely common process not under voluntary control, is strictly taboo. Outlines of sanitary pads in clothing are hidden, tampons are concealed in clever cases, and any visible bloodstain causes extreme embarrassment to a menstruating woman and those with whom she interacts. Women are under a great deal of social pressure to hide the fact they are menstruating and nearly all women employ some form of menses management..

Before the advent of sanitary napkins, nearly all women in the United States caught expelled endometrial tissue and blood on pieces of cloth or cotton batting. These cloths were rinsed after use and reused. Some women today still employ cloths in menses management, but most U.S. women use some sort of disposable menstrual protection.

The first sanitary pads were developed in the 1920s. These consisted of gauze-wrapped cotton pads that attached to an elastic belt worn around the waist. As new materials became available, the pads changed, adding adhesive so the belt was no longer needed, including a plastic liner to reduce the possibility of soaking through the pad, and incorporating polyester fibers that could draw liquid away from the skin's surface. Today's sanitary pads would seem exotic to the women who welcomed the first belted pads of the 1920s.

Sanitary pads have recently obtained a new function—covering the odor of menstruation. Menstrual blood has no odor on exit from the body but, in contact with air, will allow the growth of bacteria. Rarely is this odor noticeable, but many pads now include some type of deodorant. Mini-pads or "panty liners" are now advertised for everyday use as a method for reducing odor (i.e., "staying fresh"). Some feminists have been alarmed by this trend, because the implication of this product is that a woman's body is unclean every day (not just during her period, as women used to be told). Women are encouraged to be constantly vigilant so that the odors of their womanhood do not offend others. Besides the message that is implied by deodorant pads, the ingredients found in them may be irritating to women. One popular sanitary pad has been associated with skin irritation of the vulva, probably due to its odor-fighting ingredients.

Tampons, absorbent plugs inserted in the vagina, have also been in use for thousands of years. Before they became a consumer product, tampons were made of cloth or sponge and inserted into the vagina to absorb menstrual blood. These types of tampons, like cloth sanitary pads, could be rinsed and reused almost indefinitely. Disposable tampons, introduced in the 1920s, are made up of cotton fibers or a blend of cotton and rayon and are designed to expand to fill the vaginal opening, in much the way sponges can.

While tampons and pads are called "sanitary products," they are not especially sanitary. Neither are sterilized, although users may perceive them to be cleaner than reusable products. Disposable tampons have been associated with the sometimes fatal Toxic Shock Syndrome (TSS, discussed below). Although the bacteria causing this illness are not *introduced* by tampons, disposable tampons do not provide more protection from TSS than reusable tampons. Disposable tampons are safer than reusable types *only* when a vaginal infection is already in existence—in this case, users of reusable tampons may be continually reintroducing the infectious organism, thus prolonging the infection. Most of the time, disposable tampons and pads are primarily useful because of their convenience, the way disposable diapers are. Disposable menstrual products are also much more widely available than reusable products, which are generally only found in "health food" stores or via mail order.

Besides the commonly used pads and tampons, some alternative methods for dealing with menstrual blood exist as well. A menstrual cup (Figure 8.3), which is typically made of rubber or latex and shaped like an upside-down bell, is inserted like a tampon and emptied and rinsed when full. Some women use a diaphragm in the same manner. Both are as effective as tampons, although both require experience before women know the appropriate time to remove and empty them.

Women's self-help health groups in the 1970s experimented with methods of menstrual extraction, sometimes called "the 60-second period." Menstrual extraction consists of insertion

FIGURE 8.3   A Reusable Menstrual Cup

of a flexible plastic rod, called a cannula, through the cervix and the application of a minimal amount of suction, usually with a large, needleless syringe, to remove the endometrial lining. This procedure is fairly painless and simple. When scheduled immediately before the onset of menses, menstrual extraction can eliminate or drastically reduce the amount of menstrual bleeding that occurs. Currently, menstrual extraction is not performed on normally cycling women at medical facilities and is only practiced by women in advanced self-help groups. These groups have monitored the health of women who have engaged in the process, and there is no evidence for long-term health problems associated with frequent extraction of the endometrium; however, research on this technique is limited.

SUMMARY

Displaying evidence of menses is considered taboo, and women use various methods to hide menstrual blood. Reusable menstrual pads, tampons, and menstrual cups are as effective and as sanitary as disposable products. Menstrual extraction, which uses suction to remove endometrial tissue before the start of a woman's period, is a technique used to reduce menstrual bleeding but with little research to support its safety.

MENSTRUATION AND THE ENVIRONMENT

Many women experience disruptions in their menstrual cycle during illness, periods of stress, or changes in diet or living situation. Considering that the menstrual cycle is a complex series of interrelated events, and that many of these events are affected by changing levels of one or more hormones, it is reasonable to expect that certain changes in women's lives could impact their cycle.

Figure 8.4 summarizes some potential environmental effects on the menstrual cycle.

Menstruation and Exercise

Female athletes, coaches, and scientists have found that intense exercise may disrupt the menstrual cycle. On average, about 28% of competitive female athletes do not have monthly periods. This condition is called athletic amenorrhea. Even more women in athletics may have oligomenorrhea, which are relatively long cycles of greater than 35 days.

FIGURE 8.4   Summary of the Environmental Factors That May Influence Menstruation

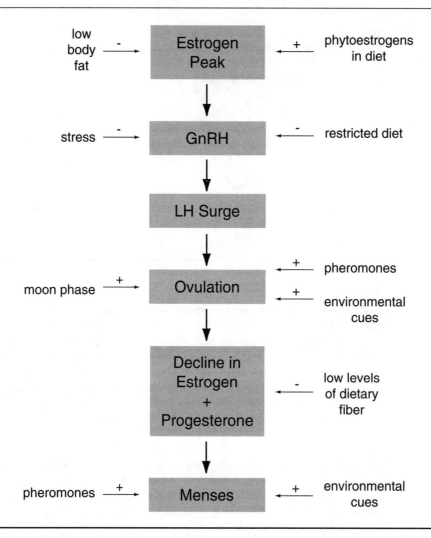

Women in some sports are more susceptible to athletic amenorrhea than others—among cross-country runners, as many as 57% do not menstruate regularly.

The most common explanation for athletic amenorrhea is that women below a threshold body fat mass are not physiologically able to menstruate. Fat tissue stores estradiol and helps convert circulating androgens into estrogens. When fat mass drops, estradiol levels may be too low to trigger ovulation. This hypothesis is supported by evidence that menarche is delayed in girls with fat mass lower than 17%. Some research has shown that adult women below 22% body fat will not sustain menstruation, although these studies have been criticized for their indirect measures of fat mass.

More recent analysis has indicated that athletic amenorrhea is not caused by excessive leanness in and of itself. Many female athletes with extremely low body fat menstruate—the very thin winner of the Boston Marathon in 1996, Uta Pippig, was menstruating on the day of the race. Instead, the diet of amenorrheic athletes seems to play a role in the cessation of menses. Surveys indicated that amenorrheic athletes consume less fiber but more protein than their menstruating peers. High fiber intake increases the amount of estradiol excreted from the body. If lean women have already low levels of estradiol, the estradiol decline that occurs at the end of luteal phase may not be large enough to trigger menstruation if these hormones are not rapidly excreted from the body.

Amenorrhea is not itself a health concern. However, because amenorrhea is usually a sign of an underlying problem, such as ovarian failure, it should be monitored closely. Amenorrheic athletes are usually quite lean and often have low levels of estrogen. Since estrogen helps to maintain bone, amenorrheic athletes have significantly lower bone density than menstruating athletes. This lowered bone density contributes to a three-fold increase in the risk of bone stress fractures among these women. Evidence exists that when amenorrhea lasts more than 3 years, this bone loss cannot be reversed. Amenorrhea in athletes can be treated by reducing the intensity of the training regimen or increasing fat levels. Athletic women who are amenorrheic should consult a nutritionist or sports doctor in order to maintain their active lifestyle without compromising future bone health.

Menstruation and Diet

Women on restricted diets often experience changes in their menstrual cycle, including amenorrhea, longer cycles, or more irregular cycles. The causes of amenorrhea in these women are not clear—as with athletes, amenorrheic dieters have low levels of estradiol, which inhibits ovulation.

Certain components of a woman's diet may directly influence ovarian hormone levels in the bloodstream. Phytoestrogens, which are estrogen-like substances produced by plants such as soybeans, are one such dietary component. Preliminary research has indicated that ingested phytoestrogens may have a protective effect against breast cancer, heart disease, and osteoporosis in postmenopausal women. Although no studies have been performed on the effect of phytoestrogens on menstruation directly, it is not unreasonable to assume that a sudden increase in phytoestrogen ingestion could influence the cycle.

Vegetarians excrete more estrogens than non-vegetarians, and high carbohydrate, low fat diets also reduce levels of estradiol and progesterone in the bloodstream. Again, while studies haven't linked this type of diet to characteristics of the menstrual cycle, we would expect that a sudden change in the levels of carbohydrate and fat would also affect the progress of the cycle.

Menstruation and Stress

The association of restrictive dieting and intense exercise with amenorrhea may be magnified by the effect of stress. Several studies of amenorrheic athletes and dancers have shown that menses will return when they discontinue competing or performing for a short period of time, even without gaining weight or fat mass.

Competitive athletes or performers are under mental stress when training for an event and may experience injury and muscle soreness when training is intense. Under conditions of psychological stress or physical pain, the body increases its production of a class of chemicals called *endorphins*. Endorphin receptors are found in the hypothalamus, and other locations. In rats, the production of GnRH is inhibited when endorphins bind to receptors in the hypothalamus. If the same is true in humans, the onset of a stressful event or the experience of acute or chronic pain may cause disruptions in the menstrual cycle via this pathway.

Menstrual Synchrony

Women who live together often find that the date of onset of their periods becomes more similar during their time together. This phenomenon, called menstrual synchrony, has been hypothesized to be due to the influence of pheromones. Pheromones are chemicals that are produced by one individual to influence the behavior of another. Pheromones are a common method of communication among animals. For example, female moths release pheromones as a signal to males of their sexual readiness and many mammals use pheromones stored in scent glands to mark the boundaries of their territory. Pheromonal communication has never been directly demonstrated in humans, so the subject of menstrual synchrony has received keen interest from researchers seeking to show that humans should include odors in our list of nonverbal tools for communication.

Menstrual synchrony has been studied almost exclusively in young women living in college dormitories and other group living quarters. Even in these environments, where contact with other women is relatively intimate and occurs over long periods of time, a trend toward synchronization is not very strong. In general , studies have shown trends toward synchrony among roommates who are close friends but not among roommates who are not close.

Only two studies have attempted to measure the direct effect of possible pheromones on the timing of menstruation. In these studies, sweat from the underarms of a donor woman was applied daily to the upper lips of regularly cycling volunteers. When compared to controls, these women's cycles did tend to experience more changes and move closer to the donor's cycle pattern. However, the experimental subjects' cycles did not change markedly and certainly did not exactly parallel the donor's cycle. When one considers how intense the contact was between the secretions of the donor and the women in the experiment, the influence of pheromones on menstrual synchrony appears to be quite weak.

■ DISCUSSION EXERCISE 1

1.1. Can you think of an alternative hypothesis to explain the trend towards menstrual synchrony among close friends?

SUMMARY

Figure 8.4 summarizes the environmental influences, including exercise, nutrition, stress, and other environmental factors, that may affect the menstrual cycle. Most of these influences seem to cause a change in the levels or rate of hormone production of hormones. Little evidence exists that the timing of the menstrual cycle is influenced by chemicals secreted by other women.

THE MENSTRUAL CYCLE, MOOD, AND PERFORMANCE

Your value system influences whether you see that irritability (i.e., being more quick to express anger at injustices) as a problem worthy of medical attention.

"The Curse"—PMS

Women have long been aware of the cyclic changes that occur in their bodies as their menstrual cycle progresses. The part of the cycle that has received the most attention, mostly negative, is the premenstrual phase. Hippocrates felt that menstruation was *caused* by premenstrual distress. Menses, he thought, was a process that removed agitated blood from the brain of an overly sensitive woman. More recent physicians have switched the relationship—antisocial behavior in women is thought to be caused by menses. In 1890 Icard described premenstrual women as subject to "kleptomania, pyromania . . . suicidal mania, erotomania, nymphomania, delusions, . . . illusions, hallucinations, and melancholia." Studies as recent as 1953 sought a link between a hypothesized substance thought to be produced premenstrually ("menotoxin") and a host of behavioral and physical disorders.

FIGURE 8.5   Some Proposed Symptoms of PMS

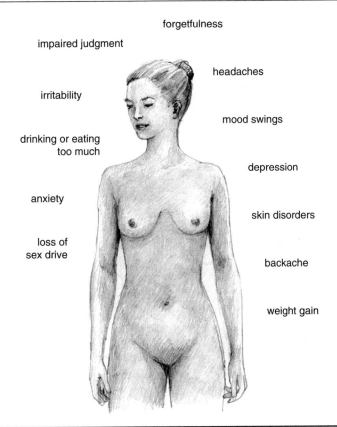

forgetfulness

impaired judgment

headaches

irritability

mood swings

drinking or eating
too much

depression

anxiety

skin disorders

loss of
sex drive

backache

weight gain

Modern studies of the premenstrual phase have investigated commonly held beliefs about the physical and psychological changes that occur before menses. In this section, we attempt to sort out these aspects of the premenstrual period and discuss the ways in which beliefs about women's nature have shaped the questions asked by scientists about this part of the cycle.

What Is Premenstrual Syndrome?   A syndrome is a group of loosely related symptoms—women who are diagnosed with PMS may have some, but not necessarily all, of these symptoms (Figure 8.5). PMS has been variously described, but most sources include the following symptoms: water retention, irritability, tension, marked spontaneous emotionality, low motor coordination, changes in eating habits, lowered judgment, and fatigue. You may notice that many of these symptoms are value loaded. For example, your value system influences whether you see irritability (i.e., being more quick to express anger at injustices) as a problem worthy of medical attention. Many feminists have noted that it is only in comparison to supposedly noncyclic, unemotional men that periodic displays of emotion and the expression of strong feelings are considered inappropriate.

The application of this loose definition of PMS understandably varies. Nearly all women experience some premenstrual changes, but depending on the source, anywhere from 1% to 90% of women could be classified as having PMS. The American Psychiatric Association's Diagnostic and Statistical Manual does not include Premenstrual Syndrome in its latest edition because of the difficulty in applying these definitions. Instead, it defines a different condition, Premenstrual Dysphoric Disorder (PDD), which is a depression that intensifies before menses in 3% to 5% of women.

While women's magazines and news programs have covered the "curse of PMS" and self-help sections of bookstores are lined with manuals on how to minimize the effects of PMS, the emotional and behavioral consequences of this syndrome have proven difficult to demonstrate. Among women who feel they suffer from PMS, about 50% have patterns of mood changes, fatigue, and emotionality that vary in a pattern unrelated to the menstrual cycle. Recalling that you felt bad before your last period may occur simply because menses serves as a good time marker—women may be less likely to recall anger or irritation that is not associated with a clear physical event.

Women have also learned since childhood that menstruation is an unpleasant occurrence, which may affect their perceptions of their physical and emotional state premenstrually. In a classic study performed in 1977, researchers misled undergraduate women into believing that the researchers could predict when their next period was due. Regardless of where they *actually* were in their cycle, the women who were told that their next period was due in 1 or 2 days reported significantly more pain, water retention, and changes in eating habits than women who were told their period would occur in 7 to 10 days. Other surveys have indicated that women who describe themselves as PMS sufferers are much more likely to make urgent doctor's appointments during menses but less likely to do so during the few days prior to menstruation. If these premenstrual symptoms described above were primarily biological in origin, the opposite results would be expected. Clearly, cultural expectations about the symptoms of menses affect women's perceptions of these symptoms.

Among those women whose psychological states do vary with the menstrual cycle, few other effects besides low energy and depression are clearly associated with the days before menses. Tests of task performance, memory, mental agility, and attention rarely show any relationship with the premenstrual phase in these women. Despite perceptions of inadequacy, women with PMS do not seem to differ in any aspect of performance from women who do not report PMS.

■ DISCUSSION EXERCISE 2

2.1. One problem with studies on premenstrual emotional and behavioral changes is the difficulty in finding control groups with which to compare menstruating women. Brainstorm a list of all possible control groups for studies on cycle characteristics.

2.2. None of these groups is a perfect control. Describe the inadequacies of each control group you listed.

What Causes PMS?   While PMS may or may not be a true syndrome, many women do experience physical changes premenstrually. These physical changes may influence women's psychological states and contribute to the cyclic pattern of premenstrual depression seen in some women.

Recall that both estradiol and progesterone levels begin quite high and fall dramatically during the premenstrual phase of the cycle. The level changes in these hormones obviously affect organs and tissues in the reproductive tract, but they may affect non-reproductive tissues as well.

The most often reported symptom of the premenstrual phase is fluid retention or "bloating." Bloating is often described as a feeling of heaviness, especially in the breasts, hands, and feet. This condition is probably related to the rapid decrease of progesterone in the bloodstream, because ingesting additional progesterone reduces the degree of bloating. However, the mechanism by which fluid retention is linked to progesterone is unknown. The amount of water retained in the tissues often causes an increase in body weight of 1–5 pounds.

In 60% of women who experience migraines, these headaches are associated with the onset of menses. Migraines in these women seem to be triggered by the sudden drop in estrogen levels—if estrogen levels are boosted premenstrually, the incidence of migraine diminishes.

Among athsma sufferers, the premenstrual phase is a time of increased susceptibility to severe attacks. While the exact mechanism of this relationship is unclear, attacks may be triggered when hormones that affect the mucus membranes in the uterus also stimulate mucus membranes inside the respiratory tract.

Many other physical symptoms that may occur premenstrually, such as fatigue and weakness, are nearly identical to the symptoms of individuals who are experiencing sleep deprivation. Several studies have indicated that women have more active dream sessions premenstrually and spend more time in light sleep stages during this phase relative to other parts of the cycle. Once again, a biological trigger for this phenomenon has not been described, although researchers have hypothesized that mild pain associated with increased prostaglandin levels or water retention may cause changes in sleep patterns. Alternatively, women who are aware of the imminence of their periods and associate it with negative outcomes may premenstrually feel more anxiety, which can also cause changes in sleep patterns.

All of these physical symptoms have the potential to impact women psychologically. After all, experiencing breast soreness, gaining weight, and feeling fatigued may all contribute to a woman's mood state. The studies of the causes of psychological symptoms of PMS have taken two directions: one set attempts to test the hormonal basis of these emotions and behavior, and the other seeks to compare the characteristics of women who have PMS to women without this syndrome. Most of the studies in the first group test a cross-section of women—if hormones influence emotional state, then all cycling women should experience some mood fluctuations. The studies in this group that have shown cyclic mood changes have all been criticized for their technique. Nearly all use an assessment tool patterned on the "Menstrual Distress Questionnaire," a survey that clearly includes the expectation that menstruation is in some way a hardship. Women in these studies may experience the onstage effect (see Chapter 2), which would cause them to exaggerate the negative aspects of the premenstrual and menstrual phase. Studies that use more neutral assessments find no predictable pattern of mood changes in women who do not claim to have PMS and only weak patterns in those that do. *No studies have demonstrated a difference in hormonal environment between women with PMS and those without.*

Studies that have investigated the psychological differences between women who report PMS and those who don't show a more intriguing pattern of results. Women who are diagnosed with PMS experience more negative life events, are more likely to respond strongly to stressful events, and have more concerns about self-control than women without symptoms. These women are also likely to have learned that menses is a negative experience and to expect more painful periods, even though in some (but not all) studies self-reported menstrual pain does not differ between women in PMS and non-PMS groups.

"Treatment" of PMS Because PMS is a syndrome with a number of symptoms, no treatment is 100% effective for all women who are diagnosed with this condition. Treatment with hormones to eliminate menses or reduce hormonal fluctuations may eliminate some of the symptoms. Certain drugs may relieve uncomfortable bloating, reduce the severity of headaches, decrease pain during menses, or act as antidepressants. However, most tests of these treatments demonstrate that a large number of patients in the control group taking a placebo in place of the drug also respond positively. This result indicates that when a woman's problems are taken seriously and attended to with care, she will often respond by feeling more in control of her own body, which is itself therapeutic. Most of the popular treatments of PMS, such as modifications of diet, establishment of a regular exercise program, or changes in work patterns or recreational activities, may also reduce the negative aspects of the premenstrual phase by helping women take more control over their life circumstances.

Many women suffer from depression premenstrually. This depression is real, but it is important to understand that many life events may contribute to its existence. While hormones may trigger the emotional and behavioral symptoms of PMS, these symptoms are also related to a woman's lack of control over her own body, stressful living and working situations, and socialized beliefs about the negative aspects of menses. Medical treatments may help some women with PMS, but social factors that improve women's ability to control important aspects of their lives may be just as helpful and may elevate the experience of menses for all women.

Other Changes in the Menstrual Cycle

Our culture's historically influenced view of menstruation has led to a focus on the negative aspects of the menstrual cycle. One wonders how much interest would exist in studies of PMS if we had long viewed the cycle as a wondrous, rather than sinister, event. Because of this historical lens, most studies of physical and emotional changes are centered on demonstrating the negative symptoms of the "paramenstruum," the period before and during menstruation.

The other part of the cycle that has received the most attention is ovulation, this time because of the role of the menstrual cycle in preparation for pregnancy. These studies have centered on sexual responsiveness, sensory acuity, and jealousy, testing the hypothesis that women will be more receptive to sexual activity and more upset by the possible loss of male support when they are most fertile. In general, the results have supported this hypothesis, but these studies have also illustrated that fluctuations occur throughout the cycle. For example, sexual arousal reaches a peak around ovulation and again premenstrually. Sexiness is not usually considered a symptom of PMS, however.

Interestingly, when men are included in studies of mood fluctuations over time, their moods are as changeable and as varied as women's. Among men, as among women, individuals differ greatly in the degree and frequency of mood swings experienced. Men's emotional states are just as unpredictable as women's, but these changes cannot be linked to another obvious physical cycle and so have been much less well studied. Our expectations of what constitutes appropriate male behavior could be made more realistic if we understood that men's emotional lives change on a daily, weekly, and monthly basis, just as women's do.

– Clearly, the large changes that occur in hormone levels and reproductive physiology throughout the menstrual cycle have an impact on women's lives. However, studies of the positive changes associated with the menstrual cycle are rarely discussed and even less likely to be studied. The few studies that investigate the totality of women's moods throughout the cycle indicate that positive feelings are the norm, and that occasional times of heightened emotional sensitivity are normal responses to bodily rhythms. Instead of setting aside one portion of the cycle as a period of "illness," we could view the entire cycle as a continuum that allows women to be in touch with many different areas of human emotional experience throughout their reproductive lives.

■ DISCUSSION EXERCISE 3

3.1. What strategies do you think should be adopted in the study and treatment of PMS? Why?

3.2. Is it worthwhile to study cyclic changes in women's physiological and psychological lives? Why? Which areas deserve more research and which do you think should be dropped from a research agenda?

SUMMARY

PMS is an illness without a single biological cause and with many associated symptoms. The real physical changes that occur premenstrually, social attitudes about menstruation, and the level of support women receive all impact the the occurrence and severity of PMS. The most effective treatments seem to be those which acknowledge the reality of a woman's experience and help her take control over aspects of her life that are effected negatively by the cycle. Very little research has been done on positive changes that occur, both premenstrually and throughout the cycle. A view of the menstrual cycle that recognizes its importance and honors the changes it makes in women's lives might minimize negative experiences of menstruation.

MENSTRUAL DISORDERS

Dysmenorrhea

Dysmenorrhea, or pain and cramping in the abdomen during menses, is extremely common in women. Nearly 75% of women surveyed in various studies experience some discomfort on at least the first day of menses, and some find the pain debilitating. Primary dysmenorrhea, which occurs without any sign of disease, is associated with prostaglandin production by the endometrium. In fact, a relationship can be seen between the amount of menstrual flow and the occurrence of dysmenorrhea—the more endometrial tissue expelled, thus more prostaglandin, the more pain experienced.

Recall that prostaglandin causes uterine contractions—the uterine muscles can become fatigued, and lactic acid, a waste product of metabolism occurring without enough oxygen, can build up in the muscles and cause soreness (see Chapter 7 for a description of lactic acid buildup in skeletal muscles). As with skeletal muscle soreness, any action that increases blood flow to the uterus, carrying away the lactic acid, can relieve pain. Deep massage of the muscles of the lower back and sexual activity, especially orgasm, which opens the cervix to allow tissue passage, help to relieve the pain of dysmenorrhea. There are also anti-prostaglandin drugs on the market that help reduce the amount and tension of uterine contractions.

Diet may also play a role in dysmenorrhea. Prostaglandins are derived from fatty acids ingested in food. The fatty acids in fish lead to the production of less biologically active prostaglandins than the fatty acids in vegetables and other meat products. Studies indicate that women who have higher fish intakes report less pain during menses.

Secondary dysmenorrhea occurs in association with a disease, such as endometriosis. Secondary dysmenorrhea is alleviated by treating the underlying problem.

Endometriosis

In some women, endometrial tissue can be found outside the uterus, either on its outer surface, on the ovaries, or on other structures inside the abdominal cavity. This "misplaced" endometrial tissue responds to changes in hormone levels in the same ways as endometrial tissue inside the uterus. The buildup and regression of this tissue over the course of a menstrual cycle may cause debilitating pain and infertility in some affected women. This condition is known as *endometriosis*.

Endometrial tissue is found outside the uterus for two possible reasons. When women menstruate, most of the tissue is expelled from the body through the cervix and vagina. However, the uterus also opens into the body cavity via the oviducts. In virtually all women observed during menses, a small amount of endometrial tissue is expelled into the body cavity rather than through the vagina of (called retrograde menstruation). Typically, this tissue is simply lost—immune cells recognize it as an invader and clean it out of the body cavity. In some women, however, the immune system misses this invader and the endometrial tissue establishes itself as cysts on other organs. In other women, endometriosis occurs when undifferentiated cells in the abdominal cavity transform into endometrial cells under hormonal stimulation. The exact mechanism and trigger of this transformation in unknown.

Endometriosis has popularly been termed the "career woman's disease." This tag came from the perception that the condition primarily affected childless white women in their 30s. In fact, endometriosis is common throughout race and class groups—it may be that the disease was associated with professional women in their 30s because this was the first group to gain enough power to demand treatment for this painful condition. Endometriosis is actually a more common significant health problem for women than breast cancer. Even though it is rarely lethal, endometriosis can have serious negative impacts on women's lives but receives very little research funding.

Endometriosis is a progressive disease and is not easily eliminated. Pain from the cyclic changes can be reduced by hormonal treatments that inhibit menses. If this treatment is unsuccessful, or if women with endometriosis are attempting to become pregnant, the only current therapy is surgery to remove endometrial cysts from internal body surfaces. In extremely debilitating cases, the uterus and ovaries may be removed, because these are the organs most likely to have endometrial cysts implanted on their surfaces.

Toxic Shock Syndrome

Toxic shock syndrome (TSS) is associated with menstruation because it is associated with a product for menstrual management—tampons. TSS is a severe reaction to exposure to bacterial toxins. TSS can occur in any individual as a result of infections, but it is unusual in menstruating women in that no sign of infection may be present before its onset. The toxin that results in TSS is produced by the bacteria *Staphylococcus aureus*, a species that is not uncommon on skin and can be found in the vaginas of 10% of healthy women. Tampons increase the risk of TSS, probably by providing a good environment for growth—they are moist, allow air flow into the vagina by holding it open, and have numerous internal surfaces. Each year, somewhere from 1 to 17 of every 100,000 menstruating women develop TSS.

In menstruating women, TSS can develop suddenly and without advance warning. The symptoms are high fever, vomiting or diarrhea, fainting or dizziness, and a sunburn-like rash. Tampon users who experience some or all of these symptoms should seek medical help immediately. If untreated, TSS can cause dangerously low blood pressure and result in death.

TSS has been associated with tampons with higher absorbency ratings, and one way to reduce the risk of tampon-associated TSS is to use smaller, less absorbent tampons. Leaving tampons in for long periods of time may also contribute to TSS risk. Certain brands of tampons that had higher than average instances of TSS association have been pulled from the market, but no tampon is completely risk free.

SUMMARY

Dysmenorrhea, or pain at menses, is associated with repeated strong contractions of the uterus and can be treated by increasing blood flow to the area or by taking anti-prostaglandin drugs. Endometriosis results from the establishment of endometrial tissue on the outer surface of the uterus or elsewhere in the body cavity. Endometriosis is a progressive disease, but symptoms may be alleviated by treatment with hormones or surgical removal of endometrial cysts. Toxic shock syndrome is a potentially fatal poisoning associated with the growth of bacteria on tampons.

MENSTRUATION AND CULTURE

Throughout this chapter we have seen how contemporary views of menstruation have affected the scientific study of this cycle as well as women's subjective experience of menses. In this section, we will briefly discuss the origins and maintenance of cultural stereotypes about menses and propose a new view of this universal cycle.

Menstrual Taboos

Many cultures in the past restricted women's activities during menses and viewed menstrual blood with a mixture of fear and disgust. Menses is, after all, bleeding that occurs without wound and without any negative health consequences. All cultures have also recognized the relationship between menses and reproduction. Thus, menstruation and menstrual blood were represented as powerful forces belonging only to women. The origin of menstrual taboos is thought to derive from its perceived power—in patriarchal (male-headed) societies, men needed to subdue women and their powerful menstrual excretions in order to maintain social order. Contact with women during menses or with their menstrual blood, it was feared, could physically drain the strength from men. In many cultures this fear has meant that menustrating women were either completely isolated from the rest of a village and ensconced in a "menstrual hut" or that their participation in activities that sustained the community (e.g. hunting, gathering, food preparation) was banned.

In some cultures, fear of the power of menstrual blood transformed into a belief that menstrual blood and menstruating women were "unclean." The Roman Pliny, whose works provide some of the basis for Western science, said of menstrual blood:

> Contact with it turns new wine sour, crops touched by it become barren, grafts die, seeds in gardens are dried up, the fruit of trees falls off, the edge of steel and the gleam of ivory are dulled, hives of bees die, even bronze and iron are at once seized by rust, and a horrible smell fills the air; to taste it drives dogs mad and infects their bites with an incurable poison.
> (Delaney et al., *The Curse*, p. 7)

In Judeo-Christian tradition, menstruating women have been banned from participating in religious ceremonies and from having sexual relations during their periods and for 7 days afterwards. Menstruating women had to take a ritual bath in order to become clean enough to fully participate in the religious life of their communities.

While in most technological societies restrictions on menstruating women's activities no longer exist, these taboos have exerted long lasting effects on our views of menstruation. Menstruation is no longer seen as a threat to male power, but today it still may act as a limitation on a woman's ability to access the power that is traditionally held by males.

Modern Menstrual Taboos

Most women understand that menses does not place any real limitation on women's physical or mental activities. The research presented in this chapter shows that even during the premenstrual phase, which may exacerbate the symptoms of depression in some women, all women are as capable of successfully completing tasks as they are elsewhere in the cycle. The realization, made clear in the last two decades, that menstruation does not place true limits on women has represented a great leap forward. No longer will men be able to say that women are incapable of acting in positions of power due to their "raging hormones." Unfortunately, however, the abolishment of this myth has not abolished another more subtle myth—that women can succeed in sharing power with men only if they conform to the menses-free state of men. Of course, being menses-free is not possible (at least without drugs or surgery) for premenopausal women, so women have been required to attempt to completely hide menstruation and the monthly changes that accompany the cycle.

An examination of menstrual management product advertisements illuminates this trend. In nearly all ads, women appear in tight-fitting clothes, happily engaged in active movement. The implication of these ads is that the ideal menstruating woman is indistinguishable from non-menstruating women, despite the fact that she may be experiencing water retention, cramps, and the fear that someone will discover her menstrual status. The need to hide menstruation probably still derives from the taboo of uncleanliness— menstrual blood is no more dangerous to health than the oils and sweat that coat our skin, but the sight (or even knowledge) of it still causes fear, shame, and disgust. When was the last time you heard a woman announce in public that she was menstruating or witnessed someone walking to the bathroom openly carrying a tampon or pad with her? The replacement of menstrual taboos with modern menstrual denial does not remove from women the burden of protecting society from their own biology.

Fairness to the Menstrual Cycle

The menstrual cycle is neither a curse nor a blessing, but it is an integral part of being a woman. Consider, as Carol Tavris has, how our treatment of menstrual changes would differ if we considered female reproductive processes as normal:

> Women and men would regard changes in mood, efficiency, and good humor as expected and normal variations, not as abnormal deviations from the (impossible) male ideal of steadiness and implacability. . . . We would regard the changes of menstruation. . . as normal, not as failures, losses, deficiencies, and weaknesses. Menstrual cramps . . . will pass. We would not confuse normal physical changes with symptoms of a disorder or a disease. We can protest the mindless application of the term "PMS" and speak instead of the variety of premenstrual changes in women *and* of hormonal changes in men.
>
> (*The Mismeasure of Woman*, pp. 168–169)

Women should not be required to be like idealized men in order to be taken as seriously as men are. The dismantling of all menstrual taboos will go a long way towards giving the biological differences of women and men equal value and allowing women to succeed on their own terms.

■ DISCUSSION EXERCISE 4

4.1. How did you learn about menstruation? Do you think there should be different approaches to teaching about menstruation than what you experienced?

4.2. When was the last time you were "taught" about menstruation? Do you think that women (and men) would have fewer problems with menstruation if it was discussed after menarche or when they are adults?

■ POINTS FOR ANSWERS TO DISCUSSION EXERCISES

Discussion Exercise 1:

The menstrual cycle may become linked to other cycles in the environment. We have already learned that lunar cycles may have an influence on menstruation. Close friends may synchronize simply because they are aware of each other's cycle.

Discussion Exercise 2:

2.1. Possible control groups: men, non-menstruating women (either premenarche, postmenopause, or for some reason incapable of menstruation), women on hormonal birth control, menstruating women at different parts of their cycle.

2.2. Men do not experience the same social environment as women and moods may be influenced by the cycle of important women in their lives.

(a) Non-menstruating women—if premenarche or postmenopause are of different age group/generation than menstruating women. Women not capable of menstruation are inherently different—their health history is clearly different from women who do menstruate and this may affect them psychologically.

(b) Women on hormonal birth control—these women experience a constant hormonal environment but may be fundamentally different from women not on hormonal birth control. They are less likely to belong to particular religious groups, may have different attitudes about sex, may be less likely to be concerned about a possible pregnancy, etc.

(c) Menstruating women at different parts of their cycle—as discussed in the text, women in our culture have learned to associate negative experiences with their menses so they may report more positive feelings during other parts of the cycle. These studies also rarely control for other stressful life events that may have just happened to correspond with the premenstrual phase.

REFERENCES

Arendt, E. A. (1993).Osteoporosis in the athletic female: Amenorrhea and amenorrheic osteoporosis. *In the athletic female.*

Asso, D. (1983). *The real menstrual cycle.* John Wiley and Sons.

Bancroft, J., & Rennie, D. (1995). Perimenstrual depression: Its relationship to pain, bleeding, and previous history of depression. *Psychosomatic Medicine, 57*(5), 445–452.

Belsey, E. M., & Pinol, A. P. (1997). Menstrual bleeding patterns in untreated women. Task Force on Long-Acting Systemic Agents for Fertility Regulation. *Contraception, 55*(2), 57–65.

Berg, D. H., & Coutts, L. B. (1994). The extended curse: Being a woman every day. *Health Care for Women International, 15*(1), 11–22.

Blume, J. (1970). *Are you there, God? It's me, Margaret.* Dell Publishers.

Boston Women's Health Collective. (1992). The new our bodies, ourselves. Simon and Schuster.

Boyd, N. F., Lockwood, G. A., Greenberg, C. V., Martin, L. J., & Tritchler, D. L (1997). Effects of a low-fat high-carbohydrate diet on plasma sex hormones in premenopausal women: Results from a randomized controlled trial. Canadian Diet and Breast Cancer Prevention Study Group. *British Journal of Cancer, 76*(1), 127–135.

Cassidy, A. (1996). Physiological effects of phyto-oestrogens in relation to cancer and other human health risks. *Proceedings of the Nutrition Society, 55*(1B), 399–417.

Cockerill, I. M., Wormington, J. A., & Nevill, A. M. (1994). Menstrual-cycle effects on mood and perceptual-motor performance. *Journal of Psychosomatic Research, 38*(7), 763–771.

Coutts, L. B., & Berg, D. H. (1993). The portrayal of the menstruating woman in menstrual product advertisements. *Health Care for Women International, 14*(2), 179–191.

Crowther, D. L. (1994). Is there a link between the consulting patterns of premenopausal women and the menstrual cycle? *Family Practice, 11*(4), 402–407.

Cutler, W. B., Friedmann, E. & McCoy, N. L. (1996). Coitus and menstruation in perimenopausal premenopausal women. *Journal of Psychosomatic Obstetrics & Gynaecology, 17*(3), 149–157.

Delaney, J., Lupton, M. J., & Toth, E. (1976). *The curse: A cultural history of menstruation.* E. P. Dutton and Co., Inc.

Deutch, B. (1995). Menstrual pain in Danish women correlated with low n-3 polyunsaturated fatty acid intake. *European Journal of Clinical Nutrition, 49,* 508–516.

Eason, E. L., & Feldman, P. (1996). Contact dermatitis associated with the use of Always sanitary napkins. *Canadian Medical Association Journal, 154*(8), 1173–1176.

Facchinetti, F., Neri, I., Fava, M., & Genazzani, A. R. (1994). Menstrual-related mood changes in patients with oligomenorrhea. *Gynecologic & Obstetric Investigation, 38*(2),122–126.

Finn, C. A. (1996). Why do women menstruate? Historical and evolutionary review. *European Journal of Obstetrics, Gynecology, & Reproductive Biology, 70*(1), 3–8.

Golub, S. (1992). *Periods: From menarche to menopause.* Sage Publishers.

Golub, S. (1983). *Lifting the curse of menstruation.* The Haworth Press.

Hatcher, R. (1992). *Contraceptive technology, 1990 – 1992. (15th rev. ed.).New York:* Irvington Press.

Krug, R., Finn, M., Pietrowsky, R., Fehm, H. L., & Born, J. (1996). Jealousy, general creativity, and coping with social frustration during the menstrual cycle. *Archives of Sexual Behavior, 25*(2), 181–199.

MacGregor, E. A. (1997). Menstruation, sex hormones, and migraine. *Neurologic Clinics, 15*(1), 125–141.

Marbaix, E., Kokorine, I., Donnez, J., Eeckhout, Y., & Courtoy, P. J. (1996). Regulation and restricted expression of interstitial collagenase suggest a pivotal role in the initiation of menstruation. *Human Reproduction,11* (Suppl 2), 134–143.

Marshall, J. C., & Griffin, M. L. (1993). The role of changing pulse frequency in the regulation of ovulation. *Human Reproduction, 8* (Suppl 2), 57–61.

Mira, M., Abraham, S., McNeil, D., Vizzard, J., Macaskill, P., Fraser, I., & Llewellyn-Jones, D. (1995). The inter-relationship of premenstrual symptoms. *Psychological Medicine, 25*(5), 947–955.

Morgan, M., Rapkin, A. J., D'Elia, L., Reading, A., & Goldman, L. (1996). Cognitive functioning in premenstrual syndrome. *Obstetrics & Gynecology, 88*(6), 961–966.

O'Brien. (1987). P. M. S. *Premenstrual syndrome.* Blackwell Scientific Publications.

Oral, E., & Arici, A. (1997). Pathogenesis of endometriosis. *Obstetrics & Gynecology Clinics of North America, 24*(2), 219–233.

Ruble, D. N. (1977). Premenstrual symptoms: A reinterpretation. *Science, 197,* 291.

Scutt, D., & Manning, J. T. (1996). Symmetry and ovulation in women. *Human Reproduction, 11*(11), 2477–2480.

Speroff, L., Glass, R. H., & Kase, N. G. (1994). *Clinical gynecologic endocrinology and infertility,* (5th ed.). Williams and Wilkins.

Strassmann, B. (1996). The evolution of endometrial cycles and menstruation. *Quarterly Review of Biology, 71*(2), 181–220.

van Dessel, H. J., Schipper, I., Pache, T. D., van Geldorp, H., de Jong, F. H., & Fauser, B. C. (1996). Normal human follicle development: An evaluation of correlations with oestradiol, androstenedione and progesterone levels in individual follicles. *Clinical Endocrinology, 44*(2), 191–198.

Weller, L., &Weller, A. (1993). Human menstrual synchrony: A critical assessment. *Neuroscience and Biobehavioral Reviews, 17*(4), 427–439.

Woods, N. F., Lentz, M., Mitchell, E. S., Heitkemper, M., & Shaver, J. (1997). PMS after 40: Persistence of a stress-related symptom pattern. *Research in Nursing & Health, 20*(4), 329–340.

Woods, N. F., Lentz, M., & Mitchell, E. S. (1995). Social pathways to premenstrual symptoms. *Research in Nursing & Health, 18*(3), 225–237.

CHAPTER 9

Remarkably, your parents together could have made over 64 trillion genetically different children, with you being only one of the possibilities!

OOGENESIS
AND FERTILIZATION

INTRODUCTION

When a new baby is born, friends and relatives remark about the baby's resemblance to either one or both parents. Though babies sometimes do resemble one parent more than the other, we all are the product of equal numbers of our mother's and our father's genes working together to make a functioning human being. This chapter will explore how it is that your parents each contributed half of their genes to you via the process of gametogenesis (the making of gametes or egg cells and sperm cells) and how these genes are united at fertilization. Additionally, this chapter describes how you can predict when you will be fertile, how twins arise, and whether or not it is possible to time fertilization so that it results in the conception of a child of a desired sex.

OOGENESIS

Oogenesis, the formation and development of female gametes, occurs in the ovaries and results in the production of egg cells. A small percentage of these egg cells will be ovulated and an even smaller percentage fertilized. Remarkably, some of the work of oogenesis is performed while the female baby is still *in utero*. Even before she is born, a female baby begins the process of making the gametes that she can pass on to her children.[1] After beginning oogenesis *in utero*, a female baby's gametic progenitor (predecessor) cells wait to complete the process until puberty. Hormonal changes at puberty stimulate further development and maturation of one of these cells per menstrual cycle. The egg cell, which undergoes this stimulation, is ovulated. At ovulation, however, the egg cell pauses again, only to complete development if fertilized.

Oogenesis begins 4–6 weeks after fertilization. At this time primordial germ cells begin migrating around the wall of the fetal gut. These cells come to rest in the embryonic region that will become the gonads, called the gonadal ridge. After the seventh week, the gonadal ridges of a female will develop into the paired ovaries, which produce the egg cells. In a male, the gonadal ridges develop into the testicles that will produce the sperm. Once at the female baby's developing gonadal ridge these cells are called oogonia. Upon completion of this migration, oogonia undergo many successive rounds of mitosis to increase their number.

Mitosis

Mitosis is a process that cells undergo in order to duplicate all 46 of their chromosomes so that the cell can make copies of itself (Figure 9.1). Chromosomes carry genes and are found in the nucleus of a human cell. Prior to mitosis, each chromosome is duplicated and the two exact copies are attached to each other. These identical copies are called sister chromatids and are attached at a region called the centromere. The process of mitosis then separates the two sister chromatids from each other and places them into two separate cells. This process can be likened to making a photocopy from one original, then stapling the two copies to each other and later separating the copies for distribution.

One round of mitosis produces two daughter cells, which are genetically identical to the parent cell. Ultimately, rapid mitotic proliferation seeds the developing gonads with around seven million genetically identical gametic progenitor cells, now called primordial oocytes. It is these primordial oocytes which begin the next step in oogenesis while a female baby is still *in utero*.

Meiosis

The next step in oogenesis involves a process called meiosis (Figure 9.2). Meiosis, like mitosis, is a mechanism for parent cells to pass chromosomes to daughter cells. However, we now make a critical distinction about the types of chromosomes present in the primordial oocytes (and in all cells except the gametes). We now think of the 46 chromosomes present as 23 pairs of chromosomes. Additionally, we make a critical distinction about the origin of these chromosomes. One member of each pair of your 46 chromosomes originated in your mother's egg cell, which was fused with your father's sperm cell, carrying the other member of each pair. These paired chromosomes, called homologous pairs, are chromosomes that carry the same genes along their length but not necessarily the same forms (alleles) of those genes.

For example, on a particular human chromosome lies the gene that codes for the production of phenylalanine hydroxylase, an enzyme that metabolizes (breaks down) the amino acid phenylalanine. A particular person could have an allele for a properly functioning enzyme on one member of the homologous pair and an allele for a nonfunctional form of the enzyme on the other member of the homologous pair. Alternatively, a person could have one functional enzyme on each chromosome or one nonfunctional form of the enzyme on each chromosome of the homologous pair.

In fact, approximately 1 of every 12,000 newborns have a homologous pair of chromosomes in which both members of the pair contain the nonfunctional, recessive allele, and, therefore, can not break down this amino acid. If untreated, phenylalanine will build up in the baby's developing brain and lead to convulsive seizures and mental retardation. Next time you drink a diet soda, look for the warning, "phenylketonurics: contains phenylalanine." This tells people who carry both recessive alleles that the product contains phenylalanine (in the artificial sweetener), and they should not drink it. Most people who carry

FIGURE 9.1   Mitosis in Depth

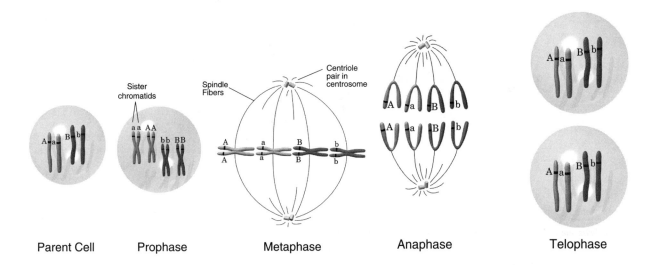

| Parent Cell | Prophase | Metaphase | Anaphase | Telophase |

Mitosis can be broken down into four phases called prophase, metaphase, anaphase and telophase in order to isolate the significant events taking place during the movement of chromosomes to their respective daughter cells. Keep in mind that the goal of mitosis is to produce two genetically identical daughter cells from one original parent cell. Because chromosomes have many hundreds of genes along their length, moving chromosomes around moves the genes on them around as well.

Shown above is the parent cell's nucleus prior to mitosis. Only 4 of the 46 human chromosomes are drawn. The band around each chromosome indicates the location of two hypothetical genes A and B. A and a are alleles of the A gene, and B and b are alleles of the B gene.

Prior to prophase, all of the chromosomes in the parent cell are duplicated and the duplicates attached to each other. These chromosomes are now composed of two sister chromatids, which are exact copies of each other. During prophase, the sister chromatids prepare for their separation and distribution into daughter cells.

To affect equal distribution, the chromosomes line up across the middle (equator) of the cell. At this time, the fibers of the spindle apparatus attach themselves to each sister chromatid. Spindle fibers are proteins that are assembled from the centrosomes at each pole of the cell. Inside each centrosome is a pair of centrioles that are required for the formation of the spindle.

The actual distribution of chromatids in a dividing cell is accomplished by the spindle fibers when they successively decrease their own length in order to pull the copies of each chromosome with them to the poles of the cell.

Telophase of mitosis is characterized by the reappearance of the nuclear membrane around each set of chromosomes. Directly on the heels of telophase, a cell reforms around each nucleus. Both nuclei now contain an exact copy of the parent cell's chromosomes.

both recessive alleles are aware of this because newborns are routinely screened for this disorder. A simple pin prick to the heel of a newborn allows hospital employees to check the blood cells thus obtained for the presence of the two recessive alleles.

It is the job of meiosis to separate these members of a homologous pair from each other. Once this is accomplished, there is one copy of each chromosome (numbered 1–23) in every gamete. In this fashion, half of a person's genes are physically placed into each gamete, thus each child you have will carry half of your genes.

It is possible for you to have made gametes which contain only those chromosomes you obtained from your mother, only chromosomes you obtained from your father, or any other combination of maternal and paternal chromosomes. This is why some children resemble one grandparent more than the other and why no two siblings are exactly alike (excluding twins, which will be discussed later).

FIGURE 9.2   Meiosis in Depth

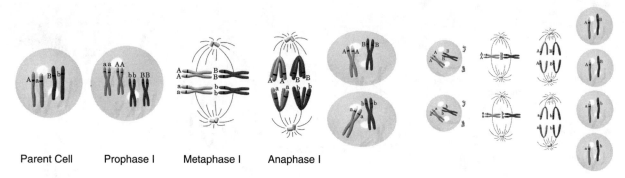

Parent Cell   Prophase I   Metaphase I   Anaphase I

Telophase I   Meiosis II

Meiosis occurs in the gametic progenitor cells and reduces the number of chromosomes in a cell by one half. The reduction in chromosome number is accomplished via two separate divisions, meiosis I and meiosis II. Meiosis I is preceded by chromosomal duplication, forming chromosomes composed of sister chromatids, and consists of prophase I, metaphase I, anaphase I, and telophase I. The result of meiosis I is to separate the homologous pairs of chromosomes from each other. Meiosis II consists of prophase II, metaphase II, anaphase II, and telophase II. Meiosis II is very similar to mitosis and results in the separation of sister chromatids from each other.

This parent cell shows only 2 of the 23 homologous pairs of chromosomes found in humans. The chromosomes of this cell will be duplicated prior to entering prophase I.

At prophase I the homologous chromosomes align and may undergo crossing over. Crossing over results in the transfer of segments of chromosomes from one homolog to the other. At prophase I the chromosomes are composed of sister chromatids.

Metaphase I of meiosis is strikingly different from metaphase of mitosis because the homologous pairs of chromosomes align with their partners across the equator. Instead of having 46 chromosomes across the equator as we saw in mitosis, meiotic cells have 23 homologous pairs of chromosomes across the equator. This pairing occurs such that one member of each pair faces the top pole of the cell and the other member of each pair faces the bottom pole of the cell. It is completely random which member of each pair will face the top (or bottom) pole for each meiosis.

The homologous pairs of chromosomes are separated from each other during anaphase I resulting in two daughter cells at telophase I. Each of these daughter cells then undergoes meiosis II, consisting of prophase II, metaphase II, anaphase II, and telophase II. Meiosis II is very similar in that it separates the sister chromatids from each other.

An analogy we have found helpful for illustrating this point deals with shoes. A pair of shoes is analogous to a homologous pair of chromosomes in the sense that the two shoes are similar in size, shape and style, but are not exactly similar in that they fit different feet. (Compare this to the pair of homologous chromosomes, which carry the same genes but possibly different alleles of those genes.) If one were to ask 23 students to take off their shoes and place them (in pairs) in a row across the front of a classroom, they might line up their shoes so that the left shoes were all one side, and all the right shoes were on the other side. The students could then separate the left shoes from the right shoes, just like meiosis separates homologous chromosomes. This would produce one pile of shoes (gametes) containing all left shoes and another pile of shoes containing all right shoes. Different piles of shoes would result if the very first pair of shoes was rotated so that the left shoe and right shoe exchange places but the other 22 pairs of shoes stayed as they were. When the shoes of a pair were separated from each other this time, one pile would have 22 right shoes and 1 left shoe together, and the other pile would have 22 left shoes and 1 right shoe together. The students could continue making different combinations of left and right shoes for the rest of their lives, because there are 2^{23} (over 8 million) possible ways to line up these pairs of shoes.

The same is true of maternal and paternal chromosomes, and if you think about this for a while, you will probably find it fascinating, and somewhat unnerving, to consider that each of your parents was able to produce over 8 million gametes other than the ones which combined to make you. The odds of you receiving the particular combination of chromosomes you received is 1/8 million x 1/8 million or 1/64 trillion. Remarkably, your parents together could have made over 64 trillion genetically different children, with you being only one of the possibilities!

Pauses During Oogenesis

The process of meiosis, which began in the developing ovaries of the female baby, does not proceed directly to the point where the homologues are separated. There are two stops along the way, the first of which occurs when the cells pause at a stage called prophase I for around 13 years, until a girl reaches sexual maturity. Once paused at prophase I, the developing egg cells are called primary oocytes. This pause in meiosis allows the primary oocytes and ovaries more time to grow and develop. By the time she is born, a girl's ovaries contain all the cells that will ever develop into eggs in the form of these primary oocytes paused at prophase I.

Initially, the developing ovaries contain about seven million primordial oocytes, many of which undergo atresia (degeneration) *in utero* so that at birth most girls have around one million primary oocytes left in their ovaries. Some of these primary oocytes will also undergo atresia prior to puberty, thus depleting her stock a little more. Commencing at puberty, a single primary oocyte per menstrual cycle overcomes the first pause in meiosis and will be ovulated. Those primary oocytes that are not selected for ovulation until close to menopause can thus stay in prophase I for 45–55 years (gestation to menopause). For fertile women, each menstrual cycle sees one of these egg cells proceeding from prophase I to metaphase II when the second stop in meiosis occurs. It is at this meiotic stage, around day 14 of the menstrual cycle, that the developing egg cell will be ovulated. It takes a secondary oocyte around 3 days to move from the ovary at ovulation through the oviduct, uterus, and cervix and to exit the body through the vagina. If however, there are sperm present in the oviduct and the secondary oocyte is fertilized, meiosis begins again from metaphase II.

During the meioses of oogenesis (versus spermatogenesis), an interesting type of cellular division occurs. Instead of the equal division of the parent cell into two daughter cells the spindle apparatus, whose fibers serve to pull the chromosomes apart, forms eccentrically (off center), resulting in one small cell and one large cell (Figure 9.3). The smaller cell is called a polar body and does not have enough nutrients to undergo any further development. Therefore, it is normally broken down and reabsorbed. The large cell receives the majority of the cytoplasmic nutrients and organelles and is thus better prepared to proceed with meiosis and, should fertilization occur, early development. The increased proportion of cytoplasm and cytoplasmic organelles found in this larger cell also helps to compensate for the very small amount of cytoplasm contributed by the sperm. Sperm cells have very little cytoplasm. For example, mitochondria, cellular organelles which convert the food you eat into ATP (a form of energy your cells can utilize), are largely inherited along with the egg's cytoplasm. Consequently, chromosomes are inherited in equal proportions from both of your parents, most of the cytoplasm and its resident organelles are inherited along with the egg cell.

Scientists believe that the developing egg cell pauses at metaphase II until it is fertilized in order to have twice as much DNA available. Recall that chromosomes have many hundreds of genes along their length and that genes are made of DNA. Genes are instructions for the production of proteins. These proteins can function as structural units in

FIGURE 9.3   Meiosis From an Eccentric Spindle and Polar Body Formation

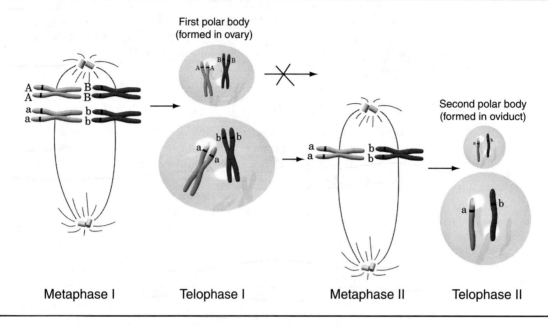

First polar body
(formed in ovary)

Second polar body
(formed in oviduct)

Metaphase I   Telophase I   Metaphase II   Telophase II

During the meiosis of oogenesis (versus spermatogenesis), the spindle apparatus forms eccentrically (off center), resulting in one small cell and one large cell. The smaller cell, a polar body, does not have enough nutrients to undergo any further development and is normally broken down and reabsorbed. The large cell receives the majority of the cytoplasmic nutrients and organelles and is better prepared to proceed with meiosis and, should fertilization occur, early development.

cells, similar to bricks in a building, or they can be involved in transporting other molecules, or they can function as enzymes which facilitate the synthesis and breakdown of all the molecules found in cells. You are probably aware that you need to provide your body with proteins, sugar, and fat through your diet. It is the enzymes made by your genes which convert all of these nutrients into a form your body can use to make energy in addition to helping to synthesize many of the proteins which you cannot obtain from your diet. At metaphase II, a developing oocyte has 23 chromosomes that are each composed of two sister chromatids. These exact copies of each other are not separated until anaphase II. The presence of twice as much DNA allows for the production of two times as much protein while this egg cell prepares for fertilization. If fertilized, an egg cell will need to have a very large available supply of proteins in order to keep up with the metabolic demands of early development. The pause at metaphase II allows the developing egg cell to build up reserves in the event that fertilization does occur. If this secondary oocyte is not fertilized, it exits the body at this meiotic stage.

SUMMARY

Primordial germ cells migrate to the site of the developing ovaries while a female baby is in utero. Once at the gonadal ridges, these oogonia proliferate rapidly by mitosis providing a stock of genetically identical cells, the primordial oocytes, some of which will then undergo meiosis. Meiosis begins in utero and pauses at prophase I until puberty. At puberty, one of these primary oocytes per menstrual cycle will move from prophase I to metaphase II. These secondary oocytes can either move out of the body or, if fertilized, finish meiosis producing a fertilized egg cell capable of producing a functioning human being (Figure 9.4).

MISTAKES IN GAMETOGENESIS

When one really looks at the data in terms of producing healthy babies, the biological clock ticks just as loudly for men as it does for women.

Gametogenesis does not always work flawlessly and, when mistakes do occur, they can be passed on to children. These mistakes are either mistakes in meiosis, which result in a gamete having the wrong number of chromosomes, or changes to the DNA of a particular gene (point mutations), which result in the origin of new forms of that gene (alleles), not expressed in either parent.

Mistakes that result in an egg cell or a sperm cell with either more than one chromosome of a homologous pair or no chromosome of a homologous pair are caused by nondisjunction. Nondisjunction occurs when members of a homologous pair fail to disjoin from each other. (Imagine the effects of tying the laces of a pair of shoes together so that they could not be separated from each other.) If a nondisjunctive gamete is involved in fertilization, the fertilized egg cell will have too many or too few chromosomes. While having the wrong number of chromosomes is normally incompatible with life, there are some situations where a viable offspring can result. A common form of mental retardation is Down's syndrome, which sometimes results when an individual receives two copies of chromosome 21 from one gamete and one copy of chromosome 21 from the other gamete (Figure 9.5).

Using chromosome specific probes, it is possible to show that persons with Down's syndrome most often inherited their extra chromosome 21 maternally, i.e., from the egg cell. It has been known for some time that the incidence of Down's syndrome births increases with maternal age, and this finding has led researchers to coin the term "maternal age effects."

Concern about chromosomal mutations associated with maternal age has been exacerbated by cultural influences that define women's roles in our society as mothers and caretakers for other people and has led, in part, to the notion of a biological clock. The ticking of the biological clock is meant to imply that women who put off having children until their careers and finances are in place are jeopardizing their children's health and risking not being able to have children at all. This clock was presumed not to be ticking in men, who were therefore able to devote as much time and attention to their careers as they felt necessary. The idea of only women having a biological clock promotes the cultural norm of women having their children young and taking care of their husbands, while the men advance their careers and earning potentials.

But is this true? Is there a biological clock that ticks only for women? Resoundingly no! Recent research shows that while the reproductive life span of women is indeed shorter than that of men, it is not so short as to preclude a woman from waiting until her 30s or even 40s to have healthy babies. Addtionally, in terms of genetic defects, men as well as women show obvious but different age effects.

While we have seen that there appears to be a maternal age effect leading to increased levels of chromosomal nondisjunction with age during oogenesis, we can now turn our attention to errors at the level of the gene, which are more likely to occur during spermatogenesis and appear to increase in frequency with paternal age.

The very mechanisms by which females and males produce their gametes leave them susceptible to different types of mutations. Women begin making their gametes very early in life and hence may be more susceptible to chromosomal mutations such as nondisjunction. However, the close association of these homologues may afford them some protection against gene damage due to environmental factors. Men have testicles containing gametic progenitor cells that do not undergo meiosis and sperm production until puberty. This facet

FIGURE 9.4   Oogenesis Summary

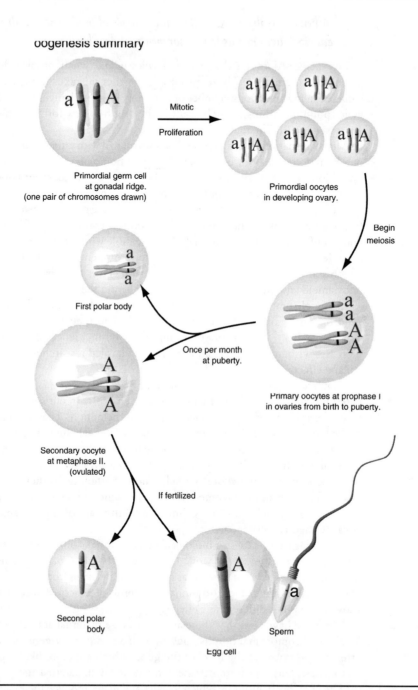

Primordial germ cells migrate to the site of the developing ovaries while a female baby is in utero. Once at the gonadal ridges, these oogonia proliferate rapidly by mitosis providing a stock of genetically identical cells, the primordial oocytes, some of which will then undergo meiosis. Meiosis begins in utero and pauses at prophase I until puberty. At puberty, one of these primary oocytes per menstrual cycle will move from prophase I to metaphase II. These secondary oocytes can either move out of the body or, if fertilized, finish meiosis producing a fertilized egg cell capable of producing a functioning human being.

FIGURE 9.5   Nondisjunction

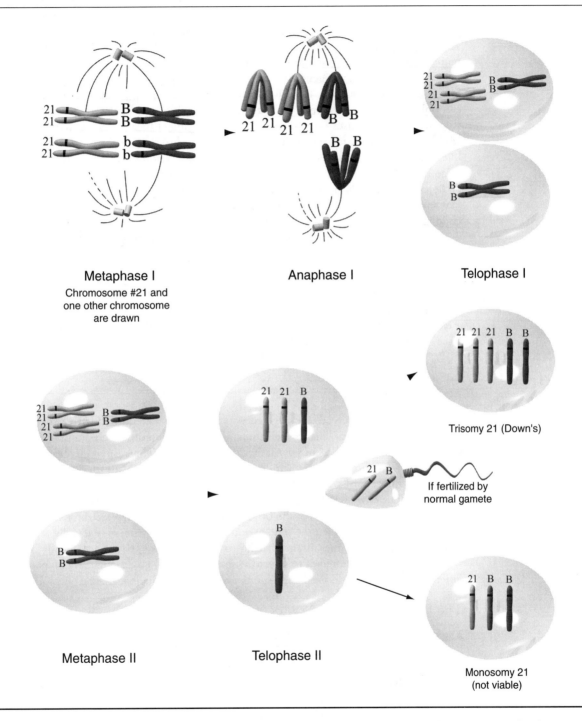

Metaphase I
Chromosome #21 and
one other chromosome
are drawn

Anaphase I

Telophase I

Trisomy 21 (Down's)

If fertilized by
normal gamete

Metaphase II

Telophase II

Monosomy 21
(not viable)

Nondisjunction occurs when chromosomes fail to separate during meiosis. This can result in gametes with too many or too few chromosomes. This figure shows one way in which nondisjunction can occur at chromosome 21 and the possible outcomes of fertilization of a nondisjunctive egg cell by a normal sperm cell.

of male gametogenesis causes men a unique set of problems not seen in women. Essentially, males begin each meiosis anew (as compared to women, who start meiosis *in utero*). Males are thus beginning meiosis from gametic progenitor cells that have been exposed to 13 or more years of environmental mutagens, which can damage the DNA of these cells. Consequently, when meiosis occurs from these cells, the resulting sperm cells have an increased number of genetic point mutations. These mutations affect individual genes either by changing the protein the gene codes for, or stopping the gene from coding for any protein at all. Moreover, these mutations accumulate over a man's lifetime leading to what can only be described as a paternal age effect. Females, having already moved past the step in meiosis that uses progenitor cells, are not subject to such cumulative effects. So while mothers may be more likely to pass on errors in chromosome number (at least to their live born offspring), fathers are more likely to pass on mutations that affect the genes directly by the creation of new mutations. Importantly, errors in chromosome number can be detected prenatally by a host of diagnostic tests, while most disorders associated with new mutations cannot. This has led contemporary researchers to advise men to have their children before age 40. Therefore, when one really looks at the data in terms of producing healthy babies, the biological clock ticks just as loudly for men as it does for women.

SUMMARY

Mistakes in gametogenesis occur in the making of eggs as well as in the making of sperm. Nondisjunction during meiosis resulting in gametes with too few or too many chromosomes occurs more commonly in females than in males and appears to increase in frequency with age. The creation of new alleles occurs more commonly in sperm cells than in egg cells because males produce sperm from cells that are exposed to many different mutagens over the course of a man's lifetime. The effects of these point mutations are cumulative and, therefore, increase in number as a man ages.

FERTILIZATION

When you were conceived, the egg cell your mother ovulated fused with a sperm cell's nucleus from your father. The egg cell contained 23 of your mother's chromosomes and the sperm nucleus contained 23 of your father's chromosomes. This fusion, therefore, left you with 23 pairs of chromosomes, which then underwent millions of rounds of mitosis to produce all the cells of your body.

In this section, we will first consider the anatomy of egg and sperm cells, the journey each cell takes in order to meet the other, and the process of fertilization itself. Further, we will attempt to pin down the time period during which a woman is actually fertile and how that fertility, in some instances, leads to multiple births (twinning). Finally, we will see how some couples attempt to select the sex of their child by capitalizing on purported differences between male-producing sperm and female-producing sperm.

The Egg Cell

The egg cell is the only cell in humans capable of developing into a new individual. Once fertilized, this single cell can give rise to every type of cell found in an adult human. In fact, some species of plants, insects, lizards, and fish are able to reproduce from eggs that become activated without sperm in a process called *parthenogenesis*. In other organisms, some frogs for example, sperm activate the eggs but are not absolutely required for development. This is evidenced by the fact that frog egg cells can be stimulated to develop experimentally by pricking them with a needle.

Parthenogenesis is not, however, possible in humans for two reasons. First, the sperm cell contributes the centrosome, containing a pair of centrioles, which is originally located at the base of the sperm tail. Centrioles are required for the formation of the spindle apparatus,

which separates chromosomes during mitosis and meiosis. This pair of centrioles contributed by the sperm duplicates itself and one pair moves to each pole of the egg cell in order to nucleate a spindle. Sometime after being ovulated the egg cell loses its centrioles, and, therefore, they must be supplied by the sperm at fertilization. Rarely, centrosomes will form *de novo* (from scratch) in human egg cells. When this occurs, the egg cell may duplicate its DNA and begin dividing. This self-activated embryo is only able to sustain itself for a brief time, and what results is an unusual tumor of the ovary called a *teratoma*.

Teratomas are normally benign tumors composed of rudimentary bone and nerve and may have well-developed skin, hair, and teeth. Teratomas have chromosomes derived only from the woman in whose body they reside, so they are examples of parthenogenesis since development began in the absence of sperm. There are however, some tissues a teratoma cannot make, like skeletal tissues, and further development of those tissue types is prevented. Why this parthenogenic tumor can develop no further seems to involve a phenomenon called *imprinting*.

Imprinting of chromosomes (the second reason that parthenogenesis is not possible in humans) is thought to provide our cells with a mechanism for insuring that a fertilized egg cell receives one maternally inherited chromosome and one paternally inherited chromosome. Imprinting involves the addition of methyl groups (CH_3) to some genes on some chromosomes in order to inactivate them. Women methylate certain genes and men methylate others. During gametogenesis, the imprint from your parents is erased, and your own imprint, based on your sex, is placed on the chromosomes you will donate to your gametes. It appears that proper fetal development requires one maternally and one paternally imprinted chromosome.

A nice example is provided by the imprinting of genes involved in early human development and placental development. It appears that genes that regulate early human development are targets for imprinting (and inactivation) by males and genes that regulate proper placental development are targets for imprinting (and inactivation) by females. This means that genes on chromosomes derived from fathers are responsible for the proper formation of the placenta and that genes on chromosomes inherited from mothers aid in early fetal growth. One chromosome of each homologous pair must be from a female and the other must be from a male in order to direct early development.

Thus, proper fetal development requires a spindle apparatus for cell division as well as genetic input from chromosomes inherited from a female and chromosomes inherited from a male. The sperm's contribution of a centrosome and the imprinting of different genes in males than in females prevent parthenogenesis in humans.

Recall that the egg cell at the time of ovulation is paused at metaphase II of meiosis. It is smaller in size than the period at the end of this sentence. Human egg cells can be much smaller than the egg cells of other organisms because offspring can obtain nutrients from their mothers during intrauterine development. Chicken eggs, frog eggs, and the eggs of other nonmammals must be quite large in order to provide nourishment for the developing embryo until it is able to feed itself. This nourishment comes in the form of yolk in the egg cell's cytoplasm, which is rich in fats and carbohydrates. When you fry an egg for breakfast, you are actually eating the chicken's enormous unfertilized ovulated egg cell (yolk) along with some extracellular material (egg white).

The anatomy of a human egg cell is shown in Figure 9.6. Surrounding the human egg cell is the egg coat, or *zona pellucida*. The zona is a translucent, non-cellular matrix rich in glycoproteins (proteins covalently bound to carbohydrates) made and secreted by the cell itself. This protective layer aids in shielding the egg from mechanical damage and acts as a species-specific barrier to sperm, admitting only those sperm that are of the same species as the egg itself. This specificity is maintained in large part by the zona glycoprotein ZP3. This glycoprotein binds with receptors on the heads of sperm from the human species only.

FIGURE 9.6   The Egg Cell

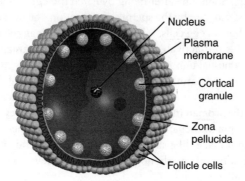

Surrounding the human egg cell plasma membrane is the zona pellucida. The zona pellucida contains ZP3 glycoproteins that aid egg and sperm binding. Just under the plasma membrane of the egg cell are secretory vesicles containing hydrolytic enzymes called cortical granules. Cortical granules secrete their enzymes outward to alter the ZP3 glycoproteins, thereby preventing the binding of more than one sperm to the zona pellucida. Follicle cells are present outside the zona to help nourish the developing oocyte.

Just under the plasma membrane of the egg cell one finds secretory vesicles containing hydrolytic enzymes (enzymes that digest protein) surrounded by membranes. These cortical granules migrate to their position underneath the plasma membrane after being modified and sorted by the Golgi apparatus. From this position, the granules secrete their enzymes outward toward the zona to alter its composition.

Follicle cells (derived from the ovary) are present outside the zona to help nourish the developing oocyte. The egg cell and surrounding follicle cells in the ovary are called the follicle. When the ovarian follicle bursts at ovulation, the egg cell and some of the surrounding cells are released.

Inside the egg cell are the organelles required to begin protein synthesis should fertilization occur and many mitochondria to provide the energy required for the very active egg cell.

The Sperm Cell

At ejaculation, the sperm cell is composed of a small head containing the DNA, a midpiece that has mitochondria wrapped around it in order to provide energy for the journey to the oviduct, and a tail (flagellum) to help propel the sperm. Additionally, at the tip of the sperm lies the Golgi-derived acrosomal vesicle. This vesicle is full of enzymes that act in concert with the constituents of the zona pellucida to form a path the sperm can follow to reach the egg cell's membrane (Figure 9.7).

The Journeys of the Egg and Sperm Cells

From its position in the oviduct, the egg cell will beckon batches of sperm toward itself by secreting a chemical attractant.

When the follicle bursts at ovulation, the egg cell and some surrounding follicle cells are released. The egg cell is moved from the ovary to the oviduct by the fimbriae. Inside the oviduct, the egg cell is propelled by the increased muscular activity of the oviduct and the subsequent increased current of fluids leading down the oviduct, which occur around the

FIGURE 9.7   The Sperm Cell

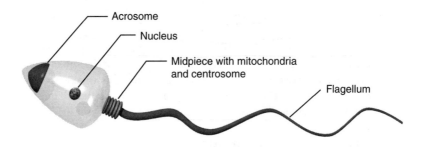

The sperm cell consists of the sperm head, neck, and tail. The sperm head contains the nucleus, its chromosomes, and the acrosome filled with enzymes to help the sperm tunnel through the egg cell's zona pellucida. The neck of the sperm contains mitochondria and the tail is used for propulsion.

time of ovulation. From this position in the oviduct, the egg cell will beckon batches of sperm toward itself by secreting a chemical attractant.

Sperm cells and the accompanying secretions typically found in an ejaculate are collectively called semen. After ejaculation into the vagina, a large percentage of the sperm will become lost or die. Of the roughly 300 million sperm ejaculated, only about 200 manage to reach the site of fertilization in the oviduct. Initially, sperm must survive the acidic (low pH) conditions of the upper vagina. The natural acidity of the upper vagina works to help prevent bacterial infections in women and can also kill sperm. When sperm are ejaculated, they are surrounded by glandular secretions from the male reproductive tract which help decrease the pH of the vagina. In fact, it takes less than 10 seconds for the semen and vaginal secretions to buffer each other, allowing the sperm to survive.

Also present in the semen are substances that interact with the walls of the upper vagina, helping the walls to contract in order to propel the sperm to the cervix. Once inside the cervix, most of the sperm will swim into the many miniature folds present in the walls of the cervix and, will make it no further. At the time of ovulation, however, hormonal changes have resulted in a change in the cervical mucus, from a thick, paste-like mucus to a less viscous, stringy type of mucus, which both facilitates movement of sperm through the cervix and toward the uterus and prolongs the life of the sperm. Once in the uterus, sperm are thought to propel themselves toward the oviducts. Sperm can be helped on this part of their journey by contractions of the smooth muscles of the uterus if female orgasm has recently occurred. In moving through the uterine cavity to the oviduct, roughly half the sperm head toward an ovary that did not/will not ovulate, and there will be no egg for them to fuse with. The oviducts themselves undergo muscular contractions around the time of ovulation, and these contractions allow the sperm to move toward the upper portion of the oviduct to wait for an egg cell to be ovulated. It takes about 1/2 hour to move a sperm from the upper vagina to the oviduct.

Once in the oviduct, sperm accumulate in the isthmus where they remain motionless until the egg sends out a chemical signal. The chemical beckons a subpopulation of sperm to move toward the egg and attempt fertilization. This signal is a follicular factor that enhances the motility of only those sperm that will be physiologically able to penetrate the egg's zona pellucida. At a given time only 2% to 12% of all sperm in the oviduct are actually able to fertilize an egg cell. These sperm have been previously capacitated, a phenomenon which involves changes in the plasma membrane of the sperm cell in the region which covers the acrosome. These glycoprotein and lipid changes to the sperm plasma membrane allow the acrosomal reaction to occur. Capacitation is absolutely required for fertilization to occur and can be accomplished *in vitro* (in glass or test tube) by placing sperm in contact with uterine tissue for several hours. The state of capacitation is temporary, lasting from 50 minutes to 4 hours. Once a population of cells loses capacitation, it no longer displays chemotaxis (movement in response to a chemical) toward the egg. Serially, small batches of sperm from a single ejaculate are capacitated in preparation for chemotaxis toward the egg cell. If no egg cell is present to secrete the follicular factor required for chemotaxis, a new batch is readied. In this manner, the egg cell selectively recruits sperm for fertilization.

The Process of Fertilization

If sperm arrive in the oviduct more than 3 to 5 days before ovulation, or 1 day after ovulation, they will die within a few hours. Around the time of ovulation cervical secretions allow sperm to survive in the oviduct for 3 to 5 days. If intercourse occurs from 3 to 5 days prior to ovulation, on the day of ovulation, or up to 1 day after ovulation, fertilization may occur. If intercourse occurs more than 24 hours after ovulation, the egg cell will already be breaking down, and due to changes in the cervical mucus which occur after ovulation, it is less likely that sperm will be present in the oviducts.

Assuming both sperm and egg are present, the sperm cell must move through the follicular cells and then pass through the zona pellucida to reach the plasma membrane of the egg cell. Getting through the zona pellucida requires binding of the sperm plasma membrane receptor to the egg cell's ZP3 glycoprotein. This binding triggers the release of the acrosomal enzymes from the sperm head. These sperm enzymes interact with the egg cell's zona pellucida to allow the formation of a tunnel through the zona pellucida toward the egg cell's plasma membrane. Once through this tunnel, the sperm plasma membrane and the egg plasma membrane fuse. In response to this fushion, the cortical granules of the egg cell release their contents into the zona pellucida where they modify the many thousands of ZP3 glycoproteins present to prevent any more sperm from binding. After egg and sperm membrane fusion, microvilli ("tiny hairs") on the surface of the egg cell allow the egg cell to envelope the sperm and draw the sperm cell nucleus and centrosome into the egg.

The egg cell now rapidly moves from metaphase II through meiosis II and, consequently, the second polar body is released. Sperm and egg nuclei fuse and their chromosomes undergo a round of DNA synthesis so that all 46 chromosomes are now composed of sister chromatids. The centrioles divide and nucleate the formation of a new spindle apparatus, on which the newly duplicated chromosomes move to the metaphase plate to begin the mitotic divisions of early development.

SUMMARY

Fertilization generally occurs in the oviduct when the egg cell binds through its species specific receptor on the zona pellucida to a sperm cell. This binding stimulates the release, from the capacitated sperm's acrosomal vesicle, of enzymes that interact with the zona pellucida to help clear a path for the sperm. Once through the zona pellucida, the sperm plasma membrane and the egg plasma membrane fuse, and the sperm nucleus and centrosome are drawn into the egg cell. In response to the binding of the sperm and egg plasma membranes, the cortical granules of the egg cell release their contents into the zona pellucida where they modify the many thousands of ZP3 glycoproteins present to prevent any more sperm from binding. The binding of the sperm and egg plasma membranes also stimulates the egg cell to finish meiosis II, resulting in the production of the second polar body. At this time, the sperm and egg chromosomes duplicate themselves, then move on the newly formed spindle to the metaphase plate to begin mitosis (Figure 9.8).

FIGURE 9.8 Fertilization

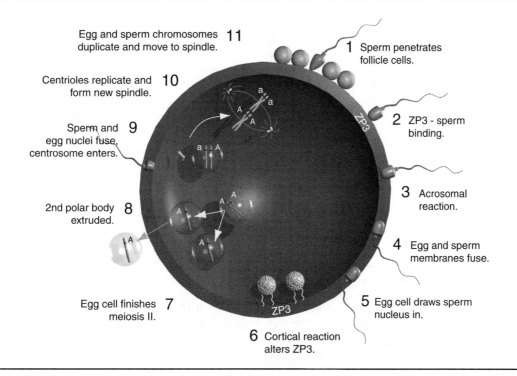

Egg and sperm chromosomes **11**
duplicate and move to spindle.

Centrioles replicate and **10**
form new spindle.

Sperm and **9**
egg nuclei fuse,
centrosome enters.

2nd polar body **8**
extruded.

Egg cell finishes **7**
meiosis II.

1 Sperm penetrates
follicle cells.

2 ZP3 - sperm
binding.

3 Acrosomal
reaction.

4 Egg and sperm
membranes fuse.

5 Egg cell draws sperm
nucleus in.

6 Cortical reaction
alters ZP3.

Fertilization generally occurs in the oviduct where the sperm cell finds its way through the layer of follicle cells that surround the egg cell (1). Once through the follicle cells, the egg cell's ZP3 binds to the sperm cell's receptor (2). This binding stimulates the release, from the capacitated sperm's acrosomal vesicle, of enzymes that interact with the zona pellucida to clear a path for the sperm (3). Once through the zona pellucida, the sperm plasma membrane and the egg plasma membrane fuse (4) and the egg cell envelopes the sperm nucleus (5). In response to the binding of the sperm and egg plasma membranes, the cortical granules of the egg cell release their contents into the zona pellucida where they modify the many thousands of ZP3 receptors present to prevent any more sperm from binding (6). The binding of the sperm and egg plasma membranes also stimulates the egg cell to finish meiosis II (7), resulting in the production of the second polar body (8). At this time, the egg and sperm nuclei fuse and the sperm centrosome enters (9). Next, the centrioles replicate (10). Finally, the egg and sperm chromosomes duplicate and move to the newly formed spindle to being mitosis (11).

FERTILITY

From a more pragmatic standpoint, it is important for sexually active women to know exactly when during their cycle they are fertile. To date, the most powerful indicator of fertility seems to be the presence of thin, very dense, stringy cervical mucus that has both the consistency and appearance of raw egg white. Lining the cervix are crypts or folds which produce this mucus and secrete it before ovulation, hence the presence of this mucus gives advance indication that ovulation is approaching. Stringy mucus of this type is arranged in parallel strands which function as channels for the sperm to move through, preventing the sperm from becoming stuck in the folds of the cervix. In the absence of this type of mucus, sperm will die within a few hours. When it is present, they can live anywhere from 3 to 5 days. Most researchers now believe that fertility starts at the beginning of mucus discharge (allowing sperm passage through the cervix), continues each day that mucus is present, and for 3 days past mucus secretion. Chapter 12 addresses methods for determining whether cervical mucus is the type associated with fertility or the type that actually blocks sperm passage.

A recent study by A. J. Wilcox (1995) helps to narrow down the period of fertility. This study indicates that the fertile time for a woman consists of the 5 days prior to ovulation and the day of ovulation itself. In this study, the probability of conception ranged from 10% when intercourse occurred 5 days before ovulation to 33% when it occurred on the day of ovulation. This does not mean that a couple will experience a pregnancy if they have unprotected intercourse during this time period. Wilcox estimates that only 37% of all ovulatory menstrual cycles will produce a pregnancy and that not all cycles are ovulatory (around 63% of cycles are ovulatory). Furthermore, it is generally accepted that as few as 30% of all human conceptions survive to birth, with a large majority of these failures lost in the very early stages of pregnancy.

TWINNING

Some fertilizations result in multiple births (twins), which can arise in one of several manners. Twinning can result from the fertilization of two separate eggs by two separate sperm. In order for this to occur, a woman must ovulate more than one egg in a particular menstrual cycle. Usually, both of these eggs are ovulated within the same 24-hour period. The children resulting from this type of fertilization, called dizygotic twinning, are genetically no more similar than nontwin siblings. Monozygotic twins arise when one egg cell is fertilized by one sperm cell if the fertilized egg cell divides one extra time very early on in development. Cells of a two-celled embryo can separate and each cell may develop into a complete fetus, yielding twins who carry identical chromosomes and genes. Monozygosity can also arise later in development when a group of cells called the inner cell mass subdivides itself forming two separate groups of cells which then develop independently into two identical individuals. Very rarely, the two inner cell masses fail to separate completely, giving rise to conjoined (Siamese) twins. In the United States, around 1 in every 88 births results in twins. Interestingly, different racial groups experience different rates of twinning, with African Americans having the highest rate in the United States at 1 in every 70 births. There is even some evidence of a genetic component to twinning. Some scientists believe that a certain region on the X chromosome may be associated with increased frequency of multiple ovulation in women whose X chromosome bears this region.

Less common mechanisms of twinning are still speculative, because it appears that not all monozygotic twins arise as a result of one egg cell being fertilized by one sperm. Some scientists believe that fertilization of the second polar body by a different sperm than the sperm that fertilizes the mature egg cell can occur. This second polar body is most often degraded, but the fact that it is produced in the oviduct only in response to fertilization has led many scientists to hypothesize that this second polar body may itself be fertilized and result in twin babies. These babies would have identical genetic contributions from the egg cell (remember that the second polar body is produced after anaphase II, which separates the identical sister chromatids into two separate daughter cells), but different paternal contributions from each of the sperm. These two individuals would be (on average) 3/4 genetically identical. Finally, some investigators estimate that many of us began as a member of a twin, with the other member of the pair not surviving early gestation. It is estimated that for every pair of live born twins, 10 to 12 twin pregnancies occurred but ultimately resulted in single births.

SEX SELECTION

Is it possible to influence the sex of your child by timing sexual intercourse in relation to ovulation, or by changing the environment of the female reproductive tract to favor female-producing sperm over male-producing sperm (or vice versa)? Some researchers (e.g., Shettles and Rorvik, 1989) believe that it is possible to exploit what they see as the differences between X-bearing sperm and Y-bearing sperm in an attempt to favor fertilization by one or the other. Recall that human males have one X chromosome and one Y chromosome that are separated from each other during meiosis. Males can either make sperm with an X chromosome or sperm with a Y chromosome and thereby determine the sex of a child. If a sperm bearing an X chromosome fertilizes an egg cell (which nearly always has one X chromosome) a female child results, and if a sperm bearing a Y chromosome fertilizes the egg cell, a male child results. Shettles and Rorvik believe that since X-bearing sperm are heavier (the X chromosome has more genes on it than the Y chromosome) they move toward the egg more slowly. They also believe that X-bearing sperm are heartier and, therefore, less susceptible to environmental extremes such as a high pH. They believe it is possible to exploit the differences in agility and response to pH in order to select for sperm of one type or the other.

According to Shettles and Rorvik, in order to exploit the differing agilities of X-bearing and Y-bearing sperm and have an X-bearing sperm fertilize the egg cell, a couple should have sexual intercourse prior to ovulation so that the X-bearing sperm will have a chance to reach the egg cell before it degenerates. To have a Y-bearing sperm cell fertilize the egg cell, a couple should have sexual intercourse as close to the time of ovulation as possible so that the quicker Y-bearing sperm will arrive at the oviduct at the same time as the egg, before any of the slower X-bearing sperm have made it to the oviduct.

To exploit the different responses to pH, couples should again time intercourse in relation to ovulation and also artificially alter the pH of the female reproductive tract by using douches of high or low pH. Around the time of ovulation, cervical mucus is at its most alkaline, which allows the Y-bearing sperm to survive, again suggesting that more males will be conceived if intercourse occurs around the time of ovulation. Alkaline douches made of a quart of water with two tablespoons of baking soda may help make the environment even more alkaline thus aiding the Y-bearing sperm. Intercourse a few days before ovulation would again favor X-bearing sperm as they would be more likely to survive the more acidic environment prior to ovulation. Acidic douches (1 quart of water and 2 tablespoons of white vinegar) may help make the environment more acidic and thus favor the X-bearing sperm.

All of this is quite interesting but more folklore than science, and it seems to be a case of applying cultural norms to gametes. The egg cell has been likened to the stable but passive female, while the sperm cell resembles the active, agile male. Indeed, there are very few scientists who support these claims. In fact, several studies have shown that pH has little effect on sperm motility and that there is no association between the sex of the baby and the timing of intercourse in relation to ovulation.

REFERENCES

Bordson, B. L., & Leonardo, V. S. (1991). The appropriate upper age limit for semen donors: A review of the genetic effects of paternal age. *Fertility and Sterility, 56*(3), 397–401.

Bryan, E. (1994). Trends in twinning rates. *Lancet (North American Edition), 343,* 1151–1152.

Chandley, A. C. (1991). On the paternal origin of *de novo* mutations in man. *Journal of Medical Genetics, 28*(4), 217–223.

Cohen-Dayag, A., Ralt, D., Tur-Kapsa, I., Mashiac, S., & Eisenbach, M. (1995). Sperm capacitation in humans is transient and correlates with chemotactic responsiveness to follicular factors. *Proceedings of the National Academy of Science U.S.A.*, *92*(24), 11039–11043.

Diasio, R. B., & Glass, R. H. (1971). Effects of pH on the migration of X and Y sperm. *Fertility and Sterility*, *22*, 303–305.

Gaulden, M. E. (1992). Maternal age effect: The enigma of Down syndrome and other trisomic conditions. *Mutation Research*, *296*(1–2), 69–88.

Goshen, R., Ben-Rafael, Z., Gonik, B., Lustig, O., Tannos, V., deGroot, N., & Hochberg, A. (1994). The role of genomic imprinting in implantation. *Fertility and Sterility*, *62*(5), 903–910.

Grimm, T., Meng, G., Liechti-Gallati, S., Bettecken, T., Mueller, C. R., & Mueller, B. (1994). On the origin of deletions and point mutations in Duchenne muscular dystrophy: Most deletions arise in oogenesis and most point mutations result from events in spermatogenesis. *Journal of Medical Genetics*, *31*(3), 183–186.

Shettles, L. B., & Rorvik, D. M. (1994). *How to choose the sex of your baby*. Doubleday.

Tycko, B. (1994). Genomic imprinting: Mechanism and role in human pathology. *American Journal of Pathology*, *144*(3), 431–443.

Turner, G., Robinson, H., & Wake, S. (1994). Dizygous twinning and premature menopause in fragile X syndrome. *Lancet (North American Edition)*, *334*, 1500.

Wilcox, A. J., Weinberg, C. R., & Baird, D. D. (1995). Timing of sexual intercourse in relation to ovulation. *New England Journal of Medicine*, *33*(23), 1517–1521.

CHAPTER 10

Episiotomy, surgery to increase the size of the vaginal opening during delivery, is usually performed without a woman's consent.

PREGNANCY
AND BIRTHING

INTRODUCTION

In addition to being a time of great excitement, pregnancy is a time of considerable biological change. This chapter will describe the changes a woman may experience while pregnant and during labor and delivery.

PREGNANCY AND CHANGES IN THE BODY

In order to accomplish the amazing feat of producing a baby from a fertilized egg cell, a woman's body undergoes many changes. A pregnant woman produces a new endocrine organ (the placenta) and develops the ability to communicate with the baby through an umbilical cord. Her uterus increases in size as the baby grows, and she develops the ability to produce breast milk. To accomplish all of this, many biological changes must occur. Most women will experience some or all of the normal changes discussed in this chapter. Although the list of potential symptoms seems daunting, most women do not experience all of these symptoms. In addition, most women report that, for the most part, they enjoy being pregnant.

Endocrine Changes

The major endocrine change during pregnancy is the formation of the placenta, an endocrine organ inside the uterus. The placenta is produced by the cooperative actions of

---

FIGURE 10.1   Implantation of the Trophoblast

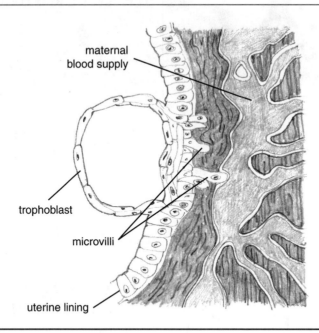

The trophoblast burrows into the lining of the uterus and begins to form the fetal portion of the placenta. To accomplish this, the trophoblast extends fingerlike projections (microvilli) into the lining of the uterus, which will be in close contact with the maternal blood supply.

the fertilized egg cell and the mother's uterus. Prior to the burrowing of the fertilized egg cell into the uterine lining (implantation), the fertilized egg cell has begun dividing and consists of about 100 cells. This ball of cells floats around in the uterus and begins to differentiate into an inner group of cells, which will become the embryo, and an outer ring of cells called the trophoblast that will become the fetal portion of the placenta. About the seventh day after fertilization, the *trophoblast* implants in the uterine wall and begins to infiltrate the uterine lining, forming finger-like projections that are able to carry blood (Figure 10.1). Maternal uterine blood vessels erode and spurt blood into the area surrounding the fetal blood vessels. This close positioning of fetal and maternal blood supplies allows the exchange of nutrients and wastes to occur. Blood cells and bacteria do not normally pass between fetal and maternal blood supplies. Substances that can be freely exchanged between the fetus and the mother include water, salt, hormones, viruses, and many drugs.

The cells of the early placenta synthesize human chorionic gonadotropin (hCG), which serves to maintain the corpus luteum. (Recall that the corpus luteum is the empty follicle present in the ovary after the ovulation of its egg cell. During a nonpregnant menstrual cycle, the corpus luteum will regress.) The continued activity of the corpus luteum results in a steady increase in the levels of progesterone and estrogen during the first 5 weeks of pregnancy. Once the placenta has established its own hormone production, the corpus luteum is no longer necessary. Consequently, hCG is only secreted during the first trimester. In order to establish its own hormone production, the placenta utilizes some maternal and some fetal precursors. This is necessary because the placenta does not have all the enzymes required to synthesize progesterone and estrogen. The placenta uses cholesterol supplied by the mother in order to synthesize progesterone. Progesterone reduces contractility of the uterus to prevent expulsion of the early fetus and prevents ovulation by suppressing LH secretion. Estrogen levels are also elevated during pregnancy. Estrogen stimulates continued uterine growth by acting on the smooth muscles of the uterus. The androgen compounds required for estrogen production are derived from the mother's blood stream in the early months of gestation. However, by the 20th week of pregnancy, the majority of estrogens are derived from fetal androgens. Regulation of placental hormone secretion is provided by GnRH, which is also synthesized by the placenta during pregnancy.

An additional hormone synthesized by the placenta is somatomammotropin, which works with estrogen, progesterone, and prolactin to stimulate development of the mother's mammary glands and, consequently, breast milk production. Near term, as the mother's estrogen level drops, prolactin is produced by the pituitary.

At term, the normal placenta is a disk-shaped structure approximately 6 or 7 inches in diameter, 1 ½ inches in thickness, and weighs a little less than 2 pounds.

Ovarian Changes

During pregnancy, the ovaries no longer undergo monthly cyclic changes seen in a non-pregnant woman. The high levels of steroid hormones produced by the placenta inhibit follicle growth and maturation by negative feedback on the hypothalamus, and ovulation ceases.

Uterine Changes

The pregnant uterus increases in size and consequently changes its position within the pelvis during pregnancy (Figure 10.2). The increase in size is about tenfold and is due to

---

FIGURE 10.2   Changes in Uterine Size, Shape, and Positioning During Pregnancy

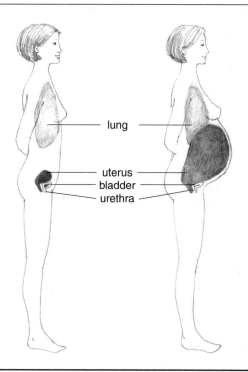

lung

uterus
bladder
urethra

During pregnancy, the uterus increases in size and consequently changes its position within the pelvis, placing stress on the diaphragm and bladder.

an increase in the number of muscle fibers, blood vessels, nerves, and lymphatic vessels in the uterine wall. The increased size causes the uterus to press against the bladder, resulting in an increased frequency of urination because the bladder holds less fluid: As the uterus continues to develop, it can begin to fill the abdominal cavity and press on the diaphragm. Shortness of breath may result if pressure on the lungs and the diaphragm occurs.

The uterus may sink downward in the pelvis several weeks before term in a process that is known as lightening or dropping. This occurs as the fetal head descends into the pelvis. Late in the pregnancy, the uterus can tighten every now and then during what are called Braxton-Hicks contractions. It is believed that these early contractions serve to strengthen uterine muscles in preparation for labor.

Cervical Changes

Increased blood flow to the cervix "softens" it during pregnancy, which allows the cervix to dilate and efface (thin out) during labor and delivery. The cervix changes color with the increased blood flow and appears bluish. The higher levels of estrogen and progesterone cause an increase in cervical secretions during pregnancy as well. Under the influence of progesterone, a thick cervical plug is formed. The so-called mucus plug blocks the entrance to the uterus and protects the fetus against bacterial infections.

Breast Changes

Very early in pregnancy, increases in ovarian estrogen and progesterone cause the breasts to swell as milk glands begin to develop. For many women this results in a feeling of tingling or throbbing, which is noticeably more severe than the breast tenderness felt premenstrually. Hormonally regulated increases in blood supply also cause the veins to become more visually prominent and the areola to darken. The small oily or sebaceous glands (glands of Montgomery) surrounding the nipples may become more prominent as well. During the later part of pregnancy, a milky fluid called colostrum may be secreted from the nipples.

Circulatory Changes

The total amount of blood in a woman's body increases by 25% during pregnancy. This increase is required to supply the growing uterus, to meet the nutritional and waste removal needs of the fetus, and to function as a protective reserve in case of hemorrhage during delivery.

Decreased blood flow to the lower extremities results from the pressure of the uterus on the blood vessels of the lower pelvis. With this decrease in the rate of flow, there is some stagnation of blood in the legs leading to abnormally dilated veins called varicose veins (Figure 10.3). Hemorrhoids are varicosities of the rectal veins, which may also occur during pregnancy when the pressure of pelvic organs on veins in the rectum causes the veins to dilate. The larger uterus also puts pressure on the lymphatic vessels of the pelvis, causing impairment of lymph drainage from the legs, which can result in swelling in the feet, ankles, and legs.

Vaginal Changes

The increased blood volume dilates blood vessels in the vaginal walls and, as a result, the lining of the vagina takes on a bluish cast. Higher estrogen levels cause the cells of the vaginal mucus to increase in size, yielding increased vaginal secretions as these cells slough off. Thickening, softening, and relaxation of the lining of the vagina increases the distensibility of the vagina in preparation for birth.

Bladder Changes

Many women find that they need to urinate more frequently during the early months of pregnancy due to the compression of the bladder by the growing uterus. Frequent urination

FIGURE 10.3 Varicose Veins

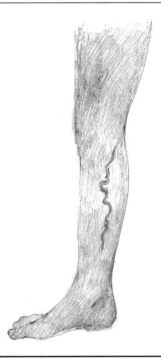

is less common during the middle of pregnancy but can reoccur near delivery when the baby descends into the pelvis.

The urethra is also distorted by the changing size and shape of the uterus. As the bladder and urethra are pulled upward by the growing uterus, the muscles that control urination are stretched and may become less efficient. This loss of efficiency may result in stress incontinence. Women who experience stress incontinence lose urine involuntarily when they cough, sneeze, or laugh, during or even after pregnancy because these muscles can be permanently damaged.

Skin Changes

Some women acquire stretch marks on their breasts and/or abdomen during pregnancy due to the tearing of the elastic tissues in the skin as the breasts and the abdomen enlarge (Figure 10.4). Dark haired women may develop a dark brown line, called the linea nigra, which extends from their naval to their pubis.

Hair growth may accelerate during pregnancy. Hair normally goes through a growing phase, followed by a resting phase, after which hair is shed and replaced by new hair. During pregnancy, fewer hairs enter the resting phase, so hair becomes thicker and grows faster. After delivery, there is a period of catching up, during which a woman's hair is lost at an increased rate.

Musculoskeletal Changes

In order to increase the size of the pelvic cavity, the joint between the pubic bones loosens, as do the joints between the sacrum and the pelvis. This loosening is in response to a hormone called relaxin, produced by the placenta and corpus luteum. The strain on the joint between the sacrum and the spine becomes greater near term as a woman attempts to

FIGURE 10.4   Stretch Marks

compensate for the increased weight in her abdomen by tilting her pelvis forward. The changes in gait caused by increased body weight can lead to backaches.

 ## Gastrointestinal Changes

The musculature of the entire intestinal tract loses much of its tone during pregnancy. As a result, peristalsis, the series of wavelike movements of the intestines, is slowed and the length of time it takes food to pass through the intestinal tract is prolonged. This decreased tonicity, when coupled with increased water retention, often leads to constipation.

"Morning sickness," or pregnancy related nausea and vomiting, is believed to be caused by increased levels of circulating hormones, decreased tonicity of the stomach, and/or alterations in maternal glucose levels. Increased estrogen accumulating in the cells of the stomach may cause stomach irritation. The loss of tone of the stomach muscles and the change in position of the stomach are conducive to the flow of intestinal contents back into the stomach. Because the fetus uses 10% of the mother's blood glucose, lowered maternal glucose levels may cause nausea and vomiting.

Heartburn is caused by regurgitation of stomach contents into the esophagus. The sphincter at the junction between the stomach and esophagus normally functions to prevent gastric acids from entering the esophagus, but its relaxed state during pregnancy allows stomach juices to enter the esophagus and cause heartburn.

Weight Changes

Weight gain is one of the most obvious symptoms of pregnancy. However, the early months of pregnancy may be accompanied by moderate weight loss because of morning sickness. Between the third and the ninth months of pregnancy, most women gain approximately 24 pounds. After subtracting the weight of the fetus, usually close to 7 pounds, the remaining weight gain consists of 4 pounds of amniotic fluid, membranes, and the placenta; 6 pounds of extra fluid distributed throughout the body; 3 pounds of fat; and 4 pounds of increased weight in the uterus and breasts.

Changes in Sleep Patterns and Requirements

When progesterone and estrogen levels are high early in pregnancy, women may require more than normal amounts of sleep. Progesterone has a sedative effect on many women and estrogen may increase REM sleep. Increased REM sleep decreases the quality of sleep. After the third month of pregnancy, hormone levels decrease enough that fatigue is lessened. Later in pregnancy, fatigue can return because it is hard to find a comfortable position for sleeping and because increases in the frequency of urination may awaken a woman several times during the night.

■ DISCUSSION QUESTION 1

1.1. Given the remarkable amount of physical changes a pregnant woman experiences, do you believe that special accommodations should be made for pregnant workers?

COMPLICATIONS OF PREGNANCY

Ectopic Pregnancy

Embryos that implant in a place other than the upper uterus initiate ectopic pregnancies. If an embryo implants too low in the uterus, the placenta may grow over the cervical opening, forming what is called *placenta praevia*. As the cervix opens during the later part of pregnancy, the placenta tears causing the woman to bleed profusely. With medical supervision, most women with placenta praevia give birth to healthy babies. When implantation occurs directly on the cervix, the embryo is usually not able to finish development and spontaneously aborts.

It is also possible, though rare, for an embryo to implant outside of the uterus. Ectopic pregnancies outside the uterine cavity occur about once in every 300 pregnancies and are a major cause of maternal death. If implantation occurs in an oviduct, the tube will eventually rupture causing severe internal bleeding. Many tubal pregnancies may be the result of scarred tubes, which result from prior infections. Implantation can also occur in the ovaries or abdomen. For this to occur, the fertilized egg cell must be swept backwards out of the oviduct and the egg and sperm must meet and fuse in the ovary or abdomen.

Preeclampsia and Eclampsia

Compromised fluid flow to tissues, including fluid flow to the fetus, can result in a disease called pregnancy induced hypertension or *preeclampsia*. Approximately 7% of women whose pregnancies progress beyond the first trimester will develop preeclampsia, which is usually not diagnosed until 20 or more weeks after conception. Decreased fluid flow results in fluid retention, which causes swelling and excessive weight gain, the first indications that a woman may have preeclampsia. The inadequate delivery of fluids to organs is attributed to constriction of the smooth muscle that lines blood vessels and is called vasospasm. Such narrowed blood vessels transport smaller volumes of fluids at a faster rate resulting in high blood pressure, or hypertension, which is the second sign of preeclampsia. Proteins secreted in response to this condition are found at high levels in the urine, a third sign of preeclampsia. The importance of universal access to good prenatal care is evidenced by the fact that, when detected early, measures can be taken to prevent preeclampsia from progressing into eclampsia.

A patient with preeclampsia is always in danger of rapidly developing eclampsia, which is distinguished by convulsions that may lead to coma. Other maternal risks of eclampsia include liver and kidney failure. The fetal risks include poor growth, premature delivery, and death.

Treatment of preeclampsia involves slowing the condition's progress in order to allow fetal growth to continue as long as possible. Bed rest is recommended in some cases of preeclampsia. This condition may also be controlled by a low salt diet or medications that help to decrease a woman's blood pressure. When severe, labor can be induced if the fetus is old enough to survive. This disease of pregnancy completely resolves when the placenta is delivered. Preeclampsia is more common with first pregnancies, multiple births, women over 40, teenagers, and women with a history of hypertension.

Gestational Diabetes

Gestational diabetes is a form of diabetes that occurs for the first time during pregnancy and resolves immediately after delivery. Approximately 3% of all pregnant women develop this condition, which is usually diagnosed in the second or third trimester. It is thought that hormonal changes during pregnancy can cause resistance to insulin, a hormone required to transport glucose across cell membranes. The increased insulin-resistant state that occurs during pregnancy is mediated by the high concentrations of the anti-insulin hormones estrogen, progesterone, somatomammotropin, and prolactin. Gestational diabetes occurs when a woman is unable to secrete enough insulin to overcome this resistance, and it results in high blood and urine glucose levels. For this reason, pregnant women normally have their urine glucose levels tested very early in the pregnancy and again around the 24th week. Approximately 50% of women who develop gestational diabetes will eventually develop adult onset (type II) diabetes. Some scientists believe that women with gestational diabetes are actually women with type II diabetes who are diagnosed for the first time when pregnant.

The risks of gestational diabetes include high birth weight babies (leading to increased rates of cesarean sections), premature delivery, and a higher incidence of fetal mortality. Treatment of gestational diabetes involves controlling dietary glucose ingestion. Preventing the accumulation of too much glucose may be facilitated by exercise, because exercise utilizes glucose present in the mother's blood stream. Insulin therapy is instituted when glucose levels cannot be managed through diet and exercise.

Spontaneous Abortions

Approximately 15% of all clearly established pregnancies result in spontaneous abortion. (Presumably there is some unknown percentage of spontaneous abortions that occur, even prior to a woman's realization that she is pregnant. These spontaneous abortions can easily be mistaken for a heavy menstrual flow.) Over half of the recognizable spontaneous abortions are thought to be the result of the fetus having too many or too few chromosomes or a chromosome that is missing genetic information. A woman with an abnormally shaped uterus is more susceptible to miscarriage, as is a woman whose cervix does not function properly or a woman with a hormonal disorder. Most miscarriages, though not all, occur between 6 and 8 weeks, with the actual expulsion of the fetus taking place 4 weeks later, between 10 and 12 weeks.

Hydatidiform Moles

Hydatidiform moles are benign trophoblastic tumors that result from a pregnancy during which the chorion (the outermost membrane which encloses the embryo) does not become vascular. Failure of the chorion to develop blood vessels results in the death of the embryo at a very early stage of development. This complication occurs approximately once in every 2,000 pregnancies. A woman with a hydatidiform mole has the symptoms of early pregnancy, however, her uterus will grow more rapidly than normal. Hydatidiform moles are generally expelled spontaneously around the 20th week. In a very small percentage of women, the hydatidiform mole becomes cancerous and invades the surrounding tissues.

PREGNANCY-RELATED TESTS

To determine if a woman is pregnant, a pregnancy test can be performed. The most common pregnancy tests are based on the detection of hCG in the blood or urine. Because hCG is produced by the placenta only when a woman is pregnant, detection of hCG is considered confirmation of pregnancy.

The presence of hCG in the blood or urine can be detected by immunoassay, which is a procedure that involves the use of an antibody-antigen reaction. Antibodies are proteins produced by the immune system in response to foreign substances, called antigens. Antibodies can also be synthesized in laboratories. When an antibody binds to its substrate in the body, the antigen is removed from circulation. The surface of a home pregnancy test contains antibodies to one sub-unit of the hCG protein, the alpha sub-unit. When urine is placed on this surface, the alpha sub-unit of hCG binds to the antibody and they move together toward the end of the test surface. In the region of the testing surface that shows the results of the pregnancy test, there are immobilized antibodies to a second sub-unit of the hCG protein, the beta sub-unit. If a woman is pregnant, these antibodies capture the antibody-hCG complex and a color change occurs, or a minus sign changes to a plus sign. If she is not pregnant, no hCG is produced or captured in the test region and no visible change occurs. An unbound antibody to hCG binds to the control region to produce a color change indicating that the test was performed properly and that all the test reagents are functioning.

This procedure can be carried out as early as several days before a woman's first missed period and does not necessitate a visit to a clinician because over-the-counter test kits are available at most pharmacies. Due to their convenience, home pregnancy test have largely replaced the "rabbit tests" of the past. Rabbits were formerly used to diagnose pregnancy by injecting urine from a potentially pregnant woman into an ear vein of a female rabbit. The presence of hCG in the urine would cause the rabbit to ovulate. Approximately 24 hours after injection, the rabbit would be killed and her ovaries would be examined for the presence of ruptured follicles.

Ultrasound

Ultrasound imaging is commonly used throughout pregnancy in order to monitor the growing fetus. This technology can be used to diagnose multiple pregnancies, problems with placenta formation, and some birth defects. Ultrasound can also help to accurately date the pregnancy and can determine the sex of the fetus. This technology uses high frequency sound waves that are above the range of sound audible to humans, so no noise is heard during this exam. As the waves travel through tissues, they are reflected back to an electronic monitor, which then forms a picture from the reflections.

Amniocentesis

Amniocentesis may be performed as early as 15 weeks into a pregnancy and involves the removal of amniotic fluid from the uterus. Fluid is removed from within the amniotic sac with a hollow needle (Figure 10.5). This fluid contains fetal cells that can be tested for certain genetic abnormalities and that can also be used to determine the sex of the fetus. Down's syndrome and neural tube defects can be detected by amniocentesis. This procedure can be carried out under local anesthesia and is relatively painless, but it has a 0.5% risk

FIGURE 10.5 Amniocentesis

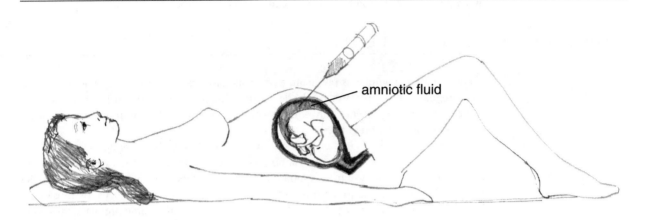

amniotic fluid

Fetal cells can be obtained from the amniotic fluid. These cells can be tested for genetic defects.

of causing miscarriage, which may result from disruption of the placenta. Due to the risk of miscarriage, this test is usually performed only if a woman has a family history of a disease or is over 35, because older women are more likely to have babies with Down's syndrome.

Chorionic Villus Sampling

Chorionic villus sampling is a procedure similar to amniocentesis that may be performed between the 6th and 12th weeks of gestation. The chorion is the vascular outer embryonic membrane and is composed entirely of fetal tissue. The chorion can be sampled by extracting cells with a needle. This can be performed through the abdomen or through the vagina and cervix (Figure 10.6). The cells obtained can be analyzed for some genetic defects, and the sex of the child can be determined. This procedure does carry a slightly higher risk of miscarriage (1.5%) than does amniocentesis, possibly because it is carried out at an earlier stage in fetal development. There is also some concern that fetal limb defects may result.

Rh Factor

In the past, couples applying for a marriage license were asked to take a blood test in order to determine their compatibility for a protein carried on the surface of their red blood cells called the Rh factor. Currently, this blood test is taken only by a pregnant woman early in her pregnancy. The Rh gene Rh$^+$ and Rh$^-$ alleles, and Rh$^+$ is dominant to Rh$^-$. If a woman has two Rh$^-$ alleles, she has no Rh protein on the surface of her red blood cells. Approximately 7% of the African American population and 15% of the white population lack the Rh factor. If the father is Rh$^+$, it is possible that the baby will be Rh$^+$ and therefore will have Rh factor on the surface of her or his red blood cells. Because there is normally no commingling of maternal and fetal blood, the mother's immune system is not exposed to the baby's red blood cells until birth. If the baby's blood enters the mother's blood stream during the birthing process, the mother's immune system will make antibodies to the Rh factor. This can cause problems in subsequent pregnancies if the mother is carrying an Rh$^+$ fetus. When this occurs, the mother's newly formed antibodies will recognize the Rh factor present on the fetal red

FIGURE 10.6   Chorionic Villus Sampling

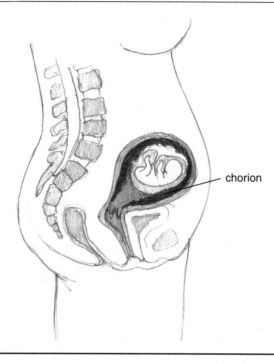

The chorion can be sampled by extracting cells with a needle. This can be performed through the abdomen or through the vagina and cervix.

blood cells as foreign. The binding of maternal antibodies to fetal red blood cells will destroy the fetal red blood cells, resulting in fetal anemia and possibly fetal death. To prevent this, Rh⁻ women are given an injection of RhoGam late in their pregnancies, which prevents the formation of antibodies against the baby's Rh factor.

Alpha-Fetoprotein

Between the 15th and 18th weeks of pregnancy, a blood test may be performed to assay the level of a protein called alpha-fetoprotein produced by the baby's liver. Large quantities of alpha-fetoprotein in the mother's blood could indicate a serious neural tube defect, anencephaly (no brain), or spina bifida (spinal cord is not fully enclosed). However, the presence of more than one fetus will raise alpha-fetoprotein levels. In addition, if the gestational age is underestimated, a normal fetus will appear to have high levels of this protein.

SUMMARY

Many changes occur during pregnancy for which there are known biological explanations. Hormonal changes can lead to the formation of the placenta, decreased ovarian activity, the formation of a mucus plug, increases in cervical and vaginal secretions, increased breast size and milk synthesis, fatigue, and increased blood volume. Increased blood volume leads to changes in the color of vascular tissues surrounding the nipples, the cervix, and the walls of the vagina. Changes in the size, shape, and positioning of the uterus can lead to increased frequency of urination, stress incontinence, shortness of breath and varicose veins in the legs and anus. Other physical changes include postural changes caused by increased abdominal weight and the loosening of the pelvic joints, increased hair growth, and stretch marks due to weight gain. A loss of tone in the gastrointestinal tract can lead to morning sickness, constipation, and heartburn.

Abnormal changes, which occur in a small percentage of pregnancies, include preeclampsia, a hypertensive disease caused by increased fluid retention that may progress into serious and potentially fatal eclampsia. Gestational diabetes can occur if the mother's cells become less able to transport glucose out of the blood stream.

Several diagnostic tests are available for pregnant women. The first test most women take is a pregnancy test to confirm that they are indeed pregnant. This test confirms the presence of human chorionic gonadotropin, which is secreted by the cells of the developing embryo. Women may also have ultrasound, amniocentesis, or chorionic villus sampling to diagnose fetal problems and to more accurately determine the age and sex of the fetus. Blood tests can also determine whether a woman has the Rh factor on her red blood cells and whether there are abnormally high levels of alpha-fetoprotein, which could indicate a fetal defect.

BIRTHING

The process of birthing involves both labor and delivery. While it is unclear exactly what causes labor to begin, there are several hypotheses. Some scientists believe that prostaglandins secreted by the placenta and the fetus stimulate labor. Prostaglandins are modified fatty acids that regulate the activities of nearby cells in a variety of ways. Prostaglandins can cause the smooth muscle of the uterus to begin contracting and the cervix to dilate. Some scientists believe the increased secretion of these chemical modulators, which occurs as the placenta enlarges, signals labor to begin. Others scientists believe that the pressure the enlarging fetus places on uterine smooth muscle stimulates contractions, or that changes in ratios of steroid hormone concentrations serve as the stimulus.

Labor normally occurs spontaneously between 37 and 42 weeks after a pregnant woman's last menstruation. On average, the entire process lasts about 12 to 14 hours for a woman giving birth to her first baby and somewhat less for subsequent deliveries.

Signs That Labor Is Imminent

There are several signs that indicate labor may be imminent. Uterine contractions normally signal the beginning of labor. However, many women experience irregular abdominal contractions known as Braxton-Hicks contractions prior to labor. These contractions are sometimes referred to as "false labor" contractions because they are not a sign that labor is imminent. For many women, especially women having a first baby, it is difficult to determine whether the contractions they are experiencing are Braxton-Hicks contractions or the kind of contractions that signal the beginnings of labor. Braxton-Hicks contractions are irregular in frequency and duration and tend to occur at the end of the day or at other times when a woman is tired. Contractions that signal labor are regular, persist during walking or other exercise, and increase in intensity, frequency, and duration with time.

The passage of the thick mucus plug blocking the cervix during pregnancy is another sign that labor is imminent. When the cervix begins to dilate, the plug loosens and is passed through the vagina. The plug may be clear, pinkish, or somewhat bloody, which is why it is sometimes referred to as the "bloody show."

Rupture of the amniotic membranes, or the "bag of waters" which has surrounded the fetus, followed by the loss of amniotic fluid, can also signal the beginning of labor. This may occur either as a gush of fluid (as much as a quart or more) or a slow trickle.

Labor and Delivery

Labor can be divided into three stages during which the cervix dilates and effaces, the baby is delivered, and the placenta is delivered. The length of time required for and the intensity of each stage differs from one woman to the next and from one pregnancy to the next in a given woman.

The First Stage: Dilation and Effacement   The first stage of labor is the longest stage, often lasting from 8 to 12 hours for a first delivery. This stage of labor involves the dilation and thinning out (effacement) of the cervix (Figure 10.7). Dilation and effacement are caused by hormonal changes and by the force of contractions on the cervix. Contractions serve to dilate and efface the uterus because they cause the muscles of the uterus to contract and shorten, which applies pressure to the baby. The baby is forced against the cervical opening, which forces the opening to enlarge. Shortening of the uterine muscle fibers tends to pull the opening of the cervix upward, helping to open the cervix as well.

Dilation of the cervix is measured in terms of centimeters, ranging from 0 cm (no dilation) to 10 cm (fully dilated). Effacement is measured in percentages, ranging from 0 percent (no effacement) to 100% (thinned out to the point of disappearing). When the cervix is 10 cm dilated and 100% effaced, the first stage of labor is complete.

The Second Stage: Delivery of the Baby   Once the cervix is fully dilated, the fetal membranes often break, and the mother begins to feel the need to bear down. This stage of labor

---

FIGURE 10.7   Dilation and Effacement of the Cervix

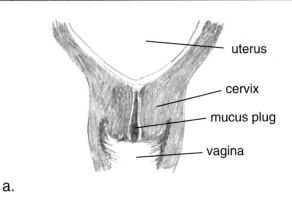
- uterus
- cervix
- mucus plug
- vagina

a.

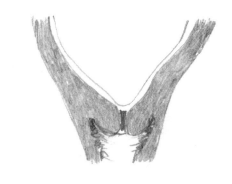

b.

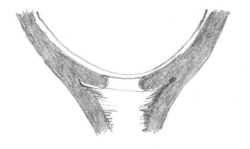

c.

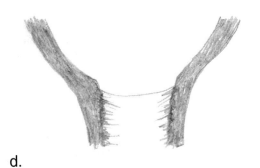

d.

a. The cervix is long and blocked by the mucus plug.
b. When labor begins, the mucus plug detaches, and the cervix is shortened.
c. During the first stage of labor, the cervix becomes effaced and dilates.
d. Dilation to 10 cm marks the beginning of the second stage of labor.

usually lasts from 1 to 2 hours and is considered to be the most painful stage of labor. As the mother contracts her abdominal muscles to push the baby out of the uterus and vagina, the force on the uterus increases dramatically. The contractions force the baby's head toward the vaginal opening until there is a bulge where the baby's head is pressing against the pelvic floor. The head can be seen moving forward with each contraction and slipping back as the contraction fades. When the head "crowns" (the top is visible), an episiotomy may be performed. After the head is born, the baby's body comes out within the next few contractions.

The Third Stage: Delivery of the Placenta   Once the baby has been delivered, the uterine cavity begins to decrease in size. As a consequence, the site of placental attachment shrivels and the placenta begins to separate from the uterine wall. Uterine contractions during this stage of labor force the placenta out of the vagina over a period of time lasting approximately 15 minutes.

After delivery, a clinician will usually massage the woman's abdomen to help the uterus to contract. Contractions of the empty uterus cause it to shrink back to its prepregnancy size and also help prevent excessive bleeding (postpartum hemorrhage). For several days after giving birth, contractions may continue to occur on their own, as well as while the baby is breast-feeding (caused by the release of oxytocin).

SUMMARY
The first stage of labor involves dilation and effacement of the cervix. Once the cervix is fully dilated, uterine contractions and abdominal pushing by the mother force the baby out of the uterus and the vagina during the second stage of labor. The third stage of labor involves delivery of the placenta.

THE MEDICALIZATION OF BIRTHING

Low-risk women with normal pregnancies are often subjected to risky procedures during labor and delivery that may be of little value to them. These procedures include episiotomies, cesarean sections, electronic fetal monitoring, and the induction of labor. While there are circumstances during which all of these procedures save lives, current data suggests that these procedures are used far too routinely.

Episiotomies

Episiotomy is a surgery that increases the size of the vaginal opening during delivery. It is usually performed without a woman's consent. Some people consider this surgery to be a form of genital mutilation. The episiotomy is the most commonly performed surgery in the West; the episiotomy rate in the United States alone is close to 80% on first vaginal births and 60% on subsequent births. This surgery involves making an incision through the perineum, the skin and muscle of the area between the vagina and the anus, in order to increase the size of the opening through which the baby can pass, and to shorten the length of the second stage of labor. The midline incision, which extends from the vagina toward the anus, is the most common. A mediolateral incision is a diagonal cut toward either side, which may prevent tearing into the rectum if the episiotomy does not hold. Figure 10.8 depicts both types of episiotomy.

Most physicians are taught that episiotomies prevent more severe tearing. However, there is no scientific evidence to support this contention. In fact, most studies show that episiotomies do not prevent more serious tearing, and in fact may *promote* tearing by compromising the integrity of the perineum. Many studies find that restricting the use of episiotomy to unusual circumstances only, such as during the delivery of a very large baby or when fetal distress is occurring, is the only justifiable use of this procedure. According to most scientists who have studied episiotomy rates, there is no defense for an episiotomy rate above 30%.

FIGURE 10.8   Episiotomy

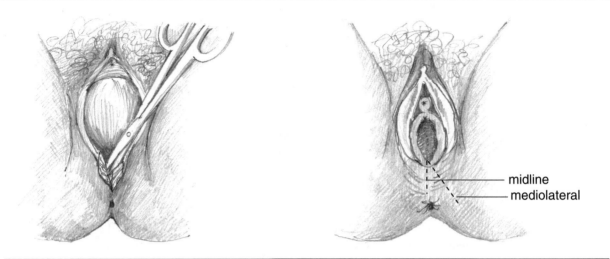

midline
mediolateral

This surgery involves making an incision through the skin and muscle of the area between the vagina and the anus in order to increase the size of the opening through which the baby can pass.

Adverse effects of episiotomy include increased incidence of severe laceration, increased maternal blood loss, longer duration of postpartum pain, delayed return to intercourse, increased frequency of stress incontinence, infection of the incision, and increased cost and psychological trauma due to scarring of the genitalia.

Cesarean Sections

Nearly 20% of all women who have delivered a baby over the past 25 years have had a cesarean section. Prior to the late 1970s, the cesarean rate was closer to 5%. Several recent studies show that up to half of all cesarean sections are unnecessary. This surgery involves making an incision directly above the pubic bone and through the abdominal and uterine walls. Cesarean sections are performed when fetal distress is thought to be occurring or when labor appears to have stalled. Cesareans used to be routinely performed when the baby was in a breech position (feet first presentation) or if a woman had a cesarean during a previous labor. There are now methods for rotating breech babies, and many women who have had cesareans in the past are able to deliver subsequent babies vaginally.

Risks of cesarean sections include fetal injury, increased maternal blood loss, infections of the incision or the uterus, and scarring. Women who have cesareans are also at increased risk of developing blood clots from bed rest, and there is an increased maternal death rate when cesareans are performed. The hospital stay after a cesarean section is close to 5 days and the cost of the surgery alone is approximately $5,000.

When a cesarean is necessary to save the life of the baby and/or the mother, women are no longer placed under general anesthesia. A regional block can be used to deaden nerve impulses to the lower body, so the mother can usually stay awake and watch the baby be delivered.

Fetal Monitoring

Fetal monitors are devices that monitor the heart rate of the fetus. Electronic fetal monitors are ultrasound devices used during labor and delivery to monitor the baby's heart rate.

This technology requires a laboring woman to wear a belt-like ultrasound device around her waist, resulting in a loss of mobility—women laboring with these monitors are less able to walk or to try a variety of laboring positions. Most studies show that electronic fetal monitoring is beneficial during a high-risk labor and delivery but of questionable benefit during the low-risk labor and delivery. Since the advent of routine fetal monitoring, cesarean section rates have doubled, in part due to the panic that ensues when the monitor shows any level of fetal distress. There is also concern that the machine takes center stage during a process in which the attention should be rightly focused on the mother and her baby.

Internal fetal monitoring is typically used during high-risk deliveries. This technology requires that an electrode be attached to the baby's head to monitor heart rates. This method requires access to the baby's scalp, so an amniotomy will be performed if the mother's water has not broken. Amniotomy is the rupture of the amniotic sac with a device called an amniohook (a long crochet type hook, with a pricked end) or an amnicot (a glove with a small pricked end on one finger).

Both types of fetal monitoring result in an increased rate of cesarean sections and operative vaginal deliveries even for low-risk women. Operative vaginal deliveries are those that require forceps or vacuum extraction delivery, which may also necessitate that an episiotomy be performed. While these technologies have been recommended only for high-risk women, they are commonly used even in low-risk situations. This may be a result of the practice of "defensive medicine," which is a response by clinicians to the ever increasing rate of malpractice suits.

Induction of Labor

When a woman's membranes rupture prior to the beginning of labor, labor is often induced in order to prevent infection. Induction of labor occurs in approximately 10 to 15% of all hospital deliveries.

Labor can be induced by the application of prostaglandins to the cervix and/or the infusion of synthetic oxytocin (pitocin) through an intravenous drip. Oxytocin is a hormone that stimulates labor and is secreted in bursts. When women are given pitocin to induce labor, it is infused at a steady rate. For this reason, pitocin induced contractions are different from natural contractions in strength and in effect. Pitocin induced contractions are stronger, more frequent, and last longer than natural contractions. This decreases the blood flow to the uterus, which serves to reduce the oxygen to the baby and may result in higher levels of fetal distress. For this reason, women who have labor induced by pitocin usually have their baby's heart beats monitored by electronic fetal monitors early in labor and by internal fetal monitors closer to the time of delivery. The monitoring, coupled with the intravenous delivery of pitocin, usually confines the mother to bed, decreasing her ability to deal with painful contractions and leading to increased use of pain medication. Induced pregnancies have higher rates of episiotomy, operative vaginal delivery, and cesarean section. The stronger contractions of induced labor can lead to rupture of the uterus, laceration of the cervix, or postbirth hemorrhage. Induction may also lead to increased infection rates because repeated cervical examinations are performed during induced labors in order to regulate the rate of cervical dilation. (During a cervical exam, a clinician inserts her or his fingers into the vagina up to the cervix in order to measure the width of dilation of the cervix and the level of effacement.) Fetal risks include suffocation from the frequent and prolonged uterine contractions, physical injury, and prematurity if the due date is not accurate.

The practice of inducing labor when a woman's water breaks prior to labor is of questionable benefit. One 1996 study conducted in five countries showed that there is no significant difference in outcome between inducing labor in women whose water has broken and waiting 4 days for labor to begin naturally. Other recent studies show that when membranes rupture before labor, 70% of women will give birth within 24 hours and 85% within 48 hours. The majority of these women would derive no benefit from induction.

It is also believed that labor can be induced by nipple stimulation, intercourse, and female orgasm, all of which stimulate the release of oxytocin causing uterine contractions and the ripening of the cervix. Intercourse with male orgasm can also stimulate labor since semen contains prostaglandins.

Midwifery

Women looking for a less invasive pregnancy experience, including those who have had negative experiences with prior pregnancies, often consult alternative care givers, such as midwives, for their medical care during pregnancy and birthing. Women without medical insurance often consider this option as well, because an uncomplicated pregnancy, labor, and hospital delivery costs close to $5,000, and a midwife assisted pregnancy, labor, and home delivery costs approximately $1,500.

Certified nurse-midwives attend graduate programs that specialize in normal pregnancy, labor, and delivery. Participating programs are approved by the American College of Nurse Midwives. The training is provided by certified nurse-midwives, usually in conjunction with a university or medical school. After earning a bachelor's degree in nursing or an RN program, students can apply to either a one-year certificate granting program or a two-year Master's program. Graduates are evaluated by the state they live in and are certified after passing exams. Certified nurse-midwives practice in conjunction with a physician and, if a pregnancy becomes high risk, refer the woman to the physician. Estimates of the number of certified nurse-midwives practicing in the United States place the number well over 4,000.

Licensed nurse-midwives are usually not nurses, although nurses are not excluded from licensure. They tend to practice in private homes or in a hospital birthing center. They receive their training in normal labor and delivery through a combination of formal schooling, correspondence courses, self study, and apprenticeships. These midwives must show that they meet or exceed the minimum requirements for the practice of midwifery by documenting their training apprenticeships and by passing state board exams. In the United States, licensure is available in 17 states.

Lay midwives obtain their training through schooling and apprenticeships. These are often midwives who practice in states without licensing opportunities. In some states they cannot charge for their services and can be prosecuted for doing so. Lay midwives, similar to licensed and certified nurse-midwives, will refer any high-risk women to an obstetrician for prenatal care. Likewise, women who develop complicating conditions during pregnancy or labor will be transferred to a hospital immediately by a responsible midwife. Midwives are often reimbursed by insurance companies for birth center and home births, but this is not always the case.

Studies show that women who give birth at home require less medication and fewer interventions than women who give birth in hospitals. There is no difference in duration of labor, occurrence of severe perineal lesions, or maternal blood loss for women who give birth at home versus those who give birth in hospitals. Neither is there any difference between their babies' birth weights, gestational ages, or overall condition. Therefore, healthy low-risk women who wish to deliver at home are not subjecting themselves or their babies to an increased risk. In fact, babies delivered by midwives are more likely to be born vaginally without induction of labor, fetal monitoring, or forceps delivery.

SUMMARY

Many medical interventions occur routinely during labor and delivery which are of questionable value for low-risk pregnancies. Episiotomies and cesarean sections are performed at alarming rates. Fetal monitoring may lead to increased intervention rates. To reduce the use of costly, unnecessary, and sometimes dangerous medical interventions during normal labor and delivery, some women chose to have their babies with the help of nurse-midwives, care givers who are trained in all aspects of normal pregnancy, labor, and delivery.

■ DISCUSSION QUESTION 2

2.1. Do you think that the training midwives receive, which focuses on normal events during pregnancy, labor, and delivery, makes them more likely to respect the ability of a woman's body to give birth without many medical interventions?

REFERENCES

Ackermann-Liebrich, U., Voegeli, T., Gunter-Witt, K., Kunz, I., Zullig, M., Schindler, C., & Maurer, M. (1996). Home versus hospital deliveries: Follow up study of matched pairs for procedures and outcome. *British Medical Journal, 313*(7068), 1313–1318.

Brown, M. A. (1995). The physiology of preeclampsia. *Clinical and Experimental Pharmacology and Physiology, 22*(11), 781–791.

Chard, T., & Macintosh, M. C. (1995). Screening for Down's syndrome. *Journal of Perinatal Medicine 23*(6), 421–436.

Davidson, J. A., & Roberts, V. L. (1996). Gestational diabetes. *Postgraduate Medicine 99*(3), 165–166, 171–172.

Deutchman, M. E., & Sakornbut, E. L. (1995). Diagnostic ultrasound in labor and delivery. *American Family Physician 51*(1), 145–154.

Gazvani, M. R., Aird, I., Wood, S. J., Thomson, A. J., & Kingsland, C. R. (1997). Changing face of ectopic pregnancy. *British Medical Journal 315*(7118), 1311–1312.

Golden, W. E., & Sanchez, N. (1996). The relationship of episiotomy to third and fourth degree lacerations. *Journal of the Arkansas Medical Association 92*(9), 447–448.

Greenwald, J. L. (1993). Premature rupture of the membranes: Diagnostic and management strategies. *American Family Physician 48*(2), 293–306.

Henderson, E., & Love, E. J. (1995). Incidence of hospital-acquired infections associated with cesarean section. *Journal of Hospital Infection 29*(4), 245–255.

Hsieh, F. J., Shyu, M. K., Sheu, B. C., Lin, S. P., Chen, C. P., & Huang, F. Y. (1995). Limb defects after chorionic villus sampling. *Obstetrics and Gynecology 85*(1), 84–88.

Hueston, W. J., & Rudy, M. (1993). A comparison of labor and delivery management between nurse-midwives and family physicians. *Journal of Family Practice 37*(5), 449–454.

Keirse, M. J., Ottervanger, H. P., & Smit, W. (1996). Controversies. Prelabor rupture of the membrane at term: The case for expectant management. *Journal of Perinatal Medicine 24*(6), 563–572.

Larson, B., & Rao, L. (1995). Childbirth in the nineties. *Prevention 47*(4), 87–91.

Lydon-Rochelle, M. (1995). Cesarean delivery rates in women cared for by certified nurse-midwives in the United States: A review. *Birth 22*(4), 211–219.

Naylor, C. D., Sermer, M., Chen, E., & Farine, D. (1997). Selective screening for gestational diabetes mellitus. *New England Journal of Medicine 337*(22), 1591–1596.

Ogueh, O., Baffour, M., Hibbert, K., & McMillan, L. (1996). Amniocentesis: The experience in a district hospital. *Clinical and Experimental Obstetrics and Gynecology 23*(3), 133–135.

Paxton, M. J. (1986). *Endocrinology: Biological and medical perspectives.* Dubuque, IA: William C. Brown.

Reilly, K. E. H. (1994). Induction of labor. *American Family Physician 49*(6), 1427–1432.

Rosen, M. G., & Dickinson, J. C. (1993). The paradox of electronic fetal monitoring: More data may not enable us to predict or prevent infant neurologic morbidity. *American Journal of Obstetrics and Gynecology 168*(3 Part I), 745–751.

Shy, K. K., Larson, E. B., & Luthy, D. A. (1987). Evaluating a new technology: The effectiveness of electronic fetal monitoring. *Annual Review of Public Health 8,* 165–190.

Smith, M. A. (1993). Preeclampsia. *Primary Care 20*(3), 655–664.

Sosa, M. E. (1997). Pregnancy-induced hypertension, preeclampsia, and eclampsia. *Journal of Perinatal and Neonatal Nursing 10*(4), 8–11.

Sperhoff, L., Glass, R. H., & Kase, N. G. (1994). *Clinical gynecologic endocrinology and infertility* (5th ed.). Baltimore, MD: Williams and Wilkins.

Sundberg, K., Bang, J., Smidt-Jensen, S., Brocks, V., Lundsteen, C., Parner, J., Keiding, N., & Philip, J. (1997). Randomized study of risk of fetal loss related to early amniocentesis versus chorionic villus sampling. *Lancet 350*(9079), 697–703.

Tal, Z., Frankel, Z. N., Ballas, S., & Olschwang, D. (1988). Breast electrostimulation for the induction of labor. *Obstetrics and Gynecology 72*(4), 671–674.

Taylor, R. N. (1997). Review: Immunobiology of preeclampsia. *American Journal of Reproductive Immunology 37*(1), 79–86.

Tussing, A. D., & Wojtowycz, M. A. (1997). Malpractice, defensive medicine, and obstetric behavior. *Medical Care 35*(2), 172–191.

Xenakis, E. M., Piper, J. M., Conway, D. L., & Langer, O. (1997). Induction of labor in the nineties: Conquering the unfavorable cervix. *Obstetrics and Gynecology 90*(2), 235–239.

CHAPTER 11

In humans, the process of milk production is an extraordinary interaction between the mother and the actions and needs of the breast feeding infant.

WOMEN POSTPARTUM

INTRODUCTION

The events of human reproduction do not end with childbirth. The physical changes of 9 months of pregnancy are dramatic, but a woman's return to the nonpregnant state is equally remarkable. After birthing, women can provide, through breast milk, the sole source of nutrition to a developing infant for up to 1 year. The birth of a baby also represents a major life change for women. The interaction between the physical and life style changes that occur postpregnancy may have profound effects on a woman's emotional state. This chapter explores the physical and psychological aspects of a woman's life after the birth of her child.

RECOVERY FROM BIRTHING

The uterus in a woman who is not pregnant is about the size of a pear. By the end of a full-term pregnancy, it will have expanded to accommodate a 6 to 10 pound baby and a 2 to 3 pound placenta. After birth, the uterus returns to firm condition (that is, it no longer extends beyond the pubic bone) within about 10 days. Because the uterus is so large after birth, women easily notice the change in size. This transformation occurs via frequent strong contractions, sometimes stimulated by oxytocin, a hormone produced during lactation.

While the uterus is shrinking, its thickened lining breaks down and is expelled in a flow called lochia. Lochia resembles a heavy menstrual flow, although it is not continuous and can last for 2 to 4 weeks after birth. The bacterial community that is found in a healthy vagina is disrupted by lochia. This change in bacterial "flora" makes this organ more susceptible to infection during this period by providing space in which infectious organisms may proliferate.

Because her body is no longer supporting the oxygen needs of the fetus, a woman's blood volume decreases by as much as 30% during the first 2 weeks postpartum. Blood volume is reduced without any outward sign of bleeding—red blood cells simply die and are not replaced. The change in blood volume that occurs during and after pregnancy is similar to the change that occurs in people moving between altitudes. When parts of the body need more oxygen than is being provided, such as at high altitudes (where oxygen supply is low) or when supporting a developing fetus (when oxygen demand is high), the bone marrow produces more red blood cells. When the oxygen levels rise, the excess blood is unnecessary and not replaced. While typically such a dramatic blood loss would cause fatigue and anemia, few postpartum women even notice the change in volume. In fact, many postpartum women notice that they feel better when their blood volume returns to prepregnancy levels.

Because of this additional blood volume, women also store extra fluid in body tissues during pregnancy. In the few weeks after birthing, these fluids are purged from the body. Many women notice that they are urinating or sweating more than usual. Dramatic changes in hormone levels (described below) may also contribute to the experience of night sweats and hot flashes that many women have at this time.

SUMMARY

The physical changes that occur in women after birth all contribute to returning to the "nonpregnant" state. These include shrinking of the uterus, loss of the uterine lining, a decrease in blood volume, and purging of excess fluids.

LACTATION

One characteristic that unites all mammals is the presence of mammary glands in females that produce milk for their infants. Human females are no different than their mammal cousins in their ability to lactate, that is, to produce milk. The milk produced by individual female mammals is unique to their species—readers who have tried both goat milk and cow milk can attest to the difference in taste and consistency between the two. Mammalian milk is an amazing substance that contains all of the nutritional components needed for early growth and development of an infant animal, including fats, proteins, carbohydrates, essential minerals, vitamins, and immune system promoters. In humans, the process of milk production is a extraordinary interaction between the mother and the actions and needs of the breast-feeding infant.

Breast Anatomy During Pregnancy and Lactation

Figure 11.1 diagrams the human breast during lactation. The structures in a lactating breast are not different than those in a nonlactating breast (see also Figure 6.1), but the mammary glands themselves are dramatically more developed. During pregnancy, estrogen produced by the placenta stimulates the production of alveoli, the milk-producing sacs of the mammary glands. At the same time, placenta-produced progesterone stimulates physiological changes in alveoli that allow milk production and increase blood flow to the gland. By midpregnancy, a woman's breasts are physiologically able to support lactation and in fact are producing colostrum, the first milk.

The external appearance of the breasts changes during pregnancy and lactation as well. The increase in mammary gland size increases the volume of the breast dramatically. The size and pigmentation of the areola around the nipple increases, covering the milk collecting

FIGURE 11.1   Diagram of Human Breast During Lactation

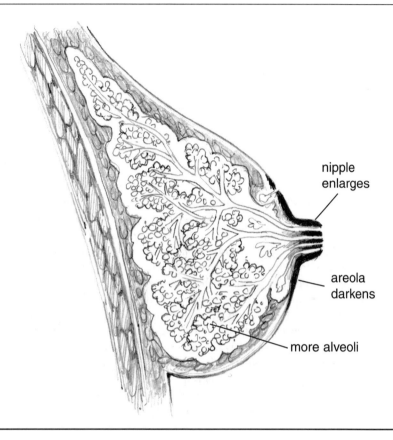

nipple
enlarges

areola
darkens

more alveoli

Notice the large size and increased extensiveness of the mammary gland and the increase in size and pigmentation of the areola.

sinuses and forming a "target" for the nursing infant to focus on. The Montgomery glands, found in the areola, produce a modified sebum and are especially important during lactation in keeping the nipple lubricated and relatively free from bacteria.

Human Breast Milk

Breast-fed babies have fewer problems with diarrhea, fewer respiratory infections, and are better protected from viral diseases than formula-fed babies.

Despite the fact that human females have been successfully providing their infants' nutritional needs for hundreds of thousands of years, many mothers in the United States and other countries have been led to believe that breast milk is inadequate and have been discouraged in the past from breast-feeding. In fact, human breast milk contains all of the essential factors needed to support a growing baby and represents the best food available for infants in nearly all situations.

Colostrum   The first milk produced after birth is called colostrum. Colostrum differs from the mature milk produced 2 to 5 days later in several ways. It is low in fat and carbohydrates but high in protein. The protein content gives the milk a thicker and more creamy appearance than the mature milk, which is thin and bluish in color.

Many of the proteins in colostrum are found in intact cells or are cytokines or immunoglobins. Cytokines provide for communication between parts of the immune system and may be necessary for effective responses to infection. Immunoglobins are antibodies—proteins that help defend the body against infection and disease. Because a baby's immune system is immature and unable to produce immunoglobins for several weeks, her or his protection against illness early in life depends on contributions of immunoglobins from the colostrum.

Colostrum provides a particular class of immunoglobins, known as IgA, to the newborn. IgA molecules are *nonspecific* antibodies and provide a first line of defense against unfamiliar pathogens. These antibodies help to prevent infection by disposing of all unknown cells. IgA is found primarily in mucus membranes, such as those that line the intestinal and respiratory tracts. IgA is only found in a baby's body after the first feeding of colostrum. Infants do not produce IgA on their own until at least 6 weeks of age.

Besides immunoglobin molecules, the colostrum also provides the baby with immune cells (i.e., white blood cells, Figure 11.2). In fact, colostrum contains as many white blood cells as adult blood. These cells include macrophages, large cells that literally eat foreign substances, and lymphocytes, cells that secrete IgA. These cells can pass into the bloodstream from the baby's intestine. Many actually survive in the intestine, where they produce IgA and help fend off diarrheal disease.

The antibiotic components of colostrum are in their highest concentrations immediately after birth. Interestingly, it seems that the more endangered the infant is, the more immunological benefits contained in the colostrum. The colostrum produced by mothers of preterm infants, babies who have especially weak immune systems, contains an extra measure of a macrophage-stimulating factor. This protein increases the number and activity of these important protective cells inside the baby's body. The amount of colostrum produced by the breast declines throughout the few days following birth. By 2 to 3 weeks after birth, it is completely replaced by mature milk.

FIGURE 11.2   White Blood Cells Found in Human Milk

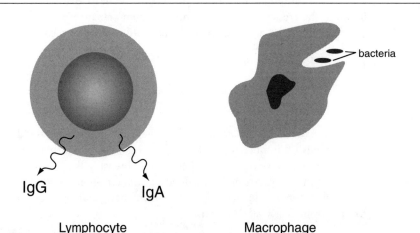

IgG   IgA

Lymphocyte   Macrophage

(a) *lymphocyte, a producer of antibodies.*
(b) *macrophage, a cell that can actively surround and ingest foreign substances*

Mature Milk   Human milk, like the milk of all mammals, consists mainly of water, protein, fat, and lactose (milk sugar), with smaller amounts of vitamins, minerals, salts, and traces of hormones. Human breast milk has the same caloric value as cow milk (about 20 calories per fluid ounce) but differs greatly in composition (Table 11.1).

Cow milk contains about three times as much protein as an equivalent measure of human milk. In order not to overload human babies with protein, cow milk is diluted by an equivalent measure of water when producing infant formula (not all brands of infant formula are made from cow milk—see below). The primary protein in cow milk is casein, a substance that aids in butter and cheese formation and will form semi-solid curds in an infant's stomach. One reason that babies on infant formula made from cow milk require fewer feedings than breast-fed infants is that these curds are harder to digest than human milk, keeping babies feeling full longer. The primary protein in human milk is whey, which does not form curds and is more digestible.

Because the component proteins differ between cow and human milk, the proportion of amino acids, the building blocks of protein, differs as well. For example, taurine is an amino acid that is found in high concentrations in human breast milk but is nearly absent in cow milk. Taurine has been shown to have a role in the development of brain tissue and is now added as a supplement to infant formula.

The amount of fat in human and cow milk is equivalent (about 50% of the calories). As with proteins, however, the types of fat differ between the two. For instance, breast milk contains more cholesterol than cow milk. Although we associate high cholesterol intake with heart disease in adults, animal studies suggest that high cholesterol intake during infancy protects against arteriosclerosis in adulthood. The ingestion of cholesterol as an infant may contribute to the development of an effective cholesterol management system that reduces the effect of dietary cholesterol later in life.

The amount of fat contained in breast milk changes over time during a feeding, from a "skim milk" at first to a very fatty milk at the end. Human breast milk also contains a fat digesting enzyme called lipase. Lipase in breast milk complements the lipase in the infant's digestive system and improves the breakdown and use of fats by the baby.

The primary sugar in milk is lactose. Although human milk has less protein than cow milk, it contains 150% of the lactose. When cow milk is diluted for infant formula, sucrose (table sugar) is often added to match the sugar content in human milk. Sucrose is broken

TABLE 11.1
COMPARISON OF NUTRIENTS IN COW MILK AND HUMAN MILK

In 100 milliliters	Cow	Human (Mature)
Calories	65	65
Fat	3.7 grams	3.7 g
Protein	3.4 g	0.9 g
Lactose	4.8 g	7.0 g
Calcium	130 milligrams (mg)	35 mg
Iron	70 mg	100 mg
Sodium	58 mg	15 mg
Vitamin A	41 micrograms (mg)	75 mg
Vitamin C	1.1 mg	5.0 mg
Vitamin D	0.02 mg	0.04 mg

down and absorbed into the bloodstream more rapidly than lactose, so babies fed on sucrose-supplemented infant formula experience more dramatic swings in blood sugar levels than babies fed on breast milk or lactose-supplemented formula.

Human breast milk also contains more of a protein called bifidus factor than cow milk or formula. The intestines of mammals contain the bacteria *Lactobacillus bifidus*, which aids in the digestion of lactose. Bifidus factor promotes the growth of this beneficial bacteria in the intestine. Large populations of *L. bifidus* can exclude more harmful bacteria from the intestine, which helps protect breast-fed babies from dangerous diarrheal disease. Due to the difference in bifidus factor levels among the milk sources, breast-fed infants have more *L. bifidus* in their gut than cow milk or formula-fed infants and are thus less likely to suffer from bacterial diarrhea.

The amounts of various vitamins and minerals in breast milk are lower than that available in cow milk, which is one reason why doctors once encouraged new mothers to feed babies infant formula, "for a more balanced diet." However, recent research has shown that although the amounts may be lower, the micronutrients in human milk are more available for absorption and are at proper levels to promote good health. For instance, calcium levels are substantially lower in human milk than in cow milk. However, the lactose in breast milk enhances the absorption of calcium, such that the amount of calcium accumulated by babies on breast milk and on formula is identical. Vitamin D is also in much higher levels in cow milk than in breast milk. However, research shows that babies fed exclusively on breast milk show no sign of Vitamin D deficiency through the first 6 months of life.

Iron is another mineral that is in low levels but easily absorbed from human milk. Interestingly, breast milk also contains two additional iron associated proteins, lactoferrin and transferrin. The role of these molecules is to bind excess unabsorbed iron in the intestines so that it may be quickly excreted. In contrast, infant formula contains very high levels of a form of iron that is poorly absorbed by the intestines. High levels of iron in the intestines promote the growth of a potentially harmful bacteria, *Escherichia coli*, which can cause diarrhea.

Infant Health and Breast Milk   Although colostrum is often considered more important for the proper development of a baby's immune system, mature milk also provides an infant protection from disease. The total concentration of antibodies and immune system factors is lower in mature milk than in colostrum, but a growing baby consumes more mature milk, and thus receives a substantial amount of immunological protection for as long as breast-feeding occurs. Breast-fed babies have fewer problems with diarrhea, fewer respiratory infections, and are protected from viral diseases than formula-fed babies. Numerous studies in both developed and developing countries indicate that the immunological benefits of breast milk enhance the survival and health of babies throughout the breast-feeding period.

One way that immunological protection in breast-fed infants is maintained is through a dynamic relationship between the mother and baby. Nursing mothers will produce antibodies to infectious agents that their baby contracts, even if the pathogen is new to the mother. This occurs after the pathogen is passed to the mother through the nipple as the infant nurses. The antibodies produced in the breast after this contact will be passed to the infant via the breast milk. As long as an infant is breast feeding, she or he continues to receive protection from an adult immune system.

The immunological benefits of breast-feeding may also extend into adulthood. Among children at risk for developing allergies—those having one or both parents with an allergy—those who were breast-fed for 6 months or more have a greatly reduced chance of developing eczema, an allergic skin rash. Allergies to pollen, dust, and animal dander, as well as asthma, are less likely among children who were breast-fed as well. This protection probably stems from the cleaning up activity of IgA in the intestine and on other mucus membranes, which prevents the absorption of potential allergy-causing substances.

Environmental Influences on Breast Milk   A woman's diet influences the taste of her breast milk. Because a woman's milk is a product of her blood supply, certain powerful flavors that are carried in blood, such as garlic, vanilla, and mint, can be transferred to breast milk. These flavors can affect the feeding experience of her child. Some mothers notice that after particular meals, their baby seems less happy during breast feedings. However, variety in a nursing woman's diet may result in her toddler being more accepting of a wide variety of solid foods.

Besides strong flavors, other compounds in a woman's body may be passed to breast milk as well. Especially worrisome is the presence of industrial waste products in human milk. The contaminants DDT, PCB, and dioxin (among others) have been found, sometimes in high levels, in breast milk. Occasionally, measured levels of these compounds in human milk are higher than the allowable limits in consumer foods. While there is good reason to suspect that ingestion of these compounds is harmful, currently there is no evidence that babies receiving them in breast milk have any measurable health problems. In fact, babies of nursing women in even the highest contaminant exposure groups have not suffered any detectable ill effects. Of course, these results do not mean that nursing women should not be concerned about chemical contamination of their milk, but so far, research indicates that the benefits of breast-feeding far outweigh the possible harm from contaminants. Nursing women can minimize their infant's exposure to these chemicals by avoiding contact with contaminants and by not engaging in crash diets during nursing. The loss of fat, which can store many of these pollutants, during a crash diet can dramatically increase the levels of these chemicals in the bloodstream, resulting in higher levels in breastmilk.

Ill mothers may also potentially transfer infectious organisms to their offspring in breast milk. Hepatitis B and HIV, the virus that causes AIDS, have both been shown to be transferred to a small percentage of children of infected mothers during breast-feeding. Women with either of these viruses may be counseled against breast-feeding their newborns.

SUMMARY
Human breast milk changes over the course of lactation from protein-rich colostrum to lactose and fat-rich mature milk. Colostrum provides many important immunological benefits to the newborn, including immune cells and antibodies. Mature human milk contains different proteins, sugars, fats, and digestive enzymes than cow milk and provides a complete source of nutrition to a developing infant. Breast-fed infants are provided with immunological benefits throughout breast-feeding via a dynamic interaction between the baby and the mother. Some environmental toxins have been found in human milk but have not been shown to negatively affect the health of a breast-fed infant.

Physiology of Lactation

[A] woman's milk production closely matches her infant's demand for milk.

Nearly all women are physiologically capable of producing milk after birth. In fact, most women can stimulate milk production even without pregnancy and birthing. The production of this life-giving and promoting substance is a process that requires both the mother and the actions of a nursing infant.

Neither the weight nor nutritional status of a woman affects her ability to lactate. Numerous studies have shown no detectable relationship between maternal BMI (body mass index, see Chapter 7) and the volume of milk produced by mothers. Even very thin mothers produce large amounts of milk. The composition of milk also does not differ much between mothers of different nutritional status—even among mothers with meager diets, the amount of fat in breast milk is not significantly less than that found in well-fed women.

Estrogen produced by the placenta during late pregnancy stimulates mammary gland development but inhibits the production of milk. Once the placenta is expelled after birth, estrogen levels drop, and milk production begins (Figure 11.3). The colostrum secreted immediately after delivery contains no mature milk but is made up of cells and residual materials (such as antibodies) from the mammary glands. With continued stimulation by the infant, the no longer suppressed, newly synthesized mature milk eventually replaces the colostrum.

Human milk is produced in the alveoli of the mammary glands (review Figure 11.1) in response to stimulation by the hormone prolactin. The prolactin present immediately postpartum declines within a few weeks after birthing. However, stimulation of the hypothalamus during nursing causes the pituitary to produce additional prolactin throughout the entire breast-feeding period (Figure 11.3). Nursing a baby ensures the continued production of milk via this method.

During milk production, the alveoli concentrate and metabolize materials passed from the bloodstream. The thinner, more watery products flow unaided from the alveoli into the collecting sinuses right behind the nipple. As these reservoirs fill between feedings, the breasts begin to feel heavy and full. The foremilk, as this thinner liquid is called, is the first milk a baby receives during a feeding but only makes up about one third of the milk passed to the infant. The thicker, creamier, and more globular hindmilk that makes up the majority of what an infant takes in must be actively ejected from the alveoli by contractions of the mammary gland.

FIGURE   11.3   **Changes in Hormone Levels During Lactation**

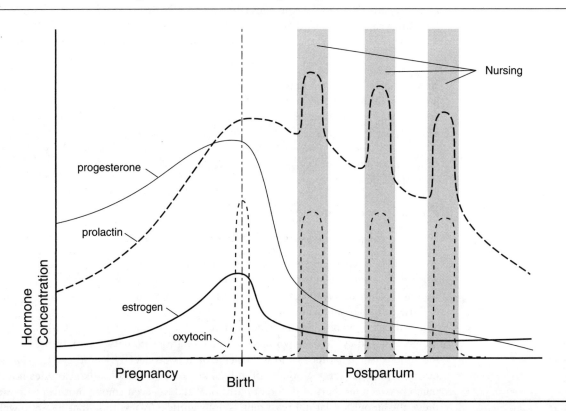

After the initial levels decline, prolactin (and thus milk) production is stimulated by suction at the breast for as long as breast-feeding continues.

The milk ejection reflex stimulates the release of hindmilk. This reflex, also called milk let down, is triggered by the hormone oxytocin. Oxytocin is produced in pulses by the pituitary gland after it is stimulated by the hypothalamus. Strong sucking action on the nipple activates nerves that trigger the hypothalamus to begin this process. The milk ejection reflex is often experienced by women as a tingling sensation and may be accompanied by slight cramping in the breast. When let down occurs, the hindmilk is literally flowing out of the breast and the baby no longer needs to suck as strenuously.

The release of oxytocin may also be triggered by emotions or environmental cues other than nursing. Some women may experience milk let down after hearing a baby cry, holding their infant, or simply sitting in the place where nursing usually occurs. Oxytocin levels have been shown to increase in response to a baby's restlessness in some 30% of women studied. Milk will begin to leak out of a woman's nipples when let down occurs without suckling. Lactating women may wear absorbent nursing pads inside their bras to absorb any leakage, and many women find that applying pressure to the nipples will stop the flow. Emotions or environmental cues may work the opposite way as well—fright or sudden shock can inhibit the milk ejection reflex and interrupt nursing. The experience of Cesarean birth (see Chapter 10) may also change the pattern of oxytocin release and diminish milk production. This occurs because oxytocin is also released during labor—interrupting its release by bypassing or shortening labor can affect subsequent milk production.

The amount of milk produced by a nursing woman is regulated by the frequency and thoroughness of feeding. Mothers of babies who feed at less than 6-hour intervals and who regularly empty the breast produce more milk than women who nurse less often and who supplement the baby's diet with infant formula. The result of this regulation is that a woman's milk production closely matches her infant's demand for milk. Most women can produce several times as much milk as they do when feeding a single infant. The mechanism for this close control of milk production is unclear but probably has to do with the frequency and duration of prolactin release as stimulated by frequent, long nursings.

Oxytocin and Behavior

Oxytocin has been called the "mothering hormone" because of the behavior it induces in animals and because it is produced in nursing women. In rats and sheep, this hormone increases a female's acceptance of her newborn offspring and triggers maternal behaviors such as nest building and grooming behaviors. However, this hormone is not unique to females; its presence during nursing does not prove the existence of a "natural" maternal role for women. Oxytocin is released in both women and men in response to various stimuli. For instance, this hormone is released after orgasm in both sexes and contributes to a feeling of relaxation and well-being in both women and men. Oxytocin appears to have a positive feedback effect—pleasurable experiences enhance its release which in turn increases and prolongs the pleasurable feeling. This hormone seems to have a general role in the positive reinforcement of a variety of beneficial behaviors. Besides stimulating maternal behaviors, oxytocin appears to increase tolerance, promote memory and learning, and function in regulating heart rate and blood pressure. Thus, this hormone appears to have many more roles than the term "mothering hormone" implies. Additionally, mothering is not a uniquely female behavior. While oxytocin stimulated during nursing may aid in bonding a mother to her child, nurturing feelings can be triggered in nonnursing women and men as well in response to an infant.

Weaning and Relactation

The dynamic interaction between a woman's milk supply and the milk demands of her infant means that a woman's body can quickly adjust to changes in the level of breast-feeding.

The process of weaning, or substituting other food sources for breast milk, depends on this dynamic interaction to support a gradual decline in milk demand by decreasing the supply. Some women opt for "child-led" weaning, meaning that they will continue to produce milk until the child no longer asks to nurse—often when the child is around 2 to 3 years old. Of course, by the time a child is a toddler, the number of nursings she or he desires may be only 2 or 3 per day, and the nursing mother's milk production is much lower than immediately after birth. Many women decide to wean a child long before she or he is a toddler, both because continued nursing requires a time commitment that may seem impossible and because prolonged nursing may be seen as "spoiling" a toddler or even a bit disturbing because of the image of breasts as sexual objects. However, there is no reason to believe that children who nurse until they are 2 or 3 years old are any less well adjusted than those who wean earlier. No matter who initiates it, a woman's milk production will adjust fairly rapidly to fewer nursings. Even when weaning is abrupt, a woman's milk supply will dry up in 7 to 10 days, because prolactin production is no longer stimulated.

Although breast-feeding is once again becoming popular among new mothers, many women opt to feed their infants formula. For this and other reasons, such as the loss of a baby at childbirth, about one half of postpartum women will be given drugs to suppress lactation. The most common drug given is bromocriptine, which suppresses prolactin production, although synthetic estrogens such as DES (diethylstilbestrol) may also be prescribed. Bromocriptine has several mild side effects, like nausea, headaches, dizziness, and vomiting. More serious side effects include heart attacks and strokes. Allowing milk supply to dry up naturally is much safer than taking a lactation-suppressing drug.

Remarkably, women can reestablish their milk supply after weaning. Even several months after regular lactation has ceased, periodic strong suction at the breast can restimulate milk production. Reestablishment of a sufficient milk supply may take several weeks of persistent training, however. When relactation is a goal and a child is already present, some women use a system by which infant formula is provided to a suckling baby via a capillary tube attached near the woman's nipple and drawing from a bag hung around the woman's neck (Figure 11.4). Women who have never lactated may also be stimulated to produce milk by a similar method. Some mothers of adopted children have prepared for their baby's arrival by using stimulation from a breast pump for several weeks to establish a supply.

SUMMARY

Preparation for milk production begins before birthing with the growth of the mammary glands, stimulated by estrogen and progesterone from the placenta. Prolactin, the hormone that triggers milk production, is produced by the placenta and declines immediately after birth. The continued production of prolactin is possible only when an infant is emptying the breast regularly. Oxytocin, the hormone that stimulates milk release, is produced in response to suckling. Oxytocin has been called the "mothering hormone" because it stimulates nurturing behaviors in nonhuman animals, but it is produced by both women and men during positive social interactions. Because the production of milk is dependent on suckling action on the breast, women closely match their milk production to their infant's needs and may be stimulated to lactate even after weaning or without giving birth.

Problems During Lactation

Sore Nipples   Many women find breast-feeding uncomfortable because their nipples become sore and the skin of the areola becomes dry and cracked. The most common cause of persistent pain has to do with the positioning of the baby and the presentation of the nipple to the infant. A baby lying at an angle to the breast will tend to stretch the nipple away from the breast much more vigorously than a suckling infant facing the breast. If the

FIGURE 11.4   The Lactaid System

The bag provides formula to the infant while she nurses at the breast. Eventually, the infant's actions will stimulate sufficient milk production from the mother.

child does not take most of the nipple and areola into her or his mouth, the pressure on the tissue is often not adequately distributed. The baby will be essentially chewing on the nipple, which can cause extreme discomfort to the mother. Most cases of painful nipples can be treated by repositioning the infant (Figure 11.5). In some cases, the infant is having difficulty latching on to a mother's breast because her nipples are flat or inverted. In this case, the nipple does not extend out from the breast when the areola is pressed on. Flat or inverted nipples can be "trained" to evert by the use of a small shield that shapes the nipple and that is worn between feedings.

Dry or cracked nipples can be treated by allowing the nipple to dry completely after a feeding. Some women find that using a hair dryer to do so is effective and comfortable.

Engorgement   One of the most common discomforts of lactation is breast engorgement, which often happens when mature milk begins production 2 to 6 days after delivery, but may happen any time during breast-feeding. Engorged breasts are literally full of milk. Tissues in the engorged breasts swell, making breasts tender and potentially interfering with blood circulation. The glands in engorged breasts are more subject to becoming plugged and/or infected because of this restricted flow.

FIGURE 11.5   Proper and Improper Positioning of Infant at the Breast

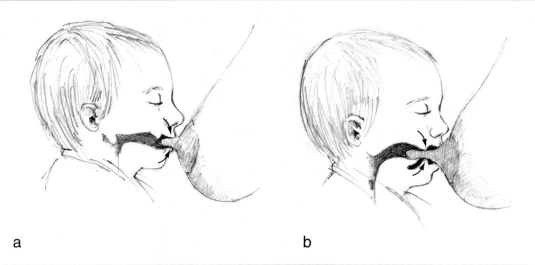

a   b

(a) The baby has not taken the entire nipple and areola into her mouth and is chewing and tugging at the nipple end. This causes nipple pain. (b) The baby has taken the entire nipple into her mouth and is massaging the nipple with her tongue rather than chewing on it. This is much more comfortable for the mother.

Engorgement with the first mature milk subsides within a few days, and this process can be hastened by allowing the infant to feed frequently. Most women find that warm water, gentle breast massage, or hand pumping of milk helps to relieve the discomfort.

Mastitis   Because a number of milk ducts (12 to 15) open at the nipple, a baby or breast pump must apply strong and varied suction in order to empty them all completely. Commonly, a duct does not empty completely over several feedings and the milk in it dries, plugging the duct outlet. As milk fills the duct but cannot flow out, the duct becomes swollen and hard. Occasionally these plugged ducts will become infected by bacteria which feed on the milk trapped there. This breast infection is called mastitis, and it results in a painful breast lump accompanied by fever and the other signs of infection.

Severe or very uncomfortable cases of mastitis are treated with antibiotics but most can be resolved through applying heat to the affected area and by allowing continued feeding. The downward pressure of milk from the rest of the gland will often dislodge the plug during nursing. Rarely, a breast infection may develop into an abscess, which is a more severe localized infection that can only be resolved by inserting a syringe to drain the duct.

Milk is sometimes retained in the alveoli of the mammary gland in a cyst called a galactocele. Galactoceles are also caused by a plugged duct, but if the plug is above the areola, drainage is more difficult, even with continued feeding. Women with a galactocele often find that the cyst grows throughout the period of lactation, which may be very frightening to both a woman and her health care provider. However, the contents of these cysts can be easily aspirated through a syringe and the cyst may in fact be eliminated by this process.

Breast Pumping and Formula

[T]he medical establishment rarely promotes breast-feeding, and in fact, has created the perception that formula feeding is the "normal" route.

When women need to be separated from infants for long periods of time, they may still be able to provide breast milk. Any action that mimics the suction of the infant at her breast can stimulate milk let down. Let down may also be promoted by looking at a photo of the baby or by being in a setting where breast-feeding typically occurs.

Manual massage of the breast can, with a little practice, empty the milk reservoirs of the breast and stimulate let down. This technique is called hand expression and requires persistent deep massage of breast tissue. Manual expression takes 20 to 30 minutes to complete.

Breast pumps are easier and less time consuming, although more expensive, than hand expression for stimulating the milk ejection reflex. Manual or battery operated breast pumps provide easily adjusted suction pressure on the nipple, while more expensive electric breast pumps closely mimic the action of sucking babies and are very effective (Figure 11.6). All pumping methods require special care that the milk does not come in contact with any infectious organisms.

Once pumped from the breast, human milk can be safely held for 6 to 10 hours at room temperature, up to 5 days in the refrigerator, and for several months when frozen. Mothers who will be separated from their infants thus can keep a supply available for their infant so that she or he may continue to be fed on demand.

There are situations when the best option for a woman is to feed her baby infant formula. In fact, in the U.S. in 1995, about 45% of 1-week-old infants were bottle fed. Although formula cannot completely replace human milk, especially the live cells and immunologic factors, in many cases it provides sufficient nutritional replacement for breast milk. In the past, formula was typically made from dried cow milk with some sugar and vitamin fortification. While some formulas still use a cow milk base, many modern formulas use only the whey protein from milk. A sucrose source (such as corn syrup), fats (such as coconut and soybean oil), and vitamin and mineral supplements are added to this base.

In modern technological societies, formula feeding does not appear to result in a serious compromise of the health of an infant. Public health in developed regions has advanced to the point where exposure to seriously debilitating diarrheal bacteria is rare and most other infectious illnesses of the infant are not life threatening. Of course, as stated earlier, even a little breast-feeding appears to be preferable to none at all in terms of future health outcomes.

FIGURE 11.6   A Variety of Manual and Mechanical Breast Pumps to Aid in Milk Expression

manual pumps   electric pump

In less developed countries, the use of formula to feed infants carries more risk. The immunological benefits of breast milk are very important in areas where sewage disposal is inadequate. The lack of clean water sources means that a formula-fed infant is exposed to a number of bacteria that can cause diarrhea. Due to these two factors, bottle-fed babies in developing countries are much more likely to die from diarrheal disease than breast-fed babies. In addition, formula is expensive. Poor women, including those in the United States, will often dilute formula to make it last, which robs the infant of the appropriate nutritional support. Among the infant children of women forced to live in poverty or in unhealthy conditions, formula can be a dangerous and inadequate substitute for breast milk.

Of major concern to proponents of breast-feeding is that it does not receive the same promotional effort as infant formula, which is produced, promoted, and sold by profit-seeking companies. Gifts and literature aimed at pediatricians and obstetricians promote particular infant formula brands. Formula manufacturers donate large amounts of money to professional doctor's organizations. Lobbyists roam the halls of government promoting formula-friendly legislation. After giving birth, mothers are contacted regularly by formula manufacturers. All of this activity by these companies has had its intended results—the medical establishment rarely *promotes* breast-feeding, and in fact, has created the perception that formula feeding is the "normal" route. Some pediatricians ask breast-feeding women to bring in their infant after 1 week for a weighing (as if a woman would be unaware that her baby is starving, a very unusual situation for breast-fed infants, *especially* if the mother has been given adequate instructions for positioning the baby at the breast). Others prescribe nutritional supplements to infants of breast-feeding mothers, giving the erroneous impression that breast milk is inadequate. In fact, surveys of breast-feeding mothers indicate that nearly half discontinue breast-feeding because they feel that their milk supply is inadequate. As we have stated, however, human milk supply is closely linked to the needs of the infant, and even mothers with poor diets can successfully provide for the nutritional needs of their children. Clearly, many of these women are not receiving adequate support, education, and counseling about breast-feeding from their health care providers. Advertising by infant formula manufacturers also contributes to increased rates of bottle feeding. For example, nearly all U.S. hospitals supply women with "discharge packets" when they leave the hospital. These packets contain rattles, diaper bags, nipples, bottles, free samples of formula, coupons for formula, and a small booklet on breast-feeding (but no nursing pads). The subtle message of these packs is "here is the set up for formula feeding when you need it." In recent surveys, 20% of breast-feeding women discontinue within the first month and nearly 50% by 3 months after birthing. This rapid decline in breast-feeding rates is no surprise when women face the realization that there is little social support for long-term breast-feeding and that their health care providers assume that they will eventually switch to formula at the same time they are being bombarded with advertisements from formula companies.

The lack of support from medical professionals toward breast-feeding is gradually changing. In late 1997, the American Academy of Pediatrics (AAP) revised their policy on breast-feeding to state that breast-feeding is the preferred method of infant nutrition for the first year of life and that no formula should be given unless medically necessary. The AAP also encouraged its member physicians to take an active role in the evaluation and teaching of breast-feeding technique in order to reduce the physical problems (such as sore nipples) that cause women to stop breast-feeding.

The choice to discontinue breast-feeding may also be economic. In a society where women need to "be like men" in order to achieve financial success, maternity leave and lactation breaks are seen as a choice made by a woman that justifiably should limit her pay and possibilities for promotion. Current law in the U.S. allows postpartum women up to 6 weeks of *unpaid* maternity leave without threat of job loss. The United States is one of only two industrialized countries that does not mandate pay during this period. For many working mothers, 6 weeks without pay is a severe hardship. For these women, prolonged breast-feeding may be seen as a luxury that they cannot afford.

Whether a woman decides to breast-feed until her child is a toddler, switches to bottle feeding at 6 weeks, or does not breast-feed at all is a decision based on social factors, economic and employment realities, personal preference, and infant health. All research indicates that breast-fed infants are healthier than formula-fed infants, but rates of breast-feeding in the U.S. will not increase unless social support for breast-feeding does as well. Until then, all new mothers deserve our emotional support, whatever their feeding choices.

■ DISCUSSION EXERCISE 1

1.1. How can society support breast-feeding? What changes in policy or beliefs would be required to trigger increases in breast-feeding rates?

1.2. When is an appropriate time to discontinue breast-feeding? Should women who breast-feed 4-year-old children be supported in the same manner as women who stop breast-feeding when their children begin to walk?

SUMMARY

Typical problems during lactation include sore nipples, engorgement, plugged ducts, and breast infections (mastitis). In most cases, frequent feedings by a baby that is properly positioned is sufficient to relieve distress. Women who are separated from their infants for extended periods may remove breast milk manually or with a pump and store it for later use. Some women opt to use infant formula, typically made from cow milk or soy products. In developed areas, the use of infant formula does not seriously impair a child's health, but where sewage treatment is poor or poverty levels are high, the use of infant formula can be deadly. Breast-feeding mothers may switch to infant formula because breast-feeding is not well promoted by health care providers.

LACTATION AND WOMEN'S HEALTH

Calcium Loss During Lactation

As women's life spans lengthen, concerns over behaviors that may impact their quality of life in old age increase. Osteoporosis is a common problem in aging women (Chapter 14). Some scientists have hypothesized that the production of milk and prolonged breast-feeding represents a significant calcium drain to a woman's body, leading to later osteoporosis. Some health care practitioners have recently begun prescribing calcium supplementation to lactating women to reduce this hypothesized problem. However, recent research has indicated that calcium supplements during lactation do not in fact stop the bone loss that occurs at this time. Both supplemented and unsupplemented women regain their original bone density at the end of lactation. As of yet, there is no evidence that prolonged breast-feeding increases a woman's risk of osteoporosis.

Lactation and Infertility

Fertility and menstruation do not return immediately after birth in both lactating and non-lactating women. However, lactation prolongs this period of amenorrhea and especially infertility during the postpartum. The length of postpartum infertility seems to be related to the amount of suckling by the infant at the breast.

Among women who are exclusively breast-feeding, the return of menses occurs approximately 4 months after birth, compared to 2 to 3 months in nonnursing mothers. The chance that a given menstrual cycle is ovulatory (i.e., an egg is released) is also decreased in nursing mothers. Ninety-five to 99% of women who are exclusively breast-feeding do not ovulate for 6 months postpartum.

The mechanism of lactational infertility is still unknown. Prolactin may have an inhibitory effect on GnRH (see Chapter 8), which would inhibit the development of follicles and ovulation. The role of prolactin in lactational infertility is supported by research that indicates that the risk of ovulation is reduced by a higher frequency of feedings, longer duration of each feed, and less supplementary feeding. All of these feeding characteristics would increase prolactin secretion in women during the postpartum period. However, no precise link between prolactin and infertility has yet been identified.

Lactation and Breast Cancer

When premenopausal women are not pregnant or lactating, the menstrual cycle induces a regular growth and regression of breast tissue (see Chapter 6). This periodic stimulation has been hypothesized to be a risk for breast cancer—the more times a cell divides, the greater chance that it will produce an error that leads to unrestricted growth (see Chapter 13). Any process that inhibits the growth and regression cycle of breast tissue, such as pregnancy and lactation, should theoretically reduce a woman's risk of breast cancer.

While early research on the link between lactation and breast cancer seemed to indicate a protective effect of breast-feeding, numerous recent studies have indicated a very weak effect, if any. Prolonged lactation seems to reduce the risk of breast cancer among women who have had children, but the reduction in risk is minimal. Pregnancy itself has a stronger protective effect, and early studies that linked lactation to breast cancer risk reduction may have not properly controlled for the effects of pregnancy.

SUMMARY

Lactation does not increase the risk of osteoporosis nor significantly decrease the risk of breast cancer. However, lactation does prolong the period of postpartum infertility, probably through some effect of prolactin on ovulation.

PSYCHOLOGICAL CHANGES DURING THE POSTPARTUM

[S]tudies have shown that married women with supportive, noncritical husbands are much less likely to suffer postpartum depression than women whose husbands criticized their appearance or infant care capabilities.

The "Baby Blues"

Many mothers experience a feeling of sadness in the few days after the birth of the baby. This emotional low is extremely common and often worries new mothers who anticipated that the birth of a child would be greeted with unbridled joy. What causes this feeling is not completely clear. Hypotheses range from the biological, such as the rapid changes in hormone levels that occur after birth, to the situational, such as fatigue from labor and from being awakened repeatedly during the night, to some combination of both factors. Feelings of sadness are not uncommon after any major life event, as individuals adjust mentally and physically to changes in their situation. In the vast majority of women, the baby blues dissipate within a day or two. However, some women find that the depression following a baby's birth may last as long as 6 months or a year.

Postpartum Depression

Even after an initial period of baby blues, it is very common for postpartum women caring for a new infant to experience periods of depression and fear. However, when the baby blues continue unabated over a period of several weeks, or are so severe as to interfere with the accomplishment of everyday activities, a woman is most likely suffering from postpartum depression. Depending on the scales used to measure depression, anywhere between 6% and 40% of postpartum women experience deep depression in the 4 to 8 weeks following birth. Approximately 2 of every 1000 postpartum women suffer disabling depression requiring hospitalization.

There are three competing theories regarding the causes of postpartum depression. Biological explanations point to the rapid loss of estrogen and progesterone at birth. As with PMS (see Chapter 8), declines in these two hormones may trigger the onset of negative emotions and behaviors in some women. However, available studies indicate that levels of these hormones in the bloodstream do not correlate directly to postpartum mood changes, and treatment with hormones is no more successful than no treatment in relieving depression. More recent biological hypotheses speculate that because estrogen and progesterone during pregnancy may affect brain function, women who experience postpartum depression do so because their brains are slower to "recover" from the effects of these two hormones.

According to psychological hypotheses about the causes of postpartum depression, a past history of depressive symptoms is directly related to the onset of depression after birth. In fact, women who generally respond negatively to life changes are more likely to see the experience of birth and child rearing in a negative light. Various studies have indicated that women who suffer from postpartum depression are less optimistic and have lower self-esteem than mothers who are depression-free.

Biological and psychological hypotheses regarding the causes of postpartum depression see this condition as due to an intrinsic property of the women who suffer from it. In contrast, sociological explanations suggest that the social support networks of affected women are causes of postpartum depression. Surveys show that women who suffer from postpartum depression are likely to implicate a range of *social* factors as influences on their feelings. For instance, studies have shown that married women with supportive, non-critical husbands are much less likely to suffer postpartum depression than women whose husbands criticized their appearance or infant care capabilities.

As with most explanations of human behavior, it is probable that all three of these factors (i.e., biological, psychological, and sociological) play a role in the onset of postpartum depression in affected women. Researchers are beginning to explore these interconnections and are finding that women with more stressful life situations and less support (sociological factors) are more likely to have low self-esteem and respond to chronic stress with depression (psychological factors). The symptoms of postpartum depression then manifest themselves biologically in the form of low levels of various brain chemicals (i.e., neurotransmitters). Drugs, such as Prozac, can relieve the symptoms of postpartum depression by influencing the synthesis and breakdown of these chemicals, but drug treatments cannot cure the underlying cause of depression. Only changes in the long-term social support of depressed women will reduce the risk of future episodes.

Interestingly, nonbirthing related depression is about twice as common among women than men. As biologists have sought biological causes for "increased sensitivity" or "lack of coping skills" in women's brains, feminists and sociologists have argued that women are more likely, for cultural reasons, to experience the chronic stressors, unreasonable expectations, and lack of support that would cause any person to feel fearful and inadequate. They point to social situations where depression is rare as evidence that this illness is not necessarily a "natural state" for women. Identifying the biological characteristics of depressed women will only allow us to treat these women's symptoms. Looking at cultures where the incidence of depression, both postpartum and in all women, is low will help to identify the social factors that benefit the mental health of all women.

■ DISCUSSION EXERCISE 2

2.1. In your experience, which explanation of the causes of postpartum depression seems to be most commonly used? Why do you think biological explanations for human behaviors seem so "correct" to the lay public?

2.2. What are some cultural factors in the United States that cause women to experience more chronic stressors than men? How might these factors be modified to improve women's mental health?

SUMMARY

Postpartum depression may be caused by hormonal changes, psychological susceptibility to stress, or lack of social support experienced by women after birthing. The experience of postpartum depression is probably related to some or all of these postpartum changes. Social factors that improve the mental health of women can be expected to decrease the incidence of depression, both postpartum and in all women.

REFERENCES

Anderson-Hunt, M., & Dennerstein, L. (1995). Oxytocin and female sexuality. *Gynecologic & Obstetric Investigation, 40* (4), 217–221.

Argiolas, A., & Gessa, G. L. (1991). Central functions of oxytocin. *Neuroscience & Biobehavioral Reviews, 15* (2), 217–231.

Baumslag, N., & Michels, D. L. (1995). *Milk, money, and madness: The culture and politics of breastfeeding.* Bergin and Garvey.

Boston Women's Health Book Collective. (1992). *The new, our bodies, ourselves.* Touchstone.

Carter, C. S., & Altemus, M. (1997). Integrative functions of lactational hormones in social behavior and stress management. *Annals of the New York Academy of Sciences, 807,* 164–174.

Daly, S. E., Kent, J. C., Owens, R. A., & Hartmann, P. E. (1996). Frequency and degree of milk removal and the short-term control of human milk synthesis. *Experimental Physiology, 81* (5), 861–875.

Daly, S. E., & Hartmann, P. E. (1995). Infant demand and milk supply. Part 1: Infant demand and milk production in lactating women. *Journal of Human Lactation, 11* (1), 21–26.

Fleming, A. S., Ruble, D., Krieger, H., & Wong, P. Y. (1997). Hormonal and experiential correlates of maternal responsiveness during pregnancy and the puerperium in human mothers. *Hormones & Behavior, 31* (2), 145–158.

Fontaine, K. R., & Jones, L. C. (1997). Self-esteem, optimism, and postpartum depression. *Journal of Clinical Psychology, 53* (1), 59–63.

Hall, L. A., Kotch, J. B., Browne, D., & Rayens, M. K. (1996). Self-esteem as a mediator of the effects of stressors and social resources on depressive symptoms in postpartum mothers. *Nursing Research, 45* (4), 231–238.

Harris, B., Lovett, L., Smith, J., Read, G., Walker, R., & Newcombe, R. (1996). Cardiff puerperal mood and hormone study. III. Postnatal depression at 5 to 6 weeks postpartum, and its hormonal correlates across the peripartum period. *British Journal of Psychiatry, 168* (6), 739–744.

Katsouyanni, K., Lipworth, L., Trichopoulou, A., Samoli, E., Stuver, S., & Trichopoulos, D. (1996). A case-control study of lactation and cancer of the breast. *British Journal of Cancer, 73* (6), 814–818.

Keverne, E. B., & Kendrick, K. M. (1994). Maternal behaviour in sheep and its neuroendocrine regulation. *Acta Paediatrica, Supplement, 397,* 47–56.

La Leche League International. (1991). *The womanly art of breastfeeding* (5th ed.). Penguin Books.

Lawrence, R. (1985). *Breast-feeding: A guide for the medical profession* (2nd ed.). C. V. Mosby.

Love, S., & Lindsey, K. (1991). *Dr. Susan Love's breast book.* Addison Wesley.

Marks, M., Wieck, A., Checkley, & Kumar, C. (1996). How does marriage protect women with histories of affective disorder from post-partum relapse? *British Journal of Medical Psychology, 69* (Part 4), 329–342.

Mennella, J. A. (1995). Mother's milk: A medium for early flavor experiences. *Journal of Human Lactation, 11* (1), 39–45.

Nissen, E., Uvnas-Moberg, K., Svensson, K., Stock, S., Widstrom, A. M., & Winberg, J. (1996). Different patterns of oxytocin, prolactin but not cortisol release during breast-feeding in women delivered by caesarean section or by the vaginal route. *Early Human Development, 45* (1–2), 103–118.

Prentice, A. M., Goldberg, G. R., & Prentice, A. (1994). Body mass index and lactation performance. *European Journal of Clinical Nutrition, 48,* Supplement 3, S78–86.

Ramos, R., Kennedy, K. I., & Visness, C. M. (1996). Effectiveness of lactational amenorrhoea in prevention of pregnancy in Manila, the Philippines: Non-comparative prospective on trial. *BMJ, 313* (7062), 909–912.

Small, R., Johnston, V., & Orr, A. (1997). Depression after childbirth: The views of medical students and women compared. *Birth, 24* (2), 109–115.

Srivastava, M. D., Srivastava, A., Brouhard, B., Saneto, R., Groh-Wargo, S., & Kubit, J. (1996). Cytokines in human milk. *Research Communications in Molecular Pathology & Pharmacology 93* (3), 263–287.

Straussberg, R., Sirota, L., Hart, J., Amir, Y., Djaldetti, M., & Bessler, H. (1995). Phagocytosis-promoting factor in human colostrum. *Biology of the Neonate, 68* (1), 15–18.

Stuver, S. O., Hsieh, C. C., Bertone, E., & Trichopoulos, D. (1997). The association between lactation and breast cancer in an international case-control study: A reanalysis by menopausal status. *International Journal of Cancer, 71* (2), 166–169.

Sugawara, M., Toda, M. A., Shima, S., Mukai, T., Sakakura, K., & Kitamura, T. (1997). Premenstrual mood changes and maternal mental health in pregnancy and the postpartum period. *Journal of Clinical Psychology, 53* (3), 225–232.

Tamaki, R., Murata, M., & Okano, T. (1997). Risk factors for postpartum depression in Japan. *Psychiatry & Clinical Neurosciences, 51* (3), 93–98.

Tay, C. C., Glasier, A. F., & McNeilly, A. S. (1996). Twenty-four hour patterns of prolactin secretion during lactation and the relationship to suckling and the resumption of fertility in breast-feeding women. *Human Reproduction, 11* (5), 950–955.

Thomas, D. B., & Noonan, E. A. (1993). Breast cancer and prolonged lactation. The WHO Collaborative Study of Neoplasia and Steroid Contraceptives. *International Journal of Epidemiology, 22* (4), 619–626.

Thurtle, V. (1995). Post-natal depression: The relevance of sociological approaches. *Journal of Advanced Nursing, 22* (3), 416–424.

Uvnas-Moberg, K., & Eriksson, M. (1996). Breast-feeding: Physiological, endocrine and behavioural adaptations caused by oxytocin and local neurogenic activity in the nipple and mammary gland. *Acta Paediatrica, 85* (5), 525–530.

Uvnas-Moberg, K. (1997). Physiological and endocrine effects of social contact. *Annals of the New York Academy of Sciences, 807,* 146–163.

Visness, C. M., Kennedy, K. I., Gross, B. A., Parenteau-Carreau, S., Flynn, A. M., & Brown, J. B. (1997). Fertility of fully breast-feeding women in early postpartum period. *Obstetrics & Gynecology, 89* (2), 164–167.

Wisner, K. L., & Stowe, Z. N. (1997). Psychobiology of postpartum mood disorders. *Seminars in Reproductive Endocrinology, 15* (1), 77–89.

CHAPTER 12

As scientists have learned more about the function of the female reproductive system, women's options when making their own reproductive choices have expanded enormously.

THE CONTROL OF FERTILITY: BIRTH CONTROL AND ASSISTED REPRODUCTION

INTRODUCTION

For thousands of years, women have sought to control their reproduction for personal, social, and political reasons. As scientists have learned more about the function of the female reproductive system, women's reproductive choices have expanded enormously. This chapter will examine the prevention of pregnancy via birth control and the inducement of pregnancy through assisted reproductive technologies.

BIRTH CONTROL

According to a recent survey by the National Center for Health Statistics, nearly 77% of sexually active women in the United States use some form of contraception, or birth control. Of those who don't, 30 to 45% do not currently desire pregnancy. Not surprisingly, 30 to 50% of pregnancies in the U.S. are unwanted or at least "unscheduled." The rate of unwanted pregnancies (and consequently, the rate of abortions) is higher in the United States than in any other developed country. Clearly, there is a need for contraceptive services in the U.S. that is not currently being met, either because women's access to birth control is limited, education is lacking, or the reliability of current, widely available forms of birth control is inadequate. In addition, the increased number of women delaying childbearing into later adulthood means that the need for safe, reliable, *reversible* forms of birth control is increasing as well. What follows is a summary of birth control methods currently in use in the U.S. and a discussion of the future of birth control technology.

General Concepts

The complexity of human reproduction allows for several different options for interfering with this process, from the blocking of sperm transport, to the inhibition of ovulation, to the removal of the fertilized egg or embryo. Figure 12.1 summarizes the primary modes of action of the most common methods of birth control.

Because of differences in how they block pregnancy, the methods illustrated in Figure 12.1 also have different levels of potential effectiveness (Table 12.1). For example, barrier methods, which attempt to block the passage of sperm into a woman's uterus, must exclude all of the approximately 250 million sperm in *each ejaculate* in order to prevent pregnancy. The chance that one or a few tiny sperm will breach the barrier is nearly impossible to eliminate, so the theoretical effectiveness of barrier methods is lower than the theoretical effectiveness of methods that attempt to stop the release of (typically) a single egg each month.

You may have noted that most of the birth control methods listed in the figure and table are female methods. There are a number of reasons for sex differences in birth control options. First, men produce many more gametes than women, which means they are more difficult to "control."

TABLE 12.1
EFFECTIVENESS OF BIRTH CONTROL
(PERCENT OF WOMEN WITH PREGNANCY DURING FIRST YEAR OF USE)

Method	Typical	Theoretical
None	85.0	85.0
Withdrawal	18.0	4.0
Barrier Methods		
Cervical Cap	18.0	6.0
Diaphragm/Spermicide	18.0	6.0
Condom	12.0	2.0
Hormonal Methods		
Combination Pill	3.0	0.1
Progestin Only Pill	3.0	0.5
Norplant	0.2	0.2
Depo Provera	0.3	0.3
IUD		
Progesterone	2.0	2.0
Copper T	1.0	0.8
Periodic Abstinence		
Calendar (Rhythm)	15.0–18.0	9.0
Ovulation	*	3.0
Symptothermal	2.0	2.0
Nonreversible Methods		
Female sterilization	0.4	0.2
Male sterilization	0.15	0.1

* Actual failure rate has not been calculated

FIGURE 12.1   Modes of Birth Control and Their Site and Method of Action

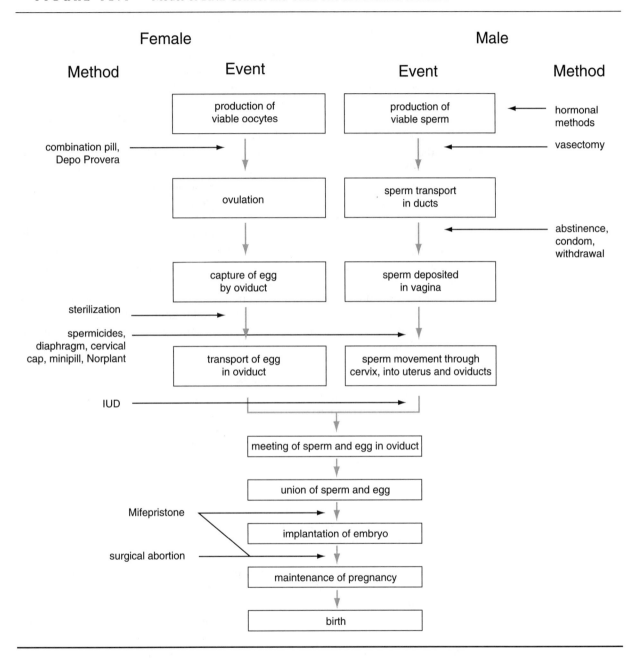

Second, most of the steps involved in fertilization and pregnancy occur inside a woman's body. Third, women typically have more interest in controlling reproduction than do their male partners. However, just because women have more options for types of birth control does not necessarily mean that the most efficient or effective birth control choices made by a sexually active couple should be a female method. For instance, because condoms are easily available and non-systemic, they can safely and easily prevent pregnancies. Condoms also carry the additional benefit of serving as excellent protection from sexually transmitted diseases. For many couples, this method of typically *male* birth control is the best choice.

Barrier Methods

[T]he effectiveness of condoms, especially those made of latex, in reducing the spread of STDs has become apparent.

Birth control methods that physically prohibit sperm from reaching the site of fertilization are known as barrier methods. Barrier methods of birth control are relatively popular among sexually active women because they are easy to obtain and do not require drugs or periodic abstinence from intercourse to be effective. However, barrier methods are more likely than other methods to fail in practice. Table 12.1 lists both the theoretical effectiveness (the maximum protection expected when the method is used by motivated couples) and the use effectiveness (the observed effectiveness when used in the "real world") of different methods of birth control. Much of the gap between the theoretical effectiveness and the use effectiveness of barrier contraceptives has to do with their typical method of use. Most will not reliably prevent pregnancy unless consistently applied a few hours (or minutes) before intercourse. Using barrier methods requires a significant amount of advance planning for sexual intercourse, which may be difficult in some relationships. Many couples find that in the excitement of sexual activity, the proper application of barrier methods is often forgotten.

Withdrawal, in which a man removes his penis from a woman's vagina before ejaculation, may be erroneously thought of as a "barrier" method of birth control, because with this method sperm is supposedly entirely prohibited from entering a woman's reproductive tract. However, as evidenced in Table 12.1, withdrawal is rather ineffective at preventing pregnancy. In reality, small amounts of sperm may be released prior to orgasm before the penis is withdrawn. Clinicians do not typically counsel women to consider withdrawal when choosing a birth control option.

Condoms are sheaths made of latex or lambskin that cover an erect penis and act as a trap for sperm. Since their introduction by the British physician, Dr. Condom, in the 1600s, they have remained the most popular method of barrier birth control. The popularity of this method has grown in recent years—nearly tripling since 1982—as the effectiveness of latex condoms in reducing the spread of STDs has become apparent. Now, according to the Centers for Disease Control, more than 20% of sexually active women rely on their partner's condom use for birth control. There is no evidence that condoms reduce the sensitivity of a man's penis during intercourse, although this is a primary reason men give for not using this method.

A female latex condom, designed as a sort of liner for the vagina, has been introduced in recent years in response to concerns about the spread of HIV, the virus that causes AIDS. The female condom provides women who have primary responsibility for birth control with a contraceptive option that also reduces their risk of contracting an STD. However, few women have adopted the female condom, probably because it is more expensive than the male condom and requires more practice to use effectively.

For increased protection against pregnancy and disease, many women use spermicides in addition to a condom. Spermicides, which may be in cream, jelly, foam, or suppository form, inactivate sperm by damaging their cell membranes. When used with a male condom, nonsuppository spermicides are simply inserted into the vagina with a plunger-type applicator. In order to act effectively, spermicides must be applied no earlier than 15 minutes and no later than 30 minutes before intercourse. The active chemical in spermicides, nonoxynol-9, is also effective in killing the bacteria that cause the common STDs gonorrhea and chlamydia. However, because nonoxynol-9 can cause open vaginal sores in some women, its use *without condoms* may actually increase the risk of transmission of other STDs, in particular HIV.

Diaphragms, which are latex domes with flexible rims (Figure 12.2), were once the most commonly used method of birth control. Margaret Sanger, founder of Planned Parenthood,

FIGURE 12.2 A Diaphragm

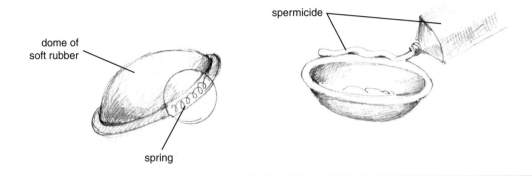

championed the distribution and use of diaphragms (a position for which she was arrested in 1918). As easier, more effective methods of birth control have become available, diaphragm use has dropped, so that now only 1.2% of women use this method. Diaphragms can be inserted up to 6 hours prior to intercourse and should be left in place for 6 to 24 hours afterwards. When filled with spermicide, a diaphragm is an effective barrier to sperm as well as to infectious organisms that could invade the cervix and upper reproductive tract. Diaphragm users experience higher rates of urinary tract infections than non-users, although the reason for this relationship is unknown. Leaving a diaphragm inserted for more than 24 hours also increases a woman's risk of experiencing toxic shock syndrome (see Chapter 8 for a description of TSS).

Cervical caps, which are smaller latex domes that cover only the cervix, work in much the same manner as diaphragms. Because cervical caps are more difficult to insert than diaphragms and because they come in only a few sizes, they are less often used as a method of birth control.

SUMMARY

Barrier methods of birth control physically block the passage of sperm from the penis into the vagina. These methods are generally not as effective, either theoretically or in practice, than hormonal methods of contraception. Condoms are the most commonly used barrier method and have the additional advantage of reducing the spread of sexually transmitted diseases. Other barrier methods may be used with spermicide to reduce the risk of some STD infections as well.

Hormonal Birth Control

The use of oral birth control pills dropped nearly 50% between 1973 and 1982 because of legitimate fears over the safety of this method. Since 1983, however, the use of combination pills has risen just as dramatically due to the development of new, safer, lower dose pills.

As our understanding of the physiology of reproductive cycles has increased, birth control methods that interfere with the normal progress of the menstrual cycle have been developed. Drugs that mimic or block the action of reproductive hormones, such as estrogen and progesterone, can prevent ovulation, make the endometrium unsuitable for embryo implantation, and inhibit the passage of sperm through the cervix. These highly effective drugs have made birth control simpler than barrier methods, and they are now an extremely popular choice among young women. However, because these drugs are systemic (i.e., circulate in the bloodstream), their effects are not uniform in all users. The side effects of hormonal birth control thus may differ from one woman to the next. In this section, we will describe some of the actions and side effects of these birth control methods, but readers should understand that this information can only supplement individualized counseling with a health care provider.

Oral Contraceptives   Oral contraceptives come in two basic forms—combination pills and progesterone-only minipills. The more commonly used combination pills contain synthetic estrogen and synthetic progesterone, which work in concert to inhibit both ovulation and fertilization. Recall from Chapter 8 that moderately high levels of estrogen inhibit GnRH synthesis. In a typical menstrual cycle, moderate levels of estrogen inhibit follicle development while *high* levels of estrogen (produced by developing follicles) trigger the events leading to ovulation. Combination pills, by *maintaining* estrogen levels at a moderate level, both stop follicles from developing and prohibit the luteinizing hormone (LH) surge necessary for ovulation. Thus, most women who take combination birth control pills rarely ovulate. The synthetic progesterone in combination pills acts as a "backup" for the estrogen component in case ovulation does occur. Progesterone with estrogen not only helps to inhibit the preovulatory LH surge, but also prevents the cervical mucus from thinning to allow sperm passage and, at levels found in the pill, makes the endometrium unfavorable for embryo implantation.

Typically, combination pills come in 28-day packets. Women take pills containing hormones for 21 days, followed by 7 days of placebo (sugar pills). Taking the placebo pills leads to a decrease in estrogen and progesterone levels, triggering menses. Because the hormone levels in the pills inhibit the proliferation of the endometrium, the menstrual periods of pill takers are typically short in duration and light in flow. In fact, the artificial menses induced by the placebo pills does not appear to be necessary. Women who wish to skip their period while on combination pills may simply skip the placebo pills. Inducing menses once a month does serve to increase a woman's confidence that she has not become pregnant and also reduces the chance that a woman who does become pregnant while on combination pills does not cause injury to her fetus by exposing it to high levels of estrogen. Additionally, all scientific studies about the safety and efficacy of combination oral contraceptives have followed women using regimens of 21 hormone-containing pills followed by 7 placebo pills. It is possible that *continuous* doses of combination pills (i.e.,, without the 7-day placebo period) may have more negative effects on women's health than have been revealed by these studies.

Combination pills come in an array of formulations containing different levels and types of estrogen and progesterone. The variety in pill types allows a woman and her clinician to choose the most appropriate formulation—one that minimizes both short and long-term side effects while ensuring effective protection. For instance, the estrogen in combination pills inhibits breakthrough bleeding (i.e., bleeding between periods) but can have negative health consequences. The best estrogen level for a woman is a moderate level that minimizes both of these effects. Other common side effects of combination pills are nausea, breast discomfort, weight gain, acne, and headaches. However, most women do not experience any of these symptoms, and many who do find that these effects diminish after two or three pill cycles.

A woman and her clinician may decide that switching to another pill formulation is the best treatment for more persistent side effects. Many recent combination pills contain "new" progesterones which are less likely than the "old" progesterones to cause acne and metabolic changes. However, recent studies have indicated that pills with these new progesterones may cause a slight increase in a woman's risk of developing estrogen-induced blood clotting problems. *Multiphasic* combination pills vary the levels of progesterone and estrogen throughout the month. These regimens have been developed in an attempt to more closely mimic a "natural" cycle and to minimize some of the side effects associated with progesterone. As of yet, there is no evidence that any one of these pill formulations significantly reduces the already low risks associated with combination oral contraceptives.

As indicated in Table 12.1, both the theoretical and use effectiveness of combination birth control pills are quite high. As long as a combination pill is taken every day, the risk of pregnancy is practically nonexistent. Missed pills can result in ovulation however, especially if they are missed immediately before or after the placebo pills. The low levels of estrogen for an extended period resulting from missed pills can trigger follicle development, eventually leading to ovulation. In general, missing two pills in a row or in the third week of the cycle greatly increases the chance of pregnancy. If this happens, a woman will usually be counseled by her health care provider to immediately begin a new packet of pills and to use additional protection for the next 7 days.

Antibiotics, drugs that kill bacteria in the body, were once thought to interfere with combination oral contraceptive effectiveness. While it is true that taking antibiotics can lower the amount of contraceptive hormones excreted in urine, the levels of hormone in the bloodstream do not change during most types of antibiotic therapy. However, clinicians will often advise women on oral contraceptives to use additional protection when on short courses of antibiotics and may avoid prescribing particular antibiotic compounds. Other compounds may interfere with the metabolism of combination birth control pills, and physicians should consider a woman's birth control wishes when prescribing additional drug therapy.

After combination oral contraceptives were introduced on the market in 1960, they quickly became one of the most popular methods of birth control. However, by the mid-1970s, studies began to reveal the negative side effects of these early pills. The use of oral birth control pills dropped nearly 50% between 1973 and 1982 because of legitimate fears over the safety of this method. Since 1983, however, the use of combination pills has risen just as dramatically due to the development of new, safer, lower dose pills. Today, birth control pills are the most commonly used form of reversible birth control. Nearly 40% of women under age 30 who use birth control are taking combination pills.

Combination birth control pills do carry some risk. Most significantly, the synthetic estrogen in these pills causes changes in the levels of certain blood clotting factors, leading to an elevated risk of blood clotting disorders and heart attack. Blood clots in the extremities and lungs, stroke, and heart attack were especially serious problems among women older than age 35 who smoked and took the first-generation, high estrogen dose (> 50 mg) pills. However, contemporary pills contain the lowest possible effective estrogen levels (around 35 mg). Most studies now indicate that current use of combination pills does increase the risk of fatal blood clots, but in women younger than 35 who do not smoke that risk increases from about 1 death per 100,000 to about 3 deaths per 100,000. (Compare this rate to the risk of death during child birth, which is approximately 6 per 100,000 births).Fatal blood clotting disorders nearly always are preceded by some warning signs, including headaches, visual disturbances, and non-fatal blood clots. Women on the pill should be counseled by their health care provider to be alert for any danger signs and to seek immediate assistance if they appear. The risk of developing a blood clotting disorder can be further minimized by not prescribing combination birth control pills to women with various risk factors, especially to those who smoke (Table 12.2). These disease risks disappear completely when combination pill use is discontinued.

In addition to short term effects on blood clotting, estrogen may have long term effects on cells with estrogen receptors. In particular, the estrogen in combination pills has been linked to an increased risk of breast cancer (see Chapter 13 for a discussion of the triggers

TABLE 12.2
CONTRAINDICATIONS TO THE USE OF COMBINED ORAL CONTRACEPTIVES

1. Any sort of blood clotting disorder
2. Markedly impaired liver function
3. Known or suspected breast cancer
4. Undiagnosed abnormal vaginal bleeding
5. Known or suspected pregnancy
6. Smokers over the age of 35
7. Before surgery or while wearing a cast

of cancer). Premenopausal breast cancer is rare, but recent studies indicate that women who have used birth control in the last 10 years and those who began use before age 20 have a slightly increased risk of being diagnosed with breast cancer before menopause. Interestingly, the cancers in these women appear to be less invasive than cancers diagnosed in non-users. While questions about the relationship between combination birth control pills and breast cancer have still not been definitively answered, it appears that unless a woman has a family history of breast cancer, her increased risk associated with the use of combined oral contraceptives is insignificant.

Estrogen also affects cervical cells. The incidence of cervical cancer appears to increase with long term (>10 years) use of combined oral contraceptives, especially among women who have been infected with HPV, the virus that causes genital warts. Cervical cancer is easily screened for during Pap smears, and long term oral contraceptive users with HPV should be especially careful to have regular pelvic examinations (see Chapter 6 for a description of Pap smears and pelvic exams).

While there are some risks associated with long term utilization of combined birth control pills, users also gain several benefits. Because estrogen inhibits the repeated cell division that typically occurs in the ovaries and uterus during the menstrual cycle, the risk of cancer of these organs is slightly lower among pill users. Pelvic inflammatory disease (PID) is 50% less common during combination pill use, probably because the cervical mucus remains thick enough to impede the passage of infectious organisms into the upper reproductive tract. (However, unlike barrier methods of birth control, hormonal birth control does not protect users from STDs.) Use of the pill also decreases discomfort before menses, reduces the incidence of dysmenorrhea, and lessens the amount of blood lost during menses. Pill use before menopause also maintains bone mass, reducing the risk of osteoporosis later in life.

The minipill, which contains only progesterone, is used by women who cannot tolerate the side effects of estrogen. As in the combination pill, the progesterone in the minipill decreases the chance that sperm will reach the upper reproductive tract and makes the endometrial lining unsuitable for embryo implantation. Progesterone also decreases the chance that the LH surge triggering ovulation will occur. However, without the additional effect of estrogen, ovulation is more likely when taking minipills than when taking combination birth control. In fact, about 40% of women on minipills ovulate regularly.

Because the effect of progesterone in the minipill on cervical mucus is relatively short lived, the minipill must be taken at the same time every day to be effective. This requirement makes this contraceptive option less attractive to many women who may have irregular daily schedules. Many of the women who choose to take minipills are lactating, because they gain additional birth control protection via lactational infertility (see Chapter 11) and because the estrogen in combination birth control pills interferes with milk production.

Without the endometrium-maintaining action of estrogen, women on minipills are more likely to experience breakthrough bleeding and irregular periods than those taking combination pills. However, because minipills do not affect ovarian function, they do not delay the return of fertility for as long a period as combination birth control pills. Women seeking pregnancy after being on combination pills may be infertile for up to a year after discontinuing use, while women on minipills are usually fertile within a month after discontinuation.

■ DISCUSSION EXERCISE 1

1.1. Research that links oral birth control pills to negative and positive health outcomes in women is always correlational. What are the problems of correlational studies (recall Chapter 2)? Design a study that would investigate unambiguously a link between combination pills and a specific health risk, such as the possible increased risk of breast cancer. Could this study be performed? Why or why not?

Norplant   In the late 1980s, a long acting method of hormonal birth control that did not require daily pill taking became available to women in the U.S. The Norplant system consists of six 3.5 cm long silicone tubes filled with a synthetic progesterone, levongesterol, which are placed under the skin of the upper arm. The powdered hormone in the tubes slowly diffuses through the silicone, producing a constant low level of progesterone in the bloodstream. The implants contain enough hormone to offer effective protection for 5 years after insertion. The progesterone in Norplant works in much the same manner as in the minipill—the LH surge is suppressed, sperm penetration is reduced, and the endometrium is made unsuitable for implantation. However, as with the minipill, about one-third of the cycles are ovulatory, and women on Norplant are very likely to experience irregular menstrual bleeding.

While Norplant is a very effective method of birth control (see Table 12.1), few women in the U.S. have opted to use it. This may be true because the long term effects of Norplant are still under study, the insertion and removal of the Norplant capsules is somewhat painful, the implants are visible as ridges on the skin surface, or breakthrough bleeding is such a common and annoying problem. Additionally, unlike most other methods of birth control, women on Norplant cannot reverse their birth control decision without a visit to a clinic or doctor's office to remove the capsules.

There are only a few known negative side effects of Norplant. The use of Norplant has been associated with an increased incidence of ovarian cysts. These cysts form when follicles stimulated by FSH to develop are not triggered to ovulate. Ovarian cysts can become large and painful, but this condition is fairly rare; most persistent follicles are reabsorbed by the ovary without causing any discomfort. Because the progesterone in Norplant makes the endometrium unsuitable for embryo implantation, the *very few* pregnancies that do occur in women using this method are likely to be ectopic, and thus potentially life threatening. However, the *rate* of ectopic pregnancies of women on Norplant is only half the rate of women who do not use birth control. Recently, Norplant has been associated with an increased risk of major depression and panic disorders. This correlation has not yet been well studied, but removal of the capsules may be performed in an attempt to relieve depressive symptoms.

Depo Provera   The compound medroxyprogesterone acetate, known by the brand name Depo Provera, is a long acting hormonal contraceptive that has fewer negative effects than Norplant. This synthetic progesterone is produced in the form of microcrystals, which are mixed with a liquid solution and injected into the muscles of the arm or buttock. Once in the bloodstream, the microcrystals dissolve slowly over a period of three months, releasing a higher level of progesterone into the bloodstream than Norplant capsules. This higher dose completely suppresses the LH surge, so unlike those on Norplant, women on Depo Provera rarely ovulate. As with other progesterone-based birth control, Depo Provera also reduces sperm transport and endometrial thickness. Because the endometrium is no longer receiving hormonal support, irregular bleeding may occur for the first few months. Nearly 60% of women no longer have periods after several injections.

Although Depo Provera has been safely in use as birth control for several decades in other countries, it was only recently approved (in 1992) in the U.S. One reason cited for the long delay in approving this drug has been the suspected link of Depo Provera to breast cancer. Depo Provera injections have been shown to increase the number of breast tumors in beagles, although this effect now seems to be unique to this particular animal. Studies in several countries have shown no, or very slight, increased incidence of breast cancer among women using Depo Provera for long periods. Depo Provera does enhance the growth of *existing* breast tumors, which may contribute to study results that showed a slight increase in breast cancer with recent use. If the risk of developing breast cancer with this method of birth control exists, it is apparently very small. As with other birth control methods that inhibit the menstrual cycle, Depo Provera use actually decreases the risk of uterine cancer, and its use may decrease the risk of ovarian cancer as well.

One common complaint of Depo Provera users has been that the drug causes weight gain. Some studies have shown that women on Depo Provera gain an average of 8 pounds within 2 years of use. In contrast, other controlled studies indicate that this is not the case, although in these studies women on Depo Provera are less likely to *lose* weight than women on combined oral contraceptives or Norplant. Depo Provera may also slow the adolescent increase in bone density; however, there is no indication that bone loss in adult women is exacerbated by Depo Provera use. Depo Provera should also not be taken when a woman is pregnant, because it suppresses the growth of the developing fetus and may interfere with the process of sex differentiation. Most clinicians will require new users to take a pregnancy test before prescribing this (or any other) form of hormonal birth control.

Like combination pills, Depo Provera inhibits regular ovarian function, and a return to fertility may be slower than with other forms of birth control. However, unlike combination pills, it can be used as birth control during lactation, because it does not interfere with milk production nor does it seem to have an adverse effect on a breast-feeding infant.

Because Depo Provera is injectable and nonreversible (for 3 months) concerns have been raised about its use in physically and psychologically dependent populations. Depo Provera has been touted as the "perfect" birth control for mentally retarded women, because it does not require daily pill taking or an understanding of barrier birth control methods. However, this use of Depo Provera begs the question of how to best deal with the sexuality of these women and what our responsibilities are to both these vulnerable members of our society and to their children. Additionally, Depo Provera can act as a form of chemical castration—reducing the sex drive of *males* who are injected with it. Depo Provera has been used in the treatment of sadomasochists, transvestites, and sexually active children and teenagers. While this drug may control dangerous or socially unacceptable behaviors, the use of Depo Provera in this way represents to many critics an unfairly deterministic and reductionist view of human sexuality. These critics argue that treating sexually "deviant" individuals with Depo Provera does nothing to solve the social problems that cause and are caused by their behaviors.

SUMMARY

Hormonal methods of birth control inhibit ovulation or cause changes in cervical mucus and the endometrium to prohibit sperm passage into the upper reproductive tract thus preventing the implantation of a fertilized egg. Combination birth control pills, which contain estrogen and progesterone, are the most commonly used form of hormonal birth control. The estrogen in combination pills causes a change in blood clotting factors that may increase a woman's risk of heart attack or stroke, although this risk is typically slight in nonsmoking women. The progesterone-only minipill eliminates many of the risks associated with combination pills but is slightly less effective, often results in breakthrough bleeding, and does not relieve dysmenorrhea. Implantable and injectable progesterone-based birth control are new to the U.S. market, have few known side effects, and are highly effective.

Intrauterine Devices

The lack of use and manufacture of IUDs has resulted from business decisions based on profit and liability, not necessarily concerns about women's health and medical options.

Some clinicians refer to intrauterine devices (IUDs) as "the perfect method of birth control." IUDs are as effective as hormonal control (see Table 12.1), are the least expensive long term birth control, have few serious side effects, do not require as much attention as barrier methods or daily pills, and affect only the target organs rather than the whole body system. Despite all of these benefits, in 1995 only 0.8% of women using birth control in the U.S. used IUDs.

IUDs, as their name implies, function when placed inside a woman's uterus. Although IUDs were once thought to prevent pregnancy by causing the abortion of fertilized eggs, it is clear that fertilization rarely occurs in the reproductive tracts of women with these devices in place. The first IUD marketed in the U.S. was the Lippes Loop (Figure 12.3a), a highly effective, inexpensive device that is still in use throughout the world. The two IUDs on the market in the U.S., the Copper T 380A (Figure 12.3b) and the Progestasert, act in slightly different ways to prevent fertilization. Any object inserted in the uterus will cause a nonspecific inflammation of the endometrium. This inflammation makes the environment in the uterus deadly to sperm. The Copper T 380A is a 4.5 cm long plastic "T" with small copper sheaths attached to its arms. These sheaths release copper atoms, increasing the spermicidal nature of the intrauterine environment. The Progestasert is also made of plastic but contains a small amount of slowly released progesterone, which changes the cervical mucus to inhibit sperm transport into the uterus—the few sperm that do reach the uterus are killed by the spermicidal environment created by the inflammation. The Copper T is effective for up to 10 years, while the Progestasert must be replaced yearly.

IUDs must be inserted by a clinician using sterile techniques to minimize the risk of infection. They are most easily inserted during or immediately after menses, when the cervix is slightly dilated. All IUDs have a "tail string" which extends out of the cervix into the vagina. The tail string is used to check on the position of the IUD and also serves as a means to extract the device. Not all women can use IUDs—about 10% are spontaneously expelled from the uterus after insertion.

One reason IUDs are not commonly used in the United States is that they have been associated with an increased risk of pelvic inflammatory disease (PID). This increased risk is associated with one IUD, the Dalkon Shield, which is now off the market (Figure 12.3c). Apparently the multifilament tail string of the Dalkon Shield provided a means for infectious bacteria to invade the uterus; however, currently available IUDs with tail strings have not been associated with an increased risk of PID. IUD-associated PID is now most likely to occur immediately after insertion, especially in women with a bacterial sexually transmitted disease such as gonorrhea or chlamydia. Clinicians can minimize the risk of PID by using careful, sterile techniques when inserting the device. Women at low risk for contracting a sexually transmitted disease are also at a low risk for PID when using an intrauterine device.

Even though available IUDs are quite safe, the unfavorable press and subsequent lawsuits about the Dalkon Shield have caused most manufacturers to stop production of IUDs and

---

FIGURE 12.3   Intrauterine Devices

a. the Lippes loop

b. the Copper T380A

c. the Dalkon shield

---

many clinicians to avoid suggesting them to patients seeking birth control. In addition, because IUDs are inexpensive and very long lasting, their manufacture does not result in large and consistent income for producers. The lack of use and manufacture of IUDs has resulted from business decisions based on profit and liability, not necessarily concerns about women's health and medical options.

IUDs are not without other negative side effects. About 15% of IUD users, primarily women who have never given birth, complain of an increase in menstrual bleeding and cramping. Smaller, progesterone-containing IUDs have minimized this effect. In fact, prolonged use of progesterone IUDs often results in amenorrhea, as the low estrogen levels resulting from follicle suppression may fail to support endometrial growth. IUDs may also perforate the uterine wall, which, although the *uterus* heals quickly, may lead to damage of other internal organs. Often an IUD that passes out of the uterus into the abdominal cavity is attacked by the immune system and becomes fused to the outside of the uterus. Many times these "lost" devices are simply left in the body with no ill effect. Lastly, it has been hypothesized that the continual irritation of the endometrium by an IUD may increase the risk of endometrial cancer, but this effect has not been demonstrated in studies.

Because non-medicated IUDs do not interfere with ovarian function, fertility is rapidly restored once one is removed. However, any pregnancy that does occur when an IUD is in place has a 50% chance of being aborted. A woman wishing to carry a pregnancy conceived with an IUD in place should have the device removed immediately to reduce the risk of spontaneous abortion, although she will still have a greater chance of losing the pregnancy.

Periodic Abstinence

A woman who is familiar with the timing of her cycle and carefully observes the signs of fertility can identify the days she should avoid intercourse if she does not desire pregnancy.

Periodic abstinence can be the least effective (Table 12.1) but also the least invasive method of birth control. Nearly 2.3% of women using birth control employ this method, many for religious reasons (e.g., periodic abstinence is the only method of birth control approved by the Catholic Church). Periodic abstinence is actually an umbrella term for many different fertility control methods, including the calendar ("rhythm"), sympto-thermal, ovulation (Billings), natural family planning, and fertility awareness methods.

All of the methods employing periodic abstinence count on these assumptions: Ovulation occurs once a month, 14 days before menses; sperm survives in the female reproductive tract for 3 to 4 days; and an egg is capable of being fertilized for only 12 to 24 hours after ovulation. By familiarity with the timing of her cycle and careful observation of the signs of fertility, a woman can identify the days she should avoid intercourse if she does not desire pregnancy—typically 5 days before and 1 day after ovulation. The calendar, or "rhythm," method relies only on a woman's awareness of the timing of her typical cycle. If her periods are very regular, than she can predict with accuracy the date she will ovulate each month and can avoid intercourse for the 5 days before and 1 day after that date. However, few women's cycles are so regular, and as is evidenced by the theoretical effectiveness of this method, this is a comparatively risky form of birth control (although in "real world" practice it is about equivalent to barrier methods). The other forms of periodic abstinence use the calendar as a guide but rely heavily on the physical changes that occur before, during, and after ovulation to pinpoint its date.

As we discussed in Chapter 8, immediately before ovulation women experience a change in their cervical mucus. Under the influence of high levels of estrogen, the mucus changes from a gummy state to a more abundant, thinner quality, similar to raw egg white. This thin, slick, and clear mucus is known as "fertile" mucus and can be recognized clinically by the ferning pattern it makes as it dries on a glass slide (Figure 12.4) and at home by its cohesiveness when stretched between two fingers. When this mucus becomes abundant enough to be present at the vaginal opening, women practicing this method know that they should abstain from intercourse. Three days after the peak of mucus production, intercourse is once again considered safe. Because of the reliance of these birth control methods on evaluation of the quality of cervical mucus, most clinicians counsel women using this method for contraception to have intercourse no more frequently than every other day during the non-fertile period. This precaution ensures that semen retained in the vagina after intercourse does not mask changes in mucus.

FIGURE 12.4   Ferning

Fertile cervical mucus forms this pattern while drying on a glass slide.

In addition to changes in mucus quantity and quality, the cervix itself changes shape and position during the fertile times of the cycle, becoming softer and higher in the vagina as the cervical os opens slightly. Some women can feel changes in the cervix by inserting one or two fingers into their vagina.

A woman's basal body temperature (BBT) also changes throughout the menstrual cycle, dropping slowly and irregularly until the day after ovulation, when a rapid rise of at least 0.5° C occurs. The temperature rise along with the changes in cervical mucus help establish when intercourse can be resumed.

In addition to these easily measured symptoms, women can use an "ovarian monitor," which is essentially a kit to measure luteinizing hormone levels excreted in urine. With this technique, a woman can identify the date of ovulation in advance of egg release.

Although few women use natural methods of birth control, recent surveys have indicated that many in the United States wish to learn more about them. Surprisingly, few clinics offer women the kind of in-depth training required to learn these methods. Many groups engaged in natural birth control education are associated with religious groups, which, although they can be excellent sources of information, may be uncomfortable settings for secular women. Curiously, little research has been done on improving the methods of fertility observation, despite keen interest from women and the lack of any negative side effects associated with periodic abstinence. Considering that fertility awareness can be very effective for women who want to avoid pregnancy and useful to those who wish to conceive, it is unfortunate that an understanding of these methods is not more widespread.

SUMMARY

Intrauterine devices prevent pregnancy by causing a nonspecific inflammation in the uterus that is toxic to sperm. IUDs may contain copper or progesterone for additional protection. While one brand of IUD has been associated with an increased risk of pelvic inflammatory disease, the brands that remain on the market provide relatively risk- and trouble-free protection for up to 10 years at a time. Natural methods of birth control rely on a woman's awareness of the signals of fertility, including changes in mucus consistency, cervix position, and body temperature. Natural methods can be as effective as nonhormonal IUDs and barrier methods.

Sterilization

Because the route from ovary to oviduct is inside a woman's abdominal cavity, tubal ligation is more complicated than vasectomy.

The most popular mode of birth control in the U.S., especially among older individuals, is irreversible surgical sterilization. Sterilization can be achieved either by prohibiting the transport of sperm from a man's testicles to his penis, or by prohibiting the passage of an egg from a woman's ovaries to her oviducts. Male sterilization, or vasectomy, is a much faster, less painful, and less expensive procedure than female sterilization, which is also known as tubal ligation. However, of the couples choosing sterilization as a method of birth control, more than 70% use female sterilization.

A vasectomy requires the severing and tying off of the two vasa deferentia that serve as passageways for sperm from the epididymus, where sperm are stored in the testicles, to the urethra, their route out of the body (Figure 12.5). This operation requires the application of localized anesthetic (such as Novocaine) and one or two small incisions to access each vas deferens. Because sperm are stored throughout the length of the vas deferens, men are not sterile immediately after a vasectomy. Most clinicians suggest that additional birth control should be used for 2 months after this procedure. Vasectomies are not completely irreversible—about 50% of operations to reanneal one or both vasa deferentia are successful.

Vasectomy is an outpatient procedure that can be performed in a doctor's office. The recovery time is minimal, and most men experience only minor pain after the anesthetic

FIGURE 12.5   Male External and Internal Genitalia

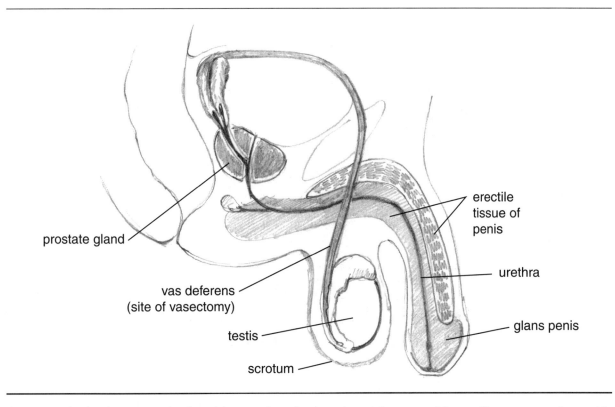

prostate gland

vas deferens
(site of vasectomy)

testis

scrotum

erectile
tissue of
penis

urethra

glans penis

Sperm are produced in the testes, stored in the epididymus, and travel to the urethra via the two vasa deferentia. Vasectomy severs the vasa deferentia, as indicated by the arrow.

wears off. Vasectomy has been associated with an increased risk of arteriosclerosis in animals, although no such relationship has been found in men. Some of the sperm produced after a vasectomy may be released into a man's body cavity, and some men produce antibodies to their own sperm after this procedure. This has been hypothesized to lead to an increased risk of autoimmune disorders, although sperm antibodies are also found in many healthy and fertile men as well and no definitive relationship has been shown between vasectomy and autoimmune disease. While studies still do not show a clear association, vasectomy also may cause a slight increase in a man's risk of prostate cancer.

Because the route from ovary to oviduct is inside a woman's abdominal cavity, tubal ligation is more complicated than vasectomy and must take place in an operating room. While there are several different varieties of operation performed, the most common is removing a section of oviduct and sealing the open ends that remain, either with mechanical clips or rings (Figure 12.6) or by coagulation, which involves essentially "melting" the tissue with electric current. Most tubal ligations require two incisions—one for the instruments used to perform the procedure inside the body cavity, and one for insertion of a laparoscope, which is a long, thin magnifier that allows the physician to observe internal organs. A newer method of tubal ligation that is becoming popular is called a "minilap," in which the physician makes a single incision for a laparoscope and a pair of forceps and pulls the oviducts out of the incision to perform the surgical procedure. This technique is easier for the physician but more painful for the woman undergoing the procedure. In both operations, the

---

FIGURE 12.6   Tubal Ligation

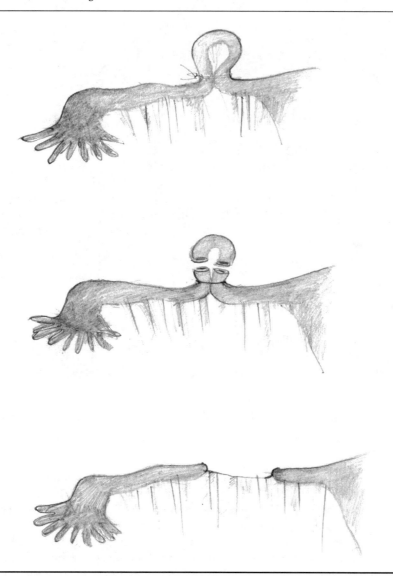

"The Pomeroy technique," a common procedure for tubal ligation. Oviducts are severed then occluded with mechanical clips or rings.

woman's abdominal cavity is filled with several liters of a gas, such as carbon dioxide, to move her internal organs away from each other allowing access to the oviducts. Generally, the woman is also positioned so that her head is lower than her abdomen, so that her internal organs will fall up and away from the reproductive tract.

Recovery time for tubal ligation is longer than that for vasectomy. Women who have a minilap usually need at least one day of bed rest, while women who undergo the more traditional procedure may experience significant discomfort as the two deep incisions heal. Tubal ligation is not associated with any health risks outside of those associated with minor surgery of the abdominal cavity. Tubal sterilizations are more difficult to reverse than vasectomies, with about a 30% success rate when the oviducts are reannealed. Reversibility is more likely when the smallest segment of oviduct is damaged, although the efficacy of the procedure as birth control decreases when less of the tube is damaged.

The Future of Birth Control Technology

In recent years, research on new female birth control methods has slowed considerably, despite the fact that there are still many targets for drugs to work on the female reproductive system. Many scientists believe that the lack of interest in contraceptive research from funding sources reflects liability concerns among drug and medical device manufacturers. Because of this fear, and due to a lack of interest in men's reproductive choices, development of safe, simple, and reversible methods of birth control for men has lagged considerably behind the progress on female birth control. This is unfortunate, because many women and men are interested in additional options that will allow the sexes to better share the risks and responsibilities of fertility control.

Most proposed methods of hormonal birth control for men interfere with the process of sperm production. High levels of testosterone, drugs that inhibit the release of LH (which, in men, stimulates sperm production), and progesterone have all been tested and shown to be effective male contraceptives. At this time, there are few studies that investigate the side effects of these drugs and the release of any to the marketplace is at least several years away. Readers may have heard of gossypol, a derivative of the cotton plant, which had been proposed as a contraceptive method that directly interferes with spermatogenesis. However, animal studies have indicated that gossypol is highly toxic, and this line of research has been abandoned.

Methods of reversible mechanical obstruction of the vas deferens by plastic plugs or clips ("vas valves") have been tested, but the side effects of their use are unknown and their effectiveness is not as high as other birth control methods. Research on male infertility has indicated that men can become infertile if they develop an allergy to their own sperm cells. Some researchers have discussed using some of the processes that occur in sperm allergy to produce a reversible method of male birth control.

With few new methods of birth control in development, women attempting to delay pregnancy until their thirties or to avoid pregnancy altogether must be either extremely committed to a non-invasive method or willing to take the risks involved in long-term use of synthetic hormones or IUDs for protection. Until a safe, convenient, inexpensive, and reliable method of birth control is easily available to all women, many unwanted pregnancies will continue to occur.

■ DISCUSSION EXERCISE 2

2.1. Why do you think methods of natural birth control/fertility awareness are not well known and rarely utilized despite their relative efficacy?

2.2. Why do women have more than twice as many sterilization procedures than men? Do you think the possibly elevated risk of prostate cancer explains the entire difference?

2.3. Why are there so many methods of female birth control and so few for men? Is this difference completely explained by the sex difference in the number of options for control?

2.4. What factors lead women to choose a particular method of birth control? Do you think there should be more birth control options?

SUMMARY

Irreversible methods of birth control (or "sterilization") include vasectomy and tubal ligation. Vasectomy, which severs the tube that allows the passage of sperm into the penis, is easier and less expensive than tubal ligation and has fewer complications. Tubal ligation, the severing of the oviducts, is more painful and complicated than male sterilization but still more than twice as common as vasectomy. Hormonal methods of male birth control may include testosterone or progesterone shots or pills, but none have been developed for market. There is little interest among pharmaceutical firms in developing new methods of contraception.

ABORTION

[N]early 50% of women in the U.S. have had an abortion, and this procedure will remain very common as long as contraceptive services are lacking, contraceptive methods are not foolproof, and sex education is wanting.

Abortions terminate approximately 1.5 million pregnancies in the United States each year. About 50% of these abortions are performed on women who were not using contraceptives. Women do not have equal access to all forms of birth control—for example, many health insurers do not provide coverage for birth control methods or provide coverage for some, but not all, methods. In addition, many women and men, especially adolescents, have not received adequate sex education and thus are not aware of their birth control options. The remaining 750,000 abortions consist of pregnancies that resulted from contraceptive failures. As long as contraceptives are not universally available, are complicated to use, and are less than 100% effective, abortion will remain a necessary option for women who wish to control their own fertility.

Ending a pregnancy becomes more complicated as time passes after conception. The simplest forms of abortion are hormonal methods that induce menstruation regardless of a woman's pregnancy status. Women can use these methods before they are certain they are pregnant, either within 2 or 3 days after unprotected (or inadequately protected) intercourse or perhaps even on a monthly basis as a prophylactic against implantation of a fertilized egg. The most commonly prescribed emergency contraceptive drug, only recently officially approved by the U.S. Food and Drug Administration (FDA), is a high dose combination oral contraceptive pill. This treatment is safely effective in stopping pregnancy only if taken within 72 hours since the failure of a contraceptive device. The high dose of hormones causes several side effects, including nausea, vomiting, breast tenderness, headache, and dizziness. Because of the unusually high hormone doses, these types of contraceptive pills are not safe to take on a monthly basis.

In recent years a chemical abortifactant called mifepristone, commonly referred to by the trade name RU486, has become available in the United States. While the FDA has not officially approved this drug in the U.S., it has been used in other countries to terminate early pregnancies. Mifepristone blocks the action of progesterone, the hormone that maintains the endometrium, and thus induces menses. Mifepristone (or other drugs like it) could thus be taken once monthly to induce menses and end any pregnancies that might have occurred. Currently, little research has been performed in the U.S. on the use of mifepristone or related drugs as a type of monthly birth control.

Until recently, research leading to the potential approval of mifepristone has been blocked in the U.S. by political opposition to abortion. When followed by treatment with prostaglandin injections or suppositories to induce uterine contractions, mifepristone can effectively end pregnancies up to nine weeks after the last menstrual period (seven weeks from conception). Unlike surgical abortions, the use of mifepristone would allow a larger number of doctors to perform safe abortions, reducing the need for women to visit protester-ringed abortion provider clinics. Activists who oppose any form of abortion have worked strenuously to keep mifepristone off the market in the U.S. to prevent this diffusion of abortions from specialized clinics to general medical offices. Despite the controversy that surrounds it, mifepristone has no known severe side effects and has been used safely in France for more than a decade. The steps required for FDA approval of mifepristone as an aborti-factant were initiated in 1994, and this drug will likely be available soon in the U.S.

Until mifepristone becomes available in this country, the most common methods of abortion will require a surgical procedure. The most frequently performed surgical abortion is vacuum aspiration. In this method, a straw-like tube called a cannula is attached to a source of gentle suction and passed through the cervix to draw the embryo or fetus and placenta out of the uterus. The cervix is manually dilated for this procedure to about 12 mm in diameter by inserting a series of cannuli of increasing size. Vacuum aspiration of the uterus takes about 5 to 15 minutes to complete but can only be performed in the first trimester, as early as 5 weeks but no more than 12 weeks after a woman's last menstrual period.

Before the advent of effective vacuum aspiration techniques, the most common abortion method was the procedure known as a D and C (dilation and curettage). Dilation of the cervix is performed with the same series of cannuli and removal of the contents of the uterus is accomplished by gentle scraping with a metal loop, called a curette. This technique is more painful and may result in slightly more complications than a vacuum aspiration, but some clinicians still use D and C's, especially during the period from 12 to 16 weeks from the last menstrual period.

Later term abortions are most commonly performed using a technique that is a kind of cross between vacuum aspiration and dilation and curettage. This procedure, called a D and E (dilation and evacuation) is used after 12 or 16 weeks because the fetus and placenta are larger and more difficult to remove from the uterus. In order to end the pregnancy effectively, a woman's cervix must be dilated to a larger diameter. Dilation is typically accomplished through the use of Laminaria sticks, strips of dried seaweed that are placed in the cervix. As these sticks absorb moisture, they expand and gradually force open the cervical os. Because this method of dilation takes place over a number of hours, it is safer and more comfortable than attempting to manually dilate the cervix with large cannuli. Once the cervix is sufficiently opened, the physician uses forceps, a curette, and vacuum suction to loosen and remove the uterine lining, placental tissue, and fetus. Oxytocin may also be given to a woman at this time to cause uterine contractions to expel retained tissue, which reduces the duration of post-abortion bleeding.

More rarely, physicians will induce labor in pregnant women who require late term abortions. These induction or instillation abortions are accomplished by either injecting saline or progesterone into the amniotic sac that surrounds the fetus or placing a progesterone suppository in the patient's vagina. In both cases, several hours after the treatment, contractions begin and the fetus and placenta are expelled. Because this technique causes a woman to experience a type of labor, this method of abortion is often the most painful of the available procedures. It is typically only used for abortions performed relatively late in pregnancy.

Early abortions have few complications but as the age of the pregnancy (and hence the invasiveness of the procedure) increases, the number of risks increases. The most common complication of surgical abortion is infection, which is true of any surgical procedure and is usually controlled with antibiotics. Some women experience heavy bleeding after an abortion, which may be a sign that some tissue remains in the uterus or that the uterus was perforated during the procedure. In most cases the bleeding stops without intervention, but women experiencing excessive bleeding after an abortion should consult their physician.

The number of abortions has declined in recent years as the number of women in the large "baby boom" generation who are seeking to postpone childbirth has dropped. However, nearly 50% of women in the U.S. have had an abortion, and this procedure will remain very common as long as contraceptive services are lacking, contraceptive methods are not foolproof, and sex education is wanting. Although many groups in the U.S. still seek to outlaw abortion or at least greatly restrict access to these procedures, we have seen in this country and others that women continue to seek abortion services even under the most repressive legal environments. Access to safe, inexpensive abortion services allows women to make decisions about their reproductive lives without endangering their own health and security.

■ DISCUSSION EXERCISE 3

3.1. Abortion may be thought of as either an elective medical procedure, like cosmetic surgery, or a required procedure, like cancer treatment. What are the consequences of considering abortion elective? What are the consequences of considering it required?

3.2. Why is abortion so highly controversial in U.S. society? Do you think there are solutions to the abortion controversy? If so, what are they? If not, why?

SUMMARY

Abortion will be a necessary component of fertility control as long as contraceptive methods are not 100% effective and women demand access to the full range of birth control options. Nonsurgical abortions include treatment with high dose oral contraceptives within 72 hours of a suspected conception or with mifepristone, a menses inducer, within 9 weeks from the last menstrual period. Surgical procedures include aspiration of the contents of the uterus and scraping of the uterine lining. Early abortions have very few complications, although risks increase for abortions occurring later in the pregnancy.

INFERTILITY

A commonly held belief is that women who "try too hard to conceive" will have trouble getting pregnant. There is little evidence for this hypothesis—it may be that women who are actively attempting to get pregnant notify more friends and relatives, and all may have unreasonable expectations about typical pregnancy rates.

Infertility is typically defined as the inability to conceive within 1 year of discontinuing contraception. In nearly 80% of heterosexual couples not using birth control, the woman becomes pregnant within 1 year. Of the remaining 20%, one half will become pregnant within the span of another year without any medical intervention, and the remainder has a fertility "problem." In 1995, 7% of heterosexual couples were considered infertile, and nearly 15% of all women (9.3 million) had used some kind of infertility service, including medical tests, drugs, surgery, or services to prevent miscarriage. The management of infertility has become a big business in the U.S. and has been accompanied by an explosion of assisted reproductive technologies (ART) that are available to infertile couples.

Figure 12.7 illustrates the sources of infertility among couples and in women alone. Although infertility is commonly thought of as a woman's health issue, male factor infertility is almost as common as female factor infertility. About 40% of cases of female factor infertility are preventable—most are caused by the long term effects of sexually transmitted disease. If an STD leads to pelvic inflammatory disease (PID), scar tissue may form in the oviducts. This scar tissue can prevent the transport of an egg to the site of fertilization and implantation, making pregnancy impossible. PID is almost entirely preventable when proper protection is taken against sexually transmitted diseases.

FIGURE 12.7   Reasons for Infertility in Couples and Women Alone

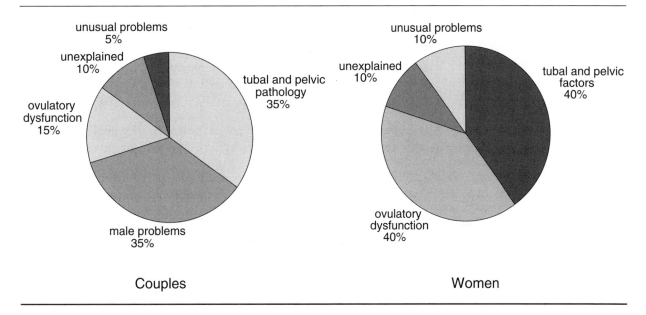

Couples

Women

STDs and Tubal Infertility

There are two main classes of STDs—those caused by bacteria and those caused by viruses (Table 12.3). Bacterial STDs can lead to PID. The two most common bacterial STDs are chlamydia and gonorrhea, of which nearly 500,000 cases *each* are reported every year. Most reported cases are found in women, because women are more likely to be screened for these diseases when they visit physicians for other reproductive services. Additionally, the number of reported cases is estimated to be less than 25% of the number of actual cases in the United States, because infection with either chlamydia or gonorrhea is very likely to go unnoticed. In fact, 75 to 80% of women infected with either of these organisms experience no symptoms. As many as 40% of women with untreated chlamydia or gonorrhea develop PID.

The risk of tubal infertility increases with each subsequent PID episode, from 12% of women becoming infertile after one attack to 54% after three bouts. The risk of PID is *doubled* by regular douching, which women may be more likely to do when a gonorrheal or chlamydial infection causes unpleasant vaginal discharge. Douching (see Chapter 6) can force bacteria present in the vagina or on the cervix into the upper reproductive tract.

Bacterial STDs can be treated with antibiotics, but prevention is more effective in reducing the risk of STD-associated PID. The best protection from all types of STD is the use of condoms for all genital to genital, genital to oral, and genital to anal contact. The use of spermicide also offers additional protection against some STD-causing organisms.

When tubal obstruction is suspected as the cause of infertility, a clinician will typically perform a hysterosalpingogram. This procedure is performed by injecting an opaque dye into the uterus while a series of X-rays are taken. The X-ray films reveal how easily and rapidly the dye leaks out of the ends of the oviducts and also help to pinpoint the location

TABLE 12.3
COMMON SEXUALLY TRANSMITTED DISEASES

Bacterial	**Viral**
Gonorrhea	Herpes
Syphilis	Genital Warts
Chlamydia	HIV/AIDS

and extent of any scar tissue or other blockages present. Alternatively, a physician may perform an insufflation test to determine the status of the oviducts. In this procedure, carbon dioxide gas is introduced into the uterus. As the gas passes out of the oviducts into the abdominal cavity, it forces the diaphragm (the muscles that separate the abdominal cavity from the chest cavity) upwards, causing pain in the chest and shoulders. If pain occurs only at relatively high gas pressures, the tubes are likely obstructed. Between 30 and 40% of previously infertile women who undergo hysterosalpingography or insufflation become fertile after this procedure, possibly because loose obstructions of the oviducts are forced out by pressure applied by the dye or gas.

Tubal obstructions that are not cleared by hysterosalpingography may be reduced in size by one of several methods. Some infertility clinics attempt to open the oviducts by performing some version of balloon tuboplasty, in which a small balloon is guided into the oviducts, inflated to flatten any obstructions, then removed. Other clinics may perform surgery to remove the tissue, either with standard surgical tools or with lasers.

When the obstruction of the oviduct is impossible to relieve, a woman may employ in vitro fertilization procedures (IVF, discussed below) to achieve pregnancy.

Ovarian Factor Infertility

Female factor infertility is as likely to be caused by reduced ovarian function as it is to be caused by tubal obstruction (Figure 12.7). Ovarian factor infertility occurs when ovulation is irregular or nonexistent. This is more likely to occur in older women (see Chapter 14 for a discussion of age-related declines in egg production).

Ovarian function can be readily diagnosed by observing changes in basal body temperature (BBT). Recall that BBT increases by about $0.5°$ C within 1 or 2 days after ovulation when progesterone levels increase. Absence of this temperature rise usually indicates the absence of ovulation.

In some women, ovarian factor infertility is the result of an abnormal corpus luteum rather than the lack of ovulation. If the corpus luteum is slow to develop, progesterone levels may remain low, and a newly fertilized egg may reach the uterus before the endometrium has developed enough to support implantation. Embryos in these conditions are often spontaneously aborted without the woman knowing that fertilization has occurred. Problems with the corpus luteum can be diagnosed by observing the timing of the LH surge and subsequent BBT rise. If the gap between these two events is more than two days, progesterone suppositories can be placed in the vagina to help initiate development of the endometrium and to support the embryo.

When a woman is ovulating rarely or irregularly, physicians often prescribe treatment with the drug clomiphene citrate (known by the trade name Clomid), human menopausal gonadotropin (hMG, known by the trade name Pergonal), or human chorionic gonadotropin (hCG). Clomiphene citrate acts by blocking estrogen binding sites on the hypothalamus. Without signals from the estrogen that is present but cannot bind, the hypothalamus triggers the continued production of follicle stimulating hormone (FSH).

Under treatment with clomiphene citrate, women are likely to ovulate several eggs per cycle. About 5% of pregnancies stimulated with the help of clomiphene citrate result in twins or triplets. Common side effects of clomiphene citrate include hot flushes, ovarian enlargement, nervousness, dizziness, and headaches.

Treatment with hMG and hCG for ovarian failure generally occurs only if clomiphene citrate has not been effective, or during IVF procedures. HMG, which is a drug purified from the urine of post menopausal women, contains FSH and luteinizing hormone (LH). HCG is purified from the urine of pregnant women and contains mostly LH. This combination of drugs is used to stimulate both follicle development and ovulation. Although only 25% of women receiving treatment with hMG and hCG become pregnant, 25% of pregnancies that do result are of twins or triplets. Roberta McCaughey, who gave birth to septuplets in late 1997, conceived these children after having been given hMG as treatment for possible ovarian factor infertility.

Because the ovaries can be super-stimulated by treatment with hMG/hCG or clomiphene citrate, enlargement of these organs may occur. Doctors often advise patients treated with ovarian stimulating drugs to avoid exercise during treatment, because sudden movements may damage overstimulated ovarian tissue. In severe cases, which occur in 1 to 2% of hMG-treated women, this overstimulation and enlargement may actually be life threatening. Ovarian enlargement may be relieved by aspirating a number of the follicles that have developed immediately after hMG treatment. When multiple oocytes are released, the risk that one will implant in the oviduct and cause an ectopic pregnancy increases as well, and physicians are watchful for this potentially life-threatening condition in treated women. Recent reports have also linked clomiphene citrate and hMG/hCG treatment with an increased risk of ovarian cancer, although these results are still tentative.

A commonly held belief is that women who "try to hard to conceive" will have trouble getting pregnant. There is little evidence for this hypothesis—it may be that women who are actively attempting to get pregnant notify more friends and relatives, and all may have unreasonable expectations about typical pregnancy rates. However, some evidence from animal studies indicates that anxiety can reduce levels of FSH and LH to the point where ovulation is inhibited. It is possible that the same process may occur in anxious women as well. While certainly there are many other reasons a woman's ovulation and fertility may be inhibited, removing pressure and stress in women's lives, especially that associated with "achieving conception," may be useful in increasing ovarian function in some women without the use of drug intervention.

Other Causes for Female Infertility

An easily observed, easily treated, but rare factor that causes female infertility is "sticky" cervical mucus. Physicians treating infertile women will often collect cervical mucus during a woman's fertile period to look for the typical ferning pattern (see Figure 12.4). If the fertile mucus does not display this pattern when dried, it may be that the woman is suffering from a low-level, chronic vaginal infection. Infection can cause the acidity of the vagina to increase. Changes in acidity cause the cervical mucus to become gummy, inhibiting sperm transport. Mucus changes caused by infection may be treated by antibiotics. Changes in cervical mucus that result from unknown causes can often be treated with low doses of estrogen or with estrogen suppositories placed in the vagina.

The daughter of a woman treated during pregnancy with diethylstilbestrol (DES, see Chapter 6) may have an unusually shaped uterus, which makes carrying a pregnancy to term more difficult. However, "DES daughters" do not have any additional problems becoming pregnant and appear to be as fertile as the general female population.

A woman with an unusually shaped or missing uterus, one who required a hysterectomy because of disease, or one who has some other uterine characteristic that makes the support of pregnancy impossible has limited options. Women in these situations may turn to a surrogate mother, a woman who is willing to be artificially inseminated by a man's sperm and to give the newborn to the infertile woman for adoption. In some cases, a surrogate mother will agree to carry an embryo produced by the mixing of sperm and egg collected from an infertile couple. These arrangements are controversial, expensive, and may become troublesome if the relationship between the surrogate and the adoptive parents breaks down. However, there have been several thousand surrogacy arrangements made in the U.S. over the past decade.

SUMMARY

Female factor infertility is the cause of approximately 50% of infertility cases. Female infertility is usually caused by either obstruction of the oviducts or ovarian dysfunction. Oviduct obstruction is highly preventable, because most cases result from scarring due to STD-associated PID. Ovarian dysfunction is more common in older women, who may no longer ovulate regularly. Anxiety may also reduce ovulation by suppressing FSH and LH release, although research has not found a direct link. Ovaries can be stimulated to release eggs by various drugs. Another less common cause of female factor infertility is a problem with cervical mucus, which may prevent the passage of sperm into the uterus. Infertility caused by a missing or abnormally shaped uterus is difficult to treat.

Male Factor Infertility

Among infertile couples, male factor infertility is almost as likely to be a cause as female factor infertility. Male factor infertility can be diagnosed by observing sperm samples (a "sperm count"), although, interestingly, this is rarely one of the first tests performed on a couple who seek infertility treatment. Sperm in samples should be plentiful, active, and not aggregated into clumps. Many cases of male infertility are due to oligospermia—low sperm production (i.e., less than 20 million sperm per milliliter of semen). The causes of oligospermia are unclear. It is known that smoking, cocaine use, excessive heat, and tight pants which hold the testicles close to the body (and thus expose them to excessive heat) can reduce sperm counts. However, many scientists are concerned that low sperm counts in men parallel low sperm counts in other species, which may be caused by industrial chemicals (found in herbicides, pesticides, and plastic) that either mimic the action of estrogen or block the action of testosterone. As of yet, no studies have confirmed a link between these synthetic chemicals and sperm production in men. If analysis of a semen sample indicates a normal sperm count but that the sperm are aggregating, the cause is likely a "sperm allergy"—i.e., the man is making antibodies to his own sperm. Treatment with cortisone may reduce the level of sperm clumping due to sperm allergy.

The semen of men with male factor infertility can be washed and motile sperm selected for by various methods. Once enough motile sperm have been collected, the simplest procedures to effect fertilization are artificial insemination (AI) or intrauterine insemination (IUI). In AI, the collected sperm are injected with a syringe into the upper vagina around the time of ovulation. IUI bypasses the cervical mucus by injecting sperm directly into the uterus. Because the passage from vagina into the uterus (through the cervix) is where the majority of sperm are "lost," this procedure results in a higher likelihood of success than AI. Both AI and IUI are relatively easy and are also commonly used by women who wish to have a child without a male partner, using sperm from a (usually unknown) donor.

Significantly more invasive than AI or IUI is a procedure known as direct intraperitoneal insemination (DIPI), in which sperm are injected into the abdominal cavity directly through the vaginal wall. In this instance, they are pulled into the reproductive tract with the ovulated egg on the suction produced by contractions of the oviducts. This procedure places a large number of sperm at the site of fertilization. DIPI has a slightly higher rate of success than AI and IUI.

"Shared" Infertility

Many cases of infertility that are due to factors unique to a *couple* are caused by a woman's immune reaction to her partner's sperm. As with sperm self-allergy, the sperm in a semen sample from an affected couple will aggregate when inside the woman's vagina and reproductive tract. The contribution of shared factors in causing infertility can be evaluated with a post-coital test. For this measure, a woman must have a sample of cervical mucus evaluated within 2 to 8 hours of intercourse. The clinician will evaluate the number of sperm in the mucus sample (note that this should not take the place of a sperm count), their appearance, and measures how well they move through the mucus. If sperm allergy is apparent, the woman will be treated with cortisone to lessen her immune response. If this treatment is unsuccessful, sperm will be collected and washed. Those that react with antibodies will be removed, and the remainder used in an AI, IUI, or DIPI procedure.

ASSISTED REPRODUCTIVE TECHNOLOGIES

Fertilization outside the body, called in vitro fertilization (IVF), was the first method of assisted reproduction developed and resulted in the world's first "test tube baby" in 1977.

When a man's sperm are of insufficient quantity or quality (i.e., weak or nonmotile), when a woman has irreversible problems that prohibit egg movement in the oviducts, or when the cause of infertility is unknown, a couple and their clinician may decide that the best strategy for achieving a pregnancy requires more aggressive techniques of bringing sperm and egg together. These intensively technical procedures require the physical removal of eggs from a woman's ovary and are collectively known as assisted reproductive technology (ART).

The "harvesting" of eggs from a woman's ovaries occurs after drug therapy to stimulate follicle development and ovulation. Typically, hMG and hCG are used to ensure that a large number of eggs are ready to be collected. In addition to these two drugs, a GnRH agonist, Luprol, is given to prevent a woman's natural LH surge. The inhibition of natural ovulation enables a physician to manually cause the ovulation of ripe eggs by suctioning the enlarged follicles from the ovary.

Eggs are harvested from the ovaries by aspiration with a needle inserted through the wall of the vagina. The physician is guided to ripe follicles using images of the ovaries produced by ultrasound examination. The eggs harvested must be evaluated by an embryologist, who removes those that have not reached metaphase II of meiosis (see Chapter 9) and are thus not capable of fertilization.

A woman with premature ovarian failure may wish to carry a pregnancy with a donated egg. Eggs for donation are harvested from young female volunteers. Incidentally, fertilization and pregnancy rates for these procedures are generally higher when donor eggs are used, probably because the donors are young and without reproductive problems.

If there is no male factor infertility and the woman has at least one intact oviduct, three to five of the harvested eggs and some collected, washed sperm may be mixed and immediately placed in the oviduct via laparoscopy. This procedure, known as gamete intrafallopian transfer (GIFT), allows for natural fertilization to occur in the oviduct and is more successful than other methods of ART. Extra eggs may be frozen indefinitely for later use in case pregnancy does not occur or if additional pregnancies are desired.

If the sperm and eggs are allowed to incubate together in a glass dish for 48 hours, fertilization will also likely occur. The sperm must be capacitated first (see Chapter 9), usually by incubation in a medium that mimics the environment of the reproductive tract. Fertilization outside the body, called in vitro fertilization (IVF), was the first method of assisted reproduction developed and resulted in the world's first "test tube baby" in 1977.

Early embryos, known as *zygotes* at this stage, can then be transferred into the oviducts (zygote intrafallopian transfer, or ZIFT) or into the uterus ("traditional" IVF). ZIFT is more likely to result in a successful pregnancy than placement in the uterus, but it requires a more invasive procedure. As with eggs, extra embryos that are not implanted may be frozen for later IVF attempts.

If male factor infertility is a problem, sperm may be aided in reaching the egg cytoplasm by a number of techniques. Weak or nonmotile sperm may have difficulty crossing the zona pellucida, which surrounds the egg (see Chapter 9). The zona may be partially abraded (partial zona dissection, PZD) to allow sperm passage, sperm may be injected underneath the zona (subzonal insemination, SUZI), or a single sperm may actually be injected into the cytoplasm of the egg (intracytoplasmic sperm injection, ICSI). Of these three techniques, ICSI is the most labor intensive and difficult but also the most likely to result in pregnancy.

After the sperm and eggs or zygotes are reintroduced into a woman's reproductive tract, she is advised to stay off her feet for at least 3 days and to refrain from exercise and intercourse until a pregnancy test is performed. A week after the transfer, her pregnancy status will be assessed via a standard pregnancy test (Chapter 10). Currently there is little information on the success of ART procedures, but the few clinics that do publish reports indicate that pregnancy results only in about 25% of ART attempts.

Critics of ART procedures have worried that the artificial processes involved increase the possibility of birth defects in developing babies. By removing the natural barriers to sperm that prohibit poorly formed sperm from reaching and fertilizing an egg, they argue, ART allows the fusion of a sperm and egg which perhaps "should not" come together. Selection against genetic problems usually occurs during early embryo development however, and currently there is little evidence that babies conceived with ART have any higher incidence of birth defects than babies conceived without such intervention.

The risks of ART are similar to those associated with artificial ovarian stimulation and with surgical procedures. In addition, about 30% of successful IVF procedures result in multiple pregnancies, which have their own risks (see Chapter 10). When ART procedures result in multiple surviving fetuses, parents may be asked to consider selectively aborting most of these to improve the chance of success of the one or two that remain. This can be an agonizing decision for many ART patients. ART procedures carry a significant financial risk as well, costing approximately $10,000 per pregnancy attempt. The pregnancies that result are almost invariably highly medically managed to ensure successful outcomes. For instance, Cesarean sections are much more common among IVF patients than among the general population. This intensive pregnancy management means that the costs of prenatal care and birthing are substantially higher for ART patients.

■ DISCUSSION EXERCISE 4

4.1. If you believed either you or your partner was infertile, do you think that you would be willing to undergo infertility testing and treatment ? Why or why not? What ethical issues do you think are involved in infertility treatment?

4.2. Do you think health insurance should cover the cost of assisted reproductive technologies? Should Medicaid cover the cost so that these treatments are available to low income couples? Should there be screening so that ART and other fertility treatments are only given to women who have the financial means to provide for any children produced?

SUMMARY

Male factor infertility is caused by problems with sperm production or by sperm allergy. These problems can often be treated by employing artificial insemination (AI), intrauterine insemination (IUI), or direct intraperitoneal insemination (DIPI), with washed, concentrated, and specially selected sperm. Couple infertility is often caused by a woman's allergy to a man's sperm and may be treated with antiallergy medications or with AI, IUI, or DIPI. Assisted reproductive technologies all require the stimulation of ovulation via drugs and the collection of eggs from the ovary. These eggs may either be mixed with sperm and reintroduced to the oviducts (GIFT) or be allowed to fertilize in the lab and transplanted into the oviducts (ZIFT) or uterus (IVF). If male sperm are rare or weak, fertilization may be stimulated by bypassing the egg's zona pellucida. Currently, most techniques of ART are expensive and have a low success rate.

REFERENCES

Abma, J., Chandra, A., Mosher, W., Peterson L., & Piccinino, L. (1997). Fertility, family planning, and women's health: New data from the 1995 National Survey of Family Growth. National Center for Health Statistics. *Vital Health Statistics* 23(19).

Alvarez, F., Brache, V., Faundes, A., Tejada, A. S., & Thevenin, F. (1996). Ultrasonographic and endocrine evaluation of ovarian function among Norplant implants users with regular menses. *Contraception*, 54(5), 275–279.

Bagshaw, S. (1995). The combined oral contraceptive. Risks and adverse effects in perspective. *Drug Safety*, 12(2), 91–96.

Billings, E., & Westmore, A. (1980). *The Billings method*. Random House.

Boston Woman's Health Collective (1992). *The new our bodies, ourselves*. Touchstone.

Cadepond, F., Ulmann, A., & Baulieu, E. E. (1997). RU486 (mifepristone): Mechanisms of action and clinical uses. *Annual Review of Medicine*, 48, 129–156.

Carr, B. R., & Ory, H. (1997). Estrogen and progestin components of oral contraceptives: Relationship to vascular disease. *Contraception*, 55(5), 267–272.

Cavero, C. (1995). Using an ovarian monitor as an adjunct to natural family planning. *Journal of Nurse-Midwifery*, 40(3), 269–276.

Collaborative Group on Hormonal Factors in Breast Cancer (1996). Breast cancer and hormonal contraceptives: Collaborative reanalysis of individual data on 53,297 women with breast cancer and 100,239 women without breast cancer from 54 epidemiological studies. *Lancet* 347, 1713–1727.

Comhaire, F. H. (1994). Male contraception: Hormonal, mechanical and other. *Human Reproduction*, 9 (2 Suppl), 22–27.

Cromer, B. A., Blair, J. M., Mahan, J. D., Zibners, L., & Naumovski, Z. (1996). A prospective comparison of bone density in adolescent girls receiving depot medroxyprogesterone acetate (Depo Provera), levonorgestrel (Norplant), or oral contraceptives. *Journal of Pediatrics*, 129(5), 671–676.

DeCherney, A. (1996). Bone-sparing properties of oral contraceptives. *American Journal of Obstetrics & Gynecology*, 174(1 Pt1), 15–20.

Division of STD Prevention (1996). *Sexually transmitted disease surveillance, 1995*. United States Department of Health and Human Services, Centers for Disease Control.

Douketis, J. D., Ginsberg, J. S., Holbrook, A., Crowther, M., Duku, E. K., & Burrows R. F. (1997). A reevaluation of the risk for venous thromboembolism with the use of oral contraceptives and hormone replacement therapy. *Archives of Internal Medicine*, 157(14), 1522–1530.

Ebi, K. L., Piziali, R. L. Rosenberg, M., & Wachob, H. F. (1996). Evidence against tailstrings increasing the rate of pelvic inflammatory disease among IUD users. *Contraception*, 53(1), 25–32.

Engel, W., Murphy, D., & Schmid, M. (1996). Are there genetic risks associated with microassisted reproduction? *Human Reproduction*, 11, 2359–2370.

Fehring, R. J., Lawrence, D. & Philpot, C. (1994). Use effectiveness of the Creighton model ovulation method of natural family planning. *Journal of Obstetric, Gynecologic, & Neonatal Nursing,* 23(4), 303–309.

Goldzieher, J. W., & Zamah, N. M. (1995). Oral contraceptive side effects: Where's the beef? *Contraception,* 52(6), 327–335.

Handelsman, D. J. (1995). Hormonal male contraception: Progress and prospects for the 21st century. *Australian & New Zealand Journal of Medicine,* 25(6), 808–816.

Hannaford, P. C., & Webb, A. M. (1996). Evidence-guided prescribing of combined oral contraceptives: Consensus statement. An International Workshop at Mottram Hall, Wilmslow, U.K., March, 1996. *Contraception,* 54(3), 125–129.

Helmerhorst, F. M., Bloemenkamp, K. W., Rosendaal, F. R., & Vandenbroucke, J. P. (1997). Oral contraceptives and thrombotic disease: Risk of venous thromboembolism. *Thrombosis & Haemostasis,* 78(1), 327–333.

Jennings, J. C., Moreland, K., & Peterson, C. M. (1996). In vitro fertilisation. A review of drug therapy and clinical management. *Drugs,* 52(3), 313–343.

Kambic, R. T., & Lamprecht, V. (1996). Calendar rhythm efficacy: A review. Advances in *Contraception,* 12(2), 123–128.

Kaunitz, A. M. (1997). Reappearance of the intrauterine device: A 'user-friendly' contraceptive. *International Journal of Fertility and Women's Medicine* 42(2), 120–127.

Kaunitz, A. M. (1994). Long-acting injectable contraception with depot medroxyprogesterone acetate. *American Journal of Obstetrics & Gynecology,* 170(5 Pt 2), 1543–1549.

Kreiss, J., Ngugi, E., & Holmes, K. (1992). Efficacy of nonoxynol-9 contraceptive sponge use in preventing heterosexual acquisition of HIV in Nairobi prostitutes. *Journal of the American Medical Association* 268, 477–482.

Moore, L. L., Valuck, R., McDougall, C., & Fink, W. (1995). A comparative study of one-year weight gain among users of medroxyprogesterone acetate, levonorgestrel implants, and oral contraceptives. *Contraception,* 52(4), 215–219.

Ortiz, M. E., Croxatto, H. B., Bardin, C. W. (1996). Mechanisms of action of intrauterine devices. *Obstetrical & Gynecological Survey,* 51(12 Suppl), S42-51.

Pasquale, S. (1996). Clinical experience with today's IUDs. *Obstetrical & Gynecological Survey,* 51(12 Suppl), S25–29.

Pfeiffer, R. A., & Witlock, K. (1984). *Fertility awareness.* Prentice Hall.

Rossing, M. A., Daling, J. R., Weiss, N. S., Moore, D. E., & Self, S. G. (1994). Ovarian tumors in a cohort of infertile women. *New England Journal of Medicine,* 331(12), 771–776.

Schlesselman, J. J. (1995). Net effect of oral contraceptiveuse on the risk of cancer in women in the United States. *Obstetrics and Gynecology,* 85(5 Part 1), 793–801.

Seleem, S., Hills, F. A., Salem, H. T., El-Nashar, E. M., & Chard, T. (1996). Mechanism of action of the intrauterine contraceptive device, Evidence for a specific biochemical deficiency in the endometrium. *Human Reproduction,* 11(6), 1220–1222.

Service, R. F. (1996). Panel wants to break R&D barrier. *Science* 272, 1258.

Shushan, A., Paltiel, O., Iscovich, J., Elchalal, U., Peretz, T., & Schenker, J. G. (1996). Human menopausal gonadotropin and the risk of epithelial ovarian cancer. *Fertility & Sterility,* 65(1), 13–18.

Siedentopf, F., Horstkamp, B., Stief, G., & Kentenich, H. (1997). Clomiphene citrate as a possible cause of a psychotic reaction during infertility treatment. *Human Reproduction,* 12(4), 706–707.

Speroff, L., Glass, R. H., & Case, N. G. (1994). *Clinical gynecologic endocrinology and infertility,* (5th ed.) Williams and Wilkins.

Stanford, J. B., Lemaire, J. C., & Fox, A. (1994). Interest in natural family planning among female family practice patients. *Family Practice Research Journal,* 14(3), 237–249.

Sturgeon, S. R., Brinton, L. A., Berman, M. L., Mortel, R., Twiggs, L. B. , Barrett, R. J., Wilbanks, G. D., & Lurain, J. R. (1997). Intrauterine device use and endometrial cancer risk. *International Journal of Epidemiology, 26*(3), 496–500.

Sturridge, F., & Guillebaud, J. (1996). A risk-benefit assessment of the levonorgestrel-releasing intrauterine system. *Drug Safety, 15*(6), 430–440.

Tarin, J. J. (1995). Subzonal insemination, partial zona dissection or intracytoplasmic sperm injection? An easy decision? *Human Reproduction, 10*(1), 165–170.

Tsang, D. C. (1995). Policing "perversions": Depo Provera and John Money's new sexual order. *Journal of Homosexuality, 28*(3–4), 397–426.

Van Os, W. A., Edelman, D. A., Rhemrev, P. E., & Grant, S. (1997). Oral contraceptives and breast cancer risk. *Advances in Contraception, 13*(1), 63–69.

Virutamasen, P., Leepipatpaiboon, S., Kriengsinyot, R., Vichaidith, P., Muia, P. N., Sekadde-Kigondu, C. B., Mati, J. K., Forest, M. G., Dikkeschei, L. D., Wolthers, B. G., & d'Arcangues, C. (1996). Pharmacodynamic effects of depot-medroxyprogesterone acetate (DMPA) administered to lactating women on their male infants. *Contraception, 54*(3),153–157.

Vrtovec, H. M., & Tomazevic, T. (1995). Preventing severe ovarian hyperstimulation syndrome in an in vitro fertilization/embryo transfer program. Use of follicular aspiration after human chorionic gonadotropin administration. *Journal of Reproductive Medicine, 40*(1), 37–40.

Wagner, K. D. (1996). Major depression and anxiety disorders associated with Norplant. *Journal of Clinical Psychiatry, 57*(4), 152–157.

Wilcox, A. J., Weinberg, C. R., & Baird, D. D. (1995). Timing of sexual intercourse in relation to ovulation. *New England Journal of Medicine 333*, 1517–1521.

CHAPTER 13

Healthy premenopausal women can reduce their risk of estrogen stimulated cancers by consuming a healthy diet and exercising.

WOMEN AND CANCER

INTRODUCTION

Finding out that you or someone you love has cancer may well be one of the most frightening experiences any of us could face. Gynecologic cancers can be even more devastating because they require a woman to discuss and allow continued inspection of body parts that are often not well understood and are considered by many to be shameful.

This chapter will describe the process by which normal cells become cancerous as well as describe the major gynecologic cancers, their frequencies of occurrence, their symptoms, and some measures which can be taken to prevent them. It is our sincere hope that an understanding of the biological basis of these cancers will allow women to face these illnesses without the added burdens of confusion and shame.

CANCER BASICS

How Do Cancers Arise?

Cancer is the unregulated division of cells. Any tissue in which cells are dividing can become cancerous. Cancers, however, occur at different rates in different tissues. (Table 13.1 shows the relative proportions of all cancers experienced by women in the United States). Cell division, the process by which cells replicate themselves, is a highly regulated process, and as such, normal cells will divide only when properly signaled. Normal skin cells, for example, grow and divide until they reach a certain size, then stop growing.

TABLE 13.1

PROPORTIONS OF VARIOUS CANCERS IN U.S. WOMEN

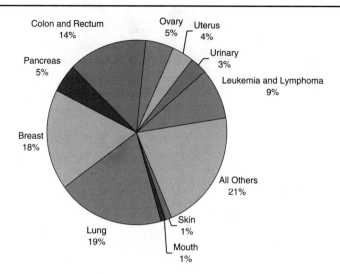

Colon and Rectum 14%
Ovary 5%
Uterus 4%
Urinary 3%
Leukemia and Lymphoma 9%
Pancreas 5%
Breast 18%
All Others 21%
Skin 1%
Lung 19%
Mouth 1%

If the skin is cut, skin cells divide to replace the damaged cells until the wound is closed, whereupon the cells discontinue division.

Carcinogenesis, the onset of cancer, normally involves cell division. Cells that are terminally differentiated, such as some nerve and muscle cells, will never divide again and are less likely to become cancerous. Tissues in which cells divide throughout the lifetime of an individual, such as breast, ovarian, and uterine tissues, are more likely sites for cancer. Estrogens secreted during the menstrual cycle stimulate cell division in breast tissue, the ovaries, and the endometrial tissues of the uterus.

A mutation (a change in the DNA sequence) in a gene that regulates cell division is often the first step in carcinogenesis. Cancer cells stop responding to signals that limit the frequency and timing of their division. Cancer cells, therefore, divide without observing any limits. A single cell with a mutation in a cell division control gene can transmit that mutation to all of its daughter cells, resulting in a growing mass of cells called a tumor.

When a tumor stays in one place and doesn't increase in size enough to impinge on the functions of nearby organs, the tumor is considered *benign*. Surgical removal of these tumors will normally result in full recovery for the affected individual. Some tumors, such as brain tumors, are inoperable if the tumor is located in a region where surgery would affect portions of the brain required to keep the person alive.

If a tumor isn't discovered and removed while it is still benign, cells of the tumor can invade neighboring tissues. Invasive tumors are considered to be *malignant*. When cancerous cells escape to other parts of the body, the cancer has *metastasized*. To accomplish this, cancer cells must loosen their attachment to their original neighbors, escape from the tissue of origin, and burrow through other tissues until they reach and enter the bloodstream or the lymphatic system (Figure 13.1). While in the blood and lymph, these cells can move to other areas of the body.

Once diffused throughout the body, cancer cells may begin to win the battle against normal cells. Cancerous cells fail to differentiate into particular cell types, such as liver cells, cervical cells or cells of the immune system. Undifferentiated cancer cells become immortal, that is, there is no limit to the number of times they can divide. In addition to being immortal, these cells incorporate nutrients at a faster rate, which translates into a further advantage for cancer cells over normal cells. Thus, the normal cells begin to die as they are deprived of nutrients and space.

FIGURE 13.1   The Spread of a Breast Cancer Cell Through the Lymphatic System.

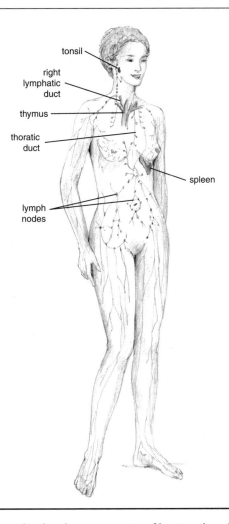

Cells from a tumor originating in the breast can detach and move to a variety of locations through the lymphatic system. The lymphatic system returns excess tissue fluid to the bloodstream and helps to protect the body from disease. Lymph nodes are masses of spongy tissue located throughout the lymphatic system. Tonsils, spleen, and thymus are lymph nodes. The function of these nodes is to filter cellular debris from the lymph. Lymph nodes also produce a high number of lymphocytes (white blood cells) that serve to clear the lymph nodes of foreign substances. When you have an infection, lymph nodes often swell as the lymphocytes and other white blood cells fight off the infectious agent. The lymphatic system can thereby transport cancerous cells around the body in a manner similar to that of the bloodstream.

Why Isn't Cancer More Common?

If a single abnormal cell can give rise to a tumor, why isn't cancer more prevalent? This question becomes even more compelling when one takes into account the number of different carcinogens (agents that cause cancers) we are exposed to over the course of our lifetimes. Luckily, not all mutations occur in genes that are important for cell division. More often, mutations occur in regions of chromosomes with no known function. Even when mutations do occur in cell cycle control genes, cancer is not inevitable. Most scientists today believe that carcinogenesis occurs after "two hits." The "first hit" is a mutation to a cell cycle control gene. Substances that cause these types of mutations are called *initiators*. However, it is only in the presence of substances called *promoters* that the mutated cell becomes actively cancerous. The "second hit" is provided by these promoters, which themselves do not change the DNA but stimulate the cell to begin dividing.

Smoking cigarettes and drinking alcohol provide both "hits" for a cell because cigarette smoke functions as an initiator and alcohol functions as a promoter. Indeed, if one adds the risk of cancer due to smoking only to the risk of cancer from drinking alcohol, the overall risk calculated is far less than the actual risk of cancer in people who both smoke and drink. It appears that supplying cells with both an initiator and a promoter yields an overall risk that is not additive but multiplicative.

In addition to the fact that individual cells seem to require "two hits" to become cancerous, human cells have repair enzymes whose job it is to constantly survey the DNA in order to find and repair any mutations. Consequently, cancers occur at a lower rate than one might expect. To put it another way, the probability that the correct gene will be mutated in the correct cell type, be exposed to the correct cancer promoter, and not be repaired by the cellular repair enzymes is actually quite slim.

SUMMARY

Normal cells become cancerous when they undergo mutations that allow them to divide in an unregulated manner, forming tumors. If cancer cells from a tumor escape their anchorage, they can move through the blood or lymph to other areas of the body. Cancer cells are less well differentiated and can outcompete normal cells for nutrients. Mutations leading to cancers are rare because human cells have many mechanisms for preventing the mutations that lead to cancers.

GYNECOLOGIC CANCERS

The major gynecologic cancers are breast cancer, cervical cancer, ovarian cancer, and uterine cancer.

Breast Cancer

Women often hear that their lifetime risk of developing breast cancer is 1 in 8. This statistic is not an accurate assessment of a woman's real risk because it assumes that all women will live to a very old age (around 100). Since women develop cancers at an increased rate as they age, those women that live long enough to celebrate their 100th birthday have a substantially higher risk of cancer than younger women. However, most women will not live this long, so assuming that all women will, and factoring in the rate of cancer for these very old women *overestimates* the average woman's risk considerably. If one were to consider all women in the United States under 75, 1 out of 40 would actually be expected to die of breast cancer before reaching age 75.

While each breast cancer differs in terms of its origin, aggressiveness, and ultimate toll, there are two general types of cancers, each of which effects a characteristic population. Older women are at risk for cancers that are induced by estrogen exposure while younger women are at risk for more aggressive cancers that often have a genetic component.

Estrogen Induced Breast Cancers   Estrogen induced breast cancers are the more common type of breast cancer and more typically affect older women. During every menstrual cycle, estrogen increases before ovulation stimulates cell division in breast tissues, thereby increasing the likelihood of cancerous mutations occurring.

Treatment of these types of cancers can involve attempts to prevent estrogen from continuing to stimulate breast cells and thereby decrease the overall toll of the disease. *Tamoxifen* is a drug that functions in preventing estrogen from binding to its receptors in breast tissue and is often taken by women who have had breast cancer in order to prevent recurrence.

The disruption of estrogen production over the course of a healthy woman's lifetime can offer some protection against ever getting the disease. For example, women who have had a break from ovulation during pregnancy have a lower risk of breast cancer. It is also the case that the very high levels of estrogen and progesterone present early in a pregnancy stimulate the differentiation of breast cells. Differentiated cells are less likely to become cancerous so pregnancy may serve to force premalignant cells into a state of terminal differentiation and thereby prevent them from becoming cancerous later on.

Some researchers think that breast-feeding (which may prolong the break from estrogen if ovulation is suppressed) reduces breast cancer risk, while others have shown that there is no association between breast-feeding and breast cancer risk (see Chapter 11).

Women with naturally lower levels of estrogen have smaller bones (see Chapter 14) and there is a correlation between smaller bones and decreased breast cancer risk.

Exercise causes the ovaries to decrease their activity and can provide a break from estrogen exposure. Women who exercise regularly have 40% lower breast cancer rates than women who don't exercise.

Diet may also play a role in decreasing a woman's estrogen exposure. Women who consume foods low in fat and high in fiber have lower blood estrogen levels before and after menopause and lower rates of breast cancer. A low fat diet is considered to be a fat intake that accounts for 10% or less of the woman's daily calories. Consumption of 35–45 grams of fiber per day constitutes a high fiber diet. One thoery, which explains why a high fiber, low fat diet decreases estrogen levels, is that this type of diet is usually rich in plant product. Some plant foods contain substances called *phytoestrogens* which are thought to act against the body's natural estrogens and thus block the onset of breast cancer and other estrogen related cancers. Phytoestrogens can be found in soy based products such as soy milk, tofu and miso, as well as in many fruits, vegetables, seeds, and berries.

Healthy premenopausal women can therefore reduce estrogen levels, and thereby reduce their risk of estrogen stimulated cancers, by consuming a healthy diet and exercising.

Environmental factors can also increase the risk for estrogen responsive cancers. The use of hormone replacement therapy, which contains estrogen (and progesterone) is thought to increase breast cancer risk (see Chapter 14). Synthetic chemicals such as the pesticides methoxychlor and endosulfan mimic the actions of estrogens and exposure may increase cancer risk.

Genetically Induced Breast Cancer   Breast cancer is relatively rare in younger women and is correlated with the prevalence of the disease among a woman's family members. High-risk families include those where three or more close relatives have had breast cancer, breast cancer in more than one generation, early onset of breast cancer, cancer in both breasts, or frequent occurrence of ovarian cancer. Only 5–10% of all breast cancers are thought to be inherited. The majority of the remaining breast cancers have environmental origins and are more preventable.

A mutation to a gene located on the long arm of chromosome 17 is responsible for the hereditary form of breast cancer and normally strikes women in their thirties and forties. The gene is called BRCA1 and around 1 in 200 women will inherit the mutated form of this gene.

BRCA1 normally functions as a tumor suppressor. When mutated, the product of this gene can't suppress tumor growth. Inheriting the disease allele of this gene essentially provides women with the "first hit" required for carcinogenesis. Hereditary cancers cause higher-grade tumors and demonstrate more aggressive growth characteristics than other cancers. While there is a genetic test for the presence of this mutant allele, only women who have a high-risk background are advised to have genetic testing. The cost of a test is around $2,500, and prevention methods, aside from breast removal, are limited.

Breast Self-Exams   To help detect cancers early, many women perform breast self-exams. Early detection and treatment increase a woman's chances for remission and cure. These exams are usually performed once a month, ideally at the same time of the cycle each month. Consistent timing helps to identify changes from one month to the next and alle-viates alarm generated by normal changes that occur throughout the cycle. The optimal time to perform a breast self-exam is one week after menstruation.

To perform a breast self-exam, begin with a visual inspection by checking in a mirror for changes in breast size and shape, dimpling, or sores. Look for scaling in the areola or nipple and discharge or puckering of the nipple. Raise your hands above your head to reveal any changes in breast contour. With your hands on your hips, lean forward to help show any dimpling.

The manual portion of the exam is best performed in the shower while your breasts are wet and soapy. Raise your right arm and feel your right breast with your left hand. Move two fingers in a circle around the surface of your breast from nipple to armpit. Perform the same exam on your left breast using your right hand. Any lumps, knots, or changes should be reported to your clinician.

If examination by you or your clinician reveals a suspicious lump (a lump that is one half inch in size, stands out, is persistent and unchanging), she or he will usually attempt to withdraw fluid from the lump to determine whether it is a fluid-filled cyst or a solid tumor. The overwhelming majority of lumps found by breast self-exam are cystic (greater than 70%), and no further treatment is necessary. If there is no fluid present, the lump will be investigated further, starting with a mammogram.

Mammography   Mammography is a procedure that generates an X-ray image of the breast. By looking at the image generated, a radiologist can determine if there are any suspicious looking areas, called lesions. The substantial majority of questionable lesions detected by mammography are benign (greater then 70%). Because mammography can detect smaller lesions than breast self-exams, the procedure can be beneficial even for women who perform monthly exams. For some women, detecting breast cancer through mammography will allow them to be successfully treated for a cancer that otherwise might have killed them. The problem, however, is determining which age group of women will most benefit from mammography. This issue is the subject of considerable debate in the scientific and medical communities.

The sensitivity of mammography is highest among women aged 50 years and older. After menopause, mammary tissue is replaced with fat, against which tumors are easily seen. For these women, the test does reduce deaths from cancer. The sensitivity of the test is decreased for younger women due to their denser breast tissues, against which tumors are difficult to discern. Consequently, mammography is less useful for detecting cancers in younger women than it is in older women.

If the sensitivity of mammography were the only problem, one might argue that it wouldn't hurt younger women to have mammograms too. However, mammography also has a high rate of false positives, which means that many women are subject to unneces-sary anxiety, pain, and expense when benign lumps must be biopsied. This experience may even lead some women to chose not to undergo mammography in the future. False negatives, on the other hand, may lead women to ignore cancerous lumps they find during breast self-exams. It is also possible that the X-rays women's breasts are exposed to during mammography may increase their risk of developing cancer.

In addition to finding breast cancer, mammography can help detect ductal carcinoma *in situ* (DCIS), a type of abnormal cell growth that may eventually become breast cancer. Most breast cancers begin in the cells lining the milk ducts, but not all abnormal cells in ducts will become cancerous. It is not readily apparent whether the early detection of these abnor-mal duct cells averts cancer deaths. As a result, some scientists and clinicians believe that women with this diagnosis may choose to have surgery that is unnecessary, or that women will worry about a condition that is not a real health risk. Other scientists and clinicians think that finding and removing DCIS is beneficial.

The National Cancer Institute recommends yearly mammography only for women over 50. Some physicians recommend mammograms for women in their forties and list the potential benefits as earlier diagnosis of fast growing tumors, reassurance of women concerned about breast cancer, and the establishment of a baseline against which future mammograms can be compared.

Treatment of Breast Cancers   A cancerous lump in the breast can be treated by surgical removal of the lump (lumpectomy) combined with radiation therapy. Radiation causes multiple mutations in cells exposed to it and is used to kill any remaining cancer cells. Radiation is necessary even after a lumpectomy because many scientists and clinicians believe that metastasis has often occurred by the time a lump is palpable (can be felt). Another treatment option is the removal of all breast, fat, and connective tissue and lymph nodes (mastectomy). The skin can be closed, leaving a flat area, or breast reconstruction over implants can be performed immediately after the mastectomy. Reconstruction can also be scheduled for a later date. A type of reconstruction that does not require implants is called the TRAM (trans rectus abdominal muscle) flap. Skin, fat and muscle in the area below the belly button is used to form a new breast. A nipple and areola can be tattooed on later.

Cervical Cancer

Thanks to a routine screening test called the Pap smear, death as a result of cervical cancer in the United States is rare. The cure rate for cervical cancer is 85–90%. Most women who die from cervical cancer are diagnosed in the later stages of the disease, often because they did not have access to a Pap smear for many years. An annual Pap smear, which costs around $25, can detect abnormal cervical cells before they become cancerous. The Pap smear, named for Dr. George Papanicolaou, who developed the test over 40 years ago, detects cells which are inflamed as a result of their exposure to the Human Papilloma Virus (HPV), also named for Dr. Papanicolaou.

There are at least 70 different strains of HPV. Different strains infect different areas of the body and generally result in benign warts on such places as the hands, feet (plantar warts), and genitals. Genital warts usually result from sexual contact (intercourse or oral-genital contact) with an infected partner, although touching the genitals with wart-infested hands can spread them. When HPV from genital warts or semen infects the cervix, the virus, instead of causing warts, causes inflammation of cervical cells. Inflammation damages cells, which must be replaced by healthy cells. As cervical cells divide to replace the damaged cells, they can undergo cancerous mutations. A Pap smear detects cells that are inflamed and may become cancerous, but not all abnormal cells will become cancerous. Most clinicians recommend that women begin having Pap smears at age 18 or when they become sexually active, which ever occurs first.

Pap Smears   The best time to schedule a Pap smear is for 1 or 2 weeks after the first day of your last menstrual period. It is a good idea to avoid using vaginal medication, douches, or contraceptives for 48 hours prior to your exam and to abstain from intercourse for 24 hours prior to your exam.

During the exam, a clinician uses a small spatula or brush to scrape cells from the cervix onto a slide and then sends them to a laboratory for microscopic examination. Most women with abnormal results have a vaginal infection that temporarily changes the shape of some of the cells lining the cervix. If there is any evidence of infection, the infection will be treated and the woman retested approximately 6 months later. If atypical cells are present after the second test, the next step is to examine the cervix with a type of microscope called a colposcope. If there is a visible abnormality on the cervix, a biopsy will be performed during which a small piece of tissue will be removed from the cervix and examined under a microscope. If these cells appear to be abnormal, the cells of the affected area of the cervix will be treated.

Some treatments of abnormal tissues include cryotherapy, where abnormal tissue is killed by freezing; laser therapy, which uses a light beam to evaporate abnormal tissue in the cervix; and loop electrosurgical excision procedure (LEEP). During LEEP, a thin electrically charged wire loop removes tissue. Conization, the surgical excision of a cone-shaped portion of the cervix, is reserved for situations where the abnormal cells appear cancerous. Conization can result in difficulty dilating during birthing. None of these treatments affect a woman's ability to become pregnant and all can usually be performed in a gynecologist's office. Hysterectomy, chemotherapy, and radiation are used when cancer is invasive.

Douching increases the risk of cervical cancer because it disrupts the normal vaginal bacterial flora allowing the virus to survive better. Douching may also force HPV from the vagina and external genitalia into the cervix.

Symptoms of cervical cancer are bleeding between periods, bleeding after intercourse, and abnormal vaginal discharge.

Ovarian Cancer

Ovarian cancer is the fourth leading cause of cancer-related deaths in women, behind breast, lung, and colon cancers. A woman's lifetime risk of being diagnosed with ovarian cancer from birth through age 60 is 1 in 55. This cancer begins in the ovaries, and, if not treated, spreads to pelvic organs, the membrane lining the abdominal cavity (peritoneum), nearby lymph nodes, and the liver. The symptoms of ovarian cancer are vague and slow to develop, thus it is rarely discovered early. It is the advanced stage at which most ovarian cancers are discovered that makes this cancer the most deadly of all cancers of the female reproductive system.

Pregnancy and birth control pills provide a break from ovulation and decrease ovarian cancer risk by 50%. Risk factors include early menopause, a high fat diet, taking fertility drugs for more than three cycles (fertility drugs stimulate cell division in the ovaries in order to stimulate ovulation), exposing the genitals to large amounts of talc, and frequent douching.

Ovarian cancer, like breast cancer, may also have a genetic component. Scientists and clinicians believe that hereditary ovarian cancer accounts for 5–10% of all ovarian cancers. If a woman's mother, sister, or daughter develops ovarian cancer, her risk increases to a 1 in 20 chance of developing the disease.

Unlike the mammograms, breast self-exams, and Pap smears of the cervix, there is no effective mass screening method that can detect ovarian cancer at very early stages. Screening for ovarian cancer involves a rectovaginal exam during which the clinician inserts his or her fingers into the anus and vagina in order to feel the ovaries. Unfortunately, by the time changes can be felt in the ovaries, the cancer has often spread. Women at risk for ovarian cancer can also have periodic CA125 level checks. CA125 is a protein secreted by cancerous cells and shed into the blood. Monitoring CA125 levels in all women is not practical because the level fluctuates normally in healthy women.

Symptoms   Because no mass screening test is currently available, women must pay attention to vague symptoms that persist longer than 3 or 4 weeks. These symptoms include abdominal swelling and/or pain, bloating and/or a feeling of fullness, loss of appetite, persistent gastrointestinal complaints such as gas, nausea, constipation and indigestion, increased frequency and/or urgency of urination, nausea, vomiting, menstrual disorders such as abnormal bleeding or postmenopausal bleeding, ongoing fatigue, and pain during intercourse. Even if you have already seen your clinician for these vague symptoms, you should insist on a thorough rectovaginal pelvic examination.

Treatments   When ovarian cancer is suspected, clinicians may explore the abdomen surgically (laparotomy) or look at the cervix through a miniature viewing device inserted through tiny abdominal incisions (laparoscopy). The surgeon can examine the region for signs of cancer and remove suspicious cells that can then be analyzed to determine if they are cancerous. If the cancer has spread, portions of the gastrointestinal tract and urinary tract can be removed. If the cancer is limited to the ovary, surgeons will usually remove the ovaries, uterus, oviducts, supporting ligaments, and possibly the lymph nodes. If only one ovary is involved, and a woman wants to be able to become pregnant, it may be possible to remove only the involved ovary and its oviduct.

Uterine Cancer

Uterine cancer occurs less frequently than breast and ovarian cancer and when detected early has a 90% cure rate. This cancer occurs most often in older women. The average age at diagnosis is 64. Risk factors for uterine cancer include infertility, early menarche, late menopause, no pregnancies, unopposed estrogen replacement therapy (ERT without progesterone), obesity, and diabetes. Some hypotheses for the causes of uterine cancers include estrogen exposure, which stimulates the cells in the endometrium to divide, and lack of menstruation, which allows cancerous cells to stay in the uterus instead of being shed. Screening for uterine cancer involves a visual and manual inspection during an annual exam. Treatment for uterine cancer often involves removal of the uterus, called hysterectomy.

Uterine fibroids are benign growths of the uterus that develop from the cells that make up the muscle of the uterus. The size, shape, and location of the fibroids can vary greatly. They can be as small as a pea, or they can grow to be so large that they fill up the entire abdomen. They can be found inside the uterus, on its outer surface, within the wall of the uterus, or attached by a stem-like structure to the outside of the uterus (Figure 13.2). Fibroids may remain small for a long time, then suddenly grow rapidly, or grow slowly for

FIGURE 13.2   Fibroids of the Uterus

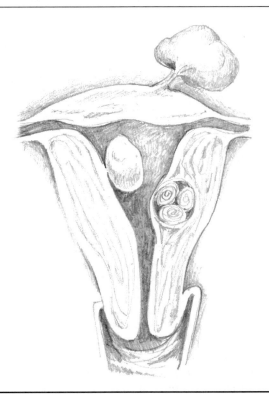

a number of years. Most fibroids produce no symptoms at all. When symptoms do occur, they can include menstrual changes, cramps, abdominal pain, and infertility. Fibroids that do not cause symptoms do not require treatment. If treatment is necessary, fibroids may respond to pharmacological treatments designed to shrink them. This condition can also be treated with electrosurgical evaporation in order to melt the embedded fibroid cells; laparoscopic myomatomy, which allows a clinician to remove embedded fibroids; and myolysis, during which a clinician uses a laser or electrified needle to burn the tissue connecting a fibroid to the uterus so that the fibroid gradually withers away.

Hysterectomies   One third of all North American women have their uterus removed by age 60. Only about 10% of these women have their uterus removed because of cancer or another life-threatening disease.

The most common reason for hysterectomy in the United States is the presence of fibroid growths in the uterus, even though many other previously described treatments are available.

Hysterectomies are also performed on women with heavy menstrual bleeding. Women should, however, be aware of alternative treatments for this syndrome such as endometrial ablation, during which the uterine lining is burned or cut away.

Hysterectomies can be performed through an incision in the abdomen or through the vagina and can include removal of the oviducts and ovaries. Vaginal hysterectomies are easier on the patient and leave the ovaries and oviducts intact. Abdominal hysterectomies, which often include the removal of ovaries, are more commonly performed.

During a hysterectomy, surgeons will often remove the ovaries in order to prevent the woman from getting ovarian cancer. However, studies show that women who have hysterectomies but keep their ovaries have lower rates of ovarian cancer than do women who have not had hysterectomies.

Even though a woman is past her childbearing years and may no longer use her ovaries and uterus for pregnancy, these organs continue to function as endocrine glands, releasing hormones for decades after menopause. Consequently, women without a uterus or ovaries have lower levels of estrogen, leading to higher cholesterol and LDL, and, therefore, show increased risk of heart disease. These women also have an increased rate of bone mass loss and, therefore, an increased risk of osteoporosis. Additionally, removal of the uterus can reduce sensation during orgasm, especially if the cervix is removed.

When the ovaries or uterus are cancerous there is good reason to remove them. Short of cancer, however, women should do what they can to preserve these organs. Even though these organs have diminished value in society, they continue to be of value to the individual woman.

SUMMARY
Breast cancers in older women tend to be hormonally induced and risk decreases with decreases in estrogen exposure. Breast cancer in younger women is less common and often has a genetic cause. Breast self-exams can help a woman find a tumor in her breast. Mammography can detect very small tumors and reduces the death rate from breast cancer in older women. Cervical cancer is caused by a sexually transmitted virus and can be prevented by having regular Pap smears. Ovarian cancer is difficult to screen for and results in vague abdominal symptoms that should be taken very seriously. Uterine cancer normally occurs in postmenopausal woman and can be treated by hysterectomy.

CANCER PREVENTION

As frightening as cancers can be, there are many preventative measures women can take to drastically decrease their risks for all cancers.

Smoking

Smoking is *the* major cause of cancer. Chemicals present in cigarette smoke can cause mutations in the cells exposed to them. Quitting smoking can reduce your cancer risk more than all other possible preventative measures combined. Lung cancer is the most common cancer in women. Female smokers are twice as likely as male smokers to get lung cancer, possibly because women's lungs are smaller and more highly impacted by cigarette smoke than the larger male lungs. Women who smoke have increased risks for all the gynecologic cancers and are more vulnerable to cancers of the larynx, esophagus, pancreas, kidney, and bladder, as well as to heart disease, osteoporosis, and premature skin damage.

Women who don't smoke may want to avoid second hand smoke. Nonsmoking women whose husbands smoke have higher cancer rates than nonsmoking women with nonsmoking husbands. While there may be other lifestyle factors involved in this relationship, limiting one's exposure to second hand smoke is sensible and may decrease cancer risks.

Diet

Fruits, vegetables, and whole grains contain phytochemicals that may reduce the risk of cancer and heart disease. Many studies have shown that increased consumption of plant foods, along with a decreased consumption of fat, is associated with a reduced risk of cancer.

The biological mechanisms underlying the anticancer properties of some fruits and vegetables are known. Antioxidants rid the body of oxygen's free radicals (unpaired electrons). Free radicals damage lipids, proteins, cell membranes, and DNA, so their removal prevents the excessive cell division associated with the replacement of damaged cells with healthy cells. Tomatoes and carrots are rich in antioxidants, as are foods rich in vitamin E such as sunflower seeds, avocado, and soybeans.

Citrus fruits are rich in detoxifiers, which remove harmful substances from the body. Strawberries and raspberries are excellent sources of ellagic acid, a substance that also may inactivate some environmental toxins.

Soy based foods contain isoflavone, a phytoestrogen now being studied to determine whether it plays a role in protecting against breast cancer and other hormone induced cancers. Garlic, onions, and leeks contain allyl sulfides that may inhibit cancers by suppressing DNA synthesis and protein synthesis. Cruciferous vegetables such as cabbage, radish, turnip, broccoli, cauliflower, kale, kohlrabi, mustard greens, and brussel sprouts have also been shown to protect against cancers.

Other Factors

Exercise reduces cancer risk, as does minimizing time spent in the sun or tanning booths. Alcohol has been identified as a risk factor for cancer although moderate intake may afford some protection against heart disease. Pesticides and industrial chemicals such as DDT, polychlorinated biphenyls (PCBs), and polybrominated biphenyls (PBBs) are known animal carcinogens that act somewhat similarly to estrogen in the body, and these chemicals have been found in unusually large amounts in the tissues of women with breast cancer. However, since studies on the cancerous effects of chemicals are performed at very high dosages in rodents, more studies need to be performed before these or any other toxic substances can be conclusively linked to human cancers.

REFERENCES

Adimora, A. A., & Quinlivan, E. B. (1995, September). Human papilloma virus infection. *Postgraduate Medicine, 98* (3), 109–120.

Ames, B. N., & Gold, L. S. (1997, June). The causes and prevention of cancer: Gaining perspective. *Environmental Health Perspective, 105 Supplement 4*, 865–873.

Atkinson, H. (1996, December 10). Estrogen, bones and breast cancer. *Health News, 2*(17), 4.

Bagga, D., Ashley, J. M., Geffrey, S. P., Wang, H. J., Barnard, R. J., Korenman, S., & Heber, D. (1995, December 15). Effects of a very low fat, high fiber diet on serum hormones and menstrual function. Implications for breast cancer prevention. *Cancer, 76* (12), 2491–2496.

Cauley, J. A., Lucas, F. L., Kuller, L. H., Vogt, M. T., Browner, W. S., & Cummings, S. R. (1996, November 6). Bone mineral density and risk of breast cancer in older women: The study of osteoporotic fractures research group. *Journal of the American Medical Association, 276* (17), 141304–141308.

Dranov, P. (1990, September). An unkind cut. *American Health, 9* (7), 36, 38–41.

Gordon, L. (1995, December 7). Removal of ovaries poses cardiovascular risks, study shows. *Medical Tribune for the Family Physician, 36* (23), 4.

Hulka, B. S. (1997). Epidemologic analysis of breast and gynocologic cancers. *Progress in Clinical Biological Research, 396*, 17–29.

Kramer, M. M., & Wells, C. L. (1995, March). Does physical activity reduce the risk of estrogen dependent cancers in women? *Medicine and Science in Sports and Exercise, 28* (3), 322–324.

Love, S. (1990, February). Breast removal and reconstruction. *Harvard Medical School Health Letter 15* (4), 3–6.

Michels, K. B., Willett, W. C., Rosner, B. A., Manson, J. E., Hunter, D. J., Colditz, G. A., Hankinson, S. E., & Speizer, F. E. (1996, February 17). Prospective assessment of breast-feeding and breast cancer incidence among 89,887 women. *Lancet 347* (8999), 431–436.

Potter, J. D., & Steinmetz, K. (1996). Vegetables, fruits and phytoestrogens as preventative agents. *IARC Scientific Publication (GKU)* (13139), 61–90.

Stavric, B. (1994, January). Antimutagens and anticarcinogens in foods. *Food and Chemical Toxicology, 32*(1), 79–90.

Struewing, J. P., Hartrage, P., Wacholder, S., Baker, S. M., Berlin, M., McAdams, M., Timmerman, M. M., Brody, L. C., & Tucker, M. A. (1997). The risk of cancer associated with specific mutations of BRCA1 and BRCA2 among Ashkenazi Jews. *New England Journal of Medicine 15, 336* (20), 141301–141306.

Weinstock, C. (1992, March). Douching danger. *American Health, 11* (2), 18.

Winchester, D. P., Osteen, R. T., & Menck, H. R. (1996, October 15). The national cancer database report on breast carcinoma characteristics and outcome in relation to age. *78* (8), 1838–1843.

Women's Health Advocate Newsletter. (1994, August). The Tamoxifen quandary, 1–6.

CHAPTER 14

The ovaries, after long years of service, have not the ability of retiring in graceful old age, but become irritated, transmit their irritation to abdominal ganglia, which in turn transmit their irritation to the brain, producing disturbances in the cerebral tissue exhibiting themselves in extreme nervousness or in an outburst of actual insanity.

A. M. Farnham (1887), *Alienist Neurologist*, 8, 532.

MENOPAUSE
AND AGING

INTRODUCTION

Menopause, or cessation of menses, is an event in a woman's life that is often anticipated with apprehension when this need not be the case. This chapter will outline the biological basis of the menopause and its effects. This chapter will also work to dispel many of the myths surrounding the menopause. It is our hope that understanding the menopause will enable women to proceed through middle-age with a clear sense that alterations in menstrual function are not a symbol of more ominous changes to occur in the future. Rather, women will know that there are physiologic reasons for some of the changes experienced during menopause, and that, for other purported changes there is no biological basis and, therefore, no guarantee that these changes will actually occur. Most important, it will be shown that the menopause can be viewed as a natural, normal portion of a healthy woman's life cycle.

MENOPAUSE AS A DISEASE STATE

Menopause has long been viewed as a disease state, during which women need to be medically treated for a variety of "symptoms." Since physicians see only the most severe types of cases, the perception is that all women suffer similarly, when in fact only 10 to 35% of women are affected enough by menopause to seek medical help. Since the women who have no trouble at menopause are less likely to seek help, there tends to be a negative bias by members of the medical community concerning menopause. This bias both reflects and reinforces the attitudes of the culture at large.

The cultural perception of menopause as a negative transition is not based on the biological changes that occur and does not have to be accepted. In fact, The Massachusetts Women's Health Study, the largest and most comprehensive study of middle-aged women, provides a powerful argument that the menopause is not and should not be viewed as a negative experience. This study found that the cessation of menses had almost no impact on the physical or mental health of the women in the study.

This is not to deny that for many women there is a degree of upheaval around the time of menopause. Many women are dealing with careers, growing children, aging parents, and the realization that this society does not value older women. This phase of life can be extremely stressful and many researchers have shown that most of the increase in "symptoms" in middle-aged women reflects social and personal circumstances, not the endocrine events of menopause.

Indeed, the menopausal transition involves social, personal, cultural, and biological dimensions. Since menopause is considered to be responsible for every mood change or feeling in a middle-aged woman (much the same as menstruation is in younger women), distinguishing those "symptoms" for which there is an actual biological basis is important in terms of predicting their likelihood of occurrence and in terms of devising strategies for dealing with these symptoms.

THE BIOLOGICAL BASIS OF THE ONSET OF MENOPAUSE

Menopause can be defined as the permanent cessation of menstruation following a decrease in ovarian activity. The median age of occurrence of menopause is 51.3 years. The perimenopause, or climacteric, includes the time period immediately before, during, and after the menopause and lasts approximately 4 years.

Prior to menopause, estrogen is secreted in large quantities by the ovaries, and in smaller quantities by the adrenal glands and fat cells (adipocytes). During the perimenopause, estrogen production by the ovaries tapers off. After menopause the circulating levels of estradiol are lowered and mainly derived from the adrenal and adipose conversion of androgens to estrogens. Postmenopausal ovarian secretion of testosterone decreases as well. As the number of ovulatory cycles gradually decreases, progesterone levels decrease because there is no corpus luteum formation during anovulatory cycles. Since all of these changing hormone levels are tied to decreasing ovarian activity, the cause of the loss of activity is an interesting question.

There are two hypotheses that attempt to explain the loss of ovarian activity. One focuses on the decreasing number of follicle cells in the ovaries, and another focuses on the hypothalamic regulation of the ovaries.

Hypothesis #1: Decreasing Number of Follicle Cells

During a woman's reproductive years, several hundred dormant follicle cells are recruited for development and one is ovulated each menstrual cycle. Because female babies are born with all of the potential egg cells they will ever have already in place in their ovaries, every menstrual cycle results in the loss of several hundred cells from this fixed supply. The number of cells recruited from dormancy is relatively constant from puberty to approximately age 37. At this time, the rate of follicle recruitment and loss accelerates more than two-fold. According to this hypothesis, there is a critical number of follicle cells which must be present in the ovary in order for consistent recruitment and loss to take place. Most women's ovaries contain more than the critical number of follicle cells until they reach their late thirties. (Of the millions of follicles present before birth, about 2500 remain by the age of 37.) When there are less than the critical number of cells in the ovaries, control mechanisms can no longer fine tune the number of cells that are recruited for development each month. This results in cycles during which too many cells develop. When too many cells develop, it may be that no dominant Graffian follicle is allowed to develop due to the increased follicular competition for LH. If this occurs, no follicle will rupture and no egg cell will be ovulated. It is also possible that the increased number of follicle cells can result in an increased secretion of LH by the hypothalamus and consequently several Graffian follicles can rupture, resulting in multiple ovulations. By the time a woman reaches menopausal age, this rapid depletion of follicle cells results in her ovaries having very few follicle cells. By age 50, a typical woman has around 1,000 follicle cells per ovary. Recruitment from this dwindling store of cells becomes sporadic; the level of estrogen secreted by the few recruited follicle cells is insufficient to cause the secretion of LH; and ovulation ceases. This level of estrogen is also too low to sustain the endometrial proliferation required for menstruation.

Hypothesis #2: Hypothalamic Changes

Some researchers believe that changes in the brain cause the ovaries to increase the number of follicle cells recruited premenopausally, thereby rapidly depleting the number of follicle cells present in the ovaries. This hypothesis predicts that changes in an aging hypothalamus lead to increased FSH production, resulting in the increased follicle recruitment and loss seen at middle age. Increased FSH levels are common in women who are entering the climacteric. Such elevated FSH levels have been assumed to be a hypothalamic response to the difficulty of recruiting follicles from a dwindling store. However, according to this hypothesis, increased FSH levels may in fact precede the rapid loss of follicle cells, be due to changes in the hormone releasing pattern of the hypothalamus, and not be contingent on the number of follicles left in the ovaries.

This hypothesis is consistent with the fact that women who have been on oral contraceptives, which suppress ovulation, do not undergo later menopause than women who have not used oral contraceptives. In research involving mice, menopause is thought to be triggered by the brain and not the ovaries. Young mice who have had their ovaries removed and replaced by the ovaries of a postmenopausal mouse remain fertile.

EFFECTS OF DECREASED OVARIAN ESTROGEN

Fewer follicle cells means less estrogen. As circulating levels of estrogen decrease, some women experience menstrual changes, hot flashes and/or vaginal changes.

Menstrual Changes

Cessation of menstruation can occur with no other menstrual changes. Indeed this is the case for approximately one third of menopausal women who simply stop menstruating. The remaining two thirds of women begin to have erratic cycles around age 45. Perimenopausal cycles vary widely from one woman to another, and from one cycle to the next for an individual woman. Some women menstruate more frequently than before. Others skip periods or have periods that are more widely spaced. Menstrual cycles can gradually become lighter, or become heavier with more clotting, or even become so heavy they result in "flooding." For most women, very heavy bleeding is normal and only rarely hints at an underlying problem such as cancer. Unfortunately, medical training focuses so heavily on pathology that many clinicians aren't aware that heavy blood loss is common at the menopause. Consequently many unnecessary hysterectomies are performed at this time. Women experiencing very heavy blood loss at the menopause might want to discuss alternatives to hysterectomy with their clinician, such as endometrial ablation or simply waiting for the flooding to pass. All of these erratic menstrual cycles may be followed by a normal cycle accompanied by ovulation. Until a woman has not menstruated for at least 1 year, she continues to be, at least potentially, fertile.

These deviations from the normal menstrual cycles are due to fluctuating estrogen levels. Recall that a menopausal woman has very few follicles developing in her ovaries. As a result, more FSH is secreted in an attempt to induce the ovaries. In this manner, FSH can make the ovaries produce enough estrogen to prepare the endometrium. However, since there are so few follicle cells, this can take longer than usual. In addition, more and more cycles become anovulatory. When ovulation does not occur, estrogen is produced, but progesterone is not. The endometrium is built up to receive an egg, but does not develop enough to separate and be extruded when no egg implants. Progesterone also has a growth limiting effect on the endometrium, so that in the absence of progesterone, the endometrium is able to increase in size much more than when the corpus luteum is secreting progesterone. Bleeding will occur when estrogen is withdrawn or when the endometrium gets so thick that the uterus can't maintain it.

Hot Flashes

Hot flashes are the most common menopausal symptom, with some estimates of the number of women who experience them being as high as 80%. Of the many women who have hot flashes during menopause, only 10% report that this symptom makes them uncomfortable enough to seek medical help. Hot flashes usually last for a few seconds to a few minutes, but they may occur hourly, or even more frequently. Most women begin to experience hot flashes in the period leading up to menopause, see an increase after cessation of menses, and a decrease again in the years following the menopause. This usually constitutes a 1 to 2 year period, but can last as long as 5 years.

The symptoms of a hot flash are the sudden reddening of the skin over the head, neck and chest accompanied by a feeling of intense body heat and profuse sweating, typically followed by a chill. Some women report an increased heart rate as well.

Body temperature is maintained by the hypothalamus. A sudden downward setting of the hypothalamic "thermostat" is thought to be the cause of hot flashes. To adjust to this new setting, heat loss mechanisms such as blood vessel dilation and sweating occur. Correspondingly, blood flow increases to the capillaries, the pulse increases, and the temperature decreases. It is thought that the decreased level of estrogen reaching the hypothalamus, for unknown reasons, causes the hypothalamus to set the body temperature lower. External triggers of hot flashes include spicy foods, high environmental temperatures, coffee, and alcohol.

While hot flashes are not a health hazard, they tend to increase in intensity at night and the ensuing sleep disturbances can be very difficult to deal with. Women with extreme sleep disturbances can become agitated, depressed, nervous, irritable, and may display memory loss.

Women with severe hot flashes can try to get through them by wearing clothes made of natural fibers such as silk, cotton and wool since these fibers will wick the moisture and heat away from the body. Dressing in layers helps too, since it allows shedding of garments when necessary.

Different cultures have different rates of and reactions to hot flashes. Hot flashes are so rare in Japan that the Japanese language has no name for them. The Japanese word for menopause, konenki, applies to both women and men, and refers to natural life changes associated with aging. Clearly, there could be genetic reasons for the decreased tendency for hot flashes in Japanese women. Alternatively, there could be cultural differences. It is easy to imagine that in cultures where the elderly are respected, it is less stressful growing old and some menopausal symptoms may be alleviated. Dietary differences may also help explain the virtual lack of hot flashes. The typical Japanese diet includes 50 milligrams of phytoestrogen per day. Because these compounds counter the effects of estrogen normally, withdrawal of estrogen at menopause may not be as drastic. Also, women in Japan often use herbal remedies for symptoms, while in the United States there has been virtually no research on nontraditional approaches to managing hot flashes.

Many American women do try herbal remedies, but it is important to remember that natural does not necessarily mean safe in all doses and combinations. It is best to consult with a health care practitioner before trying herbal or other homeopathic remedies. Substances that have gained some credibility as alleviators of hot flash duration and/or intensity include vitamin E, ginseng, black cohosh, dong quai, wild yam root, licorice root, false unicorn and evening primrose oil. Exercise can help decrease the duration and severity of hot flashes as well.

Vaginal Changes

Decreasing estrogen levels are thought to have an effect on the cells of the vagina, resulting in a thinning of the walls and a loss of elasticity in the vagina. This can lead to an increased rate of vaginal infections and a decreased level of sexual enjoyment. However, this condition can be avoided by any type of sexual activity that stimulates the vagina. It is believed that regular genital stimulation (three times per month or more) increases the circulation to the vagina enough to prevent these changes.

Emotional Distress

The link between menopause and emotional instability is more difficult to sort out. The origin of this connection can be traced as far back as the late 1800s as exemplified by the writing of A. M. Farnham who wrote that:

> The ovaries, after long years of service, have not the ability of retiring in graceful old age, but become irritated, transmit their irritation to abdominal ganglia, which in turn transmit their irritation to the brain, producing disturbances in the cerebral tissue exhibiting themselves in extreme nervousness or in an outburst of actual insanity.
>
> A. M. Farnham (1887), *Alienist Neurologist*, 8, 532.

Some women do experience emotional distress at menopause. However, emotional distress is less common among middle-aged women than among younger persons of both sexes. Several studies have found that menopausal women are not more depressed, anxious or distressed than premenopausal women their own age. Other studies have concluded that physically healthy women with positive attitudes about menopause have fewer symptoms during menopause and show little or no emotional distress. In fact, most recent studies of menopausal women find that the vast majority of women going through this transition feel as clearheaded, good-natured, useful, understood, confident, loving and optimistic as they did prior to menopause.

When women do feel depressed during the menopause it may be due to the difficulty of growing older in a culture that does not value its elderly, especially when they are women. This depression can have serious effects on the women who live with it, but there is no known biological explanation for the depression seen in the minority of women who experience it during menopause.

Libido

Another myth about menopausal women is that they lose their sex drive. In direct opposition to this, numerous studies have shown that many menopausal and postmenopausal women report an increase in libido, perhaps due to the decreased risk of pregnancy. For the most part, menopausal women have no change in sexual interest, which makes sense in light of the fact that the need for closeness and caring is life long.

The greatest influences on an older woman's sexuality are a healthy partner and a strong and intimate relationship. When a sexual problem does exist, it belongs to both partners. Overall, individuals who are sexually active early in life continue to be so in old age.

SUMMARY
Decreasing estrogen production by the ovaries, due to decreases in the number of follicle cells, leads to erratic menstrual cycles, many of which are anovulatory. Decreasing amounts of estrogen and progesterone lead to an inability to sustain the endometrium and ultimately result in the cessation of menses. Decreasing estrogen levels can also help to explain hot flashes and changes that occur to the vagina. There are no known biological reasons for decreases in emotional stability or libido to occur at menopause.

OSTEOPOROSIS

Women stooped over with osteoporosis are far more common in ads for hormone replacement therapy than in real life.

Our bones are constantly remodeling themselves. Old bone is removed and replaced with younger, stronger bone. As a woman ages, she begins to lose more bone than her body makes. The loss of bone mass is attributed to decreases in circulating estrogen levels at menopause, since many estrogen-dependent cells, growth factors, and cytokines are involved in bone formation. The process of bone thinning, called osteoporosis, weakens bones and increases the risk that they will fracture. Hip fractures and vertebral fractures are the most common complications of osteoporosis.

A hip fracture is a break in the femur (upper thighbone) just below the hip joint (Figure 14.1). Most hip fractures require extensive care, and may result in long-term disability or death as a result of complications such as pneumonia or blood clots from bed rest. Heavier women are less likely to suffer a hip fracture if they fall since fat cushions bones. Also, by virtue of the increased weight they carry, the bones of heavier women are stronger to begin with. Women with well-developed muscles are less likely to fall, as are women with good eyesight, balance and coordination. Thus, not all women with thinning bones should expect to experience a hip fracture.

Vertebral fractures can occur spontaneously as vertebrae simply collapse under the weight of the body or through coughing, lifting or other activities. When this occurs, the spine compresses downward and shortens in length. This shortening can lead to what is called a dowager's hump (Figure 14.2), resulting in a loss of several inches in height. This condition is extremely rare, with less than 5% of 70-year-olds showing vertebral collapse. Most of these women have only one or two involved vertebrae, which is generally not enough to produce the dowager's hump. Women stooped over with osteoporosis are far more common in ads for hormone replacement therapy than in real life.

FIGURE 14.1   Hip Fracture

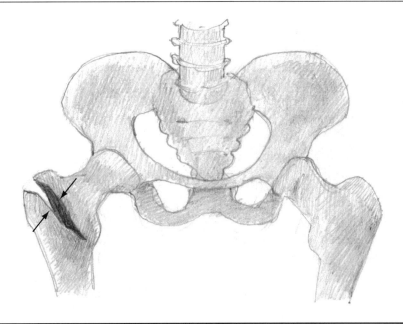

Risk Factors

One in every 5 or 6 women will develop osteoporosis. Women are four times as likely as men to develop osteoporosis. Part of the reason for the gender difference in the rate of osteoporosis is that the peak bone mass of a typical woman is approximately 30% less than the peak bone mass of a typical man. Women also lose bone mass at a younger age and at a much faster rate than men of the same age. Women lose up to 1% of their bone mass per year after age 35, and as much as 2 to 3% per year during the 15 to 20 years immediately following menopause. In contrast, men lose 0.4% of their skeletal mass per year starting at age 50.

Gender is only one of the risk factors of osteoporosis. Women of European or Asian descent are more susceptible since their bone mass is generally 10 to 15% less than that of African American women. Also at risk are women with a family history of osteoporosis since genes play a role in determining skeletal size, peak bone mass, calcium and vitamin D absorption and utilization, and vitamin D synthesis. Exercise, especially weight bearing exercise, increases bone mass and, accordingly, sedentary women are more at risk. Additionally, any condition which results in a prolonged estrogen deficiency, especially during adolescence when bones are growing, will decrease a woman's peak bone mass. Amenorrhea, induced by exercise or anorexia, will result in a decrease in the peak bone mass attained, since the estrogen increase prior to ovulation is not occurring. Women who have had a surgical menopause, for example, a hysterectomy in which their ovaries were removed, are at increased risk since the withdrawal of estrogen is more sudden and dramatic than that of a natural menopause. Because they have fewer fat cells converting androgens to estradiol, women who are very thin are at increased risk, as are women with small bones. Thin boned women have less bone mass to begin with and, as such, can tolerate less loss. Smoking and excessive alcohol or caffeine consumption can also increase risk. Smoking interferes with metabolism, alcohol is associated with dietary deficiencies and leads to falls, and high caffeine (over three cups of coffee per day) may deplete the body's store of

FIGURE 14.2   Vertebral Compression Fracture

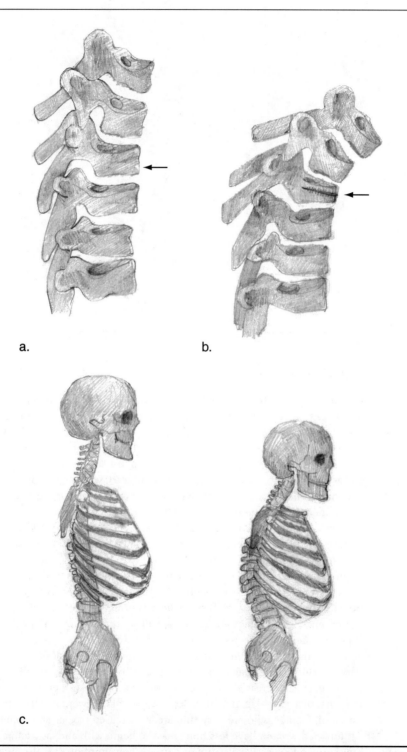

a.

b.

c.

Figure 14.2 (a) shows a normal spine, (b) shows a spine with a vertebral compression fracture, and (c) shows the change in posture that may result if many vertebrae are involved (Dowager's hump).

calcium. Finally, dietary deficiencies in calcium and vitamin D decrease overall bone mass, for reasons discussed below.

Bone Structure

Bone is living tissue, made of cells, minerals, and an organic matrix. Bone tissue is made of tiny crystals of calcium and phosphorus embedded in a matrix of protein fibers such as collagen. The calcium present in bones helps to make them hard and strong while collagen gives them flexibility.

There are two types of bone tissue. Cortical bone is the hard outer shell of bones and trabecular bone is porous, honeycomb like inner bone (Figure 14.3). Cortical bone is responsible for 80% of total bone. The long bones of the arm and leg are made of cortical bone with areas of trabecular bone at each end. Vertebrae of the spine are mostly trabecular bone with a thin cortical shell. Because of their greater surface area, bones with the most trabecular tissue are more vulnerable to thinning with age.

Bone Remodeling

Bones are constantly being broken down and reformed in a process called bone remodeling. In fact, the average adult has 10 to 30% of their bone mass replaced every year by this process. Since microfractures occur as a result of daily activities even in young bones, bone remodeling helps to keep bones healthy. To remodel bone, specialized cells called osteoclasts dig pits along the surface of the bone, in concert with other specialized cells called osteoblasts, which fill the cavities and then produce the collagen framework or matrix of the bone. The activity of osteoclasts results in bone resorption and the activity of osteoblasts results in bone formation.

In childhood and adolescence, formation exceeds resorption. Even though bones stop growing lengthwise after adolescence, bone density and strength continue to increase. By a woman's late 20s she has most likely reached her peak bone mass for trabecular bone, and peak bone mass for cortical bone is reached a few years later. Once peak bone mass is

FIGURE 14.3   Cortical Bone and Trabecular Bone

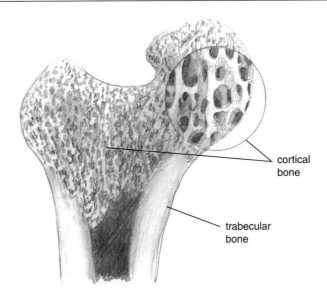

cortical bone

trabecular bone

reached, usually several years of equilibrium follow in which bone formation and resorption are about equal. By a woman's late 30s or early 40s, resorption starts to accelerate and cumulative bone loss may begin.

Following menopause, the coupling of osteoclast and osteoblast activity is driven in favor of osteoclasts and bone resorption outpaces bone formation. Because of this, there can be accelerated bone loss in all areas of the skeleton and an even more rapid loss in the trabecular bone of the spine. Due to its greater surface area, trabecular bone resorption occurs approximately six times faster than cortical bone resorption.

Hormonal Regulation of Calcium Concentrations

The amount of calcium in the body plays a major role in determining whether bone resorption or bone formation will predominate. When there is not enough calcium in the body to serve the brain, heart, nerves, muscles, blood clotting functions, and so forth, calcium from the bones is sacrificed. When needed, osteoclasts will release calcium from the matrix of the bones, leaving tiny gaps and lowered bone density in its place.

Calcium is excreted through sweat, feces, and urine at a rate of approximately 150 to 250 mg per day. Calcium absorption decreases with age and many women don't get enough calcium in their diets (see Chapter 7 for a discussion of calcium nutrition).

Estrogen   Estrogen acts to decrease loss of calcium from the bones by inhibiting the osteoclasts, aids in the absorption of dietary calcium, and may oppose the bone dissolving actions of parathyroid hormone (PTH).

Vitamin D   Vitamin D (a type of steroid hormone, Figure 14.4) is present in an inactive form in skin cells. Sunlight is required for the final step in synthesizing the partially active form of vitamin D from its inactive precursor. In its partially active form, vitamin D is stored in the liver and converted, with the help of (PTH), to its active form by the kidneys. Vita-

FIGURE 14.4   Vitamin D

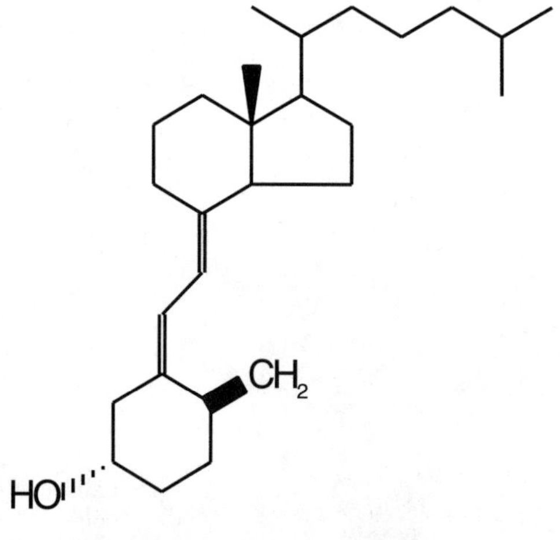

vitamin D₃

FIGURE 14.5   The Parathyroid Gland

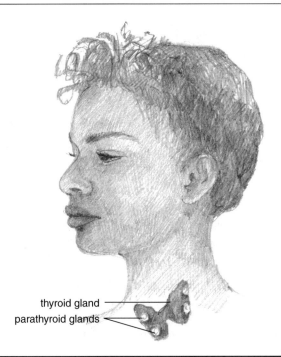

thyroid gland
parathyroid glands

min D facilitates the absorption of calcium from the small intestine and increases resorption of calcium from the kidneys, thereby lowering the amount of calcium secreted in the urine. Vitamin D can be obtained from the diet and is found in high concentrations in eggs, milk, butter, and some fish.

Parathyroid Hormone   Parathyroid hormone is a protein hormone secreted from the parathyroid gland (Figure 14.5) when the level of calcium in the blood falls below that required to meet the body's needs. Release of PTH signals the kidneys to decrease the amount of calcium secreted in the urine. PTH also stimulates the breakdown of bone so that stored calcium is released into the blood stream.

Calcitonin   Calcitonin is a protein hormone secreted from the parafollicular cells of the thyroid that serves to decrease the concentration of calcium in the blood when the level rises too high. Thus, calcitonin has the opposite effect of PTH.

Prevention of Osteoporosis

Most women can ensure that they will not experience a large degree of bone loss by getting enough calcium and exercise. Some women require pharmacological agents to help prevent bone loss.

Diet   Meeting calcium needs is very important during adolescence, when peak bone mass is being determined. This is often difficult because large numbers of women diet during adolescence, a time of rapid skeletal growth. To ensure the future health of their bones, adolescents should ingest 1500 mg of calcium per day. Premenopausal adult women require 1000 mg of calcium per day. Since decreased estrogen means more calcium will be taken from the bones, menopausal and postmenopausal women require 1500 mg of calcium per

TABLE 14.1
CALCIUM CONTENT OF SOME BASIC FOODS

1 glass of skim milk (200 mL)	=	320 mg
40 g cheese	=	320 mg
one cup of yogurt	=	180 mg
peanuts 30 g	=	50 mg
one cup of broccoli	=	70 mg

day. Table 14.1 lists some of the common sources of dietary calcium and their milligram quantities of calcium per serving.

Dietary Supplementation   Women who don't get enough calcium in their diet can increase their calcium intake with calcium supplements. Studies have shown that calcium supplementation of 1000 mg per day reduces bone loss and decreases fractures. Taking calcium supplements with milk improves absorption. Some clinicians recommend taking calcium supplements in the form of calcium carbonate (which is contained in antacids) because it is less expensive and more readily absorbed. Women who supplement with antacids should keep in mind that calcium carbonate ($CaCO_3$)is only 40% elemental calcium (Ca^{2+}), the remaining 60% of the milligram weight of calcium carbonate is carbonate (CO_3^{2-}).

To facilitate calcium absorption, women should also obtain enough vitamin D. Premenopausal women require 200 international units (IU) per day and postmenopausal women require 400 to 600 IU per day. One 8 ounce glass of milk provides 200 IU of vitamin D. Women who need to supplement vitamin D should not take more than 800 IU per day since high levels of vitamin D are toxic.

Exercise   Thick, healthy bones fracture less easily than thin ones. The size and health of bones is affected by the amount of stress placed on them. The pull of muscles and gravity on bones makes them stronger and heavier. Exercises performed against the force of gravity put stress on the long bones and increase their mass. Brisk walking is one of the best weight-bearing exercises, and many women find it relatively easy to incorporate a few long walks into their weekly schedule. Among the many other weight-bearing exercises are hiking, jogging, stair climbing, dancing, jumping rope, weight training and basketball. Swimming and bicycling, while good aerobic exercises, do not put as much stress on the bones. However, almost any type of exercise will improve muscle tone, which also helps stabilize joints and increases the flexibility of connective tissues. Most types of exercise will also decrease fracture risk by improving a woman's coordination and balance.

Pharmacological Agents   To decrease the risk of osteoporosis, some women take estrogen or estrogen and progesterone supplements after menopause. While these hormonal therapies are very effective in decreasing the rate of loss of bone mass, to have a long-term benefit, they must be taken for at least 7 years, and their protective effects are maintained only while women are on the therapy. Because there are health risks associated with hormonal therapies, many women choose to decrease their risk of osteoporosis through diet and exercise. For women who are at high risk for osteoporosis but don't want to take postmenopausal hormone supplements, there are some alternative pharmacological agents available.

Biphosphonates are phosphate salts that work by binding to bone surfaces, thereby strengthening bone and preventing resorption of bone and loss of bone density. Fosamax is the trade name for a drug that is absorbed into the matrix of bone where it inhibits osteoclasts. Fosamax has been shown to increase bone density and reduce vertebral fractures but is not as effective at preventing long bone fractures as estrogen. The benefits of the osteo-clast inhibition provided by your body's natural calcitonin can be enhanced by calcitonin injections or by using a calcitonin nasal spray. Raloxifene is a drug that counters estrogen action in the breast while mimicking it in the bone and in blood vessels. Raloxifene has not been shown to promote excess growth of uterine tissue, thus it might combat osteoporosis without increasing a woman's chances of getting cancer. However, this is a very new drug and comprehensive data about its effects in women is still forthcoming.

SUMMARY

Osteoporosis occurs when bone resorption by osteoclasts outpaces bone formation by osteoblasts. When the amount of calcium in the body is low, osteoclasts will remove calcium from the bones in order to supply the rest of the body. This results in bone thinning and an increased risk of fracture. Decreases in estrogen at menopause accelerate the rate of bone loss. Calcium levels are regulated by estrogen, vitamin D, parathyroid hormone and calcitonin. A proper diet, along with weight bearing exercise, can reduce bone loss substantially. For high risk women there are many pharmacological agents available to decrease the rate of bone loss.

HORMONE REPLACEMENT THERAPY

Women are not sex machines obligated to keep their bodies perpetually in condition for their partners.

Hormone replacement therapy (HRT) is a medically supervised drug treatment of post-menopausal women which involves supplementing hormone levels in order to compensate for the decreasing levels of ovarian hormones seen at menopause. HRT supplements both estrogen and progesterone while estrogen replacement therapy (ERT) supplements only estrogen. ERT is sometimes referred to as unopposed estrogen therapy since the proges-terone present in HRT opposes some of the actions of estrogen.

Unopposed estrogen has been prescribed to women since the 1920s when it was pro-moted as the "cure" for virtually every menopausal symptom. In the 1960s women began to question the safety of ERT and their concerns were confirmed in the 1970s when sev-eral studies showed that women taking estrogen were at an increased risk for endometrial cancer. After the results of these studies were published, progesterone was added to the therapy in order to oppose the effects of estrogen on the uterus. Progesterone acts by decreasing the number and activity of estrogen receptors. The actions of progesterone therefore decrease endometrial stimulation and a woman's chances of developing endome-trial cancer. The disadvantages of progesterone is that it counters many of the beneficial effects of estrogen and extends the period of menstrual-like bleeding for several years, until the uterus ages enough to prohibit bleeding.

Most postmenopausal women currently taking hormones are prescribed HRT. Women who have had a hysterectomy are usually prescribed unopposed estrogen since there is no chance of endometrial cancer in these women and the benefits of unopposed estrogens are thought to outweigh those of the combined estrogen and progesterone therapy.

Estimates of HRT/ERT use in the United States range from 15 to 35% of all post-menopausal women. The remaining 65 to 85% of women choose not to undergo hormone therapy either because they pass through menopause without any major discomforts, they can't afford hormone therapy, they don't want to expose themselves to the increased risk of some cancers associated with HRT/ERT, or because they are resistant to the idea that healthy women need to be medicated.

The decision of whether or not to undergo hormone replacement therapy is a difficult one and is compounded by the lack of data on the risks and benefits of the various options. Most of the available data on hormone therapies come from observational studies, not from randomized studies that are imperative in order to draw firm conclusions. During observational studies, epidemiologists find large numbers of women taking hormones and follow them for a number of years. Then they compare the disease rate in hormone users versus nonusers. Thus, it is entirely possible that the reported benefits of hormonal therapies are attributable to the lack of similarity between users and nonusers. For example, many studies have shown decreased cardiovascular risk for ERT users, but this decrease is also correlated to the higher income of hormone users. It has also been shown that women with access to hormone supplements tend to have better educations, more concern about preventative medicine, and greater inclination to exercise and use medical resources than women not on hormone therapy. These reasons alone could account for the decrease in cardiovascular risk. Therefore, this type of study does not sort out whether estrogen actually lowers the risk of heart disease or whether the type of women who have a lower risk of heart disease are the type of women who take estrogen.

Risks and Benefits of ERT and HRT

Since HRT is relatively new to the market, long-term, randomized, and observational studies are still in progress. Currently, there is considerable debate about whether the addition of progesterone decreases many of the benefits of ERT. For younger women, the Women's Health Initiative, a 15-year, large, randomized study which will be completed in 2007, should sort out many of the risks and benefits of HRT. What follows is a description of what is currently known about the effects of ERT and HRT on various symptoms of menopause.

Hot Flashes   ERT and HRT both decrease the intensity, frequency, and duration of hot flashes for most women. If ERT or HRT is used for several years, in order to alleviate the symptoms of hot flashes, women who then quit using the therapy will not normally experience a recurrence in symptoms.

Vaginal Changes   ERT and HRT improve vaginal elasticity and lubrication, thus increasing sexual pleasure in women who have experienced pain from intercourse. Since there are alternative nonpharmacologic remedies for vaginal dryness (and hot flashes), many women prefer to see if these remedies will work before setting themselves on the course of long-term hormone replacement therapy. It is also important to remember that there is nothing unhealthy about losing interest in genital sexual activity. Women are not sex machines obligated to keep their bodies perpetually in condition for their partners.

Cardiovascular Disease   Total cholesterol levels rise after menopause because of the decrease in estrogen. Along with increased cholesterol comes an increase in heart disease risk. ERT has been shown to decease heart disease risk by as much as 50%, but the decreased risk is limited to current users. In other words, to obtain the benefit of decreased heart disease risk, a woman needs to stay on ERT for her lifetime. For many women, this is a problem because the risk of breast cancer increases progressively with long-term ERT. One recent study in the New England Journal of Medicine claims that, for women at low risk of heart disease, the benefit of ERT diminishes with longer duration of use because of the increased death rate from cancer in these women.

Many scientists believe that, when it comes to cardiovascular disease, the benefits of estrogen may be opposed by the addition of progesterone, but this remains to be conclusively determined. In addition, estrogen status is not the only risk factor for heart disease in women. Other well established risk factors include high blood cholesterol, hypertension, cigarette smoking, diabetes, obesity, a high fat diet and a sedentary lifestyle. Adding lots of plant based foods to one's diet, along with exercise, can decrease the risk of heart disease. Certain plants are rich in phytoestrogens that are thought to reduce cholesterol and help prevent heart disease. Foods rich in phytoestrogens include soy beans, tofu, miso soup, roasted soy nuts, fruits, and vegetables.

Osteoporosis   ERT and HRT have both been shown to reduce a woman's risk for fractures associated with osteoporosis and to decrease the rate of bone loss in postmenopausal women. Taking hormones to decrease the risk of osteoporosis makes sense for many women. However, other women feel that the risks associated with ERT and HRT are unnecessary risks to expose themselves to. These women could try using exercise and a calcium-rich diet to decrease their risk of osteoporosis.

Breast Cancer   Estrogen increases breast cell growth and thereby increases breast cancer risk. Hormones also keep breast tissue more dense, making mammograms more difficult to read. Short-term use of ERT (less than 5 years) seems to have little effect on risk. It appears that the risk of breast cancer starts to increase after 5 or more years of estrogen use and remains elevated while taking the hormone. Use for 10 or more years may be associated with a 30 to 50% increase in risk that translates into an increased absolute risk of developing breast cancer of between 3 and 4%. If a woman stops taking hormones after long-term use, her risk returns to normal within 2 to 5 years. It is thought that the addition of progesterone neither decreases nor increases the risk of breast cancer, but this has yet to be well established.

   The cancers that develop in postmenopausal women on HRT seem to be slower growing and more curable than other breast cancers. The better prognosis may also be affected by the fact that women on hormones must visit their clinician regularly where they are closely monitored for breast changes.

Uterine Cancer   Women taking ERT have 5 to 10 times as great a chance of getting this cancer as women who take no estrogens. To put this another way, while a postmenopausal woman who does not take estrogen has one chance in 1,000 each year of getting endometrial cancer, a woman taking estrogen has 5 to 10 chances in 1,000 each year. Estrogen may also cause benign fibroid tumors of the uterus to increase in size. The addition of progesterone is thought to counter the carcinogenic effects of estrogen on the uterus. However, several recent studies have shown that women who use combined therapy of estrogen with progesterone on a long-term basis have an increased risk of endometrial cancer compared to those who are not on hormone replacement, but less than those who have used estrogen only on a long-term basis.

Other Risks and Benefits of HRT   Although these claims have been circulated widely, there is no evidence to suggest that ERT or HRT provide women with an enhanced sense of well being. Likewise, there is no conclusive evidence to support contentions that hormone replacement therapy retards Alzheimer's progression or helps to keep skin from wrinkling by slowing the breakdown of collagen. Menopause does not cause aging, aging is the cause of menopause. Consequently, it is not sensible to suggest that slowing the progress of menopause will slow the progress of aging.

SOCIAL ASPECTS OF HORMONE REPLACEMENT THERAPY

It is easier to prescribe a pill than to address the economic and social status of women.

The very phrase hormone replacement therapy implies that the postmenopausal level of estrogen is deficient and needs to be supplemented. This view of menopause corroborates the view of menopause as a disease state. There is no a priori reason to think of menopause as an estrogen deficiency disease, or to view the onset of menopause as ovarian failure, as it is often described. These are normal processes that aging women's bodies undergo.

   In this light, it seems that there is something irrational about persuading the majority of healthy women that they are not healthy and that they can only become healthy by becoming preoccupied by diseases which may or may not affect them in the future. All women need to measure their risks against their current good health, and not against gloomy predictions of future health.

To better understand the cultural significance of women being treated for estrogen deficiency, consider the justification for prescribing hormone replacement therapy for men. Studies of the effects of testosterone injections in older men show that treated males stay leaner, stronger, and more virile. Testosterone also decreases the rate of male genitalia atrophy. Without testosterone injections, an aging man's sexual desire declines, his muscles atrophy, fat collects around his abdomen and his bones lose their density. Somehow this is all seen as part of the normal aging process for men, and they are not prescribed testosterone to supplement their deficiency.

The need to "treat" older and menopausal women as diseased or dysfunctional has cultural roots. Since Western culture has only one standard of beauty for women (i.e., youthful beauty), as women age and appear less youthful, it is assumed that they should want to do everything possible to slow down this process. Males, on the other hand, are allowed two standards of beauty, one when they are young, and one when they are older. Hence men are not seen as losing their attractiveness as they age and therefore do not need to be treated.

While hormone replacement therapy can help many women, it is not without risks and it is not a panacea. The belief that all of the symptoms of menopause have biological causes encourages us to try only medical solutions rather than social change. When three quarters of elderly women are poor, and good health is correlated with higher income, taking a look at social causes seems as important as investigating biological causes for health problems in aging women. It would also be helpful to investigate the role that the lower status of older women plays in exacerbating stress, and consequently symptoms, during the menopausal years. A woman's health is related to her income, housing, nutrition, emotional stability, and support network. For the typical woman, these factors have a greater effect on health than does estrogen status. However, it is easier to prescribe a pill than to address the economic and social status of women.

It appears that many of the negative perceptions of menopausal women have cultural roots, and are yet another set of stereotypes which women must come to terms with. As we have seen throughout this text, many ideas about "women's nature" have cultural, and not biological origins. Since we have shown that women are not biologically relegated to their status as second-class citizens, social change may be the preferred avenue for improving the lives of women.

REFERENCES

Beresford, S. A., Weiss, N. S., Voigt, L. F., & McKnight, B. (1996). Risk of endometrial cancer in relation to use of estrogen combined with cyclic progestagen therapy in postmenopausal women. *Lancet, 349*(9050), 458–461.

Bergkvist, L., & Persson, I. (1996). Hormone replacement therapy and breast cancer: A review of current knowledge. *Drug Safety, 15*(5), 360–370.

Coney, Sandra. *The menopause industry.* Hunter House Publishers, 1994.

Dennerstein, L., Smith, A. M., & Morse, C. (1994). Psychological well-being, mid-life and the menopause.*Maturitas (MWN), 20*(1), 1–11.

Dennerstein, L., Smith, A. M., Morse, C., Burger, H., Green, A., Hopper, J., & Ryan, M. (1993). Menopausal symptoms in Australian women. *Medical Journal of Australia (M26),159* (4), 232–236.

Eaker, E. D., Packard, B., & Wenger, N. K. (Eds.). (1987).*Coronary heart disease in women.* New York: Haymarket Doyma.

Ewertz, M. (1996). Hormone therapy in the menopause and breast cancer risk–A review. *Maturitas, 23*(2), 241–246.

Farnham, A. M. (1887). Uterine disease as a factor in the production of insanity. *Alienist Neurologist, 8,* 532.

Ferenczy, A., & Gelfand, M. M. (1997). Endometrial histology and bleeding patterns in postmenopausal women taking sequential, combined estradiol and dyhydroprogesterone. *Maturitas, 26* (3), 219–226.

Frishman, R. G. (1996). Hormone replacement therapy for men. *Harvard Health Letter, 21*(11), 6–8.

Grodstein, F., Stampfer, M. J., Colditz, G. A., Willett, W. C., Manson, J. E., Joffe, M., Rosner, B., Fuchs, C., Hankinson, S. E., Hunter, D. J., Hennekens, C. H., & Speizer, F. E. (1997). Postmenopausal hormone therapy and mortality. *New England Journal of Medicine (NOW), 336*(25), 1769–1775.

Harby, K. (1996). Menopause: Disease state or state of nature? Implications for molecular medicine. *Elsevier Trends Journal, 2*(10), 414–417.

Hirvonen, E., Malkonen, M., & Manninen, V. (1981). Effects of different progestogens on lipoproteins during postmenopausal therapy. *New England Journal of Medicine, 304,* 560.

Horowitz, M. (1993). Cytokines and estrogen in bone: anti-osteoporotic effects. *Science, 260,* 626.

Isenbarger, D. W., & Chapin, B. L. Osteoporosis. *Postgraduate Medicine, 101*(1), 129–132, 136–137, 141–142.

Kaufert, P. A., Gilbert, P., & Tate, R. (1992). The Manitoba Project: A re-examination of the link between menopause and depression. *Maturitas, 14,* 143.

Kremer, M., Judd, J., Rifkin, B., Auszmann, J., & Oursler, M. J. (1995). Estrogen modulation of osteoclast lysosomal enzyme secretion. *Journal of Cellular Biochemistry (HNF), 57*(2), 271–279.

Kronnenberg, F. (1990). Hot flashes: epidemiology and physiology. *Annals of NY Academy of Science, 592,* 52.

Knight, D. C., & Eden, J. A. (1996). A review of the clinical effects of phytoestrogens. *Obstetrics and Gynecology, 87*(5, pt 2), 897–904.

Lindsay, R. (1993). Prevention and treatment of osteoporosis. *Lancet, 341,* 801.

MacNaughton, J., Banah, M., McCloud, P., Hee, J., & Burger, H. (1992). Age related changes in follicle stimulating hormone, leutinizing hormone, oestradiol and immunoreactive inhibin in women of reproductive age. *Clinical Endocrinology, 36,* 339.

McKinlay, J., Longcope, C., & Gray, A. (1989). The questionable physiologic and epidemiologic basis for the male climacteric: Preliminary results from the Massachusetts male aging study. *Maturitas, 11,* 103–115.

McKinlay, J. B., McKinlay, S. M., & Brambila, D. (1987). The relative contributions of endocrine changes and social circumstances to depression in middle-aged women. *Journal of Health and Social Behavior, 28,* 345.

McKinlay, S. M., & McKinlay, J. B. (1989). The impact of menopause and social factors on health (The Massachusetts Health Study). In C. B. Hammond, F. P. Heseltine, & I. Schiff (Eds.), *Menopause: Evaluation, treatment, and health concerns,* (pp. 137–161). New York: Alan R. Liss.

Oursler, M. J., Landers, J. P., Riggs, B. L., & Spelsberg, T. C. (1993). Oestrogen effects on osteoblasts and osteoclasts. *Annals of Medicine (AMD), (4),* 361–371.

Renshaw, D.C. (1983). Sex, intimacy, and the older woman. *Woman Health, 8,* 43.

Semmens, J. P., & Wagner, G. (1985). Effects of estrogen therapy on vaginal physiology during menopause. *Obstetrics and Gynecology, 66,* 15.

Sidney, S., Petitti, D. B., & Quesenberry, C. P. (1997). Myocardial infarction and the use of estrogen and estrogen-progestogen in postmenopausal women. *Annals of Internal Medicine (5A6) 127*(7), 501–508.

Sotelo, M. M., & Johnson, S. R. (1997). The effects of hormone replacement therapy on coronary heart disease. *Endocrinol Metab Clin North Am (EMC)*, 26(2), 313–328.

Sperhoff, L., Glass, R. H., & Kase, N. G. (1994). *Clinical gynecologic endocrinology and infertility* (5th ed). Baltimore: Williams and Wilkins.

Stampfer, M. J., Colditz, G. A., Willett, W. C., Manson, J. E., Rosner, B., Speizer, F. E., & Hennekens, C. H. (1991). Postmenopausal estrogen therapy and cardiovascular disease: Ten year follow-up from the Nurses' Health Study. *New England Journal of Medicine*, 325, 756.

TeVelde, E. R., & Van Leusden, H. (1994). Hormonal treatment for the climacteric: Alleviation of symptoms and prevention of postmenopausal disease. *Lancet*, 343, 654–658.

Wenger, N. K., Sperhoff, L., & Packard, B. (1993). Cardiovascular health and disease in women. *New England Journal of Medicine*, 329, 247.

Wise, P. M., Krajnak, K. M., & Kashon, M. L. (1996). Menopause: The aging of multiple pacemakers. *Science*, 273, 67–70.

Wysowski, D. K., Golden, L., & Burke, L. Use of menopausal estrogens and medroxyprogesterone in the United States, 1982–1992. (1995). *Obstetrics and Gynecology*, 85(1), 6–10.

INDEX

Abnormal sexual differentiation, 73–74
Abortion, 226–228
Acne, 91–92
    in adults, 94
Adipocytes. *See also* Fat cells (adipocytes)
    estrogen and testosterone and, 109
Adrenaline, 67
Adrenals, 67–68
Aging. *See* Menopause; Osteoporosis
    AIDS research, 6
Allele, 55
Alpha-fetoprotein, 179
Alternative hypotheses, 14
Ambiguity, gender and, 29
Amenorrhea, athletic, 137–139
American Academy of Pediatrics (AAP),
    breast-feeding policy of, 202
Aminiotomy, 184
Amino acids, twenty naturally occurring,
    52, 53

Amniocentesis, 177–178
Analytical skills, women and fields requir-
    ing, 6–7
Anatomy
    average differences between men and
        women, 82
    and basic definition of sex, 28
    evolution of male and female, 36–38
    male and female similarities, 81
Anatomy, of women's bodies, 81–105
    external, 88–95
    reproductive, 95–105
    skeletal, 83–88
Androgenization studies, gender, brain
    differences, and, 74–76
Androgens
    abnormal sexual differentiation and *in
        utero*, 73–74
    gender, brain differences, and, 74–78
    IQ and exposure to, 76

Animal models, and human research, 20–21
Anorexia nervosa, 121
    DSM-IV criteria for, 122
Anovulatory cycle, 130
Antibiotic resistance, evolution of, 31–32
Aristotle, 2
Artificial insemination (AI), 232
Asexual reproduction, 30, 31
    vs. sexual reproduction, 33
Assisted reproductive technologies (ART), 228, 233–224
Athletes, female, and eating disorders, 123
Autosomal chromosomes, 55
Autosomes, 49
Axillary hair growth, in puberty, 72

Babies. See Infants
Baby blues, 204
Bacterial STDs, 229, 230
Barr, Murray, 58
Barr body, 58
Barrier methods of birth control, 210, 212–213
Basal body temperature (BBT), 222, 230
Beauty, standards of, 93–95 Behavior
    evolution of, 38–39
    female reproductive, 40–41
    gender role, 44–48
    gene-linked, 39
    hypotheses about naturalness of, 46–48
    male reproductive, 41–42
    natural selection and, 39
    sex-associated, 28
Bifidus factor, in human milk, 194
Biological clock, 157, 158
Biology. See also Women's biology
    as a male vocation, 6
    women in field of, 5
    women's vs. men's, v–vi
Biosynthesis, of sex hormones, 68, 69
Birth control, 209–225. See also Abortion
    barrier methods of, 210, 212–213
    effectiveness of, 210
    future of, 225
    hormonal, 210, 213–219
    intrauterine devices (IUDs), 210, 219–220
    modes of, 211
    periodic abstinence, 210, 220–222
    sex differences in, 210–211
    sterilization, 210, 222–225
Birth control pills. See Oral contraceptives

Birthing, 180–186. See also Postpartum; Pregnancy
    medical procedures in, 182–185
    and midwifery, 185
    recovery from, 189–190
    signs of imminent labor, 180
Birth ratio, 60–61
Bladder, 99
    pregnancy and, 172–173
Bleier, Ruth, 78
BMI. See Body Mass Index (BMI) Body composition, 107–110
    male and female, 107–108
    oxygen delivery system to muscles, 110–111
    physiological effects of, 110–112
    roles of fat in, 111
Body fat
    sex differences and, 108–110
    in women and men, 82–83
Body Mass Index (BMI), 116, 117
    and lactation, 195
Body shape. See Body composition
Body weight. See also Weight
    and health, 115–119
Boleyn, Anne, 50
Bone remodeling, 259–260
Bone structure, and osteoporosis, 259
    Brain anatomical studies, 77–78
    androgenization and, 74–76
    female, size and intellectual capacity, 3
    gender and differences of, 74–78
    lateralization and, 76–77
    sex differences in structure, 45–46
Brain sex differences research
    on brain androgenizing, 74–78
    social implications of, 78–79
Braxton-Hicks contractions, 180
Breast cancer
    and breast self-exams, 243–244
    estrogen induced, 242–243
    genetically induced, 243
    HRT/ERT and, 265
    lactation and, 204
    mammography and, 244–245
    spread of cell through lymphatic system, 241
    treatment of, 245
Breast-feeding. See also Human breast milk; Lactation
    and estrogen induced breast cancer, 243
    support for, 202–203
Breast pumping, 200–201

Breasts. *See also* Breast cancer; Lactation
anatomy of, 95–97
anatomy of during pregnancy and lactation, 190–191
development of, 72
and hormonal changes, 96
pregnancy and, 172
Breast self-exams, 243–244
Brown, C., 123
Bulimia, 121–122
DSM-IV criteria for diagnosis of, 122
Bunions, 87, 88

Calcitonin, and calcium concentration, 261
Calcium, 112–113
hormonal regulation of, 260–261
loss during lactation, 203
in some basic foods, 262
Calendar (rhythm) method, of birth control, 210, 221
Cancer
gynecologic, 242–248
prevention, 248–249
process of, 239–241
proportions of in U. S. women, 240
rarity of, 241–242
spread of breast cancer cell through lymphatic system, 241
women and, 239–249
Carbohydrates, 114
Carcinogenesis, 240
Carcinogens, 241
and cancer prevention, 249
Cardiovascular disease. *See also* Heart disease
ERT and, 264
Career choices, gender and, 3
Catherine of Aragon, 50
Cell division, 63, 64
Cell fusion, 35
Cells, fertilization to week seven, 63–64
Cell survival strategy hypothesis, 35–36
Cervical cancer, Pap smears and, 245–246
Cervical caps, 210, 213
Cervical os, 102
Cervix, 100
dilation and effacement of, 181
labor signs, 180
pregnancy and, 172
Cesarean sections, 183
Chambers, D. W., 6
Cholesterol, 68, 69
diet and, 114
Chorionic villus sampling, 178, 179

Christian, S. S., 124
Chromosomes, 49
defined, 49
imprinting of, 161
Circulatory changes, during pregnancy, 172
Cleavage, 63
Climeractic, 23
Clinical trials. *See* Medical trials
Clitoral hood, 97, 98
Clitoridectomy, 3
Clitoris, 4, 97, 98–99
orgasms and, 101
response to masturbation and, 3
shame and, 2
Clomiphene citrate (Clomid), 20, 230–231
Clothing styles, and gender differences, 28
Code, gene for protein, 52
Colorblindness, 55
Colostrum, 191–192
Combination oral contraceptives, 210, 214–216
Condoms, 210, 211, 212
Conjoined (Siamese) twins, 166
Contraception. *See* Birth control
Control(s)
gender and, 18–19
human research and adequacy of, 19
scientific meaning of, 15
Controlled experiments, in human biology, 21
Copper T 380A (IUD), 219, 220
Corpus luteum, 134, 170
Correlational approach, scientific research and, 19–20
Cosmetics, skin inflammations and allergic reactions, 94
Courtship behaviors, 41
Cow milk, compared to human milk, 193–194
Craniology, 76
women's brains and, 3–4
Cultural biases
current, 4–10
historical, 2–4
Culture
and behavioral variations, 46
and menstruation, 146–148
and multiple genders, 30
Cycle, menstrual, 130
Cystic fibrosis (CF), 55
Cysts
in breasts, 96–97
ovarian, 103

Dalkon Shield, 219, 220
D and C (dilation and curettage) method, of abortion, 227
D and E (dilation and evacuation) method, of abortion, 227
Darwin, Charles, 3
    natural selection theory of, 32
De Beauvoir, Simone, 1, v
Deductive reasoning, 14
Delivery, labor and, 180–182
De novo centrosomes, 161
Deoxyribonucleic acid. See DNA (deoxyribonucleic acid)
Depo Provera, 210, 217–218
Depression, postpartum, 205–206
DES, effects on fetus's reproductive system, 102
Descartes, 3
Development. See also Sexual differentiation and development
    from fertilization to week seven, 63–64
    gonadal differentiation and, 65
Diabetes, overweight and, 117
Diagnostic and Statistical Manual (DSM-IV), criteria for diagnosis of eating disorders, 121, 122
Diaphragms, 210, 212–213
Diet
    and cancer prevention, 249
    cholesterol and, 114
    and estrogen induced breast cancer, 243
    and menstruation, 139
    and osteoporosis prevention, 261–262
Dietary supplementation, and osteoporosis prevention, 262
Dieting
    consequences of restrictive diets, 120
    eating disorders and restrictive, 123
    women, perception of weight, and, 119
Differentiated cells, 64
Differentiation
    duct system, 69–70
    gonadal, 65
Dilation, 181
Direct intraperitoneal insemination (DIPI), 232
Division of labor, gender, 44–45
    alternative hypotheses for, 45–46
Dizygotic twins, 2, 166
DNA (deoxyribonucleic acid)
    molecular structure of, 51
    structure/function of and sex determination, 50–52
Double-blind experiments, 21

Double helix structure, of DNA, 51
Douches, 100–101
    cervical cancer risk and, 246
    ovarian cancer risk and, 246
    PID risk and, 229
Drinking, and carcinogenesis, 242
DSM-IV. See Diagnostic and Statistical Manual (DSM-IV)
Duchenne muscular dystrophy (DMD), 56
Duct system differentiation, 69–70
Ductal carcinoma in situ (DCIS), 244
Dysmenorrhea, 145 Eating disorders
    anorexia nervosa, 121, 122
    bulimia nervosa, 121–122
    female athletes and, 123
    overcoming weight preoccupation and, 123
    and physical consequence of weight loss, 122
    and restrictive dieting, 123
    and unrealistic models of beauty, 120–121

Eclampsia, 175–176
Ectopic pregnancy, 175
Effacement, 181
Egg cell
    anatomy of, 161–162
    and cell specialization, 64
    in fertilization, 160–162
    fertilization journey of, 162–164
    and fertilization process, 164, 165
Ehrhardt, A., 76
Elizabeth I, 50
Embryo
    from fertilization to week seven, 63–64
    gonadal differentiation and development of, 65
Emotional distress, menopause and, 255–256
Endocrine changes, during pregnancy, 169–171
Endocrine system, 66–67
    adrenals, 67–68
    hypothalamus and pituitary, 67
    ovaries, 68, 69
Endocrinology, 66–67
Endometriosis, 145–146
Endometrium, 128
Endorphins, 139
Engorgement, during lactation, 199–200
Environmental factors
    breast milk and, 195
    and estrogen induced breast cancer, 243
    influencing menstruation, 138

Epidermal cancer, 90–91
Episiotomies, 182–183
ERT. *See* Estrogen replacement therapy (ERT)
Estradiol, 132, 133
Estrogen(s), 131, 132
    and calcium concentration, 260
    effects on adipocytes, 108, 109
    and fat storage, 108–109
    gender, brain differences, and, 74
    three major, 68
Estrogen induced breast cancer, 242–243
Estrogen replacement therapy (ERT), 263–265
    breast cancer and, 265
    cardiovascular disease and, 264
    hot flashes and, 264
    osteoporosis and, 265
    other risks and benefits, 265
    uterine cancer and, 265
    vaginal changes and, 264
Estrus cycle, 128
Ethical issues, using animals in scientific experiments, 20
Evaluation
    of science, 18–21
    scientific reports in media, 22
Evolution
    of gender, 38–44
    by natural selection, 31–32
    of sex chromosomes, 59–60
    of sexual reproduction, 30–36
    of two sexes, 36–38
Exercise
    and cancer prevention, 249
    and estrogen induced breast cancer, 243
    and menstruation, 137–139
    and osteoporosis prevention, 262
Experimental method, 15–16. *See also* Scientific research
    reviewing, 18–20
Experimental result, statistics and evaluation of, 16–17
Experiments, human biology and controlled, 21
External anatomy
    hair, 92–93
    skin, 89–90
    and standards of beauty, 93–95
    of women, 88–95

Fallopian tubes. *See* Oviducts Families, demands and science careers, 8
Farnham, A. M., 255
Fat, roles in body for, 111

Fat cells (adipocytes), and sex hormones, 108–110
Fats (dietary), 114–115
    chemical structure of saturated and unsaturated, 115
Fausto-Sterling, Anne, 47
Female Athlete Triad, 123
Female factor infertility. *See* Infertility
Femaleness, 4. *See also* Nature, of women
Female reproductive behavior, evolution of, 40–41
Female sexuality, and lack of cultural acceptance, 3
Ferning pattern, of cervical mucus, 221, 231
Fertility, 165–166. *See also* Assisted reproductive technologies (ART); Birth control; Infertility
Fertility awareness methods, of birth control, 221
Fertilization. *See also* Oogenesis
    and cell division, 63–64
    egg and sperm cells movement, 162–164
    egg cell in, 160–162
    and fertility, 165–166
    process of, 164, 165
    sperm cell in, 162, 163
    and twinning, 166
Fetal monitoring, 183–184
Fibroids
    tumors in breasts, 96–97
    uterine, 247–248
    uterine, and hysterectomies, 248
Folic acid, 113–114
Follicle cells, decrease in and hypothesis for onset of menopause, 252–253
Food calorie, 112
Formula feeding, and breast-feeding, 201–202
Fox, Mary Frank, 9
Freud, Sigmund, 4, 101
FSH (follicle stimulating hormone), 67, 131, 132

Gamete intrafallopian transfer (GIFT), 233
Gamete production strategies. *See* Gametes; Reproduction; Sexual reproduction
Gametes
    evolution of size of, 37
    sexes and size of, 36–37
Gametogenesis, mistakes in, 157–160
Gastrointestinal changes, during pregnancy, 174

Gaulin, S. J. C., 78
Gender
    and career choices, 3
    cultural effects on, 29–30
    evolution of, 38–44
    in mammals, 42–44
    sex and, 28–30
    in U. S. classrooms, 6–7
Gender assignment, 28–30
Gender role behaviors, in humans, 44–48
    alternative hypotheses for, 45–46
    gender division of labor, 44–45
Gender roles, skeletal anatomy and, 87–88
Gene-linked behaviors, 39
Genes
    and overweight, 118–119
    and protein production, 52–54
    on X chromosome, 54–57
    on Y chromosome, 57–58
Genetically induced breast cancer, 243
Genetic sex determination, 50
Genitalia
    development/differentiation of
        external, 70–72
    development/differentiation of
        internal, 69–70
    and sex assignment, 28
Genitalia, of women
    external, 97–99
    internal, 99–103
Gestational diabetes, 176
Girls, in U. S. classrooms, 6–7
GnRH (gonadotropin-releasing hormone),
    67, 131, 132
Gonadal ridge, 65
Gonadotropic hormones, 131
Gonadotropins, 67
Gonads
    differentiation and sex of, 65
    evolution of, 37–38
Gould, Stephen J., 98
Grafenberg, Ernest, 101
G spot, vaginal orgasm and, 101
Gynecologic cancers, 242–248

Hair, 92–93
    beauty standards and, 94–95
Hamer, Dean, 57
Hamilton, J., 5
hCG (human chorionic gonadotropin),
    230, 231
    and pregnancy, 170, 177
HDL (high density lipoprotein), 114
Health. See also Nutrition
    and overweight, 117–118

Heart disease. See also Cardiovascular
        disease
    overweight and risk factors for,
        117, 118
    studies, 5–6
    weight cycles and, 120
Hemophilia, 55–56
Hermaphrodites, 73
Hermaphroditic organisms, 36
Hidden ovulation hypothesis, 128
High density lipoprotein (HDL). See
        HDL (high density lipoprotein)
Hip fracture, osteoporosis and, 256, 257
Hippocrates, 2
History, of women's biology, 1–10
    Greek philosophers and, 2
Holton, Gerald, 8, 9
Home delivery (birth), 185
Home pregnancy tests, 177
Homosexuality, gene studies of male, 57
Hormonal birth control, 210, 213–219
Hormone replacement therapy (HRT),
        23, 263–265
    and breast cancer, 265
    and estrogen induced breast cancer, 243
    and hot flashes, 264
    osteoporosis and, 265
    other risks and benefits, 265
    social aspects of, 265–266
    and vaginal changes, 264
Hormones
    and endocrine system, 66–69
    fluctuations in and clinical trials, 5
    in menstrual cycle, 130–132, 132–134
Hot flashes, 254–255
    HRT/ERT and, 264
HRT. See Hormone replacement therapy
        (HRT)
Human breast milk. See also Lactation
    colostrum, 191–192
    environmental influences on, 195
    infant health and, 194
    mature, 193–194
Human chorionic gonadotropin (hCG).
        See hCG (human chorionic
        gonadotropin)
Human menopausal gonadotropin (hMG,
        Pergonal), 230, 231
Human Papilloma Virus (HPV), 245
Hydatidiform moles, 176–177
Hyde, Janet, 7
Hymen, 99
Hypothalamic changes, and hypothesis
        for onset of menopause, 253
Hypothalamus, 67

Hypothesis testing, logic of, 13–15
Hysterectomies, 248
    derivation of term, 1, 2
Hysterosalpingogram, 229–230

If...then...deductive test, 14
Immunoassay, 177
Imperato-McGinley, Julianne, 74
Implantation, 170
Imprinting, 161
Indifferent gonad, 65
Induction (instillation) abortions, 226
Induction of labor, 184–185
Inductive reasoning, 13–14
Infants. *See also* Birthing; Pregnancy
    breast-feeding and health of, 194
    colostrum and immune system of, 192
    delivery of, 181–182
Infertility, 228–233
    lactation and, 203–204
    male factor, 232
    other causes of female, 231–232
    ovarian factor, 230–231
    shared, 233
    sources of in couples and women
        alone, 229
    STDs and tubal, 229–230
Infundibulum, 102
Instinctive behavior, 39
Insufflation test, 230
Integument, 88. *See also* Hair; Nails; Skin
Intrauterine devices (IUDs), 210,
    219–220
Intrauterine insemination (IUI), 232
In vitro fertilization (IVF), 233–234
IQ, and androgen exposure, 76
Iron, 113

Jacklin, D., 77
Johnson, Virginia, 101

Kimura, Doreen, 78

Labia majora, 97, 98
Labia minora, 97, 98
Labor
    hypotheses about, 180
    induction of, 184–185
    signs of, 180
    stages of, 180–182
Lactation, 190–204
    breast anatomy during, 190–191
    and breast cancer, 204
    breast pumping and formula, 200–203
    calcium loss during, 203

drugs to suppress, 198
    engorgement, 199–200
    hormone level changes during, 196
    human breast milk, 191–195
    and infertility, 203–204
    mastitis, 200
    oxytocin and behavior and, 197
    physiology of, 195–197
    sore nipples during, 199
    weaning and relactation, 197–198
Lateralization, brain differences, gender,
    and, 76–77
LDL (low density lipoprotein), 114
LeVay, Simon, 57, 77–78
LH (luteinizing hormone), 67, 131, 132
Libido, menopause and, 256
Lippes Loop (IUD), 219, 220
Lochia, 189–190
Lunar cycle, menstruation and,
    129–130
Luteinizing hormone (LH). *See* LH
    (luteinizing hormone)
Lymphatic system, spread of breast
    cancer cell through, 241
Lyon, Mary, 58
Lyonization. *See* X inactivation

Macronutrients, 112
    in women's health, 114–115
Male factor infertility, 232
Male reproductive behavior, 41–42
Males. *See* Men
Male world view, in science fields, 9
Malignant tumors, 240
Mammae. *See* Breasts
Mammary glands, 95–96. *See also* Breasts
Mammography, 244–245
Margulis, Lynn, 35, 36
Mary I, 50
Masters, William, 101
Mastitis, during lactation, 200
Masturbation, clitoridectomy in response
    to, 3
Mathematics, gender and, 6–7
Media, presentation of science in, 22
Medical trials, underrepresentation of
    women in, 5–6
Meiosis, 35, 49, 152–155, 156
Melanin, environment and production of,
    89–90
Melanoma, 91
Men. *See also* Anatomy; Gender; Genitalia;
    Male reproductive behavior; Sexual
    differentiation and development
    nutrition and energy needs of, 112

oxygen delivery system to muscles, 110–111

representation in clinical trials, 5

Menarche, 73. *See also* Menstruation

Menopause. *See also* Estrogen replacement therapy (ERT); Hormone replacement therapy (HRT)

    biological basis of onset, 252–253

    decreased ovarian estrogen and, 253–256

    defined, 251, 252

    as a disease state, 252

    emotional distress, 255–256

    historical hypotheses about, 2–3

    hot flashes, 254–255

    and libido, 256

    menstrual changes, 253–254

    pathological perspectives of, 23

    vaginal changes, 255

Menses, 130

Menstrual cup, 136, 137

Menstrual cycle. *See also* Menstruation

    events in, 133

    follicular phase, 132–134

    luteal phase, 134–135

    menstrual phase, 135

    ovulation, 134

    premenstrual phase, 135

    pre-ovulatory phase, 134

Menstrual extraction, 136–137

Menstrual synchrony, 139–140

Menstruation

    changes in cycle, 144

    cultural taboos and, 146–147

    and diet, 139

    disorders of, 145–146

    and estrus cycle, 128

    events in cycle, 131

    evolutionary origin of, 127–130

    and exercise, 137–139

    hormones in, 130–132

    and lunar cycle, 129–130

    management of, 135–137

    menopause and changes in, 253–254

    and menstrual synchrony, 139–140

    and modern menstrual denial, 147–148

    phases of, 132–135

    physiology of, 130–135

    PMS and, 140–144

    puberty and, 73

    shame and, 2

    and stress, 139

    typical cycle, 130

Metaphase II, 155, 156

Metastasized cancer, 240

Metropolitan Life Insurance Company, height and weight tables of, 115–116, 117

Micronutrients, 112–114

Midwifery, 185

Mifepristone (RU486), 226–227

Milk ejection reflex (milk let down), 196, 197

Mitosis, 63, 152, 153

Mittleschmerz, 134

Money, J., 76

Monozygotic twinning, 166

Moon. *See* Lunar cycle

Müllerian duct, 70

Multiple births, 166

Multiple Risk Factor Intervention Trial (MR FIT), 6

Muscle mass, sex differences and, 108

Musculoskeletal changes, during pregnancy, 173–174

Mutation, 32

    cancer and, 240, 241–242

Nails, 89

National Institute of Health (NIH), and women in clinical trials, 5–6

Natural family planning, 221

Natural selection

    evolution by, 31–32

    and genetically based behavioral differences, 39

Nature, of women

    early ideas about, 2

    evolutionary history hypotheses about, 27–48

Non-correlational experimental approach, 21

Nondisjunction, 157, 159

Non-equivalence, between animals and humans, 20

Non-instinctual behaviors, 39

Norplant, 210, 217

Nucleotides, 52

    and order of amino acids, 52, 54

Nurse-midwives, 185

Nutrition, 112–115

    macronutrients in women's health: fat, 114–115

    and men's energy needs, 112

    vitamins and minerals in women's health, 112–114

Obesity. *See* Overweight Observer bias, 21

Offspring

    parental sex role reversals, 42

    and reproductive behavior, 40–42

Onstage effect, 21
Oogenesis, 151–156. *See also*
    Gametogenesis
    meiosis and, 152–155, 156
    mitosis and, 152, 153
    pauses during, 155–156
    summary, 158
Oral contraceptives, 214–217
Orgasms
    clitoral, 101
    G spot and vaginal, 101
    sociobiological debates about, 98–99
Osteoporosis
    bone remodeling and, 259–260
    bone structure and, 259
    defined, 256
    hormonal regulation of calcium
        concentrations and, 260–261
    HRT/ERT and, 265
    prevention of, 261–263
    risk factors, 257–259
Ovarian cancer
    symptoms, 246
    treatments, 246–247
Ovarian cycle, menstrual cycle and, 130
Ovarian factor infertility, 230–231
Ovaries, 68, 100, 103
    pregnancy and, 171
Overweight
    genes and, 118–119
    health consequences of, 117–118
    standards for defining, 115–117
Oviducts, 100, 102–103
Ovulation, 134, 144
    changes during, 128
Ovulation (Billings) method, of birth
    control, 210, 221
Oxytocin, 184
    and milk ejection reflex, 197
    positive feedback effect of, 197

Papanicolaou, George, 245
Pap smear (test), 104–105, 245–246
Parathyroid hormone, and calcium
    concentration, 261
Parthenogenesis, 160
Pelvic exams, 104–105
Pelvic inflammatory disease (PID)
    IUDs and, 219
    STDs and, 229
Pelvis, female/male differences, 83, 84–85
Penis envy, 4
Perineum, 97, 182
Periodic abstinence, as birth control, 210,
    220–222
Peritonitis, 103

"Pet hypothesis problem," 22–23
Pharmacological agents, and osteoporosis
    prevention, 262–263
Philosophers, views of female biology
    and sexuality, 3–5
Phrenology, 76
PID. *See* Pelvic inflammatory disease
    (PID)
Pitocin, 184
Pituitary, 67
Placenta, 64, 170–171
    delivery of, 182
Placenta praevia, 175
Placentation, 64
Plato, 2
PMS. *See* Premenstrual syndrome (PMS)
Postpartum
    baby blues during, 204
    depression during, 205–206
    infertility and lactation during,
        203–204
    lactation, 190–204
    recovery from birthing, 189–190
Practical significance, statistically
    significant results and, 17
Preeclampsia, 175–176
Pregnancy. *See also* Birthing; Postpartum
    bladder changes, 172–173
    body changes and, 169–175
    breast changes, 172
    cervical changes, 172
    circulatory changes, 172
    complications of, 175–177
    endocrine changes, 169–171
    gastrointestinal changes, 174
    musculoskeletal changes, 173–174
    ovarian changes, 171
    -related tests, 177–179
    skin changes, 173
    sleep patterns/requirements
        changes, 175
    uterine changes, 171–172
    vaginal changes, 172
    weight changes, 174–175
Premenstrual Dysphoric Disorder
    (PDD), 141
Premenstrual syndrome (PMS), 140–141
    causes of, 142–143
    symptoms of, 141–142
    treatments of, 143–144
Progesterone, 131, 132
Progesterone-only minipills, 210,
    216–217
Prophase I, 155
Prostaglandin, 132
Protein (dietary), 114

Proteins (intracelluar), genes and production of, 52–54
Pseudoautosomal region of X and Y chromosomes, 57–58
Pseudohermaphroditism, 73
Puberty
  breast development in, 72
  menstruation, 72–73
  pubic and axillary hair growth, 72
  skeletal growth, 72–73
Pubic hair, 72

Q angle, in women and men, 86

Random assignment, 15
Recessive alleles, 55
Reflexes, 39
Relactation, 198
Reproduction. *See also* Sexual reproduction
  asexual, 30, 31, 33, 35
  cell fusion and meiosis hypothesis, 35–36
Reproductive anatomy, of women
  breast anatomy, 95–97
  external genitals, 97–99
  internal genitals, 99–103
  and pelvic exams, 104–105
Reproductive behavior
  female, 40–41
  male, 41–42
  Reproductive processes, male vs. female, 2
  Reproductive structures, development and differentiation of, 69–72
  Results, experimental, statistics and, 16–17
Rh factor, 178–179
RNA, 52–54
Rosser, Sue V., 6
RU486. *See* Mifepristone (RU486)
Sadker, David, 6
Sadker, Myra, 6
Sagan, Dorian, 35, 36
Sanger, Margaret, 212–213
Sanitary napkins, 136
Science(s)
  analytical skills and gender in, 6–7
  controlled experiments in human biology, 21
  culture of, 7–10
  evaluation of, 18–21
  experimental method and, 15–16, 18–20
  female and male commitment to, 8
  gender and perspectives in, 8–9
  hypothesis testing, 13–15

lack of women in, 5
male world view in, 9
media presentation of, 22
process of, 13–18
sexism in, 7
social context of, 22–24
statistics and, 16–17
understanding and evaluating, 11–24
as way of knowing, 12–13

Science careers, female productivity and, 8
Scientific information
  amorality of, 13
  obtaining, 12
Scientific method, 12
  limitations of, 13
Scientific process, 11
Scientific research
  animal models and human research, 20–21
  and correlational approach, 19–20
Scientists, research and opinions/ assumptions of, 22–23
Sebaceous glands, skin and, 91
Secondary sexual characteristics, puberty and development of, 72–73
Second Sex, The (De Beauvoir), 1, v
Second sex, women as, 2
Self-esteem, high-school girls and, 7
Sex(es)
  determination of gonadal, 65
  evolution of, 27–48
  evolution of two, 36–38
  and gender, 28–30
  and reproduction hypothesis, 35–36
Sex assignment, 28
  and gender, 29–30
Sex chromosomes. *See also* X chromosomes; Y chromosomes
  evolution of, 59–60
Sex determination, 49–62
  genes and protein production, 52–54
  genetic, 50
  and modified sex ratios, 60–61
  in other species, 61–62
  and structure and function of DNA, 50–52
  and X chromosome genes, 54–57
  and X inactivation, 58–59
  and Y chromosome genes, 57–58
Sex hormones
  biosynthesis of, 68, 69
  and endocrine system, 66–69
  fat cells and, 108–110
Sex-linked genes, 55

Sex-linked inheritance, 55
  disorders and, 55–56
  and homosexuality, 56–57
Sex ratios, 37
  modified, 60–61
Sex role reversals, 42
Sex selection, 167
Sexual anatomy, 28
Sexual differentiation and development,
    63–80
  abnormal sexual differentiation, 73–74
  duct system differentiation, 69–70
  endocrine system and, 66–69
  external genitalia, 70–72
  from fertilization to week seven,
    63–64
  gender and brain differences, 74–79
  gonadal differentiation and, 65
  puberty and secondary sexual
    characteristics, 72–73
Sexual intercourse, 44
Sexuality. See also Sexual reproduction
  culture and male and female, 3
Sexually transmitted diseases (STDs)
  condoms and, 211, 212
  and tubal infertility, 229–230
Sexual pleasure, orgasms, closeness,
    and, 101
Sexual reproduction
  advantage of, 33
  evolution of, 30–36
  hypothesis I: sexual reproduction
    evolved because it increases the
    variety of offspring, 33–35
  hypothesis II: sex for reproduction is a
    side effect of a cell survival
    strategy, 35–36
  increases in variety and, 34
Sexual selection, 40–41
Sexual systems, in tamarins, 43
Shame, in women's biology, 2
Shared (couples) infertility, 229, 233
Skeletal anatomy, of women, 83–88
  bones differing with men, 83, 84
  and gender roles, 87–88
  posture, body shape, and sports injury,
    84–87
Skeletal growth, in puberty, 72–73
Skin
  acne and, 91–92, 94
  appearance of, 89–90
  cancers of, 90–91
  cross-section, 89
  environment and melanin production,
    89–90
  health and, 90

pregnancy and, 173, 174
  sebaceous glands and, 91
  tanning of, 90–92
Sleep, pregnancy and, 175
Smoking
  and cancer prevention, 249
  and carcinogenesis, 242
Social behavior, and gender differences in
    skeletal anatomy, 87–88
Social context, of science, 22–24
Social functions, of biological
    functions, 47
Social interactions, gender and, 29
Socialization vs. brain androgenization,
    studies of, 74–76
Social mammals, gender evolution
    and, 43
Society, science and, 22–24
Sociobiologists, 38
  and gender division of labor, 44–45
Sonnert, Gerhard, 8, 9
Sore nipples, during lactation,
    198–199, 200
Specialization, of cells, 64
Species, sex determination in various,
    61–62
Speculum, 104
Spermatogenesis, 155. See also
    Gametogenesis; Oogenesis
Sperm cell, 160–161
  fertilization journey of, 162–164
  and fertilization process, 164, 165
Spermicides, 210, 212
Speroff, L., 75
Spontaneous abortions, 176
Sports injury, Q angle vs. conditioning,
    86–87
SRY gene, 58, 59, 65
Stapholoccus aureus, evolution of, 31–32
Statistically significant result, 16
  experimental accuracy and, 18
  practical significance and, 17
Statistics, 16–17
STDs. See Sexually transmitted diseases
    (STDs)
Stereotypes, in women's biology, 1
Sterilization, as birth control, 210,
    222–225
Steroid hormones
  interactions, 66
  muscle mass and, 108
Stress, and menstruation, 139
Stretch marks, 172, 174
Strong inference, good controls
    and, 16
Subject expectation, 21

Subjugation, of women, and brain
size/intelligence work, 3–4
Sun, skin and exposure to, 90–91
Symptothermal method, of birth control,
210, 221

Taboos, menstrual, 146–148
Tampons, 136
Tan skin, as beauty standard, 90
Tavris, Carol, 101, 148
Teratoma, 103, 161
Testosterone
effects on adipocytes, 108, 109
and fat storage, 108–109
metabolism pathways of, 75
and muscle mass, 108
Tests, pregnancy-related, 177–180
Thelarche, 72
Tiefer, Leonore, 101
Toxic shock syndrome (TSS), 136, 146,
213
Transcription, in protein production,
52–54
Translation process, in protein
production, 54
Trophoblast, implantation of, 170
Truth table, 14, 15
Tubal infertility, STDs and, 229–230
Tubal ligation, 210, 223–225
Twinning, 166

Ultrasound, 177
"Universal Symbols" for female and
male, 29
Unsupported assertions, 14
Untested hypotheses, 14
Urethra, 99
Urinary opening, 97
Uterine cancer, 247–248
ERT and, 265
hysterectomies and, 248
Uterine wall, 64
Uterus, 100, 102
after birth, 189–190
fibroids in, 247–248
pregnancy and, 171–172

Vacuum aspiration method, of abortion,
226
Vagina, 99–101
HRT/ERT and changes in, 264
menopause and changes in, 255
pregnancy and, 172
vaginal orgasm and G spot, 101
Vaginal opening, 97, 99

Vasectomy, 210, 222–223
Vertebral fractures, osteoporosis and,
256, 258
Vertebrates, sex determination in, 61
Vestibule, of female genitals, 99
Viral STDs, 229, 230
Vitamin D, and calcium concentration,
260–261
Vitamins and minerals in women's health,
112–114
Vulva, 97–98

Wallace, Alfred Russell, natural selection
theory of, 32
Way of knowing, science as, 12–13
Weaning, 197–198
Weight. See also Body composition; Body
weight
dieting consequences, 120
eating disorders, 120–124
pregnancy and, 174–175
women's perceptions of, 119
Weight loss, eating disorders
and, 122
Wenneras, C., 8
Wilcox, A. J., 166
Wilson, Edward O., 46
Withdrawal method, of birth control,
210, 212
Wold, A., 8
Wolffian duct system, 70
Womb. See also Uterus
historical hypotheses about, 2–3
Women
and correlation approach to
studies, 19
as second sex, 2
sexual differentiation and development
in, 63–80
and weight, 119–124
X inactivation effects, 58–59
Women's biology
complexity of and medical trials, 5
history of, 1–10
and idea of second sex, 2
infant feeding and gender division of
labor, 45
as "other," 1
Women's bodies
anatomy of, 81–105
external anatomy, 88–95
muscle, fat, and health, 107–125
reproductive anatomy, 95–105
skeletal anatomy, 83–88
Wrinkles, social factors and, 93–94

X chromosomes. *See also* X inactivation
    evolution of, 59–60
    genes on, 54–57
    locations of genes on, 56
X inactivation, 58–59
XY individuals, 73–74

Y chromosomes
    evolution of, 59–60
    genes on, 57–58
Yeast infections, 100

Zona pellucida, 161